PENGUIN BOOKS

THE POISON SQUAD

Deborah Blum is the director of the Knight Science Journalism Program at MIT and publisher of *Undark* magazine (undark.org). In 1992, she won the Pulitzer Prize for a series on primate research, which she turned into a book, *The Monkey Wars*. Her other books include *The Poisoner's Handbook*, *Ghost Hunters*, *Love at Goon Park*, and *Sex on the Brain*. She has written for publications including *The New York Times*, *Wired*, *Time*, *Discover*, *Mother Jones*, *The Guardian*, and *The Boston Globe*. Blum is a past president of the National Association for the Advancement of Science, and a lifetime associate of the National Academy of Sciences.

* * *

Praise for *The Poison Squad*

"[Blum's] prose is graceful, and her book is full of vivid, unsettling detail. . . . *The Poison Squad* offers a powerful reminder that truth can defeat lies, that government can protect consumers and that an honest public servant can overcome the greed of private interests."
—Eric Schlosser, *New York Times Book Review*

"Full of fascinating detail . . . A valuable contribution to understanding the politics of food."
—*Nature*

"A detailed, highly readable history of food and drink regulation in the United States . . . [*The Poison Squad*] shows the push and pull of competing economic, political, and social interests. The journey our country has taken in establishing food, drink, and drug regulation is an important one to understand because it is still going on."
—*The Wall Street Journal*

"Blum draws from her meticulous research to recreate the battle between regulation in the name of consumer protection and production in the name of profits." —*Scientific American*

"Riveting . . . Blum isn't just telling one scientist's story but a broader one about the relationship between science and society. . . . [A] timely tale about how scientists and citizens can work together on meaningful consumer protections." —*Science Magazine*

"You've probably never heard of Harvey Washington Wiley, but he's probably the reason you aren't sick right now. . . . Pulitzer Prize–winning journalist Blum tells [Wiley's] whole story in this fascinating book." —*Lit Hub*

"Engrossing . . . Blum's well-informed narrative—complete with intricate battles between industry lobbyists and a coalition of scientists, food activists, and women's groups—illuminates the birth of the modern regulatory state and its tangle of reformist zeal, policy dogfights, and occasional overreach. . . . [A] page-turner." —*Publishers Weekly*

"Fascinating . . . The Pure Food and Drug Act of 1906 ended a century of scandal and bitter political maneuvering, with major impetus from Harvey Washington Wiley, a genuinely unknown American hero. Pulitzer Prize–winning journalist Blum offers less a biography than a vivid account of Wiley's achievements. . . . An expert life of an undeservedly obscure American." —*Kirkus Reviews*

"[A] compellingly detailed chronicle . . . Citing worrisome recent attacks on consumer-protection laws, Blum reminds readers of the twenty-first-century relevance of Wiley's cause." —*Booklist*

THE
POISON
SQUAD

One Chemist's Single-Minded

Crusade for Food Safety

at the Turn of the

Twentieth Century

———◆———

DEBORAH BLUM

PENGUIN BOOKS

PENGUIN BOOKS
An imprint of Penguin Random House LLC
penguinrandomhouse.com

First published in the United States of America by Penguin Press,
an imprint of Penguin Random House LLC, 2018
Published in Penguin Books 2019

Illustration credits appear on page 320.

ISBN 9781594205149 (hardcover)
ISBN 9780143111122 (paperback)
ISBN 9780525560289 (ebook)

Printed in the United States of America
5   7   9   10   8   6   4

DESIGNED BY AMANDA DEWEY

To Peter, who makes all things possible

CONTENTS

PART II

"I WONDER WHAT'S IN IT"

We sit at a table delightfully spread
And teeming with good things to eat.
And daintily finger the cream-tinted bread,
Just needing to make it complete
A film of the butter so yellow and sweet,
Well suited to make every minute
A dream of delight. And yet while we eat
We cannot help asking, "What's in it?"
Oh, maybe this bread contains alum or chalk
Or sawdust chopped up very fine
Or gypsum in powder about which they talk,
Terra alba just out of the mine.
And our faith in the butter is apt to be weak,
For we haven't a good place to pin it
Annato's so yellow and beef fat so sleek
Oh, I wish I could know what is in it.
The pepper perhaps contains cocoanut shells,
And the mustard is cottonseed meal;
And the coffee, in sooth, of baked chicory smells,
And the terrapin tastes like roast veal.
The wine which you drink never heard of a grape,
But of tannin and coal tar is made;
And you could not be certain, except for their shape,
That the eggs by a chicken were laid.
And the salad which bears such an innocent look
And whispers of fields that are green
Is covered with germs, each armed with a hook
To grapple with liver and spleen.
The banquet how fine, don't begin it
Till you think of the past and the future and sigh,
"How I wonder, I wonder, what's in it."

HARVEY WASHINGTON WILEY, 1899

CAST OF CHARACTERS

This account of Harvey Wiley's life and his battle for the enactment and enforcement of the United States' first national law regulating food, drink, and drugs includes many people whose lives or careers intersected with or influenced Wiley's. Among them were all U.S. presidents from Chester A. Arthur to Calvin Coolidge.

Others included:

Jane Addams: The Chicago activist and reformer, cofounder of the nation's first settlement house, also cofounded the National Consumers League.

Nelson Aldrich: This powerful and wealthy U.S. senator, a Rhode Island Republican so influential in government that the press nicknamed him "General Manager of the Nation," was a friend to many major corporations and strongly opposed the idea of regulating food and drink for safety.

Russell A. Alger: As secretary of war, he somewhat reluctantly ordered investigations into the food that had been supplied to army troops during the Spanish-American War.

Robert M. Allen: The chief food chemist for the state of Kentucky was an outspoken advocate of pure-food legislation and a valuable Wiley ally.

Carl L. Alsberg: Succeeding Wiley as chief of the USDA Bureau of Chemistry, he continued to pursue many of his predecessor's key cases, including lawsuits against the Coca-Cola Company and the producers of saccharin.

Thomas Antisell: This early USDA chief chemist investigated food adulteration during the 1860s and found it a problem but acknowledged that there was no mechanism for regulation.

J. Ogden Armour: The heir to founder Philip Armour's Armour and Company meatpacking in Chicago; he, like his father, opposed food safety regulations. The company was the basis for Upton Sinclair's fictional "Anderson" food-processing company in his bestselling novel *The Jungle*.

Ray Stannard Baker: A muckraking *McClure's* journalist, he advised his friend Upton Sinclair on proposed revisions to *The Jungle*.

Jesse Park Battershall: Author of a leading book, *Food Adulteration and Its Detection*, the nineteenth-century chemist blasted processors, bemoaned the lack of regulation, and described home purity tests that could be used by anxious family cooks.

Albert Beveridge: A progressive Republican senator from Indiana, he played a role in pushing pure-food legislation, especially the Meat Inspection Law of 1906.

Willard Bigelow: The lead chemist for the Hygienic Table Trials, also known as the Poison Squad, he was a dedicated ally of Wiley's and a dedicated chemist, once described as a "man of blue blazes and sulfurous smokes."

Charles J. Bonaparte: The U.S. attorney general under Theodore Roosevelt issued a key ruling agreeing with Wiley on whiskey-labeling requirements.

George Rothwell Brown: A *Washington Post* reporter, he made the Poison Squad experiments famous but also wrote fake news stories about them.

Joseph Gurney Cannon: The powerful and corrupt Speaker of the House opposed regulation and battled with Wiley over proposed pure-food legislation.

Russell Chittenden: As a Yale physiologist, he warned against some additives but on the Remsen Board, established after passage of the 1906 law, he was often a pro-industry defender of preservatives.

Norman J. Coleman: As commissioner of agriculture in Grover Cleveland's first term, he was a Wiley ally who initiated investigations into food purity.

Peter Collier: Wiley's predecessor as chief chemist clashed with the agriculture commissioner. Angry at being replaced, he orchestrated attacks on Wiley in an attempt to get his job back.

C. A. Crampton: A chemist on Wiley's staff, he authored a report that found potentially dangerous doses of salicylic acid in alcoholic beverages.

Chauncey Depew: A reporter's tale of corruption by this senator from New York, a wealthy former railroad lawyer and a friend of Theodore Roosevelt, caused the president to lash out at the "muckraking" press.

Grenville Dodge: A Civil War veteran and businessman, he headed the Dodge Commission investigation into allegations of adulterated army rations during the Spanish-American War.

Henry Irving Dodge: The writer worked with Willard Bigelow on "The Truth About Food Adulteration," a high-profile series for *Woman's Home Companion* magazine.

Frank Nelson Doubleday: The publishing firm founder somewhat reluctantly agreed, at his partner's urgings, to publish Upton Sinclair's novel *The Jungle*.

Herbert Henry Dow: The founder of Dow Chemical Company opposed pure-food legislation and complained that Wiley ran a "disinformation campaign" against chemical additives to food.

Frederick L. Dunlap: An ambitious, politically minded academic, he was appointed "associate chemist" as the agriculture secretary sought to undermine Wiley's authority.

Finley Peter Dunne: The humor columnist, through his fictional character Mr. Dooley, poked fun at President Roosevelt's combative habits—including the president's reaction to grisly details in *The Jungle*.

Charles P. Eagan: Army commissary general during the Spanish-American War, he became enraged at accusations that he fed "embalmed beef" to troops.

Mark Hanna: A businessman, political operative, and U.S. senator, he became a close ally and adviser to President McKinley.

Henry J. Heinz: The food processor and founder of H.J. Heinz Company advocated for pure food and decent working conditions, developed a preservative-free commercial ketchup recipe, and actively promoted his products as the safest in the country.

Albert Heller: A Chicago manufacturer, he vigorously defended food preservatives, especially his product Freezine, which used formaldehyde to slow decomposition of meat and milk.

William P. Hepburn: An Iowa congressman, he led efforts in the House to pass a pure-food law and cosponsored the Hepburn-McCumber bill, which preceded the 1906 law.

Weldon Heyburn: The U.S. senator from Idaho chaired the Committee on Manufactures from 1903 to 1913. Although not usually a reformer, he pushed food and drug legislation largely because of his dislike of false advertising by drugmakers.

August Wilhelm von Hofmann: A leading German chemist of the 1800s, his research laid groundwork for the development of coal-tar dyes, which became the leading coloring agents used in food and drink.

Harry L. Hollingworth: A Columbia University psychologist, he did precise measurements of caffeine's effects on human subjects and testified as an expert witness for Coca-Cola in a 1911 trial.

Warwick Hough: A lawyer and lobbyist for the National Wholesale Liquor Distributors Association and for Monsanto, he fought fiercely against regulation of his clients.

Burton Howard: The chief of the Chemistry Bureau's Microchemical Laboratory coauthored a study on home detection of food adulteration.

John Hurty: The Indiana state health officer crusaded against preservatives in milk and for public-health laws, successfully persuading the state to pass food safety regulations ahead of the federal government. Like Wiley, he had been on the faculty at Purdue University.

Lyman Kebler: The USDA chemist specializing in pharmaceuticals exposed many patent medicines as worthless and/or harmful. He worked particularly hard to identify the unlabeled use of stimulants in American soft drinks.

Anna "Nan" Kelton: See Anna Wiley.

Josephine Kelton: She disapproved when the much-older Wiley courted her daughter but eventually became his mother-in-law.

Edwin F. Ladd: The outspoken North Dakota food chemist successfully campaigned for a state food safety law and went on to fight for food purity on a national scale, becoming a leading critic of corporate politics at the U.S. Department of Agriculture. He was elected to the U.S. Senate in 1920.

Alice Lakey: A progressive activist from New Jersey, this Wiley ally became the influential head of the Pure Food Committee of the National Consumers League.

George Loring: The commissioner of agriculture under President Arthur, he hired Harvey Wiley as the department's chief chemist.

Isaac Marcosson: An editor at Doubleday, Page & Company with a strong interest in marketing campaigns, he enthusiastically urged publication of Upton Sinclair's *The Jungle*.

John Marshall: A professor of chemistry at the University of Pennsylvania and a nationally known toxicologist, he tested the effects of borax (with which he dosed himself), a popular early-twentieth-century food preservative, and the stimulant caffeine.

William Mason: The reformist U.S. senator from Illinois convened, in 1899, an extensive series of hearings investigating the contamination of the nation's food supply and introduced legislation, ultimately successfully, to regulate for that problem.

George P. McCabe: The Agriculture Department's industry-friendly solicitor worked against Wiley's most aggressive attempts to enforce the pure-food law.

Porter J. McCumber: A U.S. senator from North Dakota, he sponsored pure-food legislation and scheduled hearings on the issue of adulteration.

Hippolyte Mège-Mouriès: A chemist, he entered a contest to invent a butter substitute and came up with what he called *oléomargarine*, made from beef fat.

Nelson Miles: The army's commanding general called for an investigation into the quality of the food supplied to his troops in the Spanish-American War, accusing the military of feeding his men "embalmed beef."

Julius Sterling Morton: The secretary of agriculture during the second Cleveland administration was an obsessive budget cutter who suppressed Wiley's work in food safety and refused congressional money to support food safety research.

Sebastian Mueller: An executive of the H.J. Heinz Company, he defied his peers in the food-processing industry both by developing preservative-free products and advocating for pure-food legislation.

John Mullaly: The American journalist authored a mid-nineteenth-century book about the sickening practices employed by the dairy industry in New York City, from watering down milk to the use of toxic additives.

Henry Needham: A muckraking journalist and an activist, he publicly criticized Theodore Roosevelt's agriculture secretary as too close to industry, supported Wiley in his departmental battles, and helped form a pro-consumer activist group called the People's Lobby.

Charles P. Neill: President Roosevelt sent Neill, his commissioner of labor, to investigate the meatpacking industry in Chicago after *The Jungle* was published.

Algernon Paddock: A U.S. senator from Nebraska, he sponsored a proposed food-regulation law in 1891. It failed but presaged the 1906 law.

Walter Hines Page: A partner in Doubleday, Page & Company, he advocated the publication of the shocking novel *The Jungle* and helped publicize it.

S. S. Perry: As the initial chef for Wiley's Hygienic Table Trials, he ran a meticulous kitchen but was talkative and tended to let secrets slip.

David Graham Phillips: The reformist journalist, author of a book on government corruption titled *The Treason of the Senate*, and critic of what he saw as a watered-down food law infuriated President Theodore Roosevelt.

Paul Pierce: An advocate of moderation and pure food and a Wiley ally, he was a writer, editor, and publisher of *What to Eat*, later *National Food Magazine*, based in Chicago.

John F. Queeny: The founder of Monsanto Chemical Company made saccharin and the crystalline form of caffeine used in soft drinks. He steadfastly opposed regulation of industry products.

Ira Remsen: A codiscoverer of saccharin, the Johns Hopkins University chemist headed a high-priced consulting panel formed to review and often countermand Wiley's findings.

James B. Reynolds: Roosevelt sent Reynolds, an activist and a settlement house manager, along with Charles P. Neill to investigate Chicago meatpackers.

Clifford Richardson: A chemist on Wiley's staff, Richardson investigated the rampant adulteration of spices. His findings revealed revolting practices, including the use of ground shells, dirt, and rock dust.

Elihu Root: As U.S. secretary of war, he helped modernize the American military after the Spanish-American War. He also backed importation of Cuban sugar in the war's aftermath. As secretary of state, he tempered some of Roosevelt's more explosive tendencies.

Jeremiah Rusk: As secretary of agriculture in the Benjamin Harrison administration, he greatly expanded investigations of food adulteration, which he considered one of his farmer-friendly policies.

James Shepard: The South Dakota food commissioner investigated nitrates in flour, backed Wiley's pure-food cause, and opposed Agriculture Secretary James Wilson.

James S. Sherman: His canning company used saccharin as a sweetener. As a New York congressman, he opposed requiring that labels list ingredients.

Upton Sinclair: An avowed socialist, he wrote *The Jungle* to expose brutal work conditions, but its lurid descriptions of meatpacking practices shocked readers far more.

Lincoln Steffens: The muckraking journalist advised Upton Sinclair on proposed revisions to *The Jungle* and later scolded Roosevelt over an antipress speech that accused reporters of being doom-and-gloom muckrakers.

Mark Sullivan: An investigative journalist and author, Sullivan wrote about drug fraud for national magazines and also about Wiley's public campaign to win support for the pure-food bill. He included that work in his best-selling history of the United States, titled *Our Times*.

Louis Swift: The heir to the Swift & Company meatpacking firm, he rebutted all evidence of shoddy production and defended his business as "conducted in a proper and sanitary manner" during the scandal generated by publication of *The Jungle*.

Alonzo E. Taylor: A physiological chemist at the University of Pennsylvania, Taylor was a member of the Remsen Board, which reviewed Wiley's decisions.

Edmund Haynes Taylor Jr.: Known by the Kentucky honorific "Colonel," he was a distiller of aged bourbon and namesake of the Old Taylor brand, who fought the idea that blended whiskeys were of equal quality to his own products.

James W. Wadsworth: A New York Republican, he chaired the House Committee on Agriculture and preferentially called upon industry witnesses at a hearing on a meat-inspection amendment following publication of *The Jungle*.

Alex Wedderburn: In the 1890s, Wiley hired this activist-writer to produce consumer-friendly information about Chemistry Bureau findings for the public, especially concerning issues of food safety.

Anna "Nan" Kelton Wiley: A librarian at the Agriculture Department and later the Library of Congress, she married Harvey Wiley in 1910. She was known in her own right as a suffragette and longtime advocate of public health and social justice issues in general.

James Wilson: A former Iowa farmer and the secretary of agriculture through the McKinley, Roosevelt, and Taft administrations, Wilson was at first a supporter of Harvey Wiley, but later clashes over the pure-food law enforcement led him to become increasingly hostile.

John H. Young: A Northwestern University chemist specializing in pharmacology, he was a member of the Remsen Board, which served as a foil to Wiley.

INTRODUCTION

We tend these days to cast a romantic glow over the foods of our forefathers. In such rosy light, we may imagine grandparents or great-grandparents thriving happily—and solely—on farm-fresh produce and pasture-raised livestock. We may even believe that they ate and drank in a world untouched by the chemically enhanced and deceptive food manufacturing practices of today.

In this we would be wrong.

By the mid-nineteenth century, in fact, many foods and drinks sold in the United States had earned a reputation as often untrustworthy and occasionally downright dangerous.

Milk offers a stunning case in point. Dairymen, especially those serving crowded American cities in the nineteenth century, learned that there were profits to be made by skimming and watering down their product. The standard recipe was a pint of lukewarm water to every quart of milk—after the cream had been skimmed off. To improve the bluish look of the remaining liquid, milk producers learned to add whitening agents such as plaster of paris or chalk. Sometimes they added a dollop of molasses to give the liquid a more golden, creamy color. To mimic the expected layer of cream on top, they might also add a final squirt of something yellowish, occasionally pureed calf brains.

"Where are the police?" demanded New York journalist John Mullaly as he detailed such practices and worse in his 1853 book, *The Milk Trade in New York and Vicinity*. Mullaly's evidence included reports from frustrated physicians stating that thousands of children were killed in New York City every year by dirty (bacteria-laden) and deliberately tainted milk. His demands for prosecution were partly theater. Despite his and others' outraged demands for change, no laws existed to make such adulterations illegal. Still Mullaly continued to ask, when would enough be enough?

Fakery and adulteration ran rampant in other American products as well. "Honey" often proved to be thickened, colored corn syrup, and "vanilla" extract a mixture of alcohol and brown food coloring. "Strawberry" jam could be sweetened paste made from mashed apple peelings laced with grass seeds and dyed red. "Coffee" might be largely sawdust, or wheat, beans, beets, peas, and dandelion seeds, scorched black and ground to resemble the genuine article. Containers of "pepper," "cinnamon," or "nutmeg" were frequently laced with a cheaper filler material such as pulverized coconut shells, charred rope, or occasionally floor sweepings. "Flour" routinely contained crushed stone or gypsum as a cheap extender. Ground insects could be mixed into brown sugar, often without detection—their use linked to an unpleasant condition known as "grocer's itch."

By the end of the nineteenth century, the sweeping industrial revolution—and the rise of industrial chemistry—had also brought a host of new chemical additives and synthetic compounds into the food supply. Still unchecked by government regulation, basic safety testing, or even labeling requirements, food and drink manufacturers embraced the new materials with enthusiasm, mixing them into goods destined for the grocery store at sometimes lethal levels.

The most popular preservative for milk—a product prone to rot in an era that lacked effective refrigeration—was formaldehyde, its use adapted from the newest embalming practices of undertakers. Processors employed formaldehyde solutions—sold under innocuous names such as Preservaline—to restore decaying meats as well. Other popular preservatives included salicylic acid, a pharmaceutical compound, and borax, a mineral-based material best known as a cleaning product.

Food manufacturers also adopted new synthetic dyes, derived from coal by-products, to improve the color of their less appealing products. They found inexpensive synthetic compounds that they could secretly substitute into food and drink—saccharin to replace sugar; acetic acid instead of lemon juice; lab-created alcohols, dyed and flavored, to mimic aged whiskeys and fine wines. As progressive Wisconsin senator Robert M. La Follette described such practices in 1886: "Ingenuity, striking hands with cunning trickery, compounds a substance to counterfeit an article of food. It is made to look like something it is not; to taste and smell like something it is not; to sell something it is not, and so do deceive the purchaser."

No wonder, then, that when alarmed citizens began pushing for federal help in checking such fraud and fakery, they did so under the banner of purity. They saw themselves as "pure food" crusaders, fighting to clean up not only a contaminated supply chain but also a system that was dirty to its roots and protected by politicians friendly to industry. As Mullaly had done decades earlier, the new crusaders—scientists and journalists, state health officials and leaders of women's groups—loudly deplored their national government's willingness to allow such corrupt practices to continue.

The leaders of the pure-food movement united behind the idea that regulatory oversight was the only realistic answer. They'd seen many times that the country's food processors and manufacturers felt little or no responsibility to protect the food supply, especially if it meant reducing profits. Formaldehyde, for instance, had been directly linked to deaths—notably of children drinking what came to be called embalmed milk—without any move by producers to discontinue the preservative's use. The preservative's usefulness in salvaging bad milk—otherwise unsalable—was too valuable to lose.

American corporations had successfully and repeatedly blocked efforts to pass even modest food safety legislation. This especially galled consumer safety advocates because governments in Europe *were* enacting protective measures; some foods and drinks sold freely in the United States were now banned abroad. Unlike their American counterparts, European beer and wine makers were blocked from using risky preservatives in their beverages (although they could put them in products destined for U.S. sales).

At the first National Pure Food and Drug Congress, held in Washington, DC, in 1898, delegates noted that American food fraud had continued to flourish since La Follette's speech on the floor of the Senate some thirteen years earlier. How long would the country go without some policy or plan to deal with industrial food? No one knew. But surely, one delegate suggested hopefully, "this great country [must eventually] take its proper place among civilized nations and protect its citizens."

Many of the several hundred pure-food advocates at the congress saw their best chance for progress in what might have seemed an unlikely source of heroics: a small chemistry unit in the U.S. Department of Agriculture and its chief scientist, a middle-aged Indiana native who'd trained in chemistry at Harvard University.

But that was, in reality, a savvy choice.

Decades before the federal government had even considered anything resembling a food and drug administration, the Department of Agriculture (created in 1862 by President Abraham Lincoln) was tasked with analyzing the composition of American food and drink. It was the only agency to do so and that work was mostly in response to unhappy farmers who saw manufactured food undercutting their market. An 1870s complaint from a Minnesota agricultural association asked the division to investigate the "misapplication of science to deodorize rotten eggs, revive rancid butter, and dye pithy peas" green again.

But it wasn't until the Agriculture Department named Harvey Washington Wiley chief chemist in 1883—recruiting him from a job at Purdue University—that the agency began methodically investigating food and drink fraud. Although best known as an expert in sugar chemistry, Wiley had studied food fakery while still in Indiana and had warned then that "counterfeit" products could be considered a threat to public health. Upon arrival at the Agriculture Department, he promptly initiated a series of investigations of products ranging from butter to spices to wine and beer, building a detailed and sometimes horrifying portrait of the country's food supply. Those reports would lead him, in the early twentieth century, to test some of the most suspect chemical additives on human volunteers, a series of experiments dubbed the "Poison Squad" studies by the nation's newspapers.

His food and drink investigations—and the detailed criticism they contained—both infuriated manufacturers and alarmed Wiley's business-minded supervisors. But he refused, under pressure, to stop the studies. And as the pure-food advocates noted with admiration, Wiley stuck by his research—and his researchers—even when they reached conclusions that embarrassed powerful corporate and political interests.

Even worse, in the view of those interests, he publicized the findings. He steadfastly sought to inform not just government officials and lawmakers but also the public at large—including pure-food activists—about what his investigations revealed. The years of research findings, he told a congressional committee, had convinced him that polite resignation was unacceptable.

And Wiley tended to stand out anyway. He was a tall man, dark haired and dark eyed, imposing in stature, humorously charming in private, by turns ministerial and theatrical in public. He would become the best-known face of the national battle for food safety regulation at the turn of the twentieth century, building an alliance of consumer advocates and rallying them, in the face of repeated setbacks, to stay in the fight. He was America's first great food safety chemist, but his greatest contribution to the cause—even more than the scientific work he conducted and supervised, even more than his considerable ability to dramatize the cause—was "the inspired generalship he offered," wrote public-health historian Oscar Anderson Jr. Wiley, he added, "was the one leader who consistently saw the big picture," the long-term goal of strong consumer protection.

Wiley also had his imperfections. The son of a lay preacher, he tended to claim the moral high ground largely for his alliance alone. Faced with hostility, he became more rigid in his stance, often refusing to compromise even on small details. He quarreled over pictures on labels as firmly as he quarreled over toxic compounds in baked goods. His refusal to make nice, even when nitpicking, strained his alliances and, some felt, limited his effectiveness. He knew that too.

He failed, Wiley himself believed, to achieve the kind of fearlessly tough regulatory protections he wanted for his country. He could not forget or forgive the times that he'd stood up alone in—and sometimes lost—the fight against corporate interference in the law. His own criticisms of his grand achievement—the passage and enforcement of the landmark 1906 Pure Food and Drug Act—may well have undercut our perceptions of his accomplishments and caused us to undervalue his contributions.

But in that too we would be wrong.

Yes, we are still fighting for pure food. But let us recognize that we've come a wonderfully long way from the unregulated food, drink, and drug horrors of the nineteenth century. And in an era when business interests rail—as they did in Wiley's time—about government overreach and the need to eliminate regulations, we should remember how much Wiley's work laid the foundation that allows us to stand up to that. He changed the way we regulate, and he was essential in changing the way we think about food, health, and consumer protection.

It may not always serve us to cast a rosy glow over the past—or even over its heroes. But we should take care not to forget those early lessons on protecting our country—and ourselves. And as we look back to that first fierce battle for federal consumer protection, we would do well to remember what an intensely personal fight it often was. There's a remarkable and revealing story—one that illuminates where we stand today—behind the simple fact that what we now call the "pure food and drug law" was once known, coast to coast, as "Dr. Wiley's Law."

PART I

One

A CHEMICAL WILDERNESS

1844–1887

―――――●―――――

We sit at a table delightfully spread
And teeming with good things to eat.

The sixth of seven children, Harvey Washington Wiley was born on April 16, 1844, in a log cabin on a small farm in Kent, Indiana, about a hundred miles northeast of the farm where Abraham Lincoln had grown up a few decades earlier.

The humble timber dwelling was an icon of authenticity for nineteenth-century Americans, particularly because Lincoln (born in adjacent Kentucky), as well as presidents such as Andrew Jackson and Zachary Taylor, had made their log-cabin beginnings a keystone of their respective political images. In later years Wiley liked to joke about his similarly modest origins. "I am not possessed with a common prejudice that a man must be born in a log cabin to attain greatness in the United States," he said.

But like those political luminaries, Wiley grew up working the land. By age six he was driving the family cows back to the barn for milking each day. At ten he was behind a plow. His father, Preston, was one of the first Indiana farmers to grow sorghum cane, and with curious son Harvey helping, the boy learned to boil down juice pressed from the grassy grain crop into a sweet syrup. That transformation helped spur his interest in food processing and in other types of sugars, one of the inspirations for his later career.

Preston Wiley had little schooling but valued learning, another strong influence on his second-youngest child. The father, who was a lay minister as well as a farmer, had even taught himself Greek. A fierce opponent of slavery—he made a point of gathering his children around for evening readings of the powerful abolitionist novel *Uncle Tom's Cabin*—farmer Wiley also believed in acting upon one's principles. Only three miles from the Ohio River, the family farm became Indiana's southernmost stop on the Underground Railroad. Escaped slaves from Kentucky, once they'd made it across the water, knew to seek out Preston Wiley. Under cover of darkness, he would escort them safely to the next stop, eight miles northward.

Harvey Wiley was preparing for college when the Civil War broke out, and his parents, despite their antislavery stance, were determined that he continue with it. He enrolled at nearby Hanover College in 1863 but a year later decided he could no longer sit out the war. After joining the 137th Indiana Infantry, he was deployed to Tennessee and Alabama, where he guarded Union-held railroad lines and spent his spare hours studying anatomy, reciting daily from a textbook to a fellow soldier. It was only a few months later that he and many of his fellows fell ill in a plague of measles sweeping through the camp. He was still ailing when his regiment returned to Indianapolis that September. He received a discharge, went home to recuperate, and then returned to Hanover, where he earned a bachelor's and then a master of arts degree in 1867. But he had by then, influenced by his army days, determined to become a physician. In his graduation address, he spoke of his then-chosen profession with typical over-the-top exuberance. The medical man, Wiley declaimed, "can not climb to Heaven and pull down immortality," but he can help achieve a longer life "full of health and happiness and hope."

To earn money for medical school, Wiley first taught Latin and Greek at a small Christian school in Indianapolis. He spent the following summer apprenticed to a country physician in Kentucky, then enrolled in Indiana Medical College, where he earned an MD, graduating in 1871. By that time, though, he'd learned that although he admired the work of medical practitioners, he did not enjoy caring for sick people. He accepted an offer to teach chemistry in the Indianapolis public high schools and there began to appreciate the insights offered by that branch of science or, as he came to see it, the "nobility and magnitude" of chemistry. Realizing he had a passion for the rapidly advancing field, he went back to school yet again, this time to study chemistry at Harvard University, which—as was typical at the time—awarded him a bachelor of science degree after only a few months of study. In 1874 he accepted a position at Indiana's newly opened Purdue University as its first (and only) chemistry professor.

"I find so many things that I do not know as I pursue my studies," he wrote in his diary during that first year at Purdue, as he struggled to assemble a working laboratory. "My own profession is still a wilderness." During the following years, though, Wiley developed a reputation as the state's go-to scientist for analyzing virtually anything—from water quality to rocks to soil samples—and especially foodstuffs. This was accelerated by a working sabbatical in 1878 in the newly united German Empire, considered the global leader in chemical research. He studied at one of the empire's pioneering food-quality laboratories and attended lectures by world-renowned scientist August Wilhelm von Hofmann, who had been the first director of the Royal College of Chemistry in London. Von Hofmann was a pioneering industry chemist. Famed for his 1866 discovery of formaldehyde, he would later do work leading to the development of industrial dyes that the food industry embraced in the late nineteenth century. When Wiley returned to Purdue, he brought back specialized instruments for analyzing food chemistry, acquired in Germany and paid for with his own savings when the university refused to do so.

European governments—especially those of Germany and Great Britain—had been far quicker than the U.S. government to recognize and to address problems of food adulteration. In 1820 a pioneering book by chemist Fredrick Accum, titled *A Treatise on Adulterations of Food, and Culinary Poisons*, had aroused widespread public outrage when it was published in London. Accum minced no words: "Our pickles are made green by copper; our vinegar rendered sharp by sulphuric acid; our cream composed of rice powder or arrowroot in bad milk; our comfits mixed of sugar, starch and clay, and coloured with preparations of copper and lead; our catsup often formed of the dregs of distilled vinegar with a decoction of the outer green husk of walnuts, and seasoned with all-spice," he wrote.

As Accum noted, the poisonous practices of his time dated back many years. Long before the nineteenth century's new industrial dyes, merchants and processors used various colorful substances to make their wares look more enticing. Confectioners often turned to poisonous metallic elements and compounds. Green came from arsenic or copper, yellow from lead chromate, cheerful rose and pink tones from red lead. In 1830 an editorial in *The Lancet*, the British medical journal, complained that "millions of children are thus daily dosed" with lethal substances. But the practices continued, largely due to business pressures on would-be government regulators.

By midcentury, though, casualties were starting to mount in Britain. In 1847 three English children fell seriously ill after eating birthday cake decorated with arsenic-tinted green leaves. Five years later, two London brothers died after eating a cake whose frosting contained both arsenic and copper. In an 1854 report, London physician Arthur Hassall tracked forty cases of child poisoning caused by penny candies.

Three years later, twenty-one people in Bradford, Yorkshire, died after consuming candy accidentally laced with deadly arsenic trioxide—"accidentally" because the confectioner meant to mix in plaster of paris instead. Although he had noticed his workers falling ill while mixing up the stuff, the business owner had put the candy on sale anyway. He was arrested and jailed, as was the pharmacist who'd mistakenly sold him the poison in place of plaster. But they could not be convicted of any crime. Britain had no law against making unsafe—or even lethal—food products.

Fury over the Bradford incident spurred the passage in 1860 of Britain's Act for Preventing Adulteration in Food and Drink. Business interests managed to limit the fine for poisoning food to a mere £5, but at least it was a precedent.

Although not yet nearly loud enough to prod Congress, there were voices of outrage in America too, where journalists like John Mullaly railed against "milk-poison" and George Thorndike Angell, a Massachusetts lawyer and philanthropist better known for his work against cruelty to animals, loudly derided dishonest food producers. In an 1879 speech to the American Social Science Public Health Association, Angell recited a disgusting list of commercially sold foods that included diseased and parasite-ridden meat and processed animal fat passed off as butter and cheese.

"They poison and cheat the consumer; affect, and in many cases destroy, the health not only of the rich but of the poor," Angell charged, blasting dishonest food producers as little better than "the pirates who plunder our ships on the ocean or the highway men who rob and murder on the land." For good measure, he mailed the text of his speech to newspapers nationwide—and to the dismay of food processors, it received prominent display. The *American Grocer*, a trade publication, dismissed him as sensationalist and "doing a disservice to consumers." But the *Grocer* acknowledged that some problems were real, especially the too-often poisonous nature of milk and colored candy, and the reputation harm done by fraudsters. That year, in response to Angell's concerns, Virginia congressman Richard Lee T. Beale introduced legislation that would have banned

interstate commerce in chemically altered foods. A report to the
Committee on Manufactures warned: "Not only are substances of
less value commingled with those of greater, but such as are injurious
to health, and we have no doubt often destructive of life, are freely
used in manufacturing and preparing for consuming the necessaries
and luxuries of life." The bill was referred out of committee, where
it promptly died through lack of further action. But an uneasy awareness of a troubled food supply was starting to grow.

In 1881 the Indiana State Board of Health asked Wiley to examine the purity of commercially sold sweet substances, particularly
honey and maple syrup. At Purdue, Wiley had been studying potential new crops and methods for making sweeteners. Inspired by his
father's venture into sorghum, he had even worked out an improved
process for getting syrup from its woody stalks. After his studies in
Germany, Wiley possessed the right training and tools to conduct the
study, and through presentations at the American Association for the
Advancement of Science he'd gained a reputation as one of the country's leading sugar chemists. The investigation requested by the
state—and the political fallout—would serve to plunge him further
into his life's work. It was, as he later remembered, "my first participation in the fray."

A report from the National Academy of Sciences had already
warned that jars labeled "honey" were often tinted corn syrup,
with a scrap of honeycomb tossed in to complete the deception.
Corn syrup—not the much later "high-fructose" version—was a
nineteenth-century innovation. Russian chemist Gottlieb Kirchhoff
had in 1812 devised an inexpensive process for turning cornstarch
into the sugar glucose. He combined the starch with diluted hydrochloric acid and heated the mixture under pressure. The process
proved hugely profitable in the corn-rich United States. By 1881 almost two dozen factories were operating in the Midwest, turning

25,000 bushels of corn a day into sugary products. "The manufacture of sirup and sugar from corn-starch is an industry which in this
country is scarcely a dozen years old and yet is one of no inconsider-
able magnitude," Wiley wrote in his report.

In much of the English-speaking world, "corn" could mean any
kind of grain crop—barley or wheat, for example. But in English-
speaking North America it had long meant maize, a staple of indig-
enous people in the Western Hemisphere for thousands of years.
When Europeans arrived, they called it Indian corn and began growing it for themselves. By the mid-1800s corn had become a primary
crop of farmlands from Pennsylvania to Nebraska, from Minnesota
to Missouri and beyond—and engendered a whole new array of
manufactured food products.

"Corn, the new American king," Wiley wrote, "now supplies us
with bread, meat, and sugar, which we need, as well as with the
whiskey we could do without." He estimated that corn-derived glucose had about two-thirds the sweetening power of cane sugar; it
was also far cheaper, produced for less than half the cost.

Those who made and sold the sweetener often labeled it either
"corn sugar" or "corn syrup." This was after European practice.
Germany had "potato sugar," for example, and France produced a
"grape sugar." But Wiley, always a stickler for accuracy (a trait that
would over the years irritate more plainspoken colleagues, including
President Roosevelt), thought the corn-based product should be
called glucose or glucose syrup. This, he emphasized, both was the
technically accurate term and also clearly differentiated it from traditional sugars made from cane or beet. (In the twenty-first century,
amid a diabetes epidemic, many think of "glucose" in terms of human blood sugar levels. But the sugar product derived from
cornstarch—or from wheat, potatoes, and other starches—does bear
the same molecular signature.)

In Wiley's day such scientific precision could seem essential to
maintaining a sense of order in research. Chemists of the

midnineteenth century had only begun to tease out the nature of molecular bonds. In the late 1850s the German chemist Friedrich August Kekulé put forth the first theory of how atoms come together to form a molecule. Chemistry superstar Von Hofmann, then at the University of Berlin, made the first stick-and-ball models of molecules in the 1860s. In Germany, Wiley had learned to respect such precision, a point illustrated by the instruments he'd brought home with him. One of his favorites was called a polariscope (or polarimeter). At Purdue he used it to tell the difference between types of sugars by passing polarized light through sweetened substances and measuring the angle at which the light rotated. "Glucose presents several anomalies when examined with polarized light," Wiley explained, compared with the true sugars.

He was not shocked when his tests showed that a full 90 percent of his syrup samples were fakes. Shop owners had told him that these new syrups were so sweet and inexpensive that they had almost "driven all others out of the market." Testing of honey samples also turned up rampant fakery. He somewhat mockingly referred to the counterfeit product as "entirely free of bee mediation," noting that even the bit of honeycomb that producers stuck in the jar was phony, made from paraffin. In his report, Wiley found no fault with corn syrup per se—it was, after all, a natural sweetener—but he thought that a food or ingredient ought to be called what it was. To fill a bottle with "glucose" and label it as more-expensive maple syrup was to deceive the consumer. In addition to finding corn syrup masquerading as other sugars, the study turned up impurities left by the manufacturing process. There was copper from mixing tubs and some chemical remnants of charred animal bones (used as a charcoal filter), and in some samples he detected sulfuric acid.

Wiley's report, published both in the state record and in *Popular Science* in the summer of 1881, gratified those in the real maple syrup business, but it annoyed corn growers, corn-syrup manufacturers, and the bottlers of the mislabeled products—which, put together, made a far larger and more influential interest group than that consisting of maple tree tappers. Wiley, as he would for the rest of his career, had begun making powerful enemies.

Surprisingly, the group that seemed most bothered by his report was beekeepers. Instead of thanking him for exposing what the chemist called "the injury done to the honey industry" by the corn-based fakes, that industry's trade journals denounced him and the study, referring to it as "Wiley's Lie." The honey producers worried about damage to their reputations. But it became obvious as well that there were "beekeepers" who had not, of late, been bothering to keep bees.

Wiley, characteristically, doubled down. He wrote a more in-depth report for the Indiana Board of Health, stressing the importance of truthful labeling. The second report included instructions for how to detect adulterations, and it strongly recommended that Indiana set purity standards for sugar products produced and sold in the state. "The dangers of adulteration are underrated," he wrote, "when it is for a moment supposed that any counterfeit food can be tolerated without depraving the public taste, and impairing the public safeguards of human life."

Despite the political pushback, he closed with a firm call for action. It was high time, he wrote, that "the demand for honest food should be heard in terms making no denial." He wasn't afraid, as he would say throughout his career, to stand up for what he thought right. After all, he'd been raised that way.

Like Harvey Wiley, Peter Collier, chief chemist of the Department of Agriculture, was fascinated by the science of sugars and the plants from which they could be produced. Even more enthusiastic about sorghum cane than Wiley was, the Yale-educated Collier saw it as a crop of the future. He envisioned glowing copper-and-green sorghum fields across the country, a potential source of sugar as bountiful as corn or even sugarcane.

His boss, the pragmatic George Loring, did not share Collier's vision. Commissioner Loring (titled "commissioner" because the USDA was not yet a cabinet-level department) was a former Massachusetts physician with a special interest in treating the often-crippling diseases of farm animals. The sorghum disagreement between Collier and Loring might have stayed a matter of internal discussion except for one problem. Whenever Collier felt aggrieved, he had a habit of complaining about the commissioner to the Washington press. Exasperated by newspaper stories in which his chief chemist suggested that he was an idiot, Loring in 1882 sought and received permission from President Chester A. Arthur to replace Collier with a more amiable scientist. Later that year, at a December meeting of Mississippi sugarcane growers, Loring heard a speech by Harvey Wiley, who had been invited to present an overview of sugar-producing crops. It was, thought Loring, a balanced presentation. It was objective. Unlike Collier, who had become increasingly fanatic about the dreamy future of sorghum, Wiley gave each crop its due. The Purdue scientist impressed the commissioner as the reasonable man he was looking for.

Two months later, Loring offered Wiley the chief chemist job. The timing was perfect. Wiley had been feeling increasingly stifled and unappreciated at Purdue. Conservative members of the university's board of trustees hadn't cared for the negative attention his state honey and syrup study had drawn, especially from the influential corn industry. One trustee had declared publicly that scientific progress was "the devil's tool." The board even publicly disapproved of Wiley's personal life, including his regular baseball games with the college students and the high-wheel bicycle that he rode to campus daily, dressed in knee breeches. Trustees had called him into a meeting to upbraid him for making a spectacle of himself, even comparing him to a circus monkey. Wiley, as he wrote in his diary, would have taken insult if he hadn't found the scolding so amusing. Yet he admitted frustration. He had just that year been considered, but passed over, for the post of university president. For the thirty-nine-year-old bachelor, Loring's offer seemed a lifeline out of a job that increasingly felt like a trap.

But he had not anticipated that the ever-combative Collier would turn his attention from Loring to him. Furious at the loss of his job and status, Collier promptly engineered a series of attacks on his designated successor. His well-placed allies wrote to farm trade journals, denigrating the Indiana sugar studies and suggesting that their author was an inferior scientist. Collier also persuaded the senators from his home state of Vermont to visit President Arthur, demanding that Wiley be denied the position. The aggressive campaign only irritated the president and it did not win Collier his job back. But it was successful in embarrassing Wiley.

"These were the first public attacks on me and they cut to the quick," Wiley later wrote. "I felt hurt to be the victim of such insinuations and misstatements." He wrote to the same publications, attempting to defend and justify his work. Collier's faction, in turn, accused him of bragging. The best way to respond to such attacks, he would gradually come to believe, "is to go about one's business and let enemies do their worst." He began packing up for the move to Washington, DC.

In 1883, the Agriculture Department's sprawling campus was situated between the Smithsonian Institution's redbrick castle and the almost-completed Washington Monument. The grounds boasted experimental gardens, greenhouses, conservatories, and a grand, modern main building, built in the 1870s, with a stylish mansard roof. The tiny Division of Chemistry, however, was tucked into what Wiley called a "damp, illy-ventilated, and wholly unsuitable" basement.

One of the first acts of the new chief chemist was to ban smoking. Not only was the laboratory air stale already but a stray spark, he feared, would have turned the place into a bonfire.

For his living quarters, Wiley rented a bedroom from a Washington family, with whom he would happily stay for the next twenty years. Treated as a well-liked family member he frequently spent evenings helping the children with their homework. Social by nature, he accepted an invitation to join the prestigious Cosmos Club, a men-only, intellectually inclined organization whose members included Alexander Graham Bell and Mark Twain. He also joined the more casual Six O'Clock Club, which by contrast did admit women and boasted American Red Cross founder Clara Barton on its executive committee.

New to the charged political climate of Washington, Wiley scored an early coup in 1885, when Grover Cleveland became president. A dedicated Republican, Wiley knew that his job security could well depend on Democrat Cleveland's choice to replace Loring as commissioner of agriculture. The chemist started a letter-writing campaign to influential friends, urging the appointment of Norman J. Coleman, a Missouri Democrat and a longtime publisher of farm trade journals, who approved of Wiley's research. The campaign worked, and Wiley was blessed with a grateful and supportive new boss.

Coleman, who would help create a national network of agricultural experiment stations, also believed that it was a public servant's duty to champion the public interest. In fact, he wanted the chief chemist to be more aggressive in tackling food safety issues— something Wiley too had been advocating. Coleman even had a suggestion for some timely official investigations. He recommended that the Chemistry Division report on the quality and healthfulness of commercially sold milk. The scientists, he proposed, also should investigate dairy products such as butter and evaluate the new and highly suspect industry of butter substitutes.

The problems of the dairy industry had continued to fester

basically unchecked. Mullaly had written in 1853 about the practice wherein distillers housed dairy cows in stinking urban warehouses where each animal was tethered immobile and fed on the spent mash, or "swill," from the fermentation process used in making whiskey, an arrangement that enriched the owners but was linked to a host of public health problems.

In the 1850s *Frank Leslie's Illustrated Newspaper* had exposed these fly-ridden, maggot-infested milk factories, where the animals stood in their own waste, subsisting on the warm swill, which still contained residual sugar and alcohol but little nutrition. Over the cow's short, miserable life, its teeth tended to rot out before the animal stopped giving milk and was sent to slaughter—or dropped dead in the stall. Pediatricians linked swill milk to a list of childhood symptoms of ill health. "I have every year grown more suspicious of distillery milk," one doctor wrote, "whenever I have seen a child presenting a sickly appearance, loose flabby flesh, weak joints, capricious appetite, frequent retchings and occasional vomitage, irregular bowels with tendency to diarrhea and fetid breath."

The notoriously corrupt Tammany Hall government of New York City resisted reform, but finally, in 1862, passed a city ordinance outlawing swill milk, to little effect. Difficult to enforce even in the city, the new law did nothing to help manage poor dairy practices beyond its boundaries. More than two decades later a study published in the *Journal of the American Chemical Society* looked at swill milk still being produced just across the Hudson River in New Jersey and found "so numerous a proportion of liquefying colonies [of bacteria] that further counting was discontinued." A subsequent report in Indiana by that state's board of health added that a random sampling of milk found "sticks, hairs, insects, blood, pus and filth."

Under Wiley the Agriculture Department's first detailed examination of food products, *Foods and Food Adulterants* (technical Bulletin no. 13), was published in three parts in 1887. It revealed, as expected, that little had improved with regard to how milk was produced and what it contained. Wiley's investigating chemists had found a routinely thinned product, dirty and whitened with chalk. It wasn't just bacteria swimming in the milk. At least one of the samples that Wiley's crew tested had worms wriggling in the bottom of the bottle. The Division of Chemistry's findings about other dairy products were more eye opening. Much of the "butter" that the scientists found on the market had nothing to do with dairy products at all except for the fictitious name on the product.

The ability of producers to so mislead resulted from the work of several French chemists, including one of the nineteenth century's greatest, Michel Eugène Chevreul. He drew from the Greek word *margarites*, meaning pearl, and added the Latin for olive, *oleum*, to coin the term *oléomargarine*, which is what he called a glossy, whitish, semisolid that two colleagues had derived from olive oil. In 1869 inventor Hippolyte Mège-Mouriès appropriated Chevreul's terminology and applied it to a butter substitute he made from beef tallow and finely ground animal stomachs. The latter was the basis of a host of butter substitutes embraced by American food processors, which began manufacturing an inventive range of such products in 1876.

Eager to expand a new market, U.S. innovators competed to improve oleomargarine, seeking patents for variations such as "suine" (from suet) and "lardine" (made from pork fat). The industry especially took off after the powerful meatpacking interests realized the potential for profit from the by-products of slaughterhouses and canneries. Barely had the idea of oleomargarine reached the fast-growing Chicago stockyards when some processors decided that if they added just a dab of actual milk to the product, they might cast off its meaty association. Trying for a more appealing name, meatpackers like the Armour brothers and Gustavus Swift borrowed another term for margarine that was in use in Britain, one that at least sounded dairy based: "butterine." Other manufacturers didn't even bother with that terminology; they simply called their oleomargarine "butter."

In his 1883 book *Life on the Mississippi*, Mark Twain recounted overheard comments made by an oleomargarine salesman from Ohio. "You can't tell it from butter," the salesman said. "By George, an EXPERT can't. . . . You are going to see the day, pretty soon, when you can't find an ounce of butter to bless yourself with, in any hotel in the Mississippi and Ohio Valleys, outside of the biggest cities. Why, we are turning out oleomargarine NOW by the thousands of tons. And we can sell it so dirt-cheap that the whole country has GOT to take it—can't get around it, you see. Butter don't stand any show. . . . Butter's had its DAY."

The dairy industry, not surprisingly, disagreed. And furiously. Dairy organizations petitioned members of Congress, demanding action and protection from such deceptive practices. The resulting hearings in both the U.S. Senate and the House of Representatives in 1885 reflected that bitterness, taking up the issue of whether margarine should even be allowed for sale in the United States.

"We face a new situation in history. Ingenuity, striking hands with cunning trickery, compounds a substance to counterfeit an article of food," charged U.S. senator Robert La Follette. A Wisconsin Republican, La Follette was firmly in the corner of that state's numerous dairymen. They objected especially to the practice of coloring oleomargarine to make it look like butter. La Follette conveniently overlooked the fact that butter itself, when produced in the winter from cows fed on hay rather than pasture grass, turns out more white than yellow—and that in addition to diluting and adulterating milk, some dairies routinely added golden coloring to their pale butter. The new, nondairy spreads were nothing better than "counterfeit butter," the senator charged. Congressman William Grout, Republican of Vermont, went further, dubbing the products "bastard butter." Without regulation, who knew what might be in the stuff? Grout called it "the mystery of mysteries."

Patent applications for margarine listed such ingredients as nitric acid, sulfate of lime, and even sugar of lead. Congressman Charles O'Ferral, a Virginia Democrat, decried the inclusion of bromo-chloralum, a disinfectant also used to treat smallpox. O'Ferral charged that the disinfectant's purpose in margarine was "to destroy the smell and prevent detection of the putrid mass" of ground-up sheep, cow, and pig stomachs used in many recipes. Lawmakers wanted to know if other leftover bits of dead animals were finding their way into the recipes. "You do not think that you could make good oleomargarine out of a dead cat or dog?" asked Senator James K. Jones, a Democrat from Arkansas, questioning an industry representative. "It has reached the point in the history of the country where the city scavenger butters your bread," declared Congressman David B. Henderson, an Iowa Republican. Witness L. W. Morton protested. "An ounce of stale fat put into a ton of good fresh fat will spoil the whole," Morton testified, pointing out that it was common knowledge that butter also went bad.

The hearings led to the Butter Act of 1886, which passed with support from both parties and was signed by President Cleveland. But thanks to intervention from the meatpackers, the law was less than hard-hitting, imposing a tax of merely two cents a pound on margarine, leaving the imitation still cheaper to produce than the real thing. The law did define butter as "made exclusively from milk or cream" (with the possible addition of salt or dye), meaning that products like butterine had to be labeled "oleomargarine." False labelers could be fined up to $1,000—assuming they could be caught.

Members of Wiley's staff had been witnesses at the hearings, but their findings in the new Bulletin 13 series weren't issued until the next year, 1887, which made the report an anticlimax of sorts. The studies by the agriculture chemists clearly established, however, that at least a third of what was sold commercially as farm-fresh butter was oleomargarine. The bulletin also noted that thirty-seven American factories were producing more than three million pounds of oleomargarine from animal fats every month. The quality varied widely and there was at least a possibility that some animal parasites could survive the manufacturing process and be present in the spread that consumers purchased. "It is undoubtedly true that a great deal of artificial butter has been thrown on the market that is carelessly made," Wiley wrote.

Still, the Agriculture Department did not offer a blanket condemnation. The division chemists found that if animal-fat oleomargarine was made with care, the product was in many ways comparable to butter, with "nearly the same chemical composition in digestibility. There may be a slight balance in favor of butter but for healthy persons this difference can hardly be of any considerable consequence."

The primary health concerns, the investigation found, derived from dyes used to improve the look of butter and margarine. Traditional butter dyes had been vegetable products: annatto (from the fruit of a South American tree), turmeric, saffron, marigold, and even carrot juice—all benign if pure. But suppliers were adulterating the dyes. Annatto, the most popular, often had brick dust, chalk, and traces of red ocher mixed into it. Processors were also using industrial dyes such as chromate of lead, already notorious for instances of lead poisoning from eating yellow candy. Similar problems occurred in cheese, where manufacturers used red lead to enrich color. In all food products, the report warned, "the use of mineral coloring like chromate of lead is highly reprehensible."

The Division of Chemistry included in the report descriptions of several methods for testing products. With the use of a microscope and a little knowledge of what to look for, it was easy to tell if a spread was butter or margarine. At the molecular level, butter displayed long, delicate, needlelike crystalline structures. Melted, it appeared as shorter needles gathered in bundles. Beef fat crystals, by contrast, appeared as spiky, needle-studded globes, like a "sea urchin or hedgehog." Oleomargarine was a messy tumble of crystalline clumps resembling flattened cauliflowers. Complete with photos, these were handy instructions for anyone with access to a microscope but of little use to the average consumer in 1887.

That same year a New York chemist, Jesse Park Battershall, published a book called *Food Adulteration and Its Detection*, which offered easier home tests. Some, such as one to detect adulterations in tea, could be conducted in any home kitchen. Battershall recommended simply putting the "tea" into a cylinder containing cold water, capping it, and shaking it hard. Ingredients other than tea would form either a scum on the top or a sludge on the bottom. "In this way, Prussian blue (cyanide, used as dye), indigo (another dye), soapstone, gypsum, sand, and turmeric can be separated," Battershall explained. And, he added, housewives should not be too surprised to find them there.

Against the backdrop of rising public concern, and with Commissioner Coleman's support, Wiley resolved to continue raising awareness about impurities and fakery in American food products. The 1887 issues of Bulletin 13 examined three broad areas of food and beverage manufacture, dairy being only the first. The second subject had gotten far less attention—certainly nothing like congressional hearings, let alone a regulatory law—but it concerned products even more rife with fakery. "Could only a portion of the unfortunate dislike for oleomargarine be directed toward the spices?" Wiley wrote in an official letter to his boss.

Two

CHEATED, FOOLED,
AND BAMBOOZLED

1887–1896

———————◉———————

And daintily finger the cream-tinted bread,
Just needing to make it complete

A t the U.S. Customs Service laboratory in New York City, where he was a supervisor, colleagues described chemist Jesse Park Battershall as a rather shy, meticulously cautious scientist. Yet Battershall's 1887 book on food adulteration seethed with outrage over virtually every product that American grocers sold. His list included milk and butter, of course, as well as cheese, coffee, chocolate and cocoa, bread, and "baker's chemicals" (baking powders and sodas), and an appalling amount of candy laced with poisonous metallic dyes. He had tested 198 samples of candy and found that a full 115 were tainted by the use of dangerous dyes, mostly arsenic and lead chromate. Forty-one out of forty-eight samples of yellow and orange-colored candy, in fact, contained lead. He had warned of cyanide, indigo, soapstone, gypsum, sand, and turmeric in teas, but he'd also found that the leaves themselves represented a variety of cheats. In standard black and green teas, Battershall found mixtures of backyard leaves from rosebushes, wisteria vines, and trees, including beech, hawthorn, willow, elm, and poplar.

But even this paled, according to the Chemistry Division's report on spices and condiments, to the fakery involved in these products. This was not entirely a surprise. Ground, flaked, or powdered food products had long been known as easy to cut with something else or be replaced entirely by some other, cheaper powder. Ancient Roman documents tell of first-century BCE merchants selling mustard seed and ground juniper berries as pepper. In thirteenth-century England, there were tradespeople called garblers (from an old Arabic word for sieve), hired to inspect imported spices and sift out grain and grit. Predictably, some garblers, those in the employ of unscrupulous importers or merchants, did just the opposite, mixing ground twigs and sand into the spices themselves. Eventually the very word "garble" came to mean mixing things up incorrectly.

By the late nineteenth century, some countries—notably Great Britain—had laws regulating spices. Clifford Richardson, the scientist whom Wiley assigned to take the lead on the USDA spice study, noted in the bulletin that the Dominion of Canada, then still part of the British Empire, did a much better job monitoring foodstuffs than the United States did. But even so, a recent Canadian marketplace survey had found widespread and rather astonishing levels of fakery.

Richardson, writing in the bulletin, tallied up the damage: Commercially sold dry mustard registered at 100 percent adulteration, allspice at 92.5 percent, cloves 83.3 percent, and ginger 55.5 percent. The Canadian analysis also provided some specifics. For instance, scientists there had found a mixture of ground wheat chaff colored with red clay, with a little inexpensive cayenne pepper thrown in, masquerading as ground ginger. When Richardson examined American-sold "ginger," he discovered burned shells, cracker dust, ground seed husks, and dyes. He also noted that some states— Massachusetts, New York, New Jersey, and Michigan—did require spices to be tested for authenticity and purity and that the results had been appalling. In 1882 Massachusetts regulators had found 100 percent adulteration of ground "cloves," which seemed to be mostly burned seashells. The same year, the state's black "pepper" samples turned up as largely charcoal and sawdust.

When Wiley's team did its own ground pepper analysis, the chemists found it difficult to list or even figure out everything that was in the mixtures: sawdust, cereal crumbs, gypsum, potato scraps, hemp seed, and "to an astonishing extent" powdered olive stones, walnut shells, almond shells, "mineral matter," sand, soil, and more. The chemists mockingly called the spice "pepperette." A new, inexpensive product labeled "pepper dust" they found to be literal dust, apparently common floor sweepings.

"Pepper is more in demand than any other spice and is in consequence more adulterated," explained Richardson. Consumers were too trusting and didn't examine the spices they bought. With his naked eye, he'd been able to pick out crumbled crackers and charcoal in a black pepper sample. He could also pick out the crumbles of brick dust in so-called cayenne pepper. Using a microscope, he detected sawdust in the spice mixes, distinguishing the larger tree cells from the finer cellular structure of a peppercorn.

Some manufacturers took a one-size-fits-all approach to fakery. One New York firm—a purveyor of pepper, mustard, cloves, cinnamon, cassia, allspice, nutmeg, ginger, and mace—had purchased five thousand pounds of coconut shells a year for grinding and adding to every spice on that list.

Other cheats made "mustard" by mixing water with coarsely ground flour or crumbled gypsum, a mineral commonly used to make plaster. To give the resulting sludge a mustardlike tint, Martin's yellow (more technically 2,4-Dinitro-1-naphthol yellow), a coal-tar dye containing benzene (and related to naphthalene, a primary ingredient in moth balls), was added. The chemists had discovered this by adding alcohol to the "mustard" powder, separating out the dye, and analyzing its formula.

Richardson predicted that if manufacturers realized how easily this fakery could be detected, they would find another, perhaps even more harmful, chemical to substitute. With bureaucratic understatement, he noted that spices offered "large scope for inventive genius."

With Wiley's collaboration, he wrote an overtly political call to action in his conclusion to the report. It would be difficult to prevent the rise of such "manufactured" food, he said, "without some governmental action." Crooked spice processors undercut the prices of their honest competitors, leaving no economic incentive for pure products. "When proper legislation has found a place on the statute-books," the report continued, "the manufacturers will find themselves in a position where, without detriment to themselves, they can all unite in giving up the practice." Wiley underlined the point in the letter to Coleman that served as the preface to the spice report: "The necessity for some means for the suppression of the present universal sophistication of spices and condiments seems urgent." Richardson was so disgusted by his findings that he asked to be transferred to another line of research and spent the next years analyzing seeds and grasses.

The third and final Bulletin 13 report of 1887 was devoted to "Fermented Alcoholic Beverages, Malt Liquors, Wine, and Cider." That particular investigation was prompted at least in part by a growing concern about salicylic acid, a preservative that wine bottlers increasingly used—and in increasing amounts—to lengthen the shelf life of their products.

Found in plants such as meadowsweet, wintergreen, and most commonly the bark of willow trees, this natural substance had been used as a pain reliever dating back to ancient Egypt. The Greek physician Hippocrates praised it in the fifth century BCE and Native American healers knew it well. But the name "salicylic acid" or "salicin" was coined after early-nineteenth-century scientists learned to extract the pure compound from the white willow, *Salix alba*, in the early nineteenth century. They also discovered a side effect. When ingested in high doses, pure salicylic acid caused gastric bleeding.

A few decades later, in Germany, pioneering organic chemist Hermann Kolbe and lab partner Rudolf Schmitt developed an economical method for synthesizing large quantities of salicylic acid in a laboratory. They used sodium carbonate as a base for creating needle-shaped crystals that could be replicated time and time again and then ground into a fine powder. Laboratory workers learned to avoid getting a whiff of the crystalline dust, which produced almost instant irritation of the mucous membranes in the nose and set off a sneezing fit. Seeking to establish a safe dose, Kolbe used himself as a test subject, ingesting one-half to one gram daily over several days with no apparent ill effect. His conclusion was that the compound was basically safe if administered in cautious doses.

Other researchers disagreed. French chemists successfully raised safety concerns earlier, in 1881 persuading their government to ban its use as a preservative in wine. Germany also banned salicylic acid in both wine and beer made for domestic use. The Germans, however, did permit breweries to use the chemical in beers made for export to the United States. After all, American authorities had shown no interest in regulating its use. "In this country but little attention seems to have been given to the use of salicylic acid as a preservative," the Chemistry Division's report noted, somewhat sadly, in its conclusion.

The Division of Chemistry staff worried that the compound's use in alcoholic beverages could add up to a harmful dose, especially for a person who consumed several drinks a day. Authored by C. A. Crampton, one of Wiley's staffers, the fermented beverages report noted that American wines contained, on average, almost 2 grams of salicylic acid per bottle. Beers averaged 1.2 grams. But some measured higher. One case of wine contained a full therapeutic dose—3.9 grams—in every bottle tested. Not every vintner used it, but the Chemistry Division had tested seventy American wines—from Riesling to zinfandel, from New York to California—and found that more than one-fourth contained salicylic acid. The same was true for the beers and ales tested. And as a report by New York's Department of Public Health pointed out, the preservative was increasingly found not just in alcoholic beverages but in a wide range of other grocery products, upping the odds of consumers getting a stiff dose every day.

Cyrus Edson, author of the New York report, wrote to Wiley's division, requesting that the federal government take a protective stand against salicylic acid. Edson cited evidence that in addition to causing gastrointestinal bleeding, the compound could damage other organs, including the kidneys, possibly permanently. "This report closes with the recommendation that the addition of salicylic acid, even in small amounts, be absolutely prohibited by law," he wrote. "I would respectfully recommend that some action be taken by this department toward this injurious substance."

He found a receptive audience in Wiley, who was starting to worry that continual exposure to low doses of industrial chemicals— yet to be tested for safety—might indeed be a health issue. Although the chief chemist believed that "a healthy stomach can, from time to time, receive with impunity food containing small qualities of preservatives," he grew increasingly uneasy about the effects of repeating such a dose over and over. In people suffering from ill health, the elderly, the very young, and invalids with "weak or diseased stomachs," he warned that the effects of such constant dosage might be much worse. At least, he argued, there should be a requirement of accurate information on labels, which should, at a minimum, "give the name of the preservative and the quantity employed."

But Wiley also wondered what good it would do to list the ingredients in a food product if no one knew whether those ingredients were safe and in what doses. He began thinking about how he could test to see how much of such additives a person could consume safely. Would it be possible to conduct trials, not just of salicylic acid but other preservatives too, on human subjects?

In 1888 Grover Cleveland lost his bid for reelection. Before he left office, he signed a bill elevating the Agriculture Department to cabinet status. Norman Coleman became the country's first secretary of agriculture, but only for his last month in office, before making way for President Benjamin Harrison's pick, Governor Jeremiah Rusk of Wisconsin.

Like Wiley, Rusk had grown up on a midwestern farm. And like Wiley, the new secretary saw the rise in manufactured, adulterated foods as an evil that needed to be addressed. Rusk, a genial man nicknamed "Uncle Jerry" by the agency staffers, was determined to build up the department as a support system for farmers. Over his few years in the office, the USDA grew rapidly, adding staff to the Chemistry Division and field stations for research around the country. And Rusk tripled the budget for the continuing Bulletin 13 reports, from $5,000 to $15,000 yearly.

After Crampton's report on fermented beverages had rounded out the 1887 edition, Wiley published a study of lard and lard adulterants and, with the additional money from the new Republican administration, scheduled investigations into baking powders; sugar, molasses, honey, and syrup; tea, coffee, and cocoa; and canned vegetables.

The lard study again highlighted the routine nature of adulteration—and the routine false advertising that came with it. Packages of lard—labeled as the best pure hog fat—often contained cheaper fats, mostly waste products from beef manufacturing or cottonseed oil, or both. As he had earlier with oleomargarine, Wiley noted that these particular adulterations were poorly understood in terms of health effects. There was no scientific data to show that pig fat was healthier than cottonseed oil or the other way around. But packages marked "pure lard" that contained no lard lacked such ambiguity. They could be considered only another example of deceptive labeling. He also noted that the Division of Chemistry was finding unlabeled cottonseed oil in a slew of other products, especially in "olive" oils. Almost 200 million pounds of cottonseed oil were now produced in the United States and manufacturers of purportedly higher-end oil and fat products had seized upon this cheaper but "innocuous" raw material. "To do this is a fraud upon the consumer," Wiley wrote in his summary, once again recommending that the ingredients actually be listed on the packaging.

Increasingly frustrated that only a tiny readership—fellow scientists, bureaucrats, lobbyists, and legislative staffers—ever saw his technical reports, Wiley decided to try for a broader audience. In 1890 he hired Alex Wedderburn, a journalist and pure-food advocate, to write easy-to-read copy for the public—in effect, press releases or consumer brochures. And although he thought Wedderburn's first such report contained a little too much advocacy—it blasted the "utter recklessness and hard-heartedness" of food adulterers and condemned their "unlawful and dishonest methods"—he supported its publication, merely advising the writer to tone it down next time.

Not that he and his chemistry staff weren't busy supplying Wedderburn with additional ammunition. The division's 1892 investigation into coffee, teas, and cocoa, for instance, stood out for the level of inventive fraud it uncovered. Tea, as Battershall had already noted, was routinely adulterated, so much so that some manufacturers didn't bother to disguise it. The federal chemists made a point of analyzing a product proudly labeled as "Lie Tea": "This substance, as its name implied, was an imitation of tea, usually containing fragments or dust of the genuine leaves, foreign leaves, and mineral matters, held together by means of a starch solution." As for cocoa, "there is probably no more misleading or abused term in the English language." Cocoa powders contained everything from clay to sand to iron oxides (the latter used as a coloring agent). "Finely powdered tin is sometimes added to give the chocolate a metallic luster," the report added.

Coffee, long America's hot beverage of choice, had frequently been cut with all manner of adulterants ranging from tree bark, sawdust, and ground beets and acorns to relatively flavorful substitutions such as chicory root and the bitter seeds of the blue lupine flower. During the Civil War, Union troops had enjoyed the advantage of coffee that was made—at least in large part—from actual coffee beans while their Confederate counterparts made do with brews of charred wheat, corn, peas, and beans. But that was the ground product. A consumer with access to whole coffee beans and a grinder had, it was assumed, the assurance that the resulting brew was genuine.

By 1892 Wiley's staff had determined that about 87 percent of all ground coffee samples tested were adulterated. "One sample contained no coffee at all." But they'd also found that processors had devised a way to make coffee-free "beans" by pressing a mixture of flour, molasses, and occasionally dirt and sawdust into molds. The chemists discovered that the average scoop of coffee beans in Washington, DC, contained "as high as 25 percent of these artificial bodies." "Dear Sir," began one letter from a distributor to a grocer. "I send you by mail this sample of 'imitation coffee.' This is a manufactured bean and composed of flour; you can easily mix 15 percent of this substitute in with genuine coffee." A flyer from another supplier offered "coffee pellets" consisting of three-fourths filler, 15 percent coffee, and 10 percent chicory. "This makes a very desirable cup of coffee." The flyer further assured grocers it could be sold at full price and was undetectable to consumers.

Producers had also taken to coloring light-colored, inexpensive coffee beans and passing them off as costlier Java beans, recognizable by their glossy, dark appearance. The Division of Chemistry found coffee-coloring agents included charcoal, drop black (a powder made with charred bone), and finely powdered iron. They also turned up traces of more dangerous dyes, such as Scheele's green (arsenic), Prussian blue (cyanide), and chrome yellow (lead). The fake beans were usually polished to an enticing shine using glycerin, palm oil, or even Vaseline (a petroleum-based jelly patented by the British-born chemist Robert Chesebrough in 1872). "Consumers, and especially the poor, are being grossly deceived," the bulletin report concluded. "Very little pure ground coffee is sold, and even the whole coffee does not escape sophistication."

And in case any reader missed the point: "Stringent laws are certainly needed to suppress these frauds."

Lawmakers had taken only small notice of any of the Chemistry Division's food and drink bulletins. Back in 1888, Virginia congressman William H. F. "Rooney" Lee, the son of Confederate general Robert E. Lee, had introduced a bill requiring detailed labeling of products. That legislation failed, but a more powerful advocate had introduced another bill in the upper house in 1891. "The devil has got hold of the food supply in this country," declared sponsor Algernon Paddock of Nebraska, chairman of the Agriculture and Forestry Committee. Industry lobbyists and other opponents of regulation saw signs that Senator Paddock's bill was gaining support. In response, they gathered thousands of signatures on petitions aimed at blocking it. Grocers and factory owners, the National Farmers' Alliance, and the National Colored Farmers' Alliance were among the petitioners. The strongest opposition came from the southern states and their legislators, who, even decades after the Civil War, remained suspicious of any action that might further consolidate federal power. Senators from Tennessee and Georgia railed against the anticipated intrusion, suggesting that the USDA wanted to send spies and informers into the countryside to conduct unwarranted searches of homes and businesses.

Paddock responded by citing the food fraud studies from the Agriculture Department reports. He insisted that Wiley's Chemistry Division was "as nearly nonpartisan in its work as such an institution can be under our system." This was not about states' rights but about responsibility. If the federal government didn't accept its responsibility to keep the food supply honest, American citizens eventually would hold it accountable. The United States was the only Western country that lacked a national law regulating food safety, he pointed out. "Take heed when people demand bread that you continue not to give them a stone," he said, referring to flour that Wiley and his team had discovered to be cut with gypsum and rock dust. Paddock managed to wear down his opponents in the Senate, which did, rather grudgingly, pass his bill. But industry lobbyists blocked a parallel proposal from even getting a hearing on the floor of the House, effectively halting the legislation.

Wiley had advised Paddock on the food safety act at the senator's request. After the measure's failure, he pondered what he saw as a curious lack of support for reform from the public at large. In a paper titled "The Adulteration of Food," Wiley invoked the famously cynical showman P. T. Barnum, writing, "To be cheated, fooled, bamboozled, cajoled, deceived, pettifogged, demagogued, hypnotized, manicured and chiropodized are privileges dear to us all."

He sent the paper to Paddock, who agreed but encouraged him to soldier on anyway. The senator predicted that eventually consumers would come to appreciate that they could not protect themselves against systemic cheating without regulatory help. "Angry waves of popular discontent," he said, would eventually lead to change.

"A cold northeast wind and sleet makes nature look as I feel after yesterday's vote," Wiley wrote in his diary on the morning after Election Day 1892. Former president Grover Cleveland had won his old job back, meaning the well-liked secretary of agriculture Rusk was on his way out. Tired of the uncertainties of politics, Wiley considered leaving his government post. "I have thought for some time of giving it up to go into private business." But he still had such a long list of food safety investigations planned; he decided to stay and hope for the best. That hope would not last long.

The new secretary was Julius Sterling Morton of Nebraska. Like

President Cleveland, he belonged to the conservative wing of his party, often disparagingly referred to as the "Bourbon" Democrats, a reference both to bourbon whiskey and to the Bourbon dynasty in France. Like the French Bourbons in that country's bloody revolution, conservative Democrats had been swept from power with the Civil War. But the Bourbon kings returned to power in 1814 and the Bourbon Democrats had regained legislative power after Reconstruction. Morton, who had been governor of the Nebraska Territory before it became a state in 1867, was a wealthy businessman, a former newspaper editor, and a fierce believer in small government. He came to the USDA determined to make it leaner and more efficient, in keeping with the austerity policies of Cleveland's second term. Under the openhanded benevolence of Harrison appointee Rusk, Morton complained, the Agriculture Department had been "well on the way to becoming a national feed bag."

Morton was in office for a month before he called Wiley into his office to renew the chief chemist's contract and to inform him of plans for a stripped-down Division of Chemistry. The secretary wanted department chemists to concentrate only on science that could directly benefit farmers. He favored research into bettering soils, making more effective fertilizers and pesticides, and developing superior species of grains, hay, and other crops. Eliminating what he judged to be unnecessary services, Morton ordered sorghum and sugar research halted, the scientists doing that work dismissed, and USDA research stations sold off to private interests. He cut the budget for food-purity research by two-thirds. "Is there any necessity for . . . inspectors of food or seekers after adulterants in food?" he wrote in a memo to Wiley. "Would the public interest suffer if these gentlemen cease to draw salaries for what they are alleged to be doing at this time?" In 1893 Congress appropriated another $15,000, requested under Rusk, for Wiley's investigations of food adulteration, but Morton slashed that back to $5,000 and warned the chemist that he had plans to eliminate the studies entirely.

One part of Bulletin 13, an examination of canned vegetables, was still under way, and that, Morton told Wiley, would be the last. The secretary also ordered that Wiley stop sharing his division's findings with the public and recommended that Wiley get rid of the public science writer position held by Alexander Wedderburn. The Agriculture Department's mission did not include educating the public, he insisted.

To say that Wiley disagreed would be an understatement. Morton's demands led to months of exchanges with his chief chemist, during which Wiley fought to keep Wedderburn on the payroll until he could finish one last consumer piece. "It will afford me great gratification if you will show me wherein Mr. Wedderburn, during his connection with the department, has broadened the farmer's market or increased the demand or price of his products," Morton wrote to Wiley. The more people were informed about adulteration, the more they would demand untainted food, Wiley replied. "Such a consummation would be of great benefit to agriculture by relieving the farmer who sells pure foods from competition with the adulterated articles."

Morton then peppered Wiley with questions about Wedderburn's fitness to be part of the Chemistry Department. He asked how many analyses Wedderburn had done. What substances did he analyze? What chemistry school did he go to? How much experience as an analytical chemist did he have? "To your first question," Wiley replied, "None. To your second, none." The man was a talented writer with a gift for explaining science. In other words, Wedderburn was not a graduate of a chemical school and "has never had any experience as a chemist, never professed to be a chemist, and has no reputation as a chemist." Morton wrote back, "So tell me what peculiar fitness and adaptation you found in Mr. Wedderburn for the work of investigating food adulterations."

"I have endeavored in two previous communications to set plainly before you the character of Mr. Wedderburn's work," Wiley wrote, before asking if Morton was willing to throw away the paid hours that Wedderburn had already devoted to the document he was working on. The appeal to frugality worked. Morton agreed to pay the writer one final month's salary so that he could finish the promised document.

But as the secretary had feared, the result was another searing indictment of food manufacturing practices, focused on the increasing use of chemical preservatives and coal tar–derived coloring agents, which Wedderburn described as "poisonous adulterations that have, in many cases, not only impaired the health of the consumer but frequently caused death." Morton was appalled by what he saw as an attack on American business. Again, in the interest of thrift, he didn't kill the report. But he ordered a limited printing of fewer than five hundred copies and told his staff not to publicize it in any way.

Wedderburn, no longer a department employee, was free to defy Morton's order. He mailed copies of his work to farm journals and agricultural publications. This prompted a gratifying response from at least one reader, a farmer, who wrote, "The sentiment and truths contained therein can but meet the indorsement and approval of every honest man throughout our land. If there was ever a time in our history when it became the duty of the farming and laboring class of our people to organize and act in concert for the protection of their families against adulterated and poisoned food, that time is now."

Morton might have sacked Wiley too, but the chief chemist had achieved immense stature in his field, which reflected well on the department. Wiley was, at that point, president of the chemistry section of the American Association of the Advancement of Science, president of the Chemical Society of Washington, and president of the Association of Official Agricultural Chemists, which he had helped found. "President of all the chemical societies in the United States" was his new ambition, Wiley joked. The positions were certainly more gratifying, at the moment, than the position of chief chemist at the Agriculture Department.

He'd learned that the jobs of his staff members researching food adulteration were also under threat. He wrote to Morton that the services of these chemists, who earned an average of a mere $600 per year, after all, "could not be dispensed with without detriment to the public service." Morton's response was that perhaps it would make more sense to cut clerical staff. Wiley fended off that too, pointing out that the support employees, even more modestly compensated, allowed the chemists more time to do their valuable work: "The secretary can rest assured that in their retention there will be no waste of public funds."

Wearing of Wiley's apparently unlimited capacity for pushback, Morton decided the best strategy was to keep his prickly chief chemist busy. "You are hereby directed to proceed to Chicago for duty in connection with the food and cereal exhibit of the Columbian Exposition of 1893," he instructed. Wiley's job would be to promote American agriculture and the public image of the department. He added, "Your traveling expenses to and from Chicago will be paid from the fund appropriated for the investigation of the adulteration of foods."

Wiley wasn't happy about the funding but also appreciated the break from battle—and the chance to be part of the dazzle of the Chicago exposition. Six hundred miles removed from Julius Morton, he was free to conduct a series of public presentations, talks that he delivered personally, focusing on the sad state of the American food supply and his division's work in the detection of fake spices, adulterated cheese, tainted milk, and more. The exhibit he helped organize included a full-scale model of a food chemistry

laboratory, live demonstrations of analyses of everything from bread
to beer, and a public lecture series on modern chemistry. When it was
Wiley's turn to speak, he emphasized his belief that chemistry was a
science that had enormous power to improve and be part of people's
lives—and that scientists themselves should share their work with
others: "The chemist is a social being, and there is a life outside of
the laboratory as beautiful and useful as the life within. The highest
culture is not found in books, but in men. And thus to widen his
horizon and broaden his views the chemist must leave his desk and
seek the acquaintance of his fellows."

In the last week of the exposition, Wiley received a note from a
woman he'd met after one of the talks: Helen Louise Thompson, an
editor at the popular food magazine *Table Talk* ("devoted to the interests of progressive housewives"). Leaving the great fair had been
like "saying goodbye to a fairyland I never expect to see again," she
wrote. But she also wanted him to know that she was taking with
her, back to the real world, a new conviction that food additives were
a dangerous problem, one her readers needed to know about. She
asked Wiley for copies of all the old Bulletin 13 publications, and any
that might still be upcoming as well, and to write for her magazine,
proposing that he do "six or seven papers for the coming year on
food adulterations, of the kind to be of interest to the housekeeper
who does not know chicory from coffee and who really prefers cottonseed to olive oil."

With Algernon Paddock's prediction that Congress would take up
food safety regulation only when American consumers cared enough
to force action in mind, Wiley accepted. He did not consult Secretary
Morton, who, it was becoming clear, regarded Wiley as an enemy.
Morton's most recent cost-cutting move had been to reduce the division's budget for test tubes and beakers. During the process of shutting down the sugar research field stations, Morton had deliberately
sought evidence that he could use to discipline his chief chemist. After
one report from the field, the secretary charged that Wiley had

illegally spent twenty-four cents of department funds on shipping whiskey back home while inspecting research operations in Kansas. The accusation turned out to be as false as it was vindictive. "I was the manager of that company and I am very positive that no bill was ever paid for liquors, or anything else for that matter," wrote an executive at the Parkinson Sugar Company in Fort Scott, Kansas, to Morton. "To those acquainted with Dr. Wiley and his habits, the insinuation that he had liquors shipped here for his own or anybody's private use is absurd." Morton withdrew the charge without apology.

But Wiley recognized that he had to step lightly. In the year after the Columbian Exposition, the Chemistry Division's work focused almost entirely on crop research. Typical was an 1894 bulletin on the chemical composition of the cassava plant. Wiley's public speaking schedule reflected the same approach; at the Brooklyn Institute of Arts and Sciences he discussed "The Relation of Chemistry to Agriculture." Still, occasionally he could push through a small adulteration study.

In the summer of 1894, on his way to help shutter a sugar station in California, he begged a little department money to investigate wine production, especially the use of preservatives. "These are matters which relate particularly to the wholesomeness of a wine and the purity of a food product." Morton agreed to let him have a maximum of $150, which of course proved too little. Wiley spent $250 and Morton made him pay the overrun out of his own pocket.

In 1896 the secretary began requiring that he personally approve every purchase in the department. A request to restock the funnels used in experiments took two months to win his go-ahead, and only after Wiley agreed to sign a document stating "I certify that the following named articles are needed for use in the Division of Chemistry and that the public interest demands their earliest delivery." Wiley tried to economize by skimping on office supplies, but Morton complained that the chief chemist's letters, typed using a nearly spent

typewriter ribbon, were too hard to read. "The letters are all returned to you with the request that they be prepared anew."

In private, Wiley complained that Morton ran the department
with "repression, persecution, and sham reform." Even members of
Congress had noticed. In February, Congressman Chester Long of
Kansas, chairman of the House Committee on Agriculture, wrote to
Wiley directly to tell him that the secretary had once again slashed
the Chemistry Division's budget. "It is difficult usually to do anything under such circumstances but the House at present is not disposed to follow the suggestions of the Secretary of Agriculture,"
Long wrote. He hoped, sincerely, that the department's admired
chief chemist would not give up.

Three

THE BEEF COURT

1896–1899

———————◉———————

A film of the butter so yellow and sweet,
Well suited to make every minute
A dream of delight.

Wiley, as he confided in his diary, was depressed. Some of that was purely personal. His mother, Lucinda, died shortly after Morton took office in 1893. "I was plunged at once out of my long boyhood," Wiley wrote gloomily. Two years later his father, Preston, died as well, leaving him feeling further adrift and alone—an aging bachelor, renting a room in another family's house. His job now was the central focus of his life. And that too seemed to be foundering.

The election of William McKinley in 1896 brightened his outlook. McKinley was not a reformer but he was at least not a Democrat. With a Republican back in the White House wanting his own team, the chief chemist felt confident that Morton would be replaced. And when Wiley received his first-ever invitation to an inaugural ball, he allowed himself to hope it was a signal of resurgence, not just for him but also for the status of the Chemistry Division.

The early signs for that were good. McKinley appointed a former congressman, James Wilson, as the USDA's next secretary. A sixty-two-year-old professor of agriculture from Iowa State University, Wilson still farmed, growing feed corn in Iowa's Tama County, which had earned him the nickname "Tama Jim." The new secretary told Wiley immediately that his job was secure and within six months had restored full funding to the Division of Chemistry, encouraging him to begin planning new food-adulteration studies.

Perhaps it was under the influence of such a wave of renewed optimism that the chief chemist, at the age of fifty-three, took an unexpected and uncharacteristic step. He fell in love at first sight with a twenty-one-year-old USDA librarian. "I saw a young woman with a book in her hand, apparently looking for the proper place to deposit it. I was immediately struck by her appearance," he confided to a friend. She was slight, fine featured, with light brown hair and dark blue eyes. He noticed with admiration her direct, intelligent gaze. As he liked to tell the story, Wiley grabbed the arm of Edward Cutter, the library manager, and demanded to know the woman's name. The manager identified her as Anna Kelton.

"Cutter," Wiley said, "I'm going to marry that girl."

"Perhaps it would be well for you to meet the young lady before proposing matrimony," Cutter replied. Wiley greeted Anna Kelton politely, as befitted a senior official in the department, but he resolutely began plotting a courtship.

Anna "Nan" Kelton, a graduate of George Washington University, was more intent on a career. Her protective mother, Josephine, recently widowed, was even more intent in that desire. Born in Oakland, California, Anna had come with her family to Washington in 1893, when her father, Colonel John C. Kelton, was appointed governor of the Soldiers Home, a military retirement facility in the northwest quadrant of the capital. He had died of an infection just a year after taking the post, leaving his widow determined to see that her children thrived in their own right.

Wiley knew the odds were against him, but he began by politely asking Cutter if he could borrow Miss Kelton for some stenography work. From there, she gradually came to take over many of the chemistry chief's secretarial needs. Also gradually, she allowed him to escort her to the occasional play or concert. But when he called at her home, Josephine deliberately made him feel unwelcome, and he found himself again balanced between hope and discouragement.

As McKinley's presidential term began, Congress once again reluctantly considered the quality of the nation's food and beverages. The legislative attention was focused, though, on a particular beverage—and, as newspapers cheerfully pointed out, one that enjoyed legislative favor. That would be whiskey, and the rule under consideration was one setting "bonded" standards for the spirit.

The term dated to an 1868 law, which had granted distillers a delay between the time when they produced their product and when they had to pay a federal tax on it. This "bonded period" had originally been set at a year but over time was increased. It provided a financial incentive for letting spirits sit in barrels before being bottled for sale, and it resulted in aged whiskey—amber colored and more complex and mellow in taste. A distiller could charge considerably more for a well-aged bottle of spirits than for liquor straight from the still. High-end makers began to campaign for federal regulation that would do more than give them a tax-free grace period but that would also protect their profitable reputations for making the good stuff. Edmund Haynes Taylor Jr.—who bore the Kentucky honorific "colonel" and was the namesake of Old Taylor brand bourbon—was among the distillers who sought rules to distinguish products like his from, as he put it, "carelessly made whiskeys whose aim is quantity and whose objective is mere chaffering for cheapness."

Those chafferers, as Taylor called them, sometimes sold their lesser products with phony labels proclaiming them to be Taylor's brand or Jasper "Jack" Daniel's famed Old No. 7. The fakes were often made using rectified alcohol, also called neutral spirits. These were a concentrated form of ethyl alcohol, usually produced on an industrial scale by repeatedly distilling the liquid to purify it and increase its strength. To simulate whiskey, the product was diluted with water and tinted brown—often with tobacco extracts, tincture of iodine, burned sugar, or prune juice.

In 1897, after decades of complaints over the widespread adulteration and fakery of alcoholic spirits, Congress passed the Bottled-in-Bond Act, which attempted to encourage basic quality standards. The act stated that each bottle of spirits could be marked with a green "bonded" seal from the government if it was aged for at least four years in a supervised federal warehouse. Bonded whiskey was also labeled for proof (a measurement set in the United States as twice the percentage of alcohol) and the location of the specific distillery.

Makers of blended whiskeys, meanwhile, were also trying to fend off counterfeiters and set quality standards. Blended whiskeys are, as the name indicates, made from a mixture of distilled spirits. They usually contain a high-quality aged product, derived from a single distillation, to establish flavor, together with other, lesser whiskeys added for economy. Sometimes, in lower-quality blends, there are also neutral spirits added to the mix, along with dyes to enhance color.

Although they could not qualify for the bonded designation at their best, blends could be high-quality products sold at premium prices—prime targets for the counterfeit-label scam. In the nineteenth century, Canada's Hiram Walker Company, producer of Canadian Club blended whiskey, reacted to fakery in the U.S. market by hiring detectives to hunt cheats. The company took out newspaper advertisements listing the perpetrators or had the names listed on billboard posters proclaiming "A Swindle, These People Sell Bogus

Liquors." Yet inexpensive blended whiskeys were too often no better than the counterfeits. For that reason, producers of blended whiskeys were sometimes lumped together under the somewhat derogatory label "rectifiers." Wiley—who of an evening often enjoyed a glass of fine, aged bourbon—had little regard for anything called a blend and tended to dismiss any alternatives to straight whiskey as belonging to a catalog of fakes, admittedly of varying quality.

After the Bottled-in-Bond Act, Colonel Taylor and his friends began publishing advertisements touting bonded whiskey as the only "real" whiskey. Producers of blends—both good and bad—protested, to little effect at the time. But their sense of a real injustice did not end, and neither did their determination to fight for a change. The rectifiers, and their quest for equality, would lead to years of wrangling over what could rightly be called whiskey, plaguing Wiley, Wilson, and a series of presidents in the years ahead.

McKinley himself showed no interest in the topic—or in food or drink quality in general. He had other far more pressing issues, including a politically charged decision to go to war with Spain over Cuban independence in 1898. Although the conflict was brief—lasting only from April to August of that year—the aftershocks were profound. The United States became something of an imperial power, gaining former Spanish colonial possessions, including Puerto Rico, Guam, and the Philippines. And although the war was brief, it showcased so many examples of outdated and inept management of the U.S. military that McKinley was forced to replace the secretary of war, Russell Alger.

To the president's dismay, among the most stubborn scandals regarding mismanagement was one involving the quality of food fed to the troops. The story—which made newspaper headlines coast to coast—involved the shoddy state of the beef fed to American soldiers during the conflict. Testimony at the resulting hearings before the War Department would range from Wiley as an expert witness on food safety to then–New York governor Theodore Roosevelt as an aggrieved former soldier.

The "embalmed beef" scandal arose soon after the war's end in August. Major General Nelson Miles, commanding general of the army, called for an investigation of food that had been supplied to soldiers in Cuba. He'd asked all the commanders stationed in the Caribbean to write evaluations of the canned beef delivered to their regiments. Miles, citing reports of a chemical smell wafting from the product, called it "embalmed beef," a term that caught on in the nation's newspapers. The press reported that Miles had received descriptions of cans swarming with maggots and cans supposedly containing a mix of meat and charred rope. The *Chicago Tribune*—a paper particularly interested in the business of the meatpacking industry—quoted soldiers who said that often when the cans were opened they "had to retire to a distance to prevent being overcome" by the stench.

As Miles was airing his complaints, the War Department (roughly analogous to today's Department of the Army) began a general inquiry into the overall conduct of the war. At the direction of President McKinley, secretary of war Russell A. Alger appointed a long-retired Civil War officer, Major General Grenville Dodge, to lead an investigative panel that became known as the Dodge Commission. A wealthy businessman and former congressman, Dodge transported the commission aboard his own private railroad car to interview witnesses around the country. He also held numerous hearings in Washington, DC, where Miles was called to testify that December.

Miles cited a letter from one army doctor, which claimed that much of the canned beef shipped from the United States was "apparently preserved by injected chemicals to aid deficient refrigeration." The canned meat smelled like formaldehyde when opened, the doctor said, and when cooked tasted of chemical preservatives. Another officer described the canned meat as having an "unnatural, mawk-ish, sickening" odor. It was a national disgrace, Miles said, to serve chemically tainted meat with "no life or nourishment in it" to men who had put their lives at risk for their country.

Miles's angry remarks prompted an even angrier response from Brigadier General Charles P. Eagan, commissary general of subsistence, when he testified before the commission the following month. "He lies in his throat, he lies in his heart, he lies in every hair on his head and every pore in his body," said Eagan about Miles. "I wish to force the lie back in his throat, covered with the contents of a camp latrine."

In February 1899, the Dodge Commission issued a voluminous document titled "Report of the Commission Appointed by the President to Investigate the Conduct of the War Department During the War with Spain." It reflected none of the anger expressed by Eagan and Miles. Rather it contained cautious recommendations regarding army medical practices, supplies, troop movements, and more. And it did not reach a conclusion about the bad-smelling beef. The only officer punished in the wake of the hearings was Eagan, not for pro-curing distasteful meat or shipping it to the troops but for the grave offense of insulting his senior officer in public. Found guilty, Eagan, already in his late fifties, was relieved of duty until he reached the mandatory retirement age of sixty-four.

The Dodge hearings satisfied neither Miles nor the public, who remained furious that America's fighting men had been fed bad rations. Newspapers tracking the story accused the army of covering up its own substandard practices; private citizens telegraphed the White House in outrage. Under pressure, an increasingly irate President McKinley ordered the War Department to hold another inquiry on the specific question of the quality of the beef that had been supplied to U.S. troops. The *Chicago Tribune* immediately christened this second tribunal the "Beef Court." It convened in March 1899.

In anticipation, the president had summoned Secretary Wilson to the White House to ask for help with chemical analysis from Harvey Wiley's crew. "I called on Secretary Alger to request that he send me samples of the canned beef that were furnished to the soldiers last summer," Wilson wrote to Wiley, "for the purpose of determining whether any deleterious substances have been added to them in the course of preparation to more perfectly preserve them."

Wiley and his chemists had already begun to draw a precise and unappetizing portrait of all American canned beef—not just military rations. Every can they opened contained a soupy mix of meat scraps and fat. The fat was standard in canned meat production because manufacturers used it to fill spaces between the scraps. Before a can was sealed, hot fat or a boiled-bone gelatin was poured in to "fill all the interstices not occupied by pieces of meat." Finding a thick paste of gelatinous fat embedded with shreds and chunks of meat wasn't unexpected and, in fact, the chemists noted, the solid mass probably prevented some bacterial spoilage.

Wiley drew test samples from military supplies and from cans available in stores from three of the nation's biggest packinghouses, Libby, McNeil & Libby, Armour, and Cudahy, all residents of Chicago's Union Stockyards. All three had grown bigger since the oleomargarine study in the 1880s. The yards now processed close to twenty million animals a year. "Packingtown," as the locals called it, had become even more notorious for its pervasive dirt, gore, and offal.

This was a community of immigrant labor—Irish, German, Polish, Russian, anyone in desperate need of a job. The workers manned "the killing floors" for ten-hour shifts, earning perhaps ten cents an hour. Women could be hired for half that; they were employed mostly to pack the meat into boxes or cans. Children were cheaper yet; a six-year-old boy could be paid to run messages around a factory for a mere penny an hour. As the industry emphasized, Americans liked their meat inexpensive. Fresh beef could be found in the grocery store for twelve cents a pound. The average housewife could pick up three cans of corned beef for a quarter. When the War Department's Commissary Division had wanted an even better deal, the packers had found it easy to comply. Libby, McNeill & Libby alone had unloaded seven million pounds of canned meat into the military supply depots, as the army's investigating panel would note.

The Beef Court convened in the new State, War, and Navy Building on Washington's Pennsylvania Avenue. The hearing chamber was crammed with journalists, annoying both War Department officials and the meatpackers, who were angry over being portrayed publicly as poisoners of American soldiers. Roosevelt, then the thirty-nine-year-old governor of New York, appeared as a star witness early in the proceedings. At the beginning of the war, he had famously left his post as assistant secretary of the navy to form the First U.S. Volunteer Cavalry Regiment, popularly known as the Rough Riders. Bearing the rank of colonel, Roosevelt had been hailed as one of the heroes of the brief conflict, and his testimony was front-page news.

"I first knew there was trouble with the beef while we were lying off the quay in Tampa Bay," he said. "I noticed a man named Ash—I think he was from Kentucky—preparing to throw away his portion of canned roast beef. I asked him why he was throwing it away. He said, 'I can't eat it.' I told him that he was a baby and that he did not go to war to eat fancy menus and that if he was not satisfied with the rations he had better go home. He ate the meat and vomited." The governor said he had then examined the rations. "When the cans were opened, the top was nothing more than a layer of slime. It was disagreeable looking and nasty. The beef was stringy and coarse and seemed to be nothing more than a bundle of fibers."

Roosevelt stressed that the issue was that good men had been served poorly by their country, sent into war with provisions that were "uneatable, unpalatable, unwholesome . . . utterly unsafe and utterly unfit." He added that his men, unable to eat what was supplied, were half starved much of the time in Cuba. Roosevelt said he had personally quit eating the army meat rations, subsisting on beans and rice while awaiting food packages sent by his family. "I would rather have eaten my hat," he said.

Newspapers reported that Roosevelt was flushed and ill tempered by the time he finished testifying. Stamping out of the hearing room, trailed by a crowd of fascinated journalists, he turned to a friend and snapped, "It was a disgrace to our country." He was followed on the stand by dozens of equally embittered former soldiers. One after another, they described a slimy product with a chemical tang and, often, visible rot. Army cooks cited the thick greenish deposit they routinely scraped out of roast beef cans. There was also a lengthy discussion of the so-called fresh beef shipped down from the yards. One soldier marveled over a heavily preserved side of beef that, he claimed, hung in the sun for hours in a state of eerie stasis, showing no sign of decomposition. A medical officer testified that much of the beef "had an odor similar to that of a dead human body after being injected with formaldehyde, and it tasted when first cooked like decomposed boric acid." A funeral home director who had served as a soldier in Cuba also mentioned the familiar aroma of embalming chemicals. More than that, he said, the cans of beef were crowded with crystals that looked eerily like the ones that formed in corpses when he injected preservatives. "It did not look like roast beef," a corporal testified.

Eventually, expert witness Harvey Wiley came quietly to the stand. At least a few of the reporters in attendance leaned forward. The chemistry chief was in no way as famous as Governor Roosevelt, but he enjoyed a certain reputation for the trouble he had caused producers of dirty coffee and acid-laced wines. At a recent party, a food trade journal editor had refused to shake Wiley's hand, explaining that he felt no need to be civil to "the man who is doing all he can to destroy American business."

Wiley testified calmly that his staff had found traces of "all of the preservatives ordinarily employed in meat products" in the army supplies. These included "boric acid, salicylic acid, sulfites and sulfurous acid," all of them common and all considered relatively safe, although Wiley, if he had been pressed, would have admitted that he lacked data about how safe they might be and in what doses. The cans sold to the War Department had not been adulterated with the latest industrial chemicals, certainly not synthesized formaldehyde, he said. Instead, the packers had relied mostly on far cheaper sodium chloride—plain old table salt—in combination with potassium nitrate, also relatively inexpensive. Widely known as saltpeter, the latter substance was also an ingredient in gunpowder. Salts had been used this way since the Middle Ages and undoubtedly much earlier. Potassium nitrate, usually mined from guano deposits, was used not only to stop decay but also to treat disease. Eighteenth-century physicians had dosed patients with it to treat everything from asthma to arthritis. In the tiny amounts found in the cans, the compound shouldn't pose any particular risk, Wiley said.

The canned beef had been garden-variety cheap meat—stringy, gristly, poorly handled, and too quick to decompose. And rather than using preservatives too heavily, the cost-conscious meatpackers hadn't used enough salts to prevent decomposition when the cans were exposed to the Cuban heat. This lack had accounted for much of the rot and discoloration found in many cans when they were opened. Wiley speculated that eventually, the very appearance of the stuff "might produce a feeling of nausea or distaste in the person eating it." But he also gave credence to the reports of widespread illnesses blamed on the meat. Many were probably ptomaine poisoning, the general term for bacterial contamination, he said. He testified that the army should have put in place "a supervising agent to check for decay or signs of failed sterilization."

A member of his team, food chemist Willard Bigelow, also testified, reinforcing Wiley's points and adding details. Bigelow—slight, bespectacled and bearded, meticulously tidy, and intense by nature—was known as a tireless and stubborn investigator. For this analysis, he'd visited meatpacking operations not only in Chicago but also in Kansas City and Omaha. He'd run chemical analyses and taste-tested every sample. If the cans had been loaded with industrial preservatives, Bigelow testified, "the taste would be so bitter that it would soon be detected." He made it clear that he'd not enjoyed tasting meat that he judged to be from "the poorest cattle"—possibly diseased. It was terrible-quality beef, he said, but contrary to widespread rumor, it was indeed beef. He'd found no evidence that the soldiers had been dished up diced horse meat.

Perhaps the most condemnatory conclusion that the USDA chemists had reached was that the canned meat that had so disgusted soldiers in Cuba was almost exactly what U.S. consumers were finding on grocery shelves. In response, representatives from the meatpacking firms accepted none of this; they firmly defended their products. Libby issued a statement pointing out that it had been in business for twenty-five years and knew a lot more about meat and its quality than the average soldier: "We sold millions of pounds of canned meat to the government for use in the war and no cans have ever been returned to us as bad," which was true, as the War Department had destroyed the bad meat. The company suggested the real problem was lousy cooks: "All meats require pepper and salt and as the soldiers did not have any seasoning, it is likely the canned meat tasted flat to them. That may have had some effect on them." A spokesman for Augustus Swift's company declared that the packinghouse had not used embalming compounds in meat sold to the military—or to anyone else. It would be, he said, bad business.

The Beef Court concluded by issuing findings that expressed dissatisfaction with almost everyone involved, including General Miles, for raising such a fuss. The judicial panel noted that it was difficult to assess just how substandard the food had been because much of the spoiled or tainted meat was "burned or buried" rather than served to the men. The presiding officers also pointed out that the destruction of food would have left the military kitchens undersupplied if not for the fact that "the entire army was so reduced by sickness and debilitation, due to climatic influences," that many of the men hadn't been eating anyway.

There was nothing in the investigation, the panel continued, to suggest that tainted meat was the major cause of illness. The evil effects of bad water and tropical fevers were found to be the major cause: "The court finds it impossible to conclude that either the canned beef or the refrigerated beef appeared to an appreciable extent as causes of intestinal disease." Taking a cue from Wiley and Bigelow, the ruling found that supplies sent to Cuba had been no "better or worse than any other," although they were probably not suitably packaged to withstand tropical heat and perhaps were inadequately spiced or prepared in the field.

Soldiers who had served in Cuba remained unconvinced. Spanish-American War veterans insisted ever after that the meat had stunk of formaldehyde. One of them was the poet Carl Sandburg, who said years later that he could not forget the stink of the army meat. "It was embalmed," he said, "every suck of nourishment gone from it though having nevertheless a putridity of odor more pungent than ever reaches the nostrils from a properly embalmed cadaver."

The army also sought the Chemistry Division's help in investigating the death of nineteen-year-old Private Ross Gibbons of Peoria, Illinois, who had collapsed in convulsions after dining on a can of corned beef at a Tennessee training camp. A day later he died. Chemical analysis showed that the contents of the can had been saturated with the neurotoxic metal lead, which had apparently seeped out of the container itself. Lead was also found in his body.

Metal poisoning from canned goods didn't surprise Wiley. His laboratory had flagged the problem years earlier. The coffee investigation had noted that "relatively large" amounts of tin were seeping into canned foods. And in the part of Bulletin 13 investigating canned vegetables, which was printed—and promptly shelved—just before Julius Morton had shut down the food investigations, lead poisoning had been highlighted as a primary concern.

Lead solder was then the preferred method for sealing the seams of tin cans. But while European countries regulated lead levels in solder, the United States had set no standards, not even for food containers. The Chemistry Division had found that some of the solders used in tin cans were 50 percent lead. Further, the "tin" used to make cans was an unregulated alloy of whatever metals the manufacturer had handy. "In this country there is no restriction whatever in regard to character of the tin employed and as a result of this the tin of some of the cans has been found to contain as high as 12 percent of lead." The analysis also found other toxic metals including zinc and copper. Even glass containers used for canning could be contaminated. Jars were capped with lead tops and sealed with rubber pads or rings that contained sulfate of lead. Testing of jar-canned goods had found that the food inside sometimes contained higher lead levels than those found in the tin cans. As the study, overseen by the tireless Willard Bigelow, concluded: "The general result of the examination of the canned goods exposed for sale in this country leads to the rather unpleasant conclusion that the consumers thereof are exposed to . . . poisoning from copper, zinc, tin and lead."

Those earlier findings had been suppressed, but under Secretary Wilson, Wiley was again free to publicize his laboratory's food safety findings. And after the beef court, he realized that his cause was finally in the public eye. Editors were eager to feature his writing, which appeared frequently in publications that ranged from somber scientific journals to the liberal, reform-minded *Arena* to popular *Munsey's* magazine, with its circulation of more than 700,000 readers. In a *Munsey's* article, Wiley detailed his division's survey of bread and cake "flour" sold in the United States, which they had found to be liberally laced with ground white clay and powdered white rocks called "barites." Some flour, labeled as made from wheat, was really cheaper corn flour, whitened with sulfuric acid. Manufacturers made the acid-treated corn product, labeled "flour-ine," and the ground clay product, called "mineraline," specifically for sale to flour companies. In his article, Wiley quoted from a marketing bulletin that read, "Gentlemen: We invite your attention to our mineraline, which is without a doubt the greatest existing discovery. There is no flourmill man who can afford not to use it for several reasons. Your flour will be much whiter and nicer. And you will realize a profit of between $400 to $1600 per carload of shipped flour barrels."

Almost as soon as the beef court had concluded, there were new, tragic reports of not just "embalmed beef" but also "embalmed milk" causing sickness and death in places like Ohio, Nebraska, and Indiana. In June 1899 the city of Cincinnati warned citizens of "an epidemic of stomach trouble, due practically entirely to embalmed beef." More than one thousand people had fallen ill in a single week after eating beef. The Cincinnati health department had first suspected salicylic acid. As Willard Bigelow had noted in the embalmed beef hearings, this compound was increasingly popular with commercial butchers, who had discovered it could freshen the look of graying beef, setting off a chemical reaction that made old meat look newly pink for a good twelve hours. That time frame, Bigelow had said, was just long enough to move the meat out of the store and into the home kitchen.

Cincinnati's public health chemist, to his surprise, did not find salicylic acid in the samples tested. Instead he discovered two new brand-name preservatives, both of which confirmed widespread public suspicion and finally justified the use of the term "embalmed beef." One was Freezine, a sulfur-rich mixture containing a small percentage of formaldehyde. Freezine's promotional literature boasted: "Meat can be exposed for sale, returned to ice, more of the preparation applied, and still look good to the eye." The other, Preservaline, contained formaldehyde as its main active ingredient.

Cincinnati officials recommended that citizens play it safe and avoid beef altogether.

That same month, the city of Omaha reported an "embalmed milk" crisis that had led directly to the deaths of an alarming number of children. The Nebraska health department warned "all families, as far as possible, to cease the use of milk and cream furnished by local dairies." The problem again was Preservaline. The dairy industry had also discovered that formaldehyde was a useful food additive. Not only did it slow the souring of milk, but its oddly sweet taste could also mask the somewhat acrid tang of milk that had already gone bad. "It is noticeable," announced the city's public health officer, "that more infants have died in Omaha this spring than ever before." And spring, he continued, was usually "a time when the general health conditions should have been good." Following the uptick in child deaths, the department had surveyed physicians and found that almost all the recent infant deaths were related to preservatives in milk.

Hardly had the Omaha milk scandal died down when another flared in Indiana. Dairies near Indianapolis apparently weren't bothering with commercially prepared formulas like Preservaline. They were simply pouring straight formaldehyde into rotting milk. Then they sold it on the cheap to poor families and to budget-strapped facilities like orphanages. The practice had been linked to the deaths of more than two dozen children in Indianapolis orphanages.

The Indiana state health officer, Dr. John Hurty, a former professor of pharmacy at Purdue University and an old friend of Harvey Wiley, had also earned a reputation as a tireless crusader. His work for causes ranging from smallpox vaccination to pasteurization of milk would eventually lead to his election as president of the American Public Health Association. In the aftermath of the orphanage deaths, Hurty explained to journalists that the toxic compounds had proven an economic boon to dairymen, who used to have to throw out milk when it went bad. "Two drops of a forty percent solution of formaldehyde will preserve a pint of milk for several days," Hurty said. There were no safety tests available, but businessmen had gambled that the amount put into food and drink was too low to cause harm. It turned out some dairymen were adding extra drops of formaldehyde solution on the principle that it would even better preserve their product.

Hurty's department advised that even an "infinitesimal amount" of formaldehyde could be dangerous, especially to infants. "Such being the fact, it should not be used for preserving foods," he insisted. When a newspaper reporter sympathetic to the dairy industry asked him why he was making such a big deal about it, Hurty snapped back: "Well, it's embalming fluid that you are adding to the milk. I guess it's all right if you want to embalm the baby." After his press conference, the *Indianapolis News* published a cartoon showing a large glass bottle labeled "Milk" with a monster coiling from the bottle's open mouth. The creature was an evil-eyed scaly thing with jagged teeth and sharp claws. A baby in a diaper stood looking up at the monster, holding only a rattle to defend itself. "It looks like a tough battle for the little fellow" read the caption.

Hurty had been trying for years to get the Indiana legislature to pass a food safety law, arguing that it was essential due to the lack of federal action. With more victims every day—the embalmed milk epidemic would eventually kill an estimated four hundred children in the state—and a corresponding rise in public outrage, the state passed its Pure Food Law in 1898. Hurty promptly banned all use of formaldehyde in milk. He also launched a campaign to clean up dairy practices in general. Many dairies were still notoriously unsanitary, and milk routinely contained dangerous colonies of disease-causing bacteria, among other impurities. Commercially sold milk that Hurty's department had recently analyzed contained horsehair worms, flakes of moss, and traces of manure. Further, the chief health officer could "state confidently that this milk has been adulterated with stagnant water."

He strongly recommended adoption of the flash-heat process for killing microorganisms and preventing spoilage in beverages, a method developed in the 1860s by French scientist Louis Pasteur. Pasteurization had proven a success in the wine and beer industries in Europe and had more recently begun being used by European dairies to kill bacteria in their product. It was time, Hurty said, for the United States to catch up.

Four

WHAT'S IN IT?

1899–1901

———————◦———————

And yet while we eat
We cannot help asking, "What's in it?"

In 1899 U.S. senator William Mason of Illinois asked for and received permission from Secretary Wilson for Wiley to serve as scientific adviser for a new series of hearings on the country's tainted food and drink supply. Mason, a Republican from Chicago described by newspapers as "a champion of liberty," had a reputation as a progressive legislator and a reform-minded opponent of machine politics.

The Mason hearings began that very spring, with meetings scheduled not only for Washington but also for New York and Chicago. They would continue for nearly a year, encompassing fifty different sessions and almost two hundred witnesses. The Chemistry Division would be nearly overwhelmed by the need to analyze hundreds of additional samples of food and drink. State public health officials lined up to testify, from Indiana's Hurty, caught up in his state's milk scandal, to the chief chemist from Connecticut, whose laboratory had discovered that spice processors in that state were burning old rope and using the ash as filler in ground spices such as ginger. Businessmen also testified, the honest ones decrying unfair competition from fraudsters. Representatives from the cream of tartar industry warned that baking powders were tainted with aluminum. Representatives from the dairy industry testified that makers of oleomargarine (by which they meant meatpackers) were still consistently mislabeling their product as butter.

Without federal help, dairy states had little recourse; the state of New Hampshire had tried requiring that all margarine be dyed pink, but the U.S. Supreme Court had struck down that legislation in 1890, declaring it an illegal tax. Dairymen complained at the Mason hearings that margarine makers were nothing but cheats and liars. The meatpackers, in turn, accused the dairy industry of being stuck in the primitive past. Anyone, they insisted, could tell the difference between old-fashioned, often rancid butter and ever-fresh oleomargarine, which was "a product of the advanced age."

At Mason's request, the Chemistry Division's Willard Bigelow had looked again at dishonesty in the wine industry, finding the usual preservatives, such as salicylic acid, swirling through many bottles. He'd also found many bottles that were labeled as wine but were merely factory-produced ethanol colored with coal-tar dyes and flavored with fruit peels. One wine dealer, when visited by Bigelow posing as a shop owner, had asked "what distinguished label" his visitor desired. He'd taken Bigelow's list and then, while the chemist watched, filled everything from the same cask, simply pasting labels on the different bottles to identify them as claret, Burgundy, or Bordeaux.

For almost every food product, the Chemistry Division could point to a trick involved in its manufacture. Doctors continued to worry over continued reports of "grocer's itch," a side effect of the deceptive practice of grinding up insects and passing the result off as brown sugar. Sometimes live lice survived the process. Beer, which most consumers imagined to be derived from malted barley and hops, was often made from a cheaper ferment of rice or even corn grits. So-called aged whiskey often was still routinely rectified alcohol, diluted and colored brown. As Wiley had found twenty years earlier at Purdue, corn syrup was widely used as the basis for fake versions of honey and maple syrup.

Many manufacturers argued that they had to fake products to stay competitive. Detroit canner Walter Williams, of Williams Brothers, described the making of his Highland Strawberry Preserves. The jam was, he said, 45 percent sugar, 35 percent corn syrup, 15 percent apple juice made from discarded apple skins, some scraps of apple skin and cores, and usually one or two pieces of strawberry. The strawberries cost him, he added. Many comparably priced preserves were just glucose, apple juice, red dye, and timothy seed added to simulate strawberry seeds. "If we could sell pure goods, I would be pleased," Williams insisted. "I believe they should be labeled, showing their ingredients and showing the quality of the goods." But as there was no law setting such standards and as he had to compete with less scrupulous canners, there was no way for him to stay in business unless he cut costs to match.

Wiley testified that about 5 percent of all foods were routinely adulterated, with the number being much higher—up to 90 percent—in categories such as coffee, spices, and "food products made for selling to the poor." This proved to be a little too sedate a summary for some of the tabloid journals; reporters exaggerated his testimony, stating that Wiley believed 90 percent of *all* food and beverage products to be adulterated. The careless reporting dismayed Wiley, his boss Wilson, and even the president—especially after alarmed American trade representatives wrote from Europe that grocers there were talking about boycotting U.S. food entirely. Wilson had to send clarifications and copies of Wiley's actual testimony to the State Department in order to reassure importers of American food and drink.

In other testimony, Wiley concentrated on preservatives and dyes. For example, he cited the practice of improving the color of canned peas by spiking them with copper sulfate and zinc salts. In small doses, these metals might pose little risk, he said, but no one really knew what those safe doses were. As he had earlier, he also warned of a possible cumulative dose: Who could ensure that a steady diet of the stuff, over months or even years, wouldn't lead to heavy metal poisoning? Another witness, chemical physiologist Russell Chittenden of Yale University, echoed that point even more strongly, warning that most people eating canned vegetables would eventually be harmed by repeated exposure to metals. He urged that copper, in particular, be banned as an additive from American food products as soon as possible.

Wiley again emphasized that the biggest worry was for vulnerable populations: young children, people with chronic health problems, and the elderly. Those with a healthy stomach, as he put it, were unlikely to be harmed by an occasional exposure to copper or zinc. The problem was that no one was sure who would be harmed: "Many people they do hurt and the least possible amount upsets the digestion."

Unlike Chittenden, Wiley did not urge an immediate ban. Rather, Wiley told the assembled senators that such regulations needed to be grounded in good science. He urged that the government invest in studying the health effects of such additives. If risks were clearly and methodically identified, then those compounds should be removed from all food and drink. And, somewhat wearily, he once again recommended that manufacturers be required to tell consumers, on labels, what was being mixed into their products. "Were it as harmless as distilled water," he said, "there would be no excuse of its addition to food without notification to the consumer."

State food chemists also expressed dismay over the new additives. A. S. Mitchell, food chemist for the state of Wisconsin, brought to the hearings samples of three of the most popular new preservatives: Rosaline Berliner, Freezine, and Preservaline, the formaldehyde-rich culprit in the Indiana milk poisonings. He pointed out that none of them had been safety-tested; that all of them had been found in samples of commercially sold ice cream, cottage cheese, beef, chicken, pork, and shellfish; and, finally, that none of those foodstuffs bore a label listing ingredients.

With the Rosaline Berliner, Mitchell highlighted what he saw as the alarming increase in the use of its active ingredient—sodium borate, or borax. A naturally occurring mineral salt, it had been used in various forms of manufacturing for centuries. The name came from the old Arabic word *būraq*, which meant white. First discovered in the dry lake beds of Tibet, the powder, which easily dissolved in water and could be used to enhance enamel glazing, had been traded along the Silk Road as early as the eighth century CE. But its modern use had been driven by discovery of vast deposits of borax in California and by the aggressive marketing of the Pacific Coast Borax Company. A Wisconsin-born miner named Francis Marion Smith, with a natural flair for marketing his product, had founded the company. Smith, known to consumers as the "Borax King," had purchased the rights to a rich vein of borax in the Mojave region, known as the "Twenty Mule Team Mine" for the long wagon trains used to haul out the mineral deposits. On the advice of his manager, he developed a cleaning formula promoted as "Twenty Mule Team Borax" for its powerful action and then went on to market his product for that and many other uses, including as a handy preservative.

Borax was already known at that point as both a cheap and versatile preservative. It slowed fungal growth and it appeared to inhibit bacteria as well. Long before Smith's industrious marketing, food manufacturers had been gradually taking up its use. Meat producers had started using it in the mid-1870s, after British importers had complained that American bacon and ham tasted too salty. The dairy industry had followed by using borax as a butter preservative, again avoiding a salty taste. During the Mason hearings, one dairy spokesman suggested that the British had, in fact, come to prefer the slightly metallic taste of borax in butter. The meatpackers used borax to preserve everything from canned meat to oleomargarine. In a rare moment of agreement, they joined with dairy representatives in attacking complaints like Mitchell's, pointing out that refrigeration options were extremely limited when sending products overseas. One could do only so much by packing with ice; it served no one to sell slimy meat and rancid butter abroad. The meatpackers also moved to quell the suggestion that borax might not be a healthy additive. They hired toxicologist Walter Haines, from the University of Chicago, to assure the Senate that borax was safe. Haines didn't exactly stick to script. He said that he'd seen no convincing evidence that borax was harming people but refused unambiguous endorsement. For the moment, Haines explained, illnesses caused by decaying foods, the dreaded "ptomaines," seemed to him to be a far worse option.

Such scientific caution failed to satisfy preservative makers, whose position was made clear by Albert Heller of Chicago, manufacturer of the formaldehyde-infused Freezine. Yes, Heller said, Freezine was now used in everything from cream puffs to canned corned beef. But American consumers were lucky to find it there. By preventing decay, it reduced the number of illnesses caused by the ptomaines. For all he knew, it reduced other terrible diseases like cholera as well. The American public should embrace chemical preservatives, he argued, and smart consumers already did. "I wish to say that every one of us eats embalmed meat and we know it and we like it," Heller said.

In the early spring of 1900, after reviewing the hearing testimony, Senator Mason delivered a fiery speech on the Senate floor. "This is the only civilized country in the world that does not protect the consumer of food products against the adulterations of manufacturers," he charged. The country's food was full of aluminum, "sulfuric acid, copper salts, zinc and other poisonous substances." And if it wasn't contaminated with toxic substances, it was faked, disguised, or otherwise adulterated. He'd had enough and he hoped the American people and his fellow legislators felt the same, Mason said. He was proud to introduce legislation that would require safety testing of additives and substitutes and prohibit those found dangerous. Further, his pure-food bill would require accurate labeling of all ingredients. If it passed, companies that failed to comply, he added, would be fined or even taken to court. He was proud to announce that comparable legislation was being introduced in the House.

The whole parade of food and drink manufacturers—dairy, meat, eggs, flour, baking soda, beer, wine, whiskey—not to mention the chemical companies, immediately lined up against the legislation. Despite his strong language in support of the Senate bill, Mason warned Wiley privately to expect its failure. The sponsor of the House version of the bill, Congressman Marriott Brosius from Pennsylvania, was equally pessimistic. His assessment, as he also told Wiley, was that the most positive result was likely to be simply keeping the issue "before the public eye."

Within weeks, both bills were shut down in committee by legislators friendly to the different manufacturing interests. It was frustrating, Wiley wrote to Mason, because he did think public support was turning their way. He'd collected dozens of newspaper clippings about the Mason hearings and every single one of them had applauded the action of the committee.

Many people also had written directly to Wiley requesting copies of committee testimony, issues of Bulletin 13, and even a tongue-in-cheek piece of doggerel that Wiley had written for a Pure Food Congress and impulsively decided to read aloud as part of his testimony. The verses, also published in New York's *Pharmaceutical Era Weekly*, concluded pointedly:

> The banquet how fine, don't begin it
> Till you think of the past and the future and sigh,
> "How I wonder, I wonder, what's in it."

That same spring of 1900, in late May, Wiley proposed marriage to Anna Kelton. Her written answer—though not an immediate refusal—was less welcoming than he'd hoped it would be. "What worries me most of all is that I am not happier," she wrote to him. "I had always pictured to myself that love would be consuming and overwhelming in its joy and I am on the verge of tears. What is the matter with me do you think?" She was painfully aware of the great age difference, of her mother's staunch disapproval, and most of all of her own ambition to be independent and self-sustaining. "Browning's line about 'the best is yet to be' comes into my mind but still this hobgoblin thought keeps popping up and it is that I am sacrificing my ideals, however childish they may be."

Late that month, she called it off. "I am only full of reproaches for myself and for my weakness and lack of womanliness in not knowing my own mind and for letting you even this week harbor any hope of my sharing your future life," she wrote. "But oh please believe it is that same honesty in me that before you admired which now makes me tell you this before it is too late." She said she lacked that "sacred, sweet, overpowering feeling" that should accompany real love. "And so goodbye," she concluded. "Goodbye with respect and the sincerest regards, I am always yours, Anna."

Wiley couldn't bring himself to accept that as a final answer. A brief separation was pending—he'd been appointed to represent the Agriculture Department that summer in Paris, at the Exposition Universelle de 1900, and to organize an exhibit there showcasing the excellence of American wines and beers. With some difficulty, he persuaded her to wait until he returned from France, suggesting she take some time to think things over before definitively telling him no. They held on to that fragile truce until he sailed in mid-July. But he was still shipboard in the middle of the Atlantic when Anna Kelton requested and received a transfer from the Agriculture Department to the Library of Congress. "When I left for Paris I had a perfect understanding with her but I had not been here long before I received a very sensible letter from her saying that she had concluded that our agreement had better be terminated," he wrote to a friend. "At the same time I gathered from what she wrote that she had been influenced in this by her family." They thought, he knew, that it was wrong for a man of his age to court a woman in her twenties. But "I have yet to learn that loving a pretty girl in a proper way and being loved by her in return has anything blameworthy in it."

To Anna he wrote a tender good-bye letter. "You say, 'Why don't you make me love you?' Love, dear heart, does not come by making nor does it go by unmaking. . . . I want you to know, dear heart, how much zest you have brought into my life." She did not reply. But still he could not bring himself to remove her photo from the inside cover of his pocket watch.

Secretary Wilson wrote to Wiley in Paris to celebrate the good reception that he and his exhibit on alcoholic beverages had received, "which pleases me very much." Wilson also added a note of reassurance regarding job stability. The next presidential election was coming up in November. "The campaign has not yet opened up but the indications are quite good regarding Mr. McKinley's re-election."

McKinley had been forced to select a new running mate, as his popular vice president, Garret Hobart, had died in November of 1898. After much political wrangling, the party had chosen the progressive New York governor Theodore Roosevelt to take his place. McKinley's closest advisers were unenthusiastic: Roosevelt had not backed McKinley's nomination in 1894 and Roosevelt had an un-McKinley-like reputation as a reformer. But that turned out to be a major campaign advantage.

The Democrats had once again named William Jennings Bryan, who had lost to McKinley four years earlier, as their candidate. As the campaign began, Bryan fiercely attacked McKinley as a corporate insider, a president beholden to banks and railroads. As he was close to those industries, McKinley decided to keep a low profile. The president gave only one speech during the campaign. The energetic Roosevelt, by contrast, gave more than 673 speeches, in 567 cities and towns, in 24 states. On November 3, Election Day, McKinley and Roosevelt won by a wide margin. Wilson's job was secure for another four years and—as the secretary had predicted—so were both his chief chemist's job and his food safety crusade.

In 1901, shortly after McKinley's inauguration, Anheuser-Busch of St. Louis and Pabst Brewing Company of Milwaukee wrote to Wiley asking for analyses of their new "temperance beverages." These bottled malt brews, with little alcohol content, were a relatively new take on the concept of "small beer," which had been around in one form or another at least since medieval times, when it was often served to children. The big American brewers, producers of higher-alcohol beers and ales, began making temperance beverages to sell to nondrinkers and former drinkers and to curry favor from increasingly prominent anti-alcohol activists.

The Woman's Christian Temperance Union had been organized in the early 1870s with the stated goal of "achieving a sober and pure world." It was far from the first American temperance organization, but along with the Anti-Saloon League, organized in 1893, the WCTU had become one of the most strident and effective forces opposed to alcohol consumption. With its slogan, "Agitate. Educate. Legislate," the WCTU linked this cause to another growing social movement, that of women's suffrage. Frances Willard, WCTU leader, saw suffrage as a key to power. She argued that if women had the vote, they could better protect their communities from drunkenness and other vices. By 1901 the organization boasted more than 150,000 members nationwide. Its activism—and growing popularity—was making American brewers and other alcohol producers increasingly nervous.

So the brewing companies had double hopes for their temperance beverages: new markets plus the alleviation of hostilities. Wisconsin-based Pabst had two years earlier gotten the Chemistry Division to analyze its Malt Mead, seeking a stamp of approval to help market it. The lab had confirmed that the drink contained less than 2 percent alcohol. Now the company wanted Wiley's support for another new low-alcohol beverage called Nutria. Pabst intended to sell it in Indian Territory (in the eastern half of what is now Oklahoma), where tribes including the Cherokee and Muscogee had been resettled after they were forced from ancestral lands in the Southeast. Pabst's complaint was that the Department of Indian Affairs, which prohibited the sale of any alcoholic beverages in Indian Territory, had analyzed Nutria and declared it an intoxicating drink. It was shoddy chemistry, the company complained. Could Wiley's more able crew set things right? The Chemistry Division's analysis confirmed Pabst's position and Nutria went on sale in Indian Territory.

Anheuser-Busch, meanwhile, had created a drink called American Hop Ale, essentially a beer-flavored soft drink, and wanted Wiley and Bigelow to analyze it so that the company could use the official Chemistry Division findings as part of its marketing campaign. The chemists complied, and Wiley wrote to the company to inform it that the division had detected traces of alcohol in the product. This, the brewery responded, was merely a preservative. "This is our secret," a reply from Anheuser-Busch explained, but surely it didn't alter the basic nature of the beverage? "Could not a small percentage of alcohol be added to the soft stuff to make it keep?" It could, the Chemistry Division allowed, and shortly later the company launched a new near-beer campaign.

In May 1901 the Pan-American Exposition in Buffalo opened. This latest world's fair, with its dazzle of electric lighting powered by nearby Niagara Falls, sprawled across 350 acres and celebrated the new century under the slogan "Commercial well-being and good understanding among the American Republics." As part of the U.S. government's contribution, the Agriculture Department presented exhibits featuring innovations ranging from new crops to modern farm machinery. Wiley's scientific division, now renamed the Bureau of Chemistry, participated with three displays, two of which—one highlighting the sugar beet industry, the other celebrating experimental use of plant products in road building—fit the fair's theme and a third, organized by Willard Bigelow, on "Pure and Adulterated Foods," that defiantly did not.

Bigelow's exhibit was made eye-catching by some brightly dyed flags, which were labeled as exemplifying the coal-tar agents used to color food and drink. It also featured a display of faked products, ranging from vinegar to whiskey, highlighting a newly developed technique of adding soap to rectified alcohol to simulate the way aged bourbons would bead and cling on glass. But perhaps the most pointed section dealt with the rising tide of new industrial preservatives. On these shelves were not only food samples but also glass jars and beakers containing preservatives extracted from everyday foods. The exhibit divided preservatives into "undoubtedly injurious, such as formaldehyde, salicylic acid, and sulfites" and possibly injurious, such as borax and benzoic acid.

"It is claimed by those interested in their use that the amount of preservatives added to foods is so small as to be unimportant." But in this time of no food safety regulation, "small" was left entirely to the discretion of the manufacturer. Some foods were basically soaked in the new compounds. Or as Bigelow put it: "The amount added sometimes greatly exceeds that which is believed to be necessary by those who favor the use of chemical preservatives."

The popular exposition ran for seven months and attracted eight million visitors, including President McKinley, who arrived in early September to make a speech against American isolationism. On the afternoon of September 6, he stood at the head of a receiving line in the exposition's grand Temple of Music, cheerfully shaking hands with enthusiastic citizens. Reporter John D. Wells of the *Buffalo Morning News*, assigned to cover the event, stood taking notes, carefully describing each encounter. He would later recount that when one smiling young man got up to the president, he raised his right hand, which held a pistol wrapped in a handkerchief. Leon Czolgosz fired the pistol twice. The first bullet grazed McKinley's chest. The second ripped through his stomach and sent him stumbling backward. The assassin was jumped by both police and attendees and transported to the local jail; the gravely injured president was rushed by ambulance to the local hospital.

Still, doctors reassured Vice President Roosevelt and cabinet members who had rushed to Buffalo to be by McKinley's side that the wounds were not fatal. The president was expected to recover. Roosevelt departed for a working vacation in Vermont, where he was scheduled to address the state's Fish and Game League. But the local Buffalo doctors, refusing to use newfangled X-ray machines, had not successfully removed all the debris left by the fragmenting bullet or fully sterilized the internal injuries. The wounds became infected, gangrene set in, and on September 14, nine days after the shooting, McKinley died.

Roosevelt rushed back—cobbling together a trip by horse, car, and train—to take the oath of office. He received a less-than-enthusiastic welcome from reform-wary leaders of his party. "I told William McKinley it was a mistake to nominate that wild man at Philadelphia," said Senator Mark Hanna of Ohio. "Now look, that damned cowboy is president of the United States."

Czolgosz, a former steelworker and a self-proclaimed anarchist, was rapidly charged, tried, and convicted. He received the death sentence, at the unanimous recommendation of the jury, and died in the electric chair at Auburn (New York) Prison on October 29, just forty-five days after the shooting.

In the weeks after McKinley's death, Roosevelt sought at first to reassure the country: "In this hour of deep and terrible bereavement, I wish to state that I shall continue unbroken the policy of President McKinley for the peace, prosperity, and the honor of the country."

But the new president was biding his time. In February 1902, Roosevelt's administration filed an antitrust suit against a giant holding company created by a consortium that included such Gilded Age titans as J. P. Morgan, Cornelius Vanderbilt, and the Rockefellers. The *Wall Street Journal* angrily called it the greatest shock to the stock market since McKinley's assassination. By contrast, Harvey Wiley was pleased to see the president show his more volatile, reformist side and hoped to see pure food and drink become one of Roosevelt's causes. Unfortunately Wiley had stumbled already, and stumbled badly, in the opinion of the new chief executive.

Since his adventure in Cuba, Roosevelt had become a booster of the newly independent island country. With the support of Elihu Root, the secretary of war, the president proposed an agreement that would, among other things, foster economic growth by reducing the American tariff on Cuban-grown sugar. In January 1902 the House Committee on Ways and Means began hearings on the issue. Wiley, long considered an expert on the growing and processing of sugars, was called to testify.

Wiley feared that if the tariff on Cuban sugar was lowered, powerful American companies would see an opportunity for easy profit, buy up the imports, and resell them to American consumers at higher prices. The losers, he suspected, would be American farmers, undercut by the Cuban competition. He didn't want to say all of this, however, in a public hearing. He knew it wouldn't sit well with Roosevelt, but he wasn't willing to testify contrary to what he believed. So Wiley asked Secretary Wilson to get the congressional summons withdrawn. "'If I go up there I shall tell what I believe to be the truth and thus get in trouble,'" wrote Wiley, quoting himself in his conversation with the secretary.

Unfortunately for Wiley and his future relations with Roosevelt, Wilson shared the chemist's reservations about Cuban sugar and wanted those doubts to be aired in testimony before Congress. Wilson also knew he'd damage his own standing with the president if he delivered the testimony himself. As a member of the cabinet, he said, he dared not say what he thought. Wiley could. The chief chemist agreed, reluctantly, to be a witness and, characteristically, he spoke his mind. "I consider it a very unwise piece of legislation and one which will damage, to a very serious extent, our domestic sugar industry," Wiley testified. "Do you contemplate remaining in the Agricultural Department?" a legislator asked as other committee members burst out laughing.

The president was not amused. He summoned Wilson to demand that the chemist be fired on the spot. Wilson, realizing the extent of the damage he'd done to his subordinate, told the president that the chemist had been following departmental orders. It would be wrong to fire Wiley for doing what he was told, said the secretary. Grudgingly, Roosevelt agreed. He sent Wilson back with a message for the chief chemist: "I will let you off this time but don't do it again." Later that year, Roosevelt successfully negotiated a treaty that included a 20 percent tariff reduction on Cuban sugar. "I ran afoul of his good will in the first months of his administration," Wiley later wrote ruefully. "I fear that this man with whom I had many contacts after he became president never had a very good opinion of me."

Five

ONLY THE BRAVE

1901–1903

———————◦———————

Oh, maybe this bread contains alum or chalk
Or sawdust chopped up very fine
Or gypsum in powder about which they talk,
Terra alba just out of the mine

B y 1901 the Bureau of Chemistry had identified 152 "new" patent preservatives on the U.S. market. Although the term "new," the government scientists found, was often merely an advertising ploy rather than a sign of innovation. Many of these products were simply remixes of old standbys like formaldehyde or copper sulfate. The main difference was that the formulas contained these compounds in greater quantities than their predecessors—and, as a result, promised astonishing shelf life. As one advertising circular put it, a good preservative was "guaranteed to keep meat, fish, poultry, etc. for *any* length of time without ice." The idea of indestructible food products fascinated many in an era when kitchens were equipped with, at best, an icebox to delay spoilage.

The American chemical industry was quick to recognize a

lucrative market in such food- and drinking-enhancing products. In addition to preservatives, companies developed synthetic compounds to make food production cheaper. The sweetener saccharin, discovered in 1879 at Johns Hopkins University, cost far less than sugar and quickly replaced it as a cost-saving alternative. Flavoring agents such as laboratory-brewed citric acid or peppermint extracts could now be used in drinks and other products instead of fresh lemon juice or mint—again saving costs, and again crowding the farmer out of the supply chain.

The pioneering industrial chemist Charles Pfizer, who had founded his New York pharmaceutical company in 1849, now also produced borax, boric acid, cream of tartar, and citric acid for use in food and drink. Chicago's Joseph Baur, whose Liquid Carbonic Company produced the pressurized gas used in the fizzing drinks of soda fountains, had become so interested in artificial sweeteners that in 1901 he had invested in a new business in St. Louis, the Monsanto Chemical Company, to produce saccharin in large quantities. Saccharin production had also launched the Heyden Chemical Works of New York City in 1900, although that company also branched into the preservative market, producing salicylic acid, formaldehyde, and sodium benzoate for use in food and drinks. The food and drink market also attracted Herbert Henry Dow, founder at age thirty-one of the Dow Chemical Company in Midland, Michigan. Dow had been a chemistry student at the Case Institute of Technology (eventually merged into Case Western Reserve University) in Cleveland, Ohio, and in 1897 with financial backing from both friends and former professors, he'd launched his own company, Dow Chemical. The company's first venture was based on a new process Dow had invented for extracting the element bromine from brine for antiseptic use. But within a few years, Dow also made magnesium for incendiary flares, phenol for explosives, and agricultural pesticides—and was becoming a major producer of food preservatives such as sodium benzoate.

The bureau's scientists learned much of what they knew about food additives from state-employed chemists in independent-minded, agriculture-rich places like Kentucky, Wisconsin, and North Dakota, where farmers were all too aware that industry was under-cutting the fresh-food market with increasing use of artificial ingredients. Prominent examples included Indiana's outspoken John Hurty and the even more combative Edwin Ladd, analytical chemist at the North Dakota Agricultural College in Fargo. Ladd's analysis of food and drink sold in the state had led him to believe that big corporations basically regarded North Dakota as "a dumping ground for chemically-enhanced waste food products." In 1901 he launched a statewide campaign for a pure-food law, bombarding North Dakota legislators and citizens with a catalog of dismaying data.

"More than 90 percent of local meat markets in the state were using chemical preservatives and in nearly every butcher shop could be found a bottle of Freezine, Preservaline, or Iceine," he reported. "In the dried beef, in the smoked meats, in the canned bacon, in the canned chipped beef, boracic acid or borates (products of the borax industry) are a common ingredient." In almost every food product Ladd analyzed he found unlabeled industrial compounds that had never been tested for safety, although some were known toxins. "Ninety per cent of the so-called French peas we have taken up in North Dakota were found to contain copper salts." Baked goods were often loaded with "alum," a salt of aluminum and potassium, used as a preservative, in baking powders, and to whiten bread.

Ladd was particularly critical of what bottlers were passing off as "catsup" or "ketchup." (The spellings were already interchangeable.) It was often unrelated to the well-known tomato product. The cheapest of these sauces were frequently made from unwanted pumpkin skins and rinds, stewed, dyed red, and spiced up with vinegar and a little cayenne or paprika. Or ketchup was a soup of "waste products from canners—pulp, skins, ripe tomatoes, green tomatoes, starch paste, coal-tar colors, and chemical preservatives, usually benzoate of soda or salicylic acid." The North Dakota food chemistry analysis, which Ladd would issue in full the following year, revealed that 100 percent of ketchups were rich in coal-tar dyes, preservatives, and waste products. He also found similar problems in a range of other products, reporting "one hundred percent adulteration" of jams and jellies, 88 percent adulteration of canned corn, and 50 percent of canned peas. And the list went on.

Ladd sent newspapers around the state details of every adulteration finding that he'd uncovered. In response, the National Biscuit Company (later renamed Nabisco) had its legal department engage in an expensive long-distance phone call, suggesting that he tone it down. Ladd, as the local papers gleefully reported, responded by losing his temper. His secretary reported hearing his shouting: "By God, no Eastern lawyer is going to tell me what we can eat out here in North Dakota!"

Ladd's friend and colleague South Dakota food chemist James Shepard, meanwhile, had launched a similar campaign for a food safety law. To showcase the problem for state residents, Shepard created and publicized a daily meal plan to illustrate the seep of industrial chemistry into the average dinner. His menu, Shepard announced, was such that "any family in the United States might possibly use":

BREAKFAST

Sausage: coal-tar dye and borax

Bread: alum

Butter: coal-tar dye

Canned cherries: coal-tar dye and salicylic acid

Pancakes: alum

Syrup: sodium sulphite [then the spelling of sulfite]

THIS GIVES EIGHT DOSES OF CHEMICALS AND DYES FOR BREAKFAST.

DINNER

Tomato soup: coal-tar dye and benzoic acid

Cabbage and corned beef: saltpeter

Canned scallops: sulfuric acid and formaldehyde

Canned peas: salicylic acid

Catsup: coal-tar dye and benzoic acid

Vinegar: coal-tar dye

Bread and butter: alum and coal-tar dye

Mince pie: boracic acid

Pickles: coppers, sodium sulphite, and salicylic acid

Lemon ice cream: methyl alcohol

THIS GIVES SIXTEEN DOSES FOR DINNER.

SUPPER

Bread and butter: alum and coal-tar dye

Canned beef: borax

Canned peaches: sodium sulfite, coal-tar dye, and salicylic acid

Pickles: copper, sodium sulfite, and formaldehyde

Catsup: coal-tar dye and benzoic acid

Lemon cake: alum

Baked pork and beans: formaldehyde

Vinegar: coal-tar dye

Currant jelly: coal-tar dye and salicylic acid

Cheese: coal-tar dye

THIS GIVES SIXTEEN DOSES FOR SUPPER.

"According to this menu," Shepard announced to his state's newspapers, "the unconscious and unwilling patient gets forty doses of chemicals and colors per day."

But the additives were so little studied that even concerned scientists like Shepard and Ladd could only guess at what risk they might pose. There were some animal studies on these new food additives, but they were limited at best. One standard approach involved making a solution of residues from food and drink products and injecting that solution into rabbits. If the rabbits didn't die within minutes, food manufacturers would declare the material to be nonpoisonous and safe for human beings.

Wiley had long worried about this lack of guidance, lack of dosage limits, lack of basic information. If Americans consumed multiple doses of untested compounds in every meal with no assurance of their safety, he thought, then government officials like himself were failing them. The only way to fix that, he'd decided, was to devise some real public health experiments. And the most direct way to get the information would be by using human volunteers. So that same year, 1901, he asked Congress to fund a study that he described as "hygienic table trials." His plan was to sit people down at "hygienic" tables—by which he meant a clean and carefully controlled setting— and feed them precisely measured meals. Half of the diners would eat fresh, additive-free dishes. The others would receive specific doses of a chemical preservative with each meal. The diners were not to know who was consuming what. Wiley and staff would monitor the health effects, if any, from these diets.

He proposed that his human guinea pigs be tough male specimens, "young, robust fellows, with maximum resistance to deleterious effects of adulterated foods." If such individuals were sickened, he reasoned, then this would be much more of a warning flag than if the test subjects were already considered fragile. "If they should show signs of injury after they were fed such substances for a period of time, the deduction would naturally follow that children and older persons, more susceptible than they, would be greater sufferers from similar causes." The hygienic table trials, he explained in his proposal to Congress, would address "whether such preservatives should ever be used or not, and if so, what preservatives and in what quantities?" He added that the experiments could also address questions about other additives, such as food dyes. He had no idea what these experiments might find, he emphasized. But he could make a good case for giving them a try. And after all, the lawmakers were eating and drinking these unknown compounds too.

In March, Congress authorized a grant of $5,000 (about $150,000 in today's dollars) to, as the legislation put it, "enable the Secretary of Agriculture to investigate the character of food preservatives, coloring matters and other substances added to foods, to determine their relation to digestion and health, and to establish the principles which should guide their use."

The sum was only a third of what Wiley had requested, but it was a start. Now he just had to figure out how to launch the country's first food-toxicity trials involving human subjects. He had no equipment. No supplies, food or otherwise. Nor did he have any test subjects nor any assurance that anyone would sign up to be poisoned.

He needed a kitchen, a dining room, and a cook. For economy's sake, and with Wilson's permission, he decided to build his experimental restaurant in the basement at the Department of Agriculture. The resulting dining room was sparely furnished with two round tables of dark stained oak covered with white tablecloths. Six stiff ladder-back chairs gathered around each table. The china was plain white, the walls painted white and unadorned. Shelving, neatly divided into small cubbies, lined one wall and contained everything from pepper grinders to measuring tools, including a sturdy brass scale for weighing out the food.

The adjoining kitchen was furnished with cooking necessities and no more. But the area was scrupulously clean and reasonably pleasant. "Cheerful surroundings, good company, and in general an agreeable environment, tend to promote the favorable progress of digestion," he wrote. "A reversal of the conditions of the environment have exactly the opposite effect."

He wanted the meals to be wholesome, tasty, and dished out on a precise schedule: breakfast at 8:00 a.m., luncheon at noon, dinner at 5:30 p.m., "these being the customary meal-times" for civil service employees. He wanted strictly fresh ingredients with no trace of preservatives. He'd budgeted for roast beef, beefsteak, veal, pork, chicken, turkey, fish, oysters, and an array of fruits and vegetables. Cream and milk were allowed, but these had to be pasteurized to avoid both bacterial infections and unmonitored chemical preservatives. Some canned soups, fruits, and vegetables were also allowed, but only in specially ordered, preservative-free batches from selected manufacturers. "The greatest pains were taken to secure absolute freedom from antiseptics in the whole of the food consumed."

The Bureau of Chemistry recruited volunteers by posting an advertisement, circulated to government employees, promising three free meals daily in exchange for participation in the study. As the *Washington Post* put it, the U.S. government was about to "open, for the first time in history, a scientific boarding house under the direction of Prof. Wiley." To the professor's relief, volunteers applied in abundance. Young men, earning perhaps a few hundred a year, struggling to make ends meet in the nation's capital, saw a chance to stretch their budgets. Wiley, who had lived poor himself, understood that: "They are clerks, working for small salaries, and the item of free board will be a big one to them," he said.

The Chemistry Bureau also received a deluge of applications from fascinated citizens around the country: "Dear Sir," wrote one applicant. "I read in the paper of your experiments on diet. I have a stomach that can stand anything. I have a stomach that will surprise you. . . . What do you think of it? My stomach can hold anything."

Two of Wiley's chemist friends in Ohio wrote in jest to apply for positions. He wrote an amused reply, but one that probably gave them more insight into his perspective than he was willing to allow in public: "You will begin with a diet of borax garnished with salicylic acid—with a dash of alum on the side. You will then have a course in chromatics—beginning with the beautiful yellow of oleomargarine and including the green of the French canned peas. . . . Please report for duty about September 10th. Blanks for wills and coroner's certificates must be furnished by the guests." But in actual practice, he and his staff, including the ever-reliable Bigelow, decided to limit applicants to the presumably upright people who had passed the civil service exam, "so they came to us with a good character."

For the first round of experimental meals, he lined up twelve young clerks, mostly from the Agriculture Department. He'd wanted to use more but could not afford it. Still, as far as he knew, this was the largest group ever yet used in a human health experiment of this kind. The trial design was straightforward. Each compound would be studied during a six-week period, and the test subjects would be divided during that time into two different seating arrangements. For the first two weeks, those sitting at table 1 would receive untainted food and those at table 2 would be dosed with a given preservative. The scientists would track the health differences, if any, between the two groups.

They would then switch so that table 1 received the preservative and table 2 was allowed two weeks of recovery. Then back again for a final round of comparison. Critics would later point out, with justification, that two weeks wasn't sufficient time to measure an effect; that it would have been better to have maintained his control group and test group throughout. Wiley conceded that point. The hygienic table trials weren't perfect, he admitted, but they had potential to increase understanding of health effects from these mostly untested compounds. Another reason he'd kept the test periods short was to minimize any harm to his young volunteers, who'd been required to sign a liability waiver. "Did you explain that this was a dangerous process?" a congressman would ask later, during a hearing following publication of the first findings. Wiley replied that the volunteers were told about the planned procedure (although he wouldn't guarantee they understood all the implications).

The department would not have done the work, he emphasized, if he'd believed at the start that chemical compounds deliberately mixed into American food posed an immediate deadly risk. He'd gone in hoping the materials were safe, and his worst-case guess before the trials started was "that there might be some disturbance to their systems." ("So," the congressman would say, "you thought that there was nothing; but you took a release because there was danger of losing life, in a sense." That, Wiley agreed, was correct.) Test subjects could consume only what was dished out in Wiley's test kitchen. They had to refuse any other snacks or drinks: "Each individual subject pledged himself to abstain entirely from food and drink not prepared by the scientists in charge of the dining room."

As the details of the project became known, newspaper reporters covered the deprivations with a mixture of amusement and horror: "Should they become hungry between meals, they must wait until the official dinner bell rings. If they grow thirsty during working hours, they may watch the water cooler with longing eyes but nothing more. . . . They cannot even drink a friendly glass of beer."

The volunteers had to record everything they ate and drank, noting the precise amounts of every portion. They had to record their weight, temperature, and pulse rate before every meal. Twice a week they had to be examined by doctors from the Public Health and Marine Hospital Service. They had to behave in an upright way, to "pursue their ordinary vocations without any excesses and to take their ordinary hours of sleep." They also had to agree to collect their urine and feces—"every particle of their excreta," in Wiley's words—and bring it to the chemistry laboratory for analysis. In retrospect, it seems astonishing that anyone volunteered and that none of the test subjects backed out before the experiment even began.

Wiley chose the preservative borax as the first additive to test. It was one of the most widely used food preservatives. Further, the few studies conducted thus far on borax suggested that it was relatively, but not completely, benign. Here was a chance to explore the questions raised about its consumption without, he thought, putting his volunteers at too much risk.

A study published the previous year in which mice were fed varying amounts of borax and boric acid had concluded that in small doses the compounds "have no influence upon the general health of the animals." Another test with baby pigs had reached a similar conclusion. If the dose was ratcheted up, though, the compound appeared to pose some problems. There was some evidence of a disruption in metabolism; there was the occasional animal that suffered digestive upsets, nausea, and vomiting. There were also some warning signals arising from a few human studies, but those tests were idiosyncratic at best.

One of them involved a scientist mixing boric acid into his own milk for a couple weeks; he'd felt fine, he said. Another experiment, done in London, had involved dosing three young children with borax and boric acid for several months. Those results were both reassuring and a little puzzling.

Unlike Wiley, who had carefully explained his choice of sturdy test subjects, the British researchers were vague about the selection process. They had chosen a two-year-old boy, a five-year-old boy, and a four-year-old girl who "was delicate, being convalescent from pneumonia," leading to some suspicion that they'd merely selected a few children whose parents were agreeable. They had found that borax could cause some temporary nausea and diarrhea but concluded that, in the big picture, "neither boric acid nor borax in any way affected the health and well-being" of the test subjects. That is to say, the three children appeared to be okay at the end of the experiment.

Meanwhile, John Marshall, a professor of chemistry and toxicology at the University of Pennsylvania, had also dosed himself with borax, and he'd reported some severe diarrhea ("the food escapes without assimilation") and nausea. But Marshall was interested in acute toxicity and had given himself a hefty dose after being called as a witness in the trial of a butcher accused of using the preservative to restore slightly rotten meat. So, while his self-experiment suggested that a stiff dose of borax produced unpleasant symptoms, it did not predict that most Americans, receiving a daily low-level exposure while consuming products ranging from meat to milk, would become so ill.

Wiley knew his study plan was by no means perfect either. But he also believed that its design was better than anything else out there. He had a larger study group of subjects, all of comparable age and health. He would be dividing them into two groups for purposes of comparison, a far cry from one man sipping milk or the use of three random children. His tests would continue for longer and look at a greater range of doses. He still thought that he wouldn't find anything much. But if borax did pose a risk, he also thought he'd have a better chance of finding that out than any work done so far.

He struggled with the best way to deliver the borax. In the British studies, the vehicle had been milk. As the authors of the experiment with children had pointed out, this made sense because "milk forms such a large proportion of their diet." Wiley decided to try butter instead; buttered bread and rolls were a staple of the American meal and he hoped they'd be consumed with enthusiasm. He wasn't worried about the taste putting off his diners. "It is pointed out that an important point of distinction between modern preservatives and the long-established ones—salt, sugar, vinegar, and wood-smoke—is that in the small amounts used they are almost without taste and odor, and their presence in a food product would not be noticed by the consumer unless specifically proclaimed."

In November 1902, just over six months after Wiley received his grant, the dining room opened its doors for the first round of tests. In its honor, a squad member propped up a sign at the entrance to the little dining room. Like the room itself, there was nothing fancy about it, just seven black-stenciled words on a white-painted board. They read: ONLY THE BRAVE DARE EAT THE FARE.

The first snag in Wiley's tidy plan came early. His volunteers soon realized—possibly through the study's garrulous chef, S. S.

Perry—that the borax had been secreted in the butter. They quit putting butter on their bread. Wiley then quietly resorted to the British approach, serving borax-dosed glasses of milk. The diners figured that out too. "Those who thought the preservative was concealed in the butter were disposed to find the butter unpalatable and the same was true with those who thought it might be in the milk or the coffee." After a few more attempts to sneak the preservative onto the table, he decided on a straightforward approach. The table settings for the first group now included a dish of borax capsules, and either he or Bigelow or one of the other chemists stood by, monitoring to make sure that the squad members took the requisite amount. He did not take the borax capsules himself. But that didn't stop him from being referred to in the *Washington Post* as "Old Borax."

Wiley's plan had been to conduct a quietly managed study and then report the results in discreet scientific fashion. It was with some dismay that he realized his experiment had attracted the amused attention of an ambitious young reporter for the *Washington Post*, George Rothwell Brown. The son of a Washington physician, Brown, twenty-three, had started a neighborhood newspaper in the basement of his family's Capitol Hill home when he was still in high school. He'd already put in a few years reporting for the *Washington Times* when, in 1902, the *Post* hired him away. While reporting on Congress, Brown came across a dry description of Wiley's proposal while looking over the federal budget. The journalist scented a good story and hurried over to talk to Wiley and his staff.

Brown found them less helpful than he had hoped. Although he often sought to engage the public in his campaign for pure foods, Wiley feared in this case that too much showy attention might bias the study and rob it of scientific dignity. He also worried that things would go wrong and that he wouldn't be able to manage the resulting bad news.

So Wiley warned his employees against granting interviews. "I can't say anything about anything," one chemist told Brown about the experiment. Wiley also warned that volunteers would be dropped from the program if they were caught talking with journalists. Brown countered by hanging around outside the Chemistry Bureau building and following volunteers down the street. Wiley caught him several times chatting cordially with Chef Perry through a basement window.

Brown's first story was headlined DR. WILEY AND HIS BOARDERS. The *Post* published it in early November. "The kitchen at the bureau of chemistry has been painted and put in excellent condition, and the chef is ready for business." Wiley apparently didn't approve of the breezy, cheerful tone, as Brown made evident in his next story: "The authorities are apprehensive that unless the public can be brought to look upon the experiments as an enterprise undertaken by scientific men and carried out in sober earnest, with a view to deciding a question of vast import to the country at large, the results of their self-sacrificing labors and patient investigation will be partially if not entirely lost. Any suspicion or belief in the public mind that there is a humorous or insincere element or phase connected with the experiments deserving of scoffing or ridicule would be deplorable in its effect."

But Brown and his editors shared a concern that the *Post*'s readers were never going to warm up to a story about "hygienic table trials." They needed more human interest and a catchier description. He spent long hours hunting down the identities of the first group of volunteers, who were "braving the perils of a course on food preservatives." The standout among them was B. J. Teasdale, whom Brown described as "a famous Yale sprinter and a former captain in a high school cadet regiment." Teasdale had set a record in the one-hundred-yard dash. The others, none as distinguished, were "the fat boarder," "the thin boarder," the Irishman whom Brown called "the only one of the Emerald Isle's sons among the twelve subjects," and volunteers whom he identified geographically as being from Mississippi, New York, and Pennsylvania. But collectively they were a band of brothers. And, to give them credit, Brown believed that it took some courage to venture into the chemical unknown. With that in mind, he found a better name for the study. He would simply call it the "Poison Squad."

That didn't stop him from seeing that the idea of borax in food offered limitless opportunities for entertainment. As the study continued into December, he imagined, for readers of the newspaper, what that year's Christmas dinner menu might look like:

Apple Sauce.

Borax.

Soup.

Borax. Turkey. Borax.

Borax.

Canned String Beans.

Sweet Potatoes. White Potatoes.

Turnips.

Borax.

Chipped Beef. Cream Gravy.

Cranberry Sauce. Celery. Pickles.

Rice Pudding.

Milk. Bread and Butter. Tea. Coffee.

A Little Borax.

Wiley was known in the department for having a lively sense of humor; Secretary Wilson himself publicly admired it. So he could live with being called Old Borax in his city's newspaper. He could even laugh about it. He could also see the humor in the supposed holiday menu. He'd drafted a joke menu himself, although that he managed to keep a secret.

That December he'd been asked by the American Association for the Advancement of Science to help organize holiday social events for the organization's friends and for respected scientists and politicians and—as the note to Wiley read—to stand as a "representative of the best people in Washington." He'd responded with invitations to a "poison dinner" of his own, inscribed with skulls and crossbones, undertaker advertisements, and pictures of skeletons labeled "after." The invitations featured a menu of preservatives, additives, and adulterations woven into a tongue-in-cheek play on fine French dining:

MENU DU SOUPER EMPOISONNE

Le 13 Decembre 1902

Huitres queu de coq—sauce Formaldehyde (Xeres adroitment falsifie)

Hors d'ouevres varies a l'aude benzoique (Sauternes a l'aide sulfereuz)

Howards a la Nouvelle Dills aux ptomaines

Callies (perdeux) a pain brulee sauce borate de soude

Salade coucobre a l'huile de coton

Fromage aux falsifications diverses

Café artificial

Liqueurs de tête mort

Tabac—a former

Matin—Bromo-selzer a volante

Invitation du Monsieur le Docteur Wiley d'assister

a un coupfer a la Roland B. Molineux

Molineux was one of the country's more notorious cyanide murderers. A member of an aristocratic New York family—and the grandson of a decorated Civil War general—he'd been convicted in 1900 of killing two people he disliked by mailing them gifts spiked with poison.

Wiley was indeed grateful that Brown hadn't gotten his hands on a copy of that menu. But as the dismayed scientists at the Chemistry Bureau came to realize, if Brown couldn't find an element of interest in that week's work, the lively-minded journalist just made it up. For example, there was the story accusing the Chemistry Bureau of nearly starving the squad members: "F.B. Linton, who weighs out the food when Dr. Wiley is otherwise engaged, will bite a bean in half" rather than give the diners too much food. Another *Post* article reported that after only a few weeks on the borax diet, half the boarders were losing weight and the cook was so depressed that in his distraction he'd burned a turkey dinner. Another said that one of the volunteers was putting on weight and another was losing it, baffling the scientists: "Dr. Wiley is in despair." Brown reported that the volunteers also were messing with the study, relating the tale of a test subject who "in the spirit of mischief" dropped quinine into another boarder's coffee. The victim of the joke, wrote Brown, went home "prepared to die in the interests of science."

Brown's most fanciful masterpiece appeared more than six months into the Poison Squad work, in the summer of 1903. Headlined BOARDERS TURN PINK, it claimed that the steady diet of borax had wrought a marked and permanent change in the skin color of all members of the Poison Squad: "The change in the complexion of the chemical scholars has not been of an alarming character. On the contrary, each of the young men undergoing the course of treatment has blossomed out with a bright-pink complexion that would make a society bride sick with envy." The excited agricultural chemists, he added, were in the process of drafting a pamphlet about their revolutionary discovery. To Wiley's annoyance, Brown's widely distributed story—promising skin as rosy as "the inside of a strawberry"—resulted in a small deluge of letters to the Agriculture Department from women seeking the new secret to youthful skin.

By that time, the once sedate hygienic table trials had found their place in popular culture. Entertainer Lew Dockstader was performing "Song of the Poison Squad," written by S. W. Gillilan, in his minstrel shows.

O we're the merriest herd of hulks
That ever the world has seen;
We don't shy off from your
Rough on Rats or even from Paris green
We're on the hunt for a toxic dope
That's certain to kill, sans fail
But 'tis a tricky, elusive thing and
Knows we are on its trail;
For all the things that could kill
We've downed in many a gruesome wad,
And still we're gaining a pound a day,
For we are the Pizen Squad.

Rough on Rats was an arsenic-based rodent poison. Paris green, formed from copper, acetate, and arsenic, was used in pest control and as a coloring agent. Neither Wiley nor Secretary Wilson was pleased—neither by the notion that they were deliberately poisoning their volunteers nor that the Chemistry Bureau's research was now featured in musical satire.

The secretary and the chief chemist both complained repeatedly to the *Post* over the months that Brown's articles were making the department a laughingstock. They got little satisfaction. But after the BOARDERS TURN PINK story, the paper's editors had to acknowledge that their reporter had invented the whole thing. What the editors didn't catch—not then, anyway—was that Brown had missed the most important, if not the most entertaining, aspect of the Poison Squad story. By the summer of 1903, Wiley was looking at results that suggested steady ingestion of borax was not nearly as benign as had been assumed.

Six

LESSONS IN FOOD POISONING

1903–1904

————————◉————————

And our faith in the butter is apt to be weak,
For we haven't a good place to pin it
Annato's so yellow and beef fat so sleek
Oh, I wish I could know what is in it.

In 1903 Fannie Farmer was the most famous cookbook author in the United States. She had become a household name after publishing *The Boston Cooking-School Cook Book* seven years earlier. In it she had included more than recipes, written about more than preparation, presentation, and flavor. She'd also discussed food chemistry and principles of nutrition as she understood them.

"Food," the book began simply, "is anything that nourishes the body." She proceeded to explain that "thirteen elements enter into the composition of the body: oxygen, 62½ percent; carbon, 21½ percent; hydrogen, 10 percent; nitrogen, 3 percent; calcium, phosphorus, potassium, sulphur, chlorine, sodium, magnesium, iron, and fluorine the remaining 3 percent." While other chemical elements were found in food, she noted, "as their uses are unknown, [they] will not be considered." Farmer's editor at Little, Brown and Company of Boston had wondered whether women needed such chemical information. Cookbooks, replied Farmer, were an essential form of education for American women, most of whom were afforded little if any opportunity to attend college.

L ittle, Brown eventually agreed to print the book, but only if the author herself paid for the first print run. Within a year, Farmer's 1896 opus had been reprinted three times; within a decade it had sold close to 400,000 copies (and by the midtwentieth century that number would top two million). Little, Brown's hesitation worked to Farmer's advantage. She had agreed to pay for publishing the book only if she retained control of the rights. By her death in 1914, thanks to her cookbook sales, she held stock in businesses that ranged from railroad companies to chocolate factories.

In 1903 she was already financially secure. At forty-six, she could write as she chose. She chose to write a book that she would consider the most important of her career: *Food and Cookery for the Sick and Convalescent*. The idea had arisen directly out of her own struggles for good health. Born in 1857, the youngest daughter of a Boston printer, she'd suffered a collapse at the age of sixteen. Doctors diagnosed the cause as a "paralytic stroke," although later experts would wonder if the girl had suffered a polio infection. For several years Fannie was unable to walk. Her mother nursed her; her father carried her from bed to chair. She was in her twenties before she began to hobble around the house; thirty before she was independent enough to enroll as a student at the Boston Cooking School.

There, in addition to cooking techniques, students learned about germ theory—the understanding that microbes cause illness, still a cutting-edge idea in the nineteenth century—and how to apply hygienic principles. They studied the chemistry of food and read the latest research into the principles of nutrition. Within three years she was assisting the principal, and by the time she wrote her famous first cookbook, she had become the head of the cooking school.

Farmer may have been the most influential author so far to warn of impurities in the food supply. Her devoted audience—composed largely of mothers and homemakers—was particularly receptive to the warning. An entire section of *Food and Cookery for the Sick and Convalescent* was focused on the "unappetizing and unhealthful pollution" of commercially sold milk. This supposedly "pure" food, she wrote, was still filthy, still too often thinned with water, full of chalk, food dyes, and harmful microorganisms. She joined other Americans advocating for pasteurization, the pathogen-killing heat process widely used in Europe. "The pathogenic germs in milk are often causes of typhoid fever, diphtheria, scarlet fever, tuberculosis, and cholera," she warned. Some American dairies, especially in the larger cities, had begun employing the process, but it made their products more expensive. Most dairymen continued to prefer far cheaper chemical preservations. Farmer wanted to alert her devoted readers of the dangers of "borax, boracic acid, salicylic acid, benzoic acid, potassium chromate, and carbonate of soda."

Earlier cookbook authors had also warned of the risks of food fakery; nineteenth-century recipes had routinely included asides about fraudulent spices or sham coffees. But *Food and Cookery for the Sick and Convalescent* gained extra attention because of its famous author and because it was published in 1904, a year in which public awareness of food problems was increasing, partly due to press coverage of Wiley's experiments. That May the *New York Times* announced that the first group of Chemistry Bureau volunteers had officially retired from the job of "eating poisons under the direction of the Agricultural Department" and been allowed to resume their normal lives. "The ill effects of eating drugs used in preserving articles of diet are said to be visible on all members of the squad, and one or two of them appear to be on the verge of breaking down," the *Times* noted.

Wiley had turned in his borax report, nearly five hundred pages, to Secretary Wilson for review. The department had "declined to give out figures" without Wilson's approval. But the *Times* anticipated the conclusion. Its subhead read PROFESSOR WILEY HELD THE MICROSCOPE WHILE THE VOLUNTEERS WRIGGLED. The experiments, the story explained, were designed to help solve the "poison mysteries" related to eating canned and preserved foods. How much "poison"—as the paper repeatedly called borax—did the squad members consume? "It is known that each of the martyrs to science ate several ounces of poison—about the same amount fed to soldiers in Cuba in the unpleasantness with Spain." (The newspaper gave no source for this dubious comparison.) Did the study prove that preservatives were indeed poisonous? "The result shows that many preservatives are deadly, causing pronounced inflammation of the digestive tract."

In June the Department of Agriculture released its official report on the borax experiment. Wilson had hesitated to make the results public, but sensationalistic press coverage had rendered such reluctance futile. At best, the report had the potential to temper the tone of what had been written elsewhere about the trials. Titled *Influence of Food Preservatives and Artificial Colors on Digestion and Health. I. Boric Acid and Borax*, it did not throw around the word "poison." It did not suggest that volunteers were tottering toward death or had turned pink. It did state that a steady diet of borax was shown to harm the human system.

Wiley had put his volunteers through five rounds of differing dose tests. In all cases the squad members spent time eating borax-laced meals alternating with time dining preservative free. Every squad member, he said, had been tested at the start of every toxicity phase and retested after the recovery period. Whenever they were eating a "clean" diet, all men had been in solid good health. During the dosage period, all had not been so well. Only half of the test subjects had endured to the end of the fifth series of borax testing. The other half dropped out due to illness.

"The experience of the previous series having shown that the administration of increasing doses of borax produced feelings of distress in both the stomach and head," the scientists attempted to alleviate the problems by decreasing the dose in the final test series. Throughout, the high dose was three grams and the low dose was a "minute" half gram. But by the fifth round, Wiley suspected the illnesses were due to a cumulative effect: "If continued for a long time in quantities not exceeding a half gram per day, they [borax-laced capsules] cause occasional periods of loss of appetite, bad feeling, fullness in the head and distress in the stomach. If given in larger and increasing doses, these symptoms are more rapidly developed and accentuated with a slight clouding of the mental processes. When increased to three grams a day the doses sometimes cause nausea and vomiting."

Most people would never—knowingly, at least—consume three grams of borax a day, but because the product was in such a range of food products, it was possible that an enthusiastic eater might risk such a level. But the chemists had concluded that a higher, more acutely toxic dose wasn't the real issue. The issue—as Wiley himself had long worried—was chronic daily exposure with cumulative effects: "On the whole, the results show that ½ gram per day is too much for the normal man to receive regularly."

Wiley and his chemists had tested a range of foods preserved with these compounds, notably butter and meat. They calculated that a person who ate buttered bread with each meal could consume a half gram of borax and/or boric acid each day, just from the butter. More if they ate meat. Not only that, but the average consumer also would be taking in "salicylic acid, saccharin, sulfurous acid and sulfites, together with the whole list of the remaining preservatives."

Wiley speculated that the borax, and probably those others, adversely affected the kidneys, if not other organs, thus leading to "disturbances of appetite, of digestions and of health." His first Poison Squad experiment admittedly was too small and too short to yield the definitive evidence he'd have liked to find. "On the other hand, the logical conclusion which seems to follow from the data at our disposal is that the use of boric acid and equivalent amounts of borax should be restricted," especially since in many cases the food could be preserved by safer means.

He repeated his argument that consumers had a right to know what manufacturers were mixing into their food. "As a matter of public information, and especially for protection of the young, the debilitated, and the sick . . . each article of food should be plainly labeled and branded in regard to the character and quantity of the preservative employed."

By the time the report was released, the next group of volunteers was consuming salicylic acid instead of borax, and they were exhibiting worse symptoms, already showing signs of nausea and dizziness.

As songs were performed, cookbook authors worried, and the studies continued, public awareness grew and pressure built. Congress once again weighed the idea of basic protective rules, not only for food and drink but also for the unrestricted, anything-goes patent remedies and other so-called medications in the United States. Two legislators from agricultural states—Congressman William P. Hepburn of Iowa and Senator Porter J. McCumber of North Dakota—spearheaded the efforts in their respective houses. Both scheduled committee hearings on the issue and both, not surprisingly, invited Wiley as the government's leading expert on chemical additives to food and drink to testify. Wiley, keenly aware of the power of the food-processing industry to stymie legislation, proceeded with caution. He stressed the need for accurate labeling first. "The real evil of food adulteration is deception of the consumer," he said.

The American Medical Association also sent representatives to support the proposed Hepburn-McCumber legislation. So did the National Association of State Dairy and Food Departments. Wisconsin, Indiana, Texas, Louisiana, California, New Jersey, Tennessee, Vermont, Kansas, New Hampshire, West Virginia, Delaware,

Maine, New York, Illinois, Pennsylvania, and Kentucky had all crafted food legislation to try to protect their citizens. But these were a patchwork of different rules and standards. The health officers in all those states were united in thinking that this wasn't enough; there ought to be nationally consistent rules for food safety.

Kentucky's chief food chemist, Robert M. Allen, assured the Senate Committee on Manufactures, which McCumber chaired, that a national law was widely desired. Even manufacturers thought uniform federal rules would work to their benefit, he insisted. But although Allen's public persona was one of cheerful optimism, in private he was far less sure of the outcome. He wrote to Wiley that the meatpacking industry was aggressively fighting the legislation; Allen had also heard that the railroads, which held a big stake in the packing industry, were quietly working against the legislation.

Meanwhile, the processed-food industry had formed a new organization, the National Food Manufacturers Association, which was seeking a "proper" law, one that would sidestep both Wiley and his recommendations. The association offered high fees to scientists willing to testify at the hearings that preservatives were chemically harmless and that because the compounds prevented decay, they also prevented countless Americans from contracting ptomaine poisoning. The association included some three hundred members, ranging from importers of tea and coffee to fish packers and mustard purveyors to the meatpackers. And it was joined in opposing the Heyburn-McCumber legislation by the dairy industry, with its growing dependence on formaldehyde to salvage sour milk; the baking industry, which worried about limits on aluminum in products such as baking powder; the bleached flour industry; and the industrial chemical industry, with its growing investment in preservatives and aniline dyes. Whiskey blenders and rectifiers also stood in opposition to label requirements, which would have forced them to list synthetic ethanol as a key ingredient.

As Warwick Hough, the chief lobbyist for the National

Wholesale Liquor Distributors Association, once again wrote to remind Wiley, barrel-aged whiskey also contained toxic compounds. It was unfair to keep "natural poisons" off the label while forcing manufacturers who might use dyes or other materials to list them on the label. Hough urged that whiskey be removed from the legislation entirely—surely those issues could be dealt with separately. And the rectifiers were both wealthy and powerful enough that many of the bill's supporters warned Wiley that including whiskey in the regulations could doom the legislation.

Wiley feared that if whiskey was exempted, producers of other substances might lobby for exemptions too. He also worried that without the inclusion of alcoholic beverages, the bill might lose the support of the also-powerful temperance movement. Despite those fears, Wiley did eventually opt for pragmatism and recommended that the requirement for labeling the chemical constituents of whiskeys be removed from the bill. But Hepburn and McCumber overruled him on that point; they also were wary of exemptions that might weaken the bill. Exasperated, the liquor wholesalers' group urged its members to work against the legislation. Hough, ignoring Wiley's efforts on his behalf, publicly accused the chief chemist of being in league with the straight-whiskey industry, increasing the bitter relations between the two men. But Hough insisted that his message was cautionary. Wiley's known and friendly ties to the straight-whiskey industry gave the appearance of bias, Hough said, and "will seriously impair your usefulness as an officer of the government in a position which calls for the exercise of utmost impartiality."

The decision to add nostrums and over-the-counter patent medicines to the bill brought out new but equally bitter opponents. The issue of drug fakery had never been Wiley's primary cause; his focus had always been on food and drink. But as public indignation over pharmaceutical fraud had grown, the Bureau of Chemistry decided to add deceptively advertised tonics and cure-alls to the products it examined. Wiley hired a talented chemist named Lyman Kebler, a former pharmaceutical company researcher with an obsession for precise measurements, to lead the bureau's investigations into snake-oil promises. It didn't take Kebler long to find that many "medicines" were little more than flavored drinking alcohol. One of the country's most popular "women's remedies," Lydia E. Pinkham's Vegetable Compound, turned out to be 20.6 percent ethanol. The digestive tonic Baker's Stomach Bitters measured at 42.6 percent ethanol, or about 85 proof.

The Proprietary Association, an alliance representing manufacturers of such popular nostrums and "cures," struck back by calling the studies an attack on personal freedom. Its officers warned publicly that if their products became subject to regulation, government control of people's lives would know no limits. "If the Federal Government should regulate the Interstate traffic in drugs on the basis of their therapeutic value, why not regulate traffic in theology by excluding from transportation all theological books which Dr. Wiley and his assistants, upon the examination, should find to be 'misleading in any particular,'" read a communication from the association.

Both the House and Senate versions of the bill died in committee that spring. Hepburn and McCumber promised Wiley that they would reintroduce their legislation again later that year. Hepburn had written directly to Roosevelt, asking him to include a favorable reference to the proposed food and drug act in a congressional address, but the president had declined. It was an election year and he was picking his battles, Roosevelt explained. "It will take more than my recommendation to get the law passed," he added. "I understand there is some very stubborn opposition" to even the idea of a pure-food and drug act.

Wiley, looking at another round of failed legislation, now accepted that his longtime strategy of working with legislators and scientific experts was not enough. If the regulations he dreamed of were to stand a chance, he needed new allies. He already had friends in the increasingly politics-savvy community of women activists; now he further sought their help. Through the consciousness raising of

Fannie Farmer and cookbook authors like her, with their warnings that commercial foods could not be trusted, women were helping to shape the nation's opinion about the problem of food adulteration. And women-led organizations were recognized as growing agents of change, as in the case of the Woman's Christian Temperance Union.

That group had in recent years broadened its focus from opposing alcoholic beverages and promoting women's suffrage to other issues—including the movement for food and drug regulation. The organization's leaders had come to that cause by way of studies like those from the Chemistry Bureau, showing that alcohol-rich patent "medicines" contributed to the problem of drunkenness. The WCTU had also decided to tackle the problem of intoxicating substances in "tonics" and soft drinks, including the popular and famously stimulating drink Coca-Cola. WCTU had been prominent among women's groups that had pressured the beverage company to drastically reduce the amount of cocaine in its formula around 1902.

Wiley started supplying the organization's leaders with copies of Kebler's reports on patent remedies. He also began courting favor with other women's groups, volunteering to give talks—as his secretary noted, dressing up for these with respectful formality, including a top hat—and scheduling friendly meetings with their leaders. His persistence, some said his obsession, on the issue of food and drug regulation kept earning him opponents. But he was also forging new partnerships, and the drive and determination of the women's organizations gave him a fresh source of hope.

Although log cabin born and farm raised, he'd grown up with the understanding that women were strong, capable, smart, and worthy of respect. His parents had sent all three of his sisters to college, a rarity in the midnineteenth century. In his Hanover College days, he had once given an address heralding the unfettered woman of the future: "She will claim all the avenues of usefulness be opened to her, that she no longer be compelled to depend upon the bounty of a father or a friend, to marry without love or choice, to keep a crowded school which kills or wash her sister's dishes which degrades." As chief chemist, he occasionally startled his colleagues with such views. In a talk to chemists visiting from Europe, he said, "Man's highest ambition in this country is to strive to be the equal of woman."

At other times he sounded more dismissive, arguing like a privileged man of his time, echoing the sentiments of his companions. In an essay for the *Annals of the American Academy of Political and Social Science*, he wrote: "I know she is not intended by nature, taste, or by education, as a rule to follow the pursuits which are reserved for men." But he then proceeded to point out that women had intelligence, energy, and the ability to drive public opinion. Nothing was gained, Wiley went on, by excluding women "from a participation, in an organized way, in the great problems which look to the uplifting of man."

At a meeting of the Cranston, New Jersey, Village Improvement Association, where he'd been invited to speak, Wiley met the event's organizer, Alice Lakey, who would become one of his staunchest allies. Born in 1856, Lakey had once dreamed of being a concert singer, but she was sidetracked by ill health. Illness also plagued her parents. She helped look after them and, after her mother died in 1896, continued to keep house for her ailing father. Seeking to understand and alleviate both their health problems, she, rather like Fannie Farmer, developed a deep interest in nutrition. At least partly through careful devotion to a healthy diet, Lakey succeeded in becoming much stronger and, as a result, had become a dedicated advocate for nutrition, a balanced diet, and pure, untainted food and drink.

She'd joined the village association as a member of its Domestic Science Division and became association president, the post she held when Wiley came to speak. The two crusaders struck up an instant bond. Under Lakey's leadership, the Cranston Village Improvement Association petitioned Congress to pass food and drug legislation and she persuaded the New Jersey Federation of Women's Clubs to do the same. She then began a push for more support at the national level, contacting the National Consumers League and encouraging its more famous leaders to speak out on the issue.

Started in 1899 by influential social reformers Josephine Lowell and Jane Addams, the league primarily focused on helping the working poor. Addams—whose tireless work to help the disadvantaged would be honored in 1931 with a Nobel Peace Prize—had become nationally known for pioneering programs to bring education to America's low-income communities. She was the cofounder of one of the country's best-known settlement houses in Chicago, Hull House, which offered a range of classes and recreational activities for immigrant workers and also did detailed studies on the results. Addams recognized that shoddy food especially undermined the health of the poor. It took little urging from Lakey for Addams to begin to speak publicly in favor of pure-food legislation. Even the "most conservative woman," even the most traditional housewife, Addams emphasized at a national women's club convention, had a stake in the fight. It was shameful that she could not keep a "clean and wholesome" house, or feed her children safely, or buy "untainted meat" for the family dinner due to the troubled state of the American food supply.

Lakey also joined the pure-food committee of another national organization, the General Federation of Women's Clubs. Founded in 1890 by New York journalist Jane Cunningham Croly, a pioneer of American feminism, the federation linked volunteer women's clubs across the country. Like the WCTU, the federation had become interested in food and drug safety regulations some years earlier: Members had written pamphlets on "The Chemistry of Food" and invited speakers including Fannie Farmer to discuss preservatives and other issues in food science. They'd also backed state food regulations across the country. The federation members, Wiley wrote, were "the most efficient organizations now existing" in terms of political activity and good works.

"I think women's clubs of this country have done great work in whatever they have undertaken to the betterment of the condition of society," he wrote to one club president. "There is something wonderful in the power which organized effort can develop and the women of this country, through organized effort, in my opinion can secure any good thing which they demand."

Lakey urged Wiley to take a further lesson from the cookbook writers. There was a reason that domestic science was so popular among women frustrated by the lack of educational opportunities. The Chemistry Bureau's publications contained a wealth of scientific information. Why not, she asked, put that to practical use in the country's kitchens? Not only would it be helpful, but also it would serve to remind women that the simple act of assembling a meal could, far too often, put their families at risk. Her idea was to publish a guide to simple tests that home cooks might use to identify adulterated products.

There had been precedents for that in the private sector. In 1861 the Boston physician Thomas A. Hoskins had published a book called *What We Eat: An Account of the Most Common Adulterations of Food and Drink with Simple Tests by Which Many of Them May Be Detected*. "For the purpose of adding something to the means of self-protection," Hoskins explained, "I have endeavored to furnish simple directions, by which many of the more dangerous frauds in foods may be detected."

Battershall's 1887 book on food adulteration had also included many such home tests, and more recently the magazine *What to Eat* had published an article titled "How to Detect Food Adulterations," by John Peterson, food commissioner of Utah. It included several pages of instructions for testing milk, cream, ice cream, coffee, spices, sugar, salt, baking soda, cream of tartar, and extracts of lemon and vanilla. For example, Peterson advised adding a few drops of tincture of iodine to a sample of ice cream to find out if it was genuine or made from skim milk thickened with cornstarch. "A deep blue color is instantly developed if corn starch or flour is present," he wrote. He suggested introducing a little vinegar to test a sample of milk. The resultant curds should be white. If they turned "a distinct orange color," it meant the liquid had been colored with an aniline coal-tar dye. If the curds were brownish, it meant the vegetable dye annatto was present.

The test for formaldehyde and its ilk was simpler yet: "Keep the milk or cream in a warm place for forty-eight hours. If the sample is still sweet at the expiration of this time, a preservative is strongly indicated."

Because so much had already been published on the topic, Wiley wasn't sure there was a need for an official USDA report, but he admitted that the bureau's chemists could do a better job of sharing their expertise with the public. He had his staff prepare a new publication: Bulletin 100, *Some Forms of Food Adulteration and Simple Methods for Their Detection.* More than sixty pages long, it was coauthored by Willard Bigelow, now head of the bureau's food division, and Burton Howard, chief of its microchemical laboratory.

"Sir," wrote Wiley to Secretary Wilson, "I have the honor to submit for your approval a manuscript on food adulteration and simple methods for the detection of some of the more prevalent forms. This bulletin has been prepared to meet the numerous demands for non-technical information. . . . It is believed that it will be of service both to housekeepers and to dealers."

The bulletin's diplomatic introduction took pains not to accuse food processors of deliberate malice. "It is not in their interests to shorten the lives of their customers nor to impair their appetites," it noted. "We must assume they honestly believe the products they employ to be wholesome. Therefore, in judging the wholesomeness of preservatives and other products added in the preparation of foods, the subject must be treated in a conservative manner and no criminal or even dishonest motives attributed to those who disagree with us on the subject."

Among the easiest tests that the bulletin recommended was simply looking at the product. A cook could easily detect copper sulfate: "We sometimes find upon our market, pickles of a bright green hue which is not suggestive of any natural food." The same remained true for so-called fancy French peas. The report noted that of thirty-seven cans of peas examined by the bureau, thirty-five were loaded with copper sulfate.

More than half of bulletin 100 consisted of tables and charts detailing the continued problems of food adulteration in the United States. Twelve of thirteen samples of sausage had been found to contain borax. Ten of nineteen additional samples were packed with more cornstarch than meat. Coffee continued to be only partly coffee. Spices continued to be adulterated with ground coconut shells, Indian corn, almond shells, olive pits, and sawdust. Fraud was not just pervasive; it was standard practice.

Bigelow and Howard recommended that the curious cook invest in a strong magnifying glass, a small glass funnel (perhaps three inches in diameter), some filter paper, and some golden-brown "turmeric paper," heavily embedded with that spice and known to be useful in specific tests.

They also recommended that the household cook buy a few reagents, including grain alcohol, chloroform, potassium permanganate, tincture of iodine, and hydrochloric acid. These could all easily be purchased at a local pharmacy and were also useful in testing food and drink. The authors also issued a strong warning: "CAUTION: The corrosive nature of hydrochloric acid must not be forgotten. It must not be allowed to touch the skin, clothes or any metal."

Once equipped, and dressed protectively, the home cook could follow instructions to detect fakes and chemical additives in her groceries. As a typical example, the federal scientists offered this way to check for the preservative borax in meat: Macerate a tablespoon of chopped meat with hot water, press it through a bag, and then put two or three tablespoons into a sauce dish. Drip in fifteen to twenty drops of hydrochloric acid per tablespoon. Pour the liquid through the filter-paper-lined funnel. Then dip a piece of turmeric paper into the filtered liquid and dry the wet paper near a stove or lamp. "If boric acid or borax were used for preserving the sample, the turmeric paper should turn a bright cherry red."

The chemists provided several other kitchen-table experiments, but they also admitted that for some tests a laboratory was needed. "Although spices are very frequently adulterated, there are few methods that may be used by one who has not had chemical training and who is not skilled in the use of a compound microscope for the detection of the adulterants employed."

On April 30, 1904, the bustling city of St. Louis opened the gates to yet another spectacular world's fair, an exposition designed to outdo those hosted earlier by Chicago and Buffalo. Food, in its many incarnations, held a starring role. The daily *World's Fair Bulletin* announced that some of the "swellest" restaurants in the country could be found along the midway—known as the Pike—or integrated into exhibits. The fair boasted 125 eateries, ranging from the upscale, serving fifteen-course meals, to crowded snack stands. A simulated coal mine included a restaurant staffed by waiters dressed as miners. At a farm exhibit, visitors could look over a flock of chickens and pick out the specific bird they wanted roasted for their dinner.

In the midst of this cornucopia, Wiley's growing contingent of pure-food enthusiasts staged their own counter-display. They had been inspired partly by the Chemistry Bureau's modest presentation at the Pan-American Exposition, with its samples of adulterated products. This time they wanted something bigger, more dramatic, a showy staging that would garner national attention. They had spent more than a year planning a pure-food exhibit designed to shock fairgoers with its display of adulterations and dangers.

As well as the Kentucky food chemist Allen, representing the

National Association of State Dairy and Food Departments, and the tireless Alice Lakey, the organizers of the exhibit included the Chicago-based writer and editor Paul Pierce. Slender, meticulously groomed, fastidious in his habits, Pierce had for years campaigned against overeating and obesity. He considered far too many Americans—especially of the era's upper classes—to be "over-fed gluttons." Yet his interests in food and nutrition were wide-ranging and eclectic, as reflected in his magazine *What to Eat*. In its first issue, printed in August 1896, Pierce had promised that "no food or practice will be slighted" and it featured topics ranging from nine-course party menus to a discussion of the pure-food movement's battle against adulterations. "There is no more doubt that plain food is conducive to good health, than there is that pure air is good for respiratory organs," Pierce wrote in his opening essay.

In the years since he'd launched the magazine, Pierce had grown more adamant in his opposition to adulteration and fakery. The pages of *What to Eat* were increasingly packed with horror stories about chemically poisoned groceries, bitter commentary on the government's failure to protect its citizens from predatory manufacturers, and practical tips for surviving the current era of high-risk food. Like Wiley, he had become convinced that the nation's activist women, through their closely knit associations, would be key in winning the fight for regulation. "Now let the food adulterer quail, for we have the women on our side" read one of his editorials. "With a million women in our ranks fighting for such a cause, we will fear no foe that man and the might of millions in money can muster."

Wiley had successfully negotiated for an astonishingly large display space within the fair's Agriculture Palace, a pavilion surrounded by brilliant gardens that spread across twenty acres. Within that complex, the pure-food exhibit would cover two full acres. As rumors spread about their plans, Allen discovered that some unhappy food processors and manufacturers had considered seeking an injunction against the exhibit but had dropped the idea, deciding that the resulting furor would only "increase public interest" in the display.

To create the exhibit, Pierce wrote to food commissioners around the country, asking them to provide examples of adulterated, over-dyed, heavily preserved, or otherwise problematic food and drinks. As the boxes and cartons began piling up, it rapidly became obvious that two acres would hardly do justice to the problem.

The organizers decided to exhibit only two thousand different brands representing tainted food and drink sold in the United States. North Dakota sent canned meats: "While potted chicken and potted turkey are common products, I have never yet found a can in the State which really contained in determinable quantity either chicken or turkey," noted North Dakota food chemist Edwin Ladd. Minnesota and South Dakota sent sheets of silk and wool, each five feet square, brilliantly colored with coal-tar dyes extracted from strawberry syrups, ketchup, jams and jellies, and red wine. Michigan sent samples of a lemon extract in which the manufacturer had used cheap but deadly wood alcohol as the base. Illinois provided more faked extracts, such as "vanilla" made only of alcohol and brown food coloring, and a display of bottles carefully curved and carved to hide the fact that they held less than the advertised amount. Kansas offered up lemon drops colored yellow by poisonous lead chromate and chocolate faked by using burned sienna, a pigment made from oxides of iron and manganese.

Participating states provided forty brands of ketchup, labeled as a tomato product, that were mostly stewed pumpkin rind dyed red, and some fifty brands of baking powder that were largely well-ground chalk enhanced by aluminum compounds. To the fury of food industry executives, the fair's head of publicity, Mark Bennett, sent out a news release titled "Lessons in Food Poisoning," which noted: "If you want to have your faith in mankind rather rudely shaken, take the time to look about in the exhibit of the State Food Commissioners in the south end of the Palace of Agriculture."

For those who hadn't been following the issue, Bennett offered a guide to some of the continuing problems. "Maple syrup" was still likely to be mostly corn-derived glucose dyed brown; "cider vinegar" was found to be lab-made acetic acid colored with a little burned sugar; "lard" was mostly tallow (rendered mutton fat); "butter" still often turned out to be deliberately mislabeled oleomargarine; spices like "cayenne" were mostly ground nut shells; and, according to Bennett's release, "jellies and jams are any old thing," dyed any old color with coal-tar dyes. "Down a long list we might go, telling the secrets of those who are putting dollars into their pockets by putting poisons into our foods." Pierce happily reprinted Bennett's news release in his magazine.

Almost twenty million people—including President Roosevelt, who scheduled an elaborate and patriotically themed banquet—attended the fair. Roosevelt, in the midst of an election campaign to remain in office, did not mention the pure-food exhibit in his St. Louis remarks. But another attendee, the New York–based investigative journalist Mark Sullivan, made a point of doing so. Sullivan described the pure-food exhibit admiringly as "one of the most effective bits of propaganda ever achieved, for pure food or for any other purpose."

The fair also was home, in late September 1904, to the eighth meeting of the International Pure Food Congress. Secretary Wilson declined to attend but sent personal regrets and, naturally, his chief chemist. Harvey Wiley gave three speeches, one on his inspection work, one on adulteration—"The real evil of food adulteration is the deception of the consumer"—and the last on his preservative research. Regarding the latter, he put a strong emphasis on the groups most at risk. The work with borax and his current study of salicylic acid demonstrated, he said, that while exposure to such compounds was obviously survivable by healthy young men, they posed a greater risk to children, the elderly, the ill, the "least resistant."

As part of the Poison Squad tests, his staff was still evaluating the effects of salicylic acid ingestion on the bureau's volunteer diners, so Wiley held his fire on the topic of that preservative, but he urged strong protective action against the use of borax in food products. "It should not, I believe, be put in foods of any kind, except when they are plainly marked, and even not then except in special cases and for special purposes." Later that year in a speech at City College of New York, he clarified what he meant by "special purposes," emphasizing that they would be quite limited and specific. "It is true that there may be occasions where chemical antiseptics are necessary. It is far better to have food preserved with chemical antiseptics than to have no food at all. If I were going, for instance, to the North Pole—which I hope I never do—or any other long journey where access to foods would be cut off, it might be safer to use chemical preservatives in the foods which were taken along than to trust other sources."

In 1904 Wiley was taking a far tougher line on chemical additives than he had even a few years earlier. And he was further alarming his opponents within the food industry. They had reason to be alarmed, judging from the mood at September's Pure Food Congress. In his talk opening the congress, delegate James W. Bailey of Oregon hailed the unprecedented number of participants and the intensity of their advocacy.

"There are times in life when one is awed by the greatness of the occasion," said Bailey, who was the newly elected president of the National Association of State Dairy and Food Departments. "Such is my feeling today when I arise to address this, the greatest meeting ever held in the interests of pure food." The cause, he declared, had finally come of age. "Like every new idea, the pure food movement was at first thought to be merely a fad and hailed as a farce." But now the activists were getting through to the public. People were listening, and the St. Louis exhibit would, he predicted, surely change minds and spur reform. "I doubt if some of the sins of our manufacturers will be shown up more plainly on the day of judgment than they are at this exhibit." Bailey went on to predict that safe and healthy food would soon be seen as "one of the dire necessities of the land and coexistent with our welfare and happiness."

Makers of distilled spirits clashed again at the Pure Food Congress, and Wiley once again was drawn into the fight. As his friends and fellow social club members well knew, he favored good, aged bourbon—to drink and on principle. At the gathering, as in other public testimony, he continued to champion the traditional process of fermenting mash and barrel aging, citing the rich natural chemistry that produced a complex, satisfying taste that rectified whiskey could never match. He continued—despite warnings from Warwick Hough—to praise it also as a healthier drink than the lab-made and blended alternatives. As Wiley noted, aged whiskey required no dyes; it simply darkened as it aged. Barrel aging for at least four years also modified or eliminated most of the impurities, he claimed, and the old-fashioned way of making whiskey gave it certain characteristics of "health, purity, and flavor" that the artificial version could never attain.

Hough was also in attendance at the St. Louis fair, and he made it clear that he did not agree and did not appreciate the straight whiskey friendly corner of the food exhibit. Both in person and in correspondence, he once again urged Wiley to reconsider his arguments.

"I agree with you that false labeling is a deception which should be prohibited," Hough wrote to Wiley after the congress. "To brand a Bourbon whiskey as a Rye whiskey, or to assert that a whiskey is not a blend when in fact it is a blend, or to say that whiskey is ten years old, when in fact it is only five years old. But it is an equal deception for you or any of the distillers interested in the bottled in bond goods to attempt to create the impression upon the public, that the stamp on bottled in bond goods guarantees either the quality or the purity of the whiskey." The rectifiers, he said, were not finished with this fight. And the combative exhibits at the St. Louis fair had only stiffened that resolve.

Seven

THE YELLOW CHEMIST

1904–1906

The pepper perhaps contains cocoanut shells,
And the mustard is cottonseed meal;
And the coffee, in sooth, of baked chicory smells

In early November 1904, just as Theodore Roosevelt won election to the presidency in his own right, the writer Upton Sinclair traveled by train from the East Coast to Chicago, where he moved into a bare-bones settlement house, intent on researching his next novel.

The previous July, butchers had gone on a wage strike at packinghouses in nine cities, from Omaha to New York. The two-month strike failed because meatpacking firms, using a strategy developed by Chicago's famously ruthless Armour family, hired unskilled, nonunion replacements who could be paid less than the union butchers.

Sinclair, a twenty-eight-year-old son of a New York shoe salesman, was instantly sympathetic. He had barely paid for his own education at City College by writing jokes, dime novels, and magazine articles. Upon graduation in 1897, the aspiring novelist and freelance journalist had joined the worker-friendly socialist cause, partly inspired by his own struggles to make a living. He had written up a passionately pro-strike article and sent it, unsolicited, to the Kansas-based socialist newspaper, *Appeal to Reason*. In the same package Sinclair included a copy of his recent Civil War novel, *Manassas*, which had been a critical, if not commercial, success. The combination prompted the paper's editor, Julius Wayland, to make him an offer. He would print Sinclair's essay on the butchers' strike, and he would pay the writer $500 for a serialized novel telling the story of the valiant workers of Chicago's stockyards. Sinclair quickly accepted. He then persuaded his editor at Macmillan Publishing to give him another $500 contract to turn the serialized novel into a print book.

Flush with a grubstake of $1,000 (about $30,000 today), Sinclair spent seven weeks in Chicago's yards, living in a settlement house operated by a friend of Jane Addams's, often dressing in the grubby clothing of a worker to blend in. He observed and interviewed, gathering notes and sketches before returning to the East Coast, where with his wife and son he moved into a New Jersey farmhouse and settled down to write the most influential book of his prolific career.

The novel's main character was a Lithuanian immigrant, carrying that familiar dream of building a good life in America. "I will take care of us," he tells his wife. "I will work harder." In the end, the hardworking laborer is nearly destroyed by working conditions at the fictional "Anderson" meat-processing company. He eventually loses his health, family, and friends in the meatpacking industry but in Sinclair's conclusion finds some hope, at least, by embracing the brotherhood of socialism.

In February 1905 *Appeal to Reason* began serializing Sinclair's novel. By pure coincidence, the publication occurred just as other tales of troubled food production were unfolding in Congress, where advocates of pure-food legislation again sought to advance their cause. Both McCumber and Hepburn were still determined supporters of the proposed food and drug law, although Hepburn, as chair of the House Committee on Interstate and Foreign Commerce, was now mostly working with Roosevelt on railroad legislation. And a new senator from Idaho, Weldon Heyburn, had replaced McCumber as chairman of the Committee on Manufactures.

Heyburn, fifty-one, was a Republican but not in the least a Roosevelt progressive. He was an attorney who had made a living representing bankers and timber barons in his home state. During his time in the Senate, he would oppose the president on issues ranging from creation of new national forests to child labor laws. But like McCumber, he represented a frontier state—Idaho had become the forty-third state in 1890—where consumers believed, as did their counterparts in North Dakota, that their grocery stores were being treated as dumping grounds for cheap, adulterated food ginned up in the East. He also represented one of only four states in the country that had so far granted women the vote (the others were Wyoming, Utah, and Washington). Before the 1902 election, which saw Heyburn come into office, Idaho club women had met with every one of the state's political candidates to say that they would vote in a bloc against any who failed to support pure-food legislation.

Heyburn rose to the challenge. He found himself genuinely appalled by false claims made for mislabeled, largely useless products—especially those sold by the patent medicine industry. "I am in favor of stopping the advertisements of these nostrums in every paper in the country," he said. When industry representatives chastised him for supporting the proposed legislation, he replied, "The object of this bill is not to protect the dealer. It is to protect the persons who consume the articles."

The confrontational Heyburn tended to make enemies, among them Washington journalists. His press coverage was so often critical that he had fired back by describing reporters allowed into government buildings as mere guests of the state who "had no right to make disparaging remarks about senators." He had also antagonized many of his fellow lawmakers, who often, even publicly, described him as arrogant and humorless. Still, many Capitol colleagues succumbed to the force of his determination.

By January 1905 Heyburn had a food and drug bill called up before the full Senate. Two weary veterans of the fight, McCumber and Wiley attempted to temper his expectations, suggesting strategic concessions, such as to the whiskey rectifiers. Heyburn, as was typical, refused to compromise.

Food-processing industries had hardened their opposition to reform. The National Food Manufacturers Association lobbied for Heyburn to sponsor a different Senate bill, one that permitted the use of preservatives, excluded reports from the Bureau of Chemistry, and transferred regulatory authority over food and drink from the Agriculture Department to the business-friendly Department of Commerce and Labor.

Meanwhile, the blended-whiskey interests had been outraged to learn that the straight-whiskey men had secretly given financial support to the pure-food exhibit in St. Louis. Colonel Taylor himself had delivered a $3,000 check to the Kentucky food commissioner, Robert Allen, along with several cases of good bourbon to be displayed as examples of the "right" kind of whiskey. Allen had not shared that information with the other exhibit organizers, which in turn created outrage among his allies as well as the rectifiers. Paul Pierce wrote for *What to Eat* several angry pieces on the corrupting influence of Taylor and his like, but rectifiers weren't mollified.

In a story headlined LABELING RUINOUS TO LIQUOR TRADE, published in the *New York Journal of Commerce*, a major liquor distributor declared that if rectified whiskey was fully labeled as to dyes, additives, and synthetic alcohol, it would do untold damage to businessmen and government income derived from its sale. Taxes, the distributor predicted, would "suffer to an extent never dreamed of heretofore." The rectifiers' chief lobbyist, the obstreperous Hough, notified every member of Congress that his members flatly insisted on removing *any* whiskey-labeling requirements from the legislation.

Hough further sent out a circular urging all blenders, rectifiers, and distributors to stand together against such "hostile measures" before Congress. From the baking powder producers to the patent medicine industry to the meatpackers, manufacturers joined to fight any sign of food, drink, or drug regulation.

William Randolph Hearst, publisher of the *New York Evening Journal*, wrote: "There is a bill in the Senate of the United States called the Pure Food Bill. Its purpose is to prevent food adulteration, the swindling and poisoning of the public. Nobody in the Senate says a word against this bill; nobody dares go on record, of course, in behalf of adulteration. Yet it is certain that the bill will not be passed." The business of Congress was to take care of businessmen, Hearst wrote, and even some of the country's most "respectable" businessmen reaped huge profits by producing, misrepresenting, and selling adulterated, diluted, and downright faked food and drink. "Who is that shabby looking, patched-up individual trying to get on the floor of the House?" mused the editors of *Life* magazine. "O, that's old Pure Food Bill. When he first came around here he looked pretty good, but now he has been knocked around and changed so much that his friends don't know him at all. In a minute you'll see him thrown out bodily again."

As predicted, the proposed legislation collapsed in both houses within just a couple of months. "What now?" wrote the chairman of the Federation of Women's Clubs pure-food committee to Wiley. "Does this mean the [final] defeat of the Pure Food Bill or shall we keep on with our petitions and letters?" Wiley could almost imagine himself as the living incarnation of that shabby, patched-up bill described by *Life*. His advocacy for the legislation had increasingly made him a public target. An editorial in the *California Fruit Grower*, titled "Chemistry on the Rampage," had demanded, "Let somebody muzzle the yellow chemist who would destroy our appetite with Borgian tales," and the trade journal *Grocery World*, which represented the wholesalers, had chimed in: "The greater part of Dr. Wiley's time seems to be taken up in the delivering of sensational lectures on food frauds and the writing of articles on such subjects" as poisoned foods. "Dr. Wiley seems to thirst deeply for notoriety. He is happiest when looking complacently into the horror-stricken eyes of women he has just scared half to death." The journal's editors had even recommended that Wilson officially reprimand Wiley. The secretary had not done so, but he had once again called his chief chemist into his office to recommend discretion.

Wiley—somewhat to the secretary's frustration—instead returned to the lecture trail with renewed vigor. "I believe in chemistry and its application to the welfare of humanity," he told students at Cornell University. "But at the same time I can't help noticing how it is abused." He put the whole force of his personality behind the arguments, observed the muckraking progressive journalist Mark Sullivan: "On the platform the forcefulness and originality of his utterances gained from the impressiveness of his appearance: his large head capping the pedestal of broad shoulders, his salient nose shaped like the bow of an ice-breaker, and his piercing eyes compelled attention." It was a "great battle," Wiley would later write, and any battle, he thought, needed a general, someone who could coordinate the different factions into an effective army. At this moment he seemed to be the natural, perhaps the only, choice for that role. He urged the federated women's clubs to renew their activities, to protest the stalled legislation to every senator, every congressman, and every newspaper. His friends in the WCTU needed little urging to do the same. The National Association of State Dairy and Food Departments returned to the issue with increased urgency. Pushing past Allen's ties to the whiskey-distilling industry, the association joined Wiley in this new offensive push. It created a traveling exhibit, smaller but more graphic than the one at the St. Louis fair, a "chamber of horrors" that could be used to provide tangible illustration of adulterated food and drink at lectures. The state commissioners were nearing desperation. If the legislation failed yet again, their cause might die. They feared that they'd reached the critical moment, that if they didn't succeed now there might not be another chance for food and drug reform, or perhaps for any kind of consumer protection law, in their lifetimes.

The serialized version of Sinclair's novel, which he titled *The Jungle*, had a limited socialist readership, but he was counting on his editor at Macmillan to grow that audience. He mailed the installments to the publishing firm and, chapter by chapter, his editor became more dismayed. The book described diseased cattle arriving by railroad in Chicago to be butchered and sold to American housewives. "It was a nasty job killing these," Sinclair wrote, "for when you plunged your knife into them they would burst and splash foul smelly stuff into your face." Sinclair also evoked the embarrassing food scandals of the Spanish-American War: "It was stuff such as this that made the 'embalmed beef' that killed several times as many United States soldiers as all the bullets of the Spaniards; only the army beef, besides, was not fresh canned, it was old stuff that had been lying around for years in cellars."

Pickled beef had to be bathed in acid; the men working that line had their fingers eaten away by repeated exposure. Tuberculosis germs thrived in the moist, stinking air of the processing plants and spread from animal to animal, worker to worker. In the rendering rooms, there were open vats of acid set into the floor, to help break down the carcasses. Workers occasionally fell in, and "when they were fished out, there was never enough of them left to be worth exhibiting." Sometimes, Sinclair wrote, an exhausted worker, staying after hours to earn a little more, would slip into a vat and "be overlooked for days till all but the bones of them had gone out into the world as Anderson's [his thin disguise for Armour's] Pure Leaf Lard."

His editor sent chapters out for review by well-connected friends and advisers. Equally dismayed, they wrote back to insist that the descriptions couldn't be true. In late summer a new chapter recounted the ways that meat in a state of decay, even when fuzzed over with mold, could be cleaned, "dosed with borax and glycerin and dumped into hoppers and made over again for home consumption." It related that the packers routinely put out poisoned bread to keep the rat population down, and "then the rats, bread and meat would go into the hoppers together."

It was too much. His editor declared that the book was "gloom and horror unrelieved." Macmillan asked Sinclair to remove objectionable passages. Sinclair took the recommendations to some of his fellow writers, among them reformist journalists Lincoln Steffens and Ray Stannard Baker. Both those journalists had made names for themselves writing for the muckraking magazine *McClure's* with articles centered on government and corporation corruption. Both encouraged Sinclair to reject the cuts that Macmillan wanted and to keep his novel rich in the blood-spattered details of the Chicago stockyards. Steffens did warn him, though, that he should expect continued resistance and revulsion. Sometimes, the veteran journalist noted gloomily, "it is useless to tell things that are incredible, even though they may be true." Baker, whose exposés of the railroad industry had led to Roosevelt's obsession with reforming it, thought Sinclair should have written a nonfiction book instead of a novel, but he counseled his friend not to back down.

Sinclair determined that "I had to tell the truth and let people make of it what they would." In September 1905 Macmillan canceled his contract, generously offering that he keep the $500 advance. Disappointed, Sinclair shopped *The Jungle* around to other publishers but found no takers. He arranged to publish a "sustainers edition," essentially self-publishing. Issued under the Jungle Publishing Company imprint, it was offered to subscribers of the *Appeal*, and sold surprisingly well—netting him almost $4,000—but, to his disappointment, failed to gain any real national attention.

Meanwhile, other writers continued to drive interest in the subject of the country's appalling food supply. The illustrated monthly *Everybody's Magazine* published an investigation into the National Packing Company, a trust established by Armour, Swift, and Morris. Its author, investigative journalist Charles Edward Russell, then published a book, in that fall of 1905, called *The Greatest Trust in the World*, devoted to the further evils of the meatpacking industry. Its angry dissection of price-fixing, inhumane working conditions, and corrupt practices at the Chicago stockyards would help Upton Sinclair sharpen many of the demoralizing descriptions in subsequent editions of *The Jungle*. Crusading women's magazines also took aim at the toxic nature of processed food. In the spring of 1905, the *Woman's Home Companion*, a monthly magazine founded in 1873 and with a circulation approaching two million, published a three-part series titled "The Truth About Food Adulteration," written by Henry Irving Dodge. The journalist had worked in collaboration with none other than Willard Bigelow, chief of the Division of Foods at the Bureau of Chemistry. "The series is therefore a thoroughly authoritative account of this most dangerous and growing practice," read the magazine's promotional copy.

Bigelow described for Dodge some of the clever ways that American businessmen legally deceived consumers. He cited a popular product, Old Reliable Coffee, which was described on its elaborately scrolled label as "a compound of delicious drinking coffee, guaranteed to please those who like a full-bodied cup of coffee." There was not, Bigelow said, one grain of coffee inside the can. But the use of the word "compound" allowed the manufacturer to make coffee claims under both state and federal law. Bigelow encouraged Dodge to examine food samples through a microscope, revealing to the journalist the ground pumice stone in baking powder, the pulverized olive pits in spices, demonstrating the difference between a rectilinear crystal of lard and a bush-shaped crystal of beef fat. None of these fakes, Dodge wrote admiringly, escaped the department's chemistry analyst, whom he further described as a "man of blue blazes and sulfurous smokes."

Part 2 of the series was titled "How the Baby Pays the Tax: The Food Poisoner Reaches the Height of His Crime When He Attacks the Baby, upon Whose Well-Being the Fate of the Nation Depends." The story was illustrated by a drawing of a child dining at one end of a well-stocked table and a skeleton watching him from the other. The words "Glucose, Sulphate of Copper, Boracic Acid, Aniline Dyes, Benzoic Acid, Formaldehyde" were embroidered along the edge of the tablecloth. "The man who poisons food for gain builds a palace of bones upon a graveyard" was the opening sentence of Dodge's next salvo.

The focus was milk, still widely adulterated and either filthy with bacteria or poisoned with formaldehyde. Dodge cited a plethora of anecdotes to support this conclusion, from Brooklyn to Chicago, where authorities had been recently forced to condemn almost five hundred vats of milk in a single week. A doctor in New Jersey had recently blamed an uptick in child deaths on continued used of formaldehyde in milk, and another in New York had noted that unpasteurized supplies had contributed to yet another outbreak of typhoid. In the year 1904, Dodge noted, more than twenty thousand children under the age of two had died in New York City and that milk was considered a major contributor to those fatalities. "The cry 'Poisoned Milk'" rings through the land, he wrote, as it had over decades of government inaction and corruption.

Dodge had learned from a friend in the U.S. Senate that manufacturers were prepared to spend more than $250,000 to defeat any regulations and had already made major contributions to the campaigns of senators considered friendly to the cause. No wonder the proposed food legislation was going nowhere, he wrote: "The Senate does not indulge in bawling opposition to the bill. Oh no, its weapons are much more effective and more deadly. It lets the bill die." The

American government, he concluded, would rather protect wealthy business interests than protect the American people.

Also in 1905, Pierce's magazine, *What to Eat*, published a four-part series titled "The Slaughter of Americans." In his opening editor's note, Pierce wrote: "In view of the widespread adulteration of foods in America, that is adding so greatly to the death roll and causing more sickness and misery than all the other sources combined, *What to Eat* has decided to publish a series of carefully compiled articles revealing to Americans the actual condition of the food we eat today." The series provided a detailed list of the reasons that Pierce and his food-reform allies were so frustrated and angry. In one article Pierce assured his readers that butter now contained enough coal-tar dye to kill a cat. Another article in the series said that more than 400,000 infants were killed by unwholesome food and formaldehyde-tainted milk every year in the United States. A restless urgency crackled through Pierce's series and through the writings, speeches, and letters, both private and public, of all of Wiley's growing army of food-reform allies. They were fed up with foot-dragging federal lawmakers.

U pton Sinclair refused to give up on his novel. He kept shopping *The Jungle* to established publishing firms.

He suffered more rejections from publishers wary of potential lawsuits but got a meeting with Isaac Marcosson, who worked for the publishing house Doubleday, Page & Company. As a newspaper writer in Louisville, Kentucky, Marcosson had written a positive review of Sinclair's 1903 novel, *The Journal of Arthur Stirling*. He welcomed the author into his office and listened to Sinclair's promise that the hefty bundle of pages he carried was "something sensational." Marcosson lugged the manuscript home and became engrossed, staying up all night reading it. In the morning he presented it enthusiastically to his boss, Walter Hines Page.

Both Page and his partner, Frank Nelson Doubleday, needed persuading. Page shared much of Marcosson's enthusiasm but agreed
with more dubious Doubleday that the story's revolting details might
be too much for readers to stomach. Page cautioned their young employee that if they did contract for Sinclair's book, it would be with
the understanding that Marcosson would be responsible for "launch-
ing and exploiting" *The Jungle.* The publishers also insisted on sending a copy of the manuscript to the *Chicago Tribune* for an opinion
on whether the book's grisly descriptions had any basis in reality.
Tribune editors responded with a two-dozen-page rebuttal of the
packinghouse descriptions. Alarmed, Page and Doubleday called
Sinclair to their offices. But Sinclair promptly began picking apart
the *Tribune*'s critique.

For instance, the paper had denied that the tuberculosis bacte-
rium could survive on walls or floors of the packing rooms. Sinclair
pointed out that the germ could indeed survive on those surfaces and
could transfer to anything that touched them. He'd brought medical
studies to prove it, as well as other evidence to back up his story. He
further noted that the paper's owners were obviously friendly with
the meatpackers and sided with them. In fact, it would turn out that
the newspaper's management had not assigned a reporter to study
Sinclair's claims but instead passed the task on to a publicist who
worked for the meatpackers.

The *Tribune*'s fervent denial of the story made Page, also a former reporter, suspicious. As well as a book publisher, he was editor
of the business magazine *World's Work.* His journalist's instincts
told him something wasn't right about the *Tribune* report. It smelled
like a whitewash. He decided on an independent investigation. The
publishing company sent Marcosson and the company's lawyer on
an expedition to Chicago. Both men returned disgusted and horri-
fied by what they'd seen. They'd also secured multiple sources willing to provide public statements about the odious conditions in the

yards. Page became convinced and he persuaded his partner Double-day to agree. Page also decided that when *The Jungle* went on sale, he would buttress it by publishing factual reporting on the horrors of the yards in *World's Work*. Sinclair signed his book contract with the publishing firm on January 6, 1906.

R obert Allen recovered, for the most part, from the scandal re-garding his cozy deal with bourbon distillers during the pure-food exhibition in St. Louis. Allies in the movement forgave him, perhaps in recognition that he had accepted the whiskey men's $3,000 not for personal gain but to finance the exhibit. Again supported by the well-connected bourbon barons, he secured a meeting with President Roosevelt in the summer of 1905, and several prominent food reform advocates agreed to attend. Wiley wasn't among them. The chief chemist asked for and received from Wilson an assurance that the Agriculture Department officially supported the meeting. But he believed that there was more power in a delegation of private citizens, especially when the president already knew Wiley's position all too well. The delegation included Alice Lakey, food commissioners from Ohio and Connecticut, a representative of the retail grocers' association, and a representative from the H.J. Heinz Company of Pittsburgh, which was now very successfully marketing a preservative-free ketchup made from actual tomatoes. They presented their case to Roosevelt but, as Allen related with some disappointment afterward, the president remained noncommittal.

Then later that year, in November, Roosevelt invited the delegation back to the White House, revealing that he had taken the trouble to talk over their issue with a range of experts, from Wiley to Ira Remsen of Johns Hopkins University, codiscoverer of the sweetener saccharin. The president had even discussed the matter with his personal physician. The result was, the president said, that he had decided at last to support the beleaguered food and drug law in his end-of-the-year message to Congress. He told the group that he had little expectation that his advocacy would change anything— opposition to food and regulation remained both stubborn and powerful—but on December 5 Roosevelt formally announced that he was backing the legislation: "I recommend that a law be enacted to regulate interstate commerce in misbranded and adulterated foods, drinks and drugs. Such a law would protect the legitimate manufacturer and commerce and would tend to secure the health and welfare of the consuming public." The speech made it clear that the president had been following Wiley's research and its conclusions: "Traffic in foodstuffs which have been debased or adulterated so as to injure health and deceive the public should be forbidden."

Senator Heyburn promptly brought the bill back to the manufacturing committee, hoping to move it quickly to a vote by the full chamber. But the president had accurately assessed the hostility gathered against the legislation. It appeared, in fact, that Roosevelt's intervention had stirred up even stronger resistance. The Republican leader of the Senate, Nelson Aldrich of Rhode Island, had made his fortune as a wholesale grocer with strong ties to the food manufacturing industry. He now took to the floor to attack the bill as an affront to individual liberty: "Are we to take up the question as to what a man shall eat and what a man shall drink and put him under severe penalties if he is eating or drinking something different from what the chemists of the Agricultural Department think desirable?" Angrily, McCumber replied: "On the contrary, it is the purpose of the bill that a man may determine for himself what he will eat and what he will not eat. It is the purpose of the bill that he may go into the market and when he pays for what he asks for that he shall get it and not get some poisonous substance in lieu of that."

Aldrich stood unmoved. He flatly refused to bring the bill forward for a full Senate vote. Roosevelt tried to suggest, in a private meeting, that Aldrich should let the bill go forward. It would look better publicly and, after all, Aldrich didn't have to vote for it. The senator would not budge.

But in early February 1906, the Rhode Island senator was forced into an unhappy meeting with a powerful backer of the bill, the director of the American Medical Association's legislative council. The AMA was less interested in food safety than in the problem of snake-oil medicines, but the two issues were bonded together in the law. The organization wanted those patent cures regulated and was prepared, Aldrich was informed, to rally all 135,000 physicians in the country, including all of those located in the senator's home state, to get the bill passed. The doctors would, if need be, contact every patient, county by county. The AMA had a reputation for avoiding partisan politics, but its board had decided to take this legislation on as a personal cause. And according to Charles Reed, the AMA legislative council director, the senator from Rhode Island could take this as a personal warning. Shortly after that meeting, Aldrich called a more junior senator into his office—Albert Beveridge of Indiana—and told him to carry a message to Heyburn: It was now good timing for Heyburn to bring his bill up for a vote again.

Beveridge later told journalist Mark Sullivan that he had suspected that his errand was just for show. He thought that any Senate vote in favor of the bill would prove futile. The legislation was clearly destined to die in the House, where leadership was just as firmly opposed. But the Indianan obediently went to Heyburn's office. As he also recounted to Sullivan, "Heyburn said he could not believe it and said he was tired of being made a fool of by asking useless consideration [for the bill] which he had asked so many times before." Beveridge ventured the opinion that the game seemed, for the minute, to be going Heyburn's way and that he might as well take advantage of it. That afternoon Heyburn requested a vote on his bill. On February 26 the food and drug bill passed 63–4, with Aldrich abstaining. The bill then went to the House and, as predicted, Sullivan wrote, "There it slept."

Back at the Bureau of Chemistry—which Wiley had taken to calling "America's test kitchen"—the toxicity testing of preservatives continued to tell an alarming story. Bigelow remained lead chemist for the trials and Wiley himself had assumed a more hands-on role. He no longer had the help of physicians from the Marine Hospital Service, who had found the twice-weekly examinations of Poison Squad volunteers too time-consuming. So Wiley was conducting the physicals himself. As with borax in the previous trial, in the second round of tests on salicylic acid, doses were administered either in capsules or tablets. Wiley publicly acknowledged that industry-backed scientists had criticized this in the borax study, arguing that it failed to represent normal intake of the preservative, which was usually premixed into food. Yet he dismissed the criticism. "It is hardly necessary to call attention to the futility of such an objection," he added. "A preservative administered in this way at the time of the meals, as was always the case, is rapidly mixed with the contents of the stomach during the process of digestion, and could not in any way exert any injurious effect by reason of the form of its administration."

Another repeated criticism was that Wiley and his staff did not constantly monitor the men's activities and could not be sure they didn't cheat on their prescribed diets. These were working government employees who came to the test kitchen only for meals and checkups. This was a real limitation. "The attempt has been made to control, as far as possible, all conditions of the experimental work," he said, but "the difficulties attending the task are so enormous that it is not possible that complete success should be secured." Still, he thought, the chemistry crew had done enough checks, interviews, questionnaires, and follow-ups to be sure that their volunteers were not ill, taking medications, or experiencing other unusual exposures.

Again they tested the suspect preservative at varying dosages, ranging from about two hundred milligrams to a full two grams daily. Wiley again believed that although the higher dose, not unexpectedly, produced more severe effects, the real issue was the subtler risk of daily chronic exposure at low doses and an apparent cumulative effect. "Like other ordinary preservatives, it is not one that can be classified as a poison in the usual sense of the word." Salicylic acid's long history in folk medicine, as well as its use as a prescribed pharmaceutical, tended to reassure consumers that it was benign. Wiley agreed that salicylic acid was "often beneficial when prescribed by a competent physician." It was also a base for synthesizing the milder acetylsalicylic acid, an active ingredient in aspirin, with which it was sometimes confused. But, just as Wiley's lab had reported in its 1887 study of alcoholic beverages, its use as a preservative raised the risk of a cumulative overdose. When salicylic acid was mixed into either drink or food and consumed day after day, meal after meal, it became far more of a hazard than a health aid. During the months of the salicylic acid tests, the scientists had recorded chronic stomach pain, nausea, appetite loss, and weight loss in their squad members. Bigelow's written conclusion was that taken chronically, even in small quantities, salicylic acid "exerts a depressing and harmful influence upon the digestion and health and general metabolic activities of the body." The chemists again pointed out that the use of such compounds could be reduced if manufacturers would merely process foods in clean conditions.

Wiley sent Wilson an early copy of the report. It reinforced the secretary's concern that his bureau chief had become more crusader than objective chemist. The end of the salicylic acid report, in fact, came awfully close to sounding like a Paul Pierce diatribe: "The addition of salicylic acids and salicylates to foods is therefore a process which is reprehensible in every respect and leads to injury to the consumer, which though in many cases not easily measured, must finally be productive of great harm." This was not the same prudent, methodical Harvey Wiley who had spoken so judiciously about the preservative issue during the embalmed-beef hearings. Wilson had

long supported Wiley's activities, but his growing stridency was starting to alienate the chief chemist from his politically cautious boss.

As Doubleday, Page prepared to publish *The Jungle* in early 1906,
Marcosson told Sinclair that the firm wanted major revisions.
The serialized version of the novel, the last chapter of which had appeared in *Appeal to Reason* the previous November, featured too
much overwrought, preachy philosophy, including its many refer-
ences to exploitive employers preying on hapless workers. Doubleday, Page wanted to excise Sinclair's overt comparisons of worker life
to an existence in a wild forest with "the strong devouring the
weak"—the source of his title. At such a late date, after his struggles
to find a publisher, he gave in. The publisher cut thirty thousand
words and ordered an initial print run of twenty thousand copies.
Publication was set for February 26, which was, again by pure coincidence, the day the Senate passed Heyburn's food and drug bill.

Marcosson speculated that the book would either be "a sensa-
tional success or a magnificent failure." To help get the word out,
Sinclair sent an early copy to his muckraking journalist friend Baker
at *McClure's*. Marcosson sent copies to the wire services Associated
Press and United Press with a note urging them to quote at will. And
he sent extra copies to newspapers and magazines in every major
American city. The publishing company also sent a copy to President
Roosevelt, autographed by Sinclair, of course.

Eight

THE JUNGLE

1906

———◉———

And the terrapin tastes like roast veal.
The wine which you drink never heard of a grape,
But of tannin and coal tar is made.

With the legislation seeming permanently stalled in Congress, Harvey Wiley had taken to writing protest letters to newspapers and magazines, complaining about their advertising of fake remedies and fraudulent foods. Their practices weren't illegal, he acknowledged, but they were dismayingly dishonest.

To the *Washington Star* he wrote in early 1906: "I have read with regret in your issue of Monday, [January] 29th of the probably fatal illness of Buck Ewing, the celebrated catcher." Ewing, a former star player and manager for the New York Giants, had been diagnosed with Bright's disease, an inflammation of blood vessels in the kidneys, dreaded as bringing on a rapid and painful death.

But Wiley noted that the *Star* was apparently prepared to offer a solution to such a devastating diagnosis, as illustrated by "your issue of Sunday, the 28th instant, of Dr. Kilmer's Swamp Root. This remedy, which I always keep near me," he added sarcastically, "has on the carton in very large letters—Cures Brights Disease—together with every other ill that the flesh is heir to."

Perhaps, he suggested, the *Star* didn't realize that his bureau chemists had found that the Swamp Root formula was mostly drinking alcohol and turpentine, flavored with a sprinkle of herbs and spices such as cinnamon, peppermint, and sassafras. But as the newspaper's advertisement guaranteed the tonic's cure-all potency, Wiley promised to send Ewing "a marked copy of the *Sunday Star* with this absolute guarantee and I shall expect soon to hear of his entire restoration to health." Ewing died of Bright's disease in October 1906 at age forty-seven.

To *Everybody's Magazine* in New York, Wiley fired off a series of questions: Could the magazine explain how Rubifoam made teeth look "just like pearls"? In what sense was Celes, the oxygen tooth powder, "chemically perfect"? And about that Kneipp Malt Coffee, which was made from roasted barley grains. How exactly did it manage to have "real coffee flavor? Is there anything that can have the 'real coffee flavor' except coffee?" How exactly did the magazine plan to stand behind these claims?

Needling the periodicals and their advertisers provided him with an amusing respite from the seemingly never-ending and increasingly bitter legislative fight. After the encouraging vote on Heyburn's bill in the Senate, after Wiley's acceptance of his role as the public face of the campaign, the opposition had escalated the frequency and the vitriol of their attacks on him, which were also becoming more personal in tone. "My attention is called to the fact that considerable agitation is going on here looking to your removal," wrote the director of Dudley & Co. Canned Goods in New York City to Wiley. *Grocery World*, a trade paper for wholesale grocers, had published two editorials in the previous two weeks demanding that Wiley be removed from office.

Critics described him as "the nation's janitor," busily sweeping up the kitchens and pantries of its citizens; the overzealous "policeman" of the American stomach; a would-be tyrant; a shoddy scientist; a man with mental issues and delusions of grandeur. The publicist for the borax industry sent letters to news editors under a fake name, calling the Poison Squad studies deeply flawed. The whiskey rectifiers and the wholesale grocers printed a pamphlet on Wiley's work on fake honey from the early 1880s, dating back to his years at Purdue.

Repeating the old charge, it was titled "Wiley's Honey Lie" and purported to be from still-angry honey producers. The American Honey Producers League denied any knowledge of the pamphlet but the damage was done. The whiskey rectifiers suggested that he was a bourbon-soaked alcoholic receiving packets of hard cash from Taylor and his friends. Wiley started receiving sympathy notes from members of Congress. "The attacks which are being made upon you by certain representatives of the liquor interests are contemptible," wrote a Wisconsin legislator to Wiley about one circular. In a good-humored reply, Wiley called the rectifiers' diatribe "[A]bout the best one that has been issued so far. I shall take pleasure in showing it to the Secretary of Agriculture." Wilson, despite his concerns, was still standing by Wiley and had recently renewed the chemist's contract.

In late February Wiley gave a pro-legislation speech to a national convention of the canning industry, held in Philadelphia. The president of the Midwest canners' group, A. C. Frasier of Wisconsin, had invited him. Frasier, who specialized in peas processed without preservatives, found Wiley's arguments compelling. But when the chief chemist arrived at the Philadelphia train station, he found his host pacing the platform in a state of alarm. He feared for Wiley's safety, Frasier said, should he attend the meeting. "What is the matter?" Wiley asked. "Well, they say you are trying to ruin their business," Frasier replied. "I can not help what they say," Wiley replied. "I am trying to save their business." He was not going to be a government employee who ran in fear from a roomful of American businessmen. That would send a terrible message to the canners. But he agreed that it made sense to have a backdoor exit ready, just in case.

The hall was packed with canners, food jobbers, and brokers, none of them smiling. An Iowa canner, William Ballinger, stood up to explain that he was opposed to allowing Wiley to become "dictator" of his industry. "I want to declare the job too big a one for Professor Wiley and his assistants," Ballinger said. "Furthermore it has been my observation, and I want Professor Wiley to know I do not mean anything personal, that a man who lives in an atmosphere of microbes and bacilli not only becomes a crank but absolutely monomaniacal on the subject upon which he is interested."

Wiley didn't deny that he could appear to be a crank. But he defended his record and that of the Chemistry Bureau in helping, rather than trying to control, the canning industry. "The canners of this country have a serious responsibility placed on them," he said. "Let me pay you the compliment of having progressed steadily in preserving the food you can, but there should never be a relaxation of efforts to move onward as there are some things that can be bettered."

He restated his belief that the canners' mushrooming use of dyes and preservatives, often to disguise poor-quality food, was driving consumers away from American products. "Honesty is what the American public demands and canned goods will have an ever-growing market as long as people are confident that the goods are free from anything injurious."

He could stand for both consumer protection and the American businessman, Wiley insisted, and he hoped those seated in the room could respect that. "You are honest businessmen," he continued. "Is there one man in this room that wants to take one dollar from an American citizen which, if that American citizen knew what he was selling him, he would not give?" To the surprise of both Frasier and himself, Wiley received a standing ovation. Some of the leading canners even promised to back the proposed pure-food legislation. Not all of them would do so, of course. Some of the canners had already allied themselves with the hostile National Food Manufacturers Association. But even among that contingent, there were attendees who agreed with Wiley that public perception of a chemically tainted and adulterated food supply was hurting their business.

Wiley told the story of his meeting with the canners at a congressional hearing about that canners' conference, stressing that he wanted to allay legislators' concerns about political retribution if they passed a pure-food law. There were plenty of processors who would welcome uniform safety standards, he told them. He offered the examples of Pittsburgh's H.J. Heinz and the Chicago-based Reid, Murdoch and Co. The latter had written to him in mid-February, "From the newspapers we notice that the attitude of the so-called National Food Manufacturer's Association is, in some instances, taken to represent the views of manufacturers generally. We desire to state that we have no connection whatsoever and we believe that none of the large manufacturing grocers of this country are identified with it. We are unreservedly for a National Pure Food Law."

Senate passage of Heyburn's bill had rallied supporters as well as opponents. "Your wonderful tenacity of purpose and persistence seems to have at last won out triumphantly," wrote a former state food commissioner from Ohio. Charles Reed of the AMA, who had successfully threatened Nelson Aldrich in the Senate, said he planned to put similar pressure on legislators in the House. "When the Pure Food Bill begins to draw to a focus in the House, let me know," he wrote to Wiley in early March. "It is my intention to do with the House what I did with the Senate, but in addition, I propose having telegrams pour into the members from all over the United States."

In early March Frank Doubleday received a visit from a lawyer representing meatpacking titan J. Ogden Armour. The Chicago meatpacking titan had organized the industry response to Sinclair's book, publicly declaring that the products were "without blemish," privately pressuring newspapers not to review the book and libraries not to carry it. The attorney invited the publisher to lunch with Armour, the meal to be served in a private car now awaiting his pleasure at Grand Central Station. The lawyer explained that Armour wanted to offer a generous advertising contract to the publishing firm, on the condition that Doubleday, Page curtail further publication plans for *The Jungle*, in particular any plan to publish the book abroad. As it happened, Doubleday had just received an offer from an English publisher, Alfred Harmsworth, Lord Northcliffe, seeking to buy both British and European rights to *The Jungle*. Harmsworth had founded two tabloid newspapers, the *Daily Mail* and the *Daily Mirror*, and he'd become famous—or notorious, depending on one's point of view—for his sensationalistic presentation of news stories. Doubleday had been personally and patriotically disinclined to accept the offer. He had only reluctantly followed Page's lead in agreeing to publish Sinclair's book at all. If he accepted Northcliffe's deal, he worried that he would be showing the world an unsavory side of American business, and he "did not care to wash our dirty linen in all the capitals of Europe."

But the lawyer drew out of his briefcase a can of corned beef and placed it, with a smile, on the publisher's desk, a gesture meant to symbolize a lucrative relationship. Doubleday, known for his quick temper, lost it.

"This chap made me so angry," he said. "I showed him [Northcliffe's] telegram and told him we would give permission to have the book reprinted in Europe." His visitor expressed bafflement, leading the still infuriated Doubleday to insult the attorney as a moral degenerate and throw him out of his office.

The Jungle was on its way to U.S. sales of more than 150,000 in its first year of publication, which would also see it translated into more than seventeen languages. In England the rising political star Winston Churchill recommended that all citizens read it; the playwright George Bernard Shaw called it an example of "what is going on all over the world under the top layer of prosperous plutocracy." Sinclair appreciated his sudden prosperity, but he did not enjoy every aspect of his newfound celebrity.

Meatpacking interests planted stories in friendly newspapers, claiming that the young author had spent more time in Chicago whorehouses than in the yards. The hostile *Chicago Tribune* had printed an editorial titled "Investigating a Novel," which described the book as "garbage fiction," Sinclair as a "pseudo-reformer," and Roosevelt as barely interested but concerned that "the American export trade in meat would be destroyed if foreigners were led to believe that the novel dealt with facts." Sinclair was in a resentful mood, discontented even with the public's response to his book. Despite incredible sales, no one was talking about the struggles of the workingman or socialist ideals. They were talking about filthy, germ-infested food and the possibility that their morning sausage contained scraps of rat and possibly human meat as well as the standard pork. "I aimed for the public's heart," he would later say, bitterly. "And by accident I hit it in the stomach."

Beginning the first week of publication in February, letters and telegrams of outrage arrived at the White House, demanding to know how Roosevelt planned to fix the problem of the country's disgusting food supply. The president had been one of the book's earliest readers and had also been appalled. The political humorist Finley Peter Dunne, in his syndicated newspaper column "Mr. Dooley," enjoyed imagining Roosevelt's reaction to the revelations in *The Jungle* while at the White House breakfast table. Veteran journalist Dunne wrote the popular column in the person of fictional Chicago barkeeper Martin J. Dooley, who spoke in a thick Irish brogue: "Tiddy was toying with a light breakfast an' idly turn'n over the pages iv th' new book with both hands. Suddenly he rose fr'm th' table, an cryin': 'I'm pizened', begun throwin' sausages out iv th' window." In Dunne's telling, a hurled sausage struck Senator Beveridge—who had played a part in Senate passage of the food and drug bill—right in the head "an' made him a blond" before whizzing on to injure a Secret Service agent and destroy a thicket of oak trees. Fearing for the president's life, the newly blond Beveridge rushed into the White House and "discovered Tiddy in hand to hand combat with a potted ham. . . . Since thin th' Prisidint, like th' rest iv us, has become a viggytarynan."

Doubleday, Page had also sent the president early proofs of the supporting articles scheduled to appear in *World's Work*, one of them a microbiologist's detailed discussion of dangerously prolific germ cultures in Chicago processing plants and the failure of government inspectors to address the problem. Dismayed, Roosevelt asked Secretary Wilson to explain what was going on with the Inspection Division of the Department of Agriculture. Its employees were supposed to make sure that diseased animals were not sent from the slaughterhouses into production of canned, dried, smoked, and chopped meat. In *The Jungle*, which Sinclair claimed was based on his own reporting directly from the yards, the packers simply paid the government inspectors either to look the other way or stay away.

The question threw Wilson on the defensive and he replied with an attack on Sinclair's "willful and deliberate" portrayal of corrupt inspectors. An irked Roosevelt warned Wilson that his department seemed to be more interested in hiding a problem than in solving it. The president then sought less self-protective points of view, including one from Chicago progressive activist Mary McDowell, a colleague and friend of Jane Addams, who had provided housing for Sinclair during his book research. McDowell had worked for years to help packinghouse laborers, earning her the nickname "Angel of the Stockyards." She told him that the novel was based in truth, allowing for some slight exaggeration. Like Doubleday, Roosevelt did not admire the book's socialist ideas, and he wrote to Sinclair directly to tell him so, but he also decided to invite the young author to the White House in early April to discuss the realities of the stockyards.

Roosevelt told Sinclair that he was bypassing the Agriculture Department and sending two independent investigators to Chicago: his commissioner of labor, Charles P. Neill, and the social reformer James B. Reynolds, a manager of settlement houses on the East Side of Manhattan. The president invited Sinclair to meet with them and perhaps suggest avenues of inquiry. Neill and Reynolds were leaving so soon that Sinclair managed only a brief discussion on the train platform. He returned home to find a letter from a friend in Chicago, saying that packers had been alerted to the new inquiry—purportedly by the White House itself—and were busily cleaning up the factories.

Sinclair had little trust in the president. In Roosevelt's speech that spring at the annual dinner of the Gridiron Club, he'd railed against investigative journalists as "muckrakers," filling the pages of periodicals and books with dirt while "ignoring at the same time the good in the world." The president's attack wasn't inspired by Sinclair or his friends at *McClure's* but by David Graham Phillips, author of a series titled "The Treason of the Senate," running in William Randolph Hearst's magazine *Cosmopolitan*. Phillips had characterized the Senate as an "agent of interests as powerful as any invading army could be, and vastly more dangerous." The opening article focused on corrupt Republicans and attacked New York senator Chauncey Depew, Roosevelt's friend and political ally. Roosevelt wanted to respond by excoriating Phillips personally, but advisers persuaded him to deliver a broader critique of overzealous, reform-seeking writers—a category that could be interpreted to include Sinclair, Lincoln Steffens, Ray Stannard Baker, Ida Tarbell, Henry Irving Dodge, and more. In defense of his profession, Steffens, long a cordial acquaintance of the president, visited the White House the day after the Gridiron speech to criticize the intemperate language. The resolute Roosevelt brushed off the scolding and reprised the speech in expanded form before the Senate itself. There he clarified that he would not abide corruption, but that overweening journalists could do more harm than good in their eagerness to expose wrongdoing: "The men with the muck rakes

are often indispensable to the well being of society; but only if they
know when to stop raking the muck."

The president's nuances were lost on Sinclair. He took the
speeches personally, convinced that Roosevelt was a progressive only
when it suited him. He'd learned that the meatpacking interests had
quietly donated $200,000 toward Roosevelt's election campaign in
1904. He doubted that the president's investigators would or could
confirm the truths that he'd depicted in *The Jungle*—at least not
without help. He took the pragmatic step of persuading a longtime
journalist friend to meet with Neill and Reynolds in Chicago and to
arrange interviews for them with sources he had talked to for his
book. At the same time, he took the undiplomatic step of writing to
Roosevelt, expressing his fear that the government had no genuine
interest in the truth. This was prompted, at least in part, by a report
in the *Tribune* that the president planned to give another speech, this
one attacking *The Jungle*. Roosevelt wrote back dismissively, coun-
seling, "Really, Mr. Sinclair, you must keep your head." Roosevelt
himself had read hundreds of lies about his own life, and all with
"quite as little foundation" as the recent *Tribune* fabrication. To
Doubleday, Roosevelt wrote with irritation, "Tell Sinclair to go home
and let me run the country for a change."

Despite Sinclair's worries and despite the packers' efforts to polish things up before the investigators' visit, the Neill-Reynolds report
deeply dismayed the president. The facts were as bad as or worse
than the scenes in the novel. The findings read, in part: "Many inside
rooms where food is prepared are without windows, deprived of sunlight, and without direct communication with the outside air. . . .
Usually the workers toil without relief in the humid atmosphere
heavy with the odors of rotten wood, decayed meats, stinking offal
and entrails. The tables on which meat was handled, the tubs, and
other receptacles were generally of wood, most of which were water-
soaked and only half cleaned. The privies, as a rule, were sections of
workrooms, enclosed by thin wooden partitions, ventilating into the

workrooms. In a word, we saw meat shoveled from filthy wooden floors, piled on tables rarely washed, pushed from room to room in rotten box carts, in all of which processes it was in the way of gathering dirt, splinters, floor filth and expectoration of tuberculous and other diseased workers."

One dead hog had fallen out of a box cart and into a privy. Workers had simply dragged it out and sent it down the line with the other carcasses. "When comment was made to floor superintendents about these matters, it was always the reply that this meat would afterward be cooked, and this sterilization would prevent any danger from its use." But this, Neill and Reynolds noted, wasn't entirely true. A considerable amount of the meat went into sausages, uncooked and unsterilized. The leavings from the sausages were piled into a heap that also included floor sweepings of desiccated meat scraps, rope strands, and "other rubbish. Dismayed inquiry evoked a frank admission this garbage heap was to be ground up and used in making potted ham."

The factual report was, the president recognized, potentially even more explosive than *The Jungle*. The latter bore the label "fiction," after all, and had been penned by a self-avowed socialist. It could be dismissed. What Neill and Reynolds had found out could not. Roosevelt decided not to publish their report, holding it back as political leverage. But he showed some of the findings to a few trusted members of Congress, among them the reliable Albert Beveridge, asking him to draft an amendment to the Agricultural Appropriations Bill, which would impose new and more stringent federal inspections of meat on the industry. The Beveridge amendment passed the Senate on May 25 without a dissenting vote.

The appropriations bill then went to the House, where the meatpackers indeed had exceptionally good friends. The House Committee on Agriculture, chaired by a wealthy New York farmer and cattle dealer, James Wadsworth, held the necessary hearing on the Beveridge amendment. But Wadsworth filled the witness list with executives from the packinghouses and their friends. Most of the hearing was spent mocking both *The Jungle* and the Neill-Reynolds report. Congressman Charles Wharton, a Chicago Republican whose district included the yards, described the packinghouses as just as "clean and wholesome" as any home kitchen. The government inspectors, he continued, were simply not smart enough to understand how a reputable business operated.

"If a commission of men of average intelligence should investigate the meat producing businesses, they would find it conducted in a proper and sanitary manner," said Louis Swift, who had inherited Swift & Company from his father, Gustav. In turn, Neill replied that he was intelligent enough to avoid all products from the Chicago packinghouses. From the moment he had returned from the yards, he had insisted that no meat be served at his house unless it was fresh beef and mutton from local farms.

Upton Sinclair telegraphed the House committee members, asking permission to testify. They turned him down. In short order, the members voted to reject the Beveridge amendment. Wadsworth offered in its place an amendment that reduced inspections and penalties for the packing businesses and changed the funding plan for the inspection program. Beveridge's amendment had required the packers to pay into a fund that would support inspections. Wadsworth removed that burden on industry and returned it to the taxpayers. In doing so, he deliberately created a much smaller budget for inspections. Whatever Sinclair's suspicions about him, Roosevelt did recognize that the industry needed to be reformed. The message he sent to Wadsworth read, "I am sorry to have to say that this strikes me as an amendment which, no matter how intentionally, is framed so as to minimize the chance of rooting out the evil in the packing business."

Wadsworth replied that he considered the changes to be correct and appropriate. "I regret that you, the President of the United States, should feel justified, by innuendo, at least, in impugning the sincerity and the competency of a committee of the House of Representatives." He added that he had no intention of making further changes to the amendment. They conducted these exchanges in private. Publicly the legislation simply appeared stalled as usual. But by now Sinclair had had enough of political discretion. He'd become friendly with Neill and Reynolds and he knew their report was both solid and a confirmation of his own work.

In late May, Sinclair decided to leak what he knew about the Neill-Reynolds report to the *New York Times*. He stuffed a briefcase with notes, affidavits, letters, and everything he had on paper and marched off to a meeting at the newspaper. The *Times* editors recognized journalistic gold and ran the story on the front page on Monday, May 28, loaded with quotes from the government inspectors and from the novelist. "In Armour's own establishment I saw with my own eyes the doctoring of hams that were so putrefied that I could not force myself to remain near them," read a quote from Sinclair. The story quoted Neill recounting that "the pillars of the buildings were caked with flesh" and that "in these packing houses, the meat is dragged about on the floor, spat upon and walked upon." The *Times* even hunted down General Nelson Miles, who had brought the embalmed-beef complaint after the Spanish-American War. Miles's anger over the military food supply had not abated. "The disclosures about packing-house products now being exploited is no news to me," Miles declared. "I knew it seven years ago. Had the matter been taken up then, thousands of lives would have been saved."

In early June, exasperated with newspapers and with Upton Sinclair, but mostly with the members of Congress who had put him in this impossible position, Roosevelt released an eight-page summary of the Neill-Reynolds report. Newspapers printed the summary verbatim. Consumers were appalled—as were the meatpackers. The president, Armour declared, was no friend to businessmen and seemed to hold a particular dislike of those based in the heartland. "Roosevelt has a strong, personal animus against the packers of Chicago and is doing everything in his power to discredit them." Roosevelt responded by letting the packers and their friends in Congress know that he was out of patience. He wanted meat-inspection legislation on his desk in short order. If not, he would release the full report.

Within a week after Roosevelt released the Neill-Reynolds summary, even the *Chicago Tribune* was signaling the packers' defeat. On June 10 the paper ran a special report from a London correspondent headlined EUROPE THINKS U.S. LACKING IN HONOR. The sentiment on the Continent, the writer said, was in favor of sending the Chicago meatpackers to jail. By the end of the month, the British had stopped importing canned meat from the United States and both Germany and France were refusing American meat products in any form. American politicians recognized that they had to move to prevent further damage to the country's reputation and economy.

The battle-weary food and drug bill's advocates now realized the advantage of the moment. Finally circumstances were aligned in their favor. Once Roosevelt made up his mind, he honored his commitments. Heyburn, McCumber, and Beveridge in the Senate pressed the president again on broader food and drug legislation, as did Hepburn and his allies in the House. A new explosion of letters came flying from the women's clubs. The AMA's telegram campaign took off. Wiley hurried to meet with legislators and offer new findings from the Poison Squad studies, along with other research findings providing evidence of the need for change.

"The momentum of the Meat Inspection amendment carried with it the Pure Food Bill, which its enemies thought had been safely chloroformed in committee," wrote the investigative journalist Mark Sullivan. "In the end, the exposures of the packers by Roosevelt's commission, of the wholesale liquor dealers by themselves, of the patent medicines by *The Ladies' Home Journal* and *Collier's*, of food adulteration and food dyeing by Doctor Wiley and State and city food officials—the aggregate of all that worked into the strengthening of Roosevelt's hand, and was invincible."

There were still those who thought that Roosevelt and his

legislative allies compromised too much, among them the proud muckraking journalist David Graham Phillips. He'd already noted in his "Treason of the Senate" series that the New York congressman James Wadsworth had not entirely backed down from his defense of the meat industry. He'd successfully deleted the requirement that meat companies fund the inspection program. Further, Wadsworth had limited federal financing to $3 million a year when the "lowest estimate of the cost of adequate inspection" was twice that. The packers had also persuaded Wadsworth to remove a requirement that the inspections be marked with a date. The idea of that date was "so that the beef trust could not relabel three-and-four-and-five-year-old cans and furbish and 'freshen' decaying meat and work it off as good, new meat." Phillips deplored the fact that that requirement too had been deleted and warned that the planned legislation was far more corporate than consumer friendly. But in the rush to success, he doubted that he was being heard.

On June 30, 1906, Roosevelt triumphantly signed both the Meat Inspection Act and the Food and Drug Act. He presented Beveridge with the pen he'd used to sign the meat act. He did not acknowledge Sinclair's contribution, having decided, he told his friends, that the man was a crackpot. The president did not acknowledge Wiley either, not in the ceremony and not by any other gesture. Stung by the deafening silence, Wiley, after a modest interval, asked Beveridge if he would mind inquiring with the White House about whether he might also receive some token of the victory. Roosevelt's secretary replied: "Senator Beveridge spoke to me about presenting the Doctor with the pen with which the president signed the pure food bill, but on looking up the matter I found it had already been promised to Senator Heyburn, as author of the bill." Otherwise, the secretary politely continued, "it would have been a pleasure to have sent it to Dr. Wiley, to whom too much credit cannot be given for his long fight for pure food and against shams."

Roosevelt had a different view. As he would put it some years later: "The Pure Food and Drug bill became a law purely because of the active stand I took in trying to get it through Congress." Wiley and his allies had tried for years and failed, he said, because "some of them, although honest men, were so fantastically impractical that they played right into the hands of their foes." Newspapers might frequently reference the 1906 Pure Food and Drug Act as "Dr. Wiley's Law," but Roosevelt would never do so. And he worried that the doctor's uncompromising approach would only hamper, rather than help, the cause of safe food in the United States.

PART II

Nine

THE POISON TRUST

1906–1907

———◦———

And you could not be certain, except for their shape,
That the eggs by a chicken were laid.

"How does a general feel who wins a great battle and brings a final end to hostility?" Wiley would wonder, looking back on the passage of the food and drug law. "I presume I felt that way on the last day of June 1906." Bottles of champagne and Kentucky bourbon whiskey, fresh fruit and unadulterated candy, real honey and fine cheese had arrived in baskets and boxes at the Bureau of Chemistry, along with blizzards of celebratory telegrams and congratulatory letters, bearing wishes such as this one: "I have long contemplated writing you to express my admiration and encouragement in your contest for pure food, which I now express."

But Wiley, awash in that triumphant fizz of success, would later allow that he'd been too optimistic in believing that winning the legislative battle would end the hostilities. He'd gotten his hopes up, despite notes of caution mixed among the initial bravos. "I suppose you are pleased and I cannot refrain from writing my entire satisfaction in regard to the matter," wrote Wiley's old friend James Shepard,

the South Dakota chemist who had publicized the preservative problem with his cautionary "daily meal plan." However, Shepard continued, "Perhaps it is not 'time to holler' yet for we may not be out of
the woods." Shepard's assessment was accurate. The law had barely
passed, Wiley later wrote, before manufacturers united to undo its
proposed regulations "and then the real fight began."

On July 24 Wilson formally assigned his chief chemist to work
with the three other departments—Treasury, Commerce, and
Labor—to draft "for approval of the respective secretaries the rules
and regulations necessary for the enforcement of the pure food act."
They had some six months to do so; the law would not take effect
until January 1907. The new law, as the government officials recognized, was big on ideas, minimal on specifics. The legislation, Wiley
acknowledged in a letter to his friends at the American Medical Association, "is not as good as we would like it." It would take real
work to render it effective. The best thing was that it had passed at
all and that it had not—"when we consider the determined and able
efforts which have been continually made by the opponents of this
legislation"—been rendered completely toothless. Wiley's hope at
this point, he continued, was to help strengthen it into a "more perfect structure in the future."

It did at least contain a definition of what constituted adulterated
food, packed into one long sentence, one that became increasingly
grim as it wound its way to the period. First, food would be considered adulterated if "anything" was mixed into it that reduced its
quality or strength. Second, if one ingredient was surreptitiously sub-
stituted for another, as when manufacturers labeled cottonseed oil as
high quality olive oil. Third, "if any valuable ingredient has been
wholly or partially removed," as when vanilla extract contained no
actual vanilla. Fourth, if the food was "mixed, colored, coated or
stained" so as to conceal damage or fakery. The last items on the list
were pure Harvey Wiley, the fifth declaring food adulterated if it
contained "any poisonous or injurious ingredient" that might put

health at risk, and the sixth barring acceptance of food that contained diseased animals, or consisted "in whole or part, of filthy, decomposed or putrid animals or vegetable substance."

But Wiley had wanted specific numbers, scientifically valid measurements to be part of the definition. As the bill was being drafted and revised, he had tried but failed to get such specific standards written into it. He knew enforcement would be hampered by vagueness. For instance, how was one to precisely measure what a reduction "in quality or strength" meant? As it now stood, the law lacked standards by which a material could be judged "injurious to health." It offered no definition of what constituted a poison; it qualified in no way why any part of an animal should be considered "unfit for food." It did not specify how ill or weak a steer or hog could become before it was officially judged "diseased."

Further, the new Agricultural Appropriation Act, which had also passed on June 30, hadn't authorized the Agriculture Department to set such standards. The original bill had done so, early drafts explicitly ordering the department to "establish standards of purity for food products and to determine what are regarded as adulterations therein." But the industry-backed National Food Manufacturers Association had successfully lobbied for removal of that language. Wiley had tried to have the authorization restored, but whiskey lobbyist Warwick Hough had successfully outflanked him.

When the bill was being drafted and revised, Wiley had warned legislators that a failure to set standards would make it easy for manufacturers to fight regulatory efforts by attacking them as arbitrary or political. "No set of authorities can equitably execute a food law without a set of standards of purity for their guide," he wrote to Congressman James R. Mann of Illinois. At the same time, Mann, a Republican, and other members of the House of Representatives were fielding intense pressure from business interests hostile to such standards. Journalist Phillips was right when he warned that the industry could weaken even the best-intentioned legislation. "For seventeen years the people had been trying to get a law that would check the operations of what is commonly known as 'the poison trust,'" Phillips wrote, using his favorite nickname for the American food manufacturing industry. He continued, "For seventeen years, the Senate had refused to permit the 'industry' to be molested." Phillips credited the passage of even minimal regulation mostly to the toxicity studies by Wiley's Chemistry Bureau and to the efforts of his energetic network of allies. He allowed some brief admiration for the pure-food exhibit at the St. Louis World's Fair, along with published articles, speeches, letters, telegraphs, and other determined advocacy. He judged that these combined had an even larger influence than Sinclair's famous book. "A campaign was coming on and the people were in an ugly mood." He credited Roosevelt for his political savvy in forcing consumer-protection measures and noted that Congress had been pushed into a corner where it had no alternative. The food and drug legislation, as proposed by Heyburn, had seemed a relatively honest attempt at regulation, Phillips added, modeled on successful laws already in place in Europe. But by the time Roosevelt had signed the bill, Phillips wrote, it had become perverted into what he now saw as a gift to the food processors and the chemical manufacturers.

Like Wiley, Phillips pointed out that the new law failed to set standards for "deleterious" ingredients, and, he complained, it didn't name a single toxic compound to be regulated. In his assessment, the final version also had been crafted to deliberately protect unscrupulous grocers and other food purveyors, notably including a clause declaring "No dealer shall be prosecuted" for selling adulterated products if the businessman could produce a written guarantee from a manufacturer, wholesaler, "or any other party residing in the United States" that the goods were pure. In other words, Phillips noted sarcastically, a note from the grocer's mother would serve to excuse him from selling fake or chemically risky products.

Further, he pointed out, the law was written so as to make the enforcement process nearly impossibly cumbersome. If a Bureau of Chemistry analysis found adulteration or misbranding, the secretary of agriculture was required to first notify the business in question. The business owner could then demand a hearing to defend the product. If the secretary sided with the manufacturer, the matter would be dropped. If the secretary sided with the bureau's findings, he was to "certify" the evidence as correct but still couldn't take direct enforcement action. Instead, he had to recommend legal prosecution to the appropriate district attorney, who could agree or not to take on the case.

Enforcement, if any was planned, would thus require a strong collaborative and cordial relationship between the Agriculture Department and the court system. And it would require an equally collaborative relationship between Wiley, as head of the Chemistry Bureau, and Wilson as head of the department. The two men had worked together with a fair degree of harmony in the past, but the need to function in a law-enforcement capacity would necessarily force them into a different and far more politically oriented partnership. "The new, the boasted pure food law adds nothing," Phillips wrote. "The pure food men did the shouting but the poison trust got the victory."

Despite that, Wiley found himself dealing almost daily with a corporate backlash that followed passage of the law. "Naturally when the battle array was formed, the first point of attack was on me," he wrote. Hough—who was by this time drawing a salary of $40,000 a year (almost $1 million today) as a liquor lobbyist—was among the first to attack. He had pelted Wilson with complaints about Wiley's interest in the whiskey question. "The word FOOD does not include drinks and beverage," Hough wrote to the secretary in late November. Therefore, the Agriculture Department had no standing to order—as Wiley had done—that liquor ingredients be put on labels. "The kind of actions taken by the Bureau of Chemistry," Hough continued, "would cause a renewal of trade disturbances, thanks to the kind of unwarranted statements of the Chief of the Bureau of Chemistry." In early December 1906, as implementation of the law loomed, Hough wrote again demanding the secretary's reassurance that his department would not permit Wiley to "discriminate against one class or grade of whiskey against another."

Wilson had been in office since shortly after McKinley's inauguration in 1897 and owed his continued employment in part to a diplomatic ability to distance himself from such quarrels. But Hough's hectoring tone pushed him to exasperation. He told the lobbyist that he had discussed the issue of labeling whiskey ingredients with the president, and that Roosevelt had promised that the White House would review the situation. In the meantime, Wilson advised that Hough stop criticizing the Bureau of Chemistry.

"Since you have objected to my writing about Dr. Wiley's efforts which only benefit the whiskey trust," Hough snapped back, he would temporarily halt his letter-writing campaign. In return, he expected the White House to support him, and he would send a message to the blenders and rectifiers, advising them that "no general onslaught is to be made by your department upon their business" when the law goes into effect in January. He had no doubt, he continued, that the secretary would comply with that very reasonable request. Wilson, still irritated, assured Wiley that he would continue to stand up to Hough, giving the chief chemist hope that he had the support to enforce the Food and Drug Act vigorously.

In a mid-December speech at the annual dinner of Chicago's Atlas Club, Wiley assured diners that the wide-reaching new law would change both food and country for the better. He added that the warnings he'd begun to lay out in his toxicity studies would help set enforcement standards that would continue to help protect the country's citizens: "This poison squad, gentlemen, is destined to play an important role in the future history of food regulation."

In 1907 the Bureau of Chemistry published the third of the hygienic table trial studies, this one focusing on the use of sulfurous acid in food processing. In a letter to Wilson, Wiley again credited his loyal staff members for doing the excellent work: F. C. Weber for overseeing the study, Willard Bigelow for doing the food and fecal analysis, B. J. Howard for the "microscopical examination of the blood and urine."

The letter also emphasized Wiley's intensifying belief that the bureau researchers—and the scientific community in general—were just beginning to understand the risks imposed by piling one preservative after another into the American food supply. "The relations of sulfurous acid to health are perhaps of greater importance than those of the preservatives already studied—namely boron compounds and the salicylic acids and its salts," he noted. He attributed this importance—and the need for well-thought-out regulation—to the fact that the compound was so widely used. Manufacturers were devoted to it, insisting that its use "approaches a necessity."

Sulfurous acid is related to the similarly named, better-known, and highly corrosive sulfuric acid. Chemically they differ by only a few oxygen atoms, but unlike sulfuric acid, sulfurous acid is relatively easy to handle. Manufacturers especially liked the fact that it could be converted into a solid form, such as sulfite of lime, by saturating lime (another name for calcium oxide) with sulfurous acid. This could be heated and its vapors used as a fumigant. In this form it was used to preserve a bright color in dried fruit while simultaneously preventing fermentation and fending off insects. Sulfurous acid was also used to treat syrup, molasses, smoked meats, and wine, as well as to disinfect wine-making equipment. Barrels used to age a vintage were typically given a good dose of acid fumes to sterilize the wood. Sulfur dioxide could also be directly bubbled into the fermenting liquid as a preservative and anti-oxidizer. Not surprisingly, the end result could be high levels of sulfites in wine. The Poison Squad study had thus focused on those compounds and on the chemists' suspicion that exposure could carry significant risks. To test that idea, the bureau used one of the better-known salts derived from sulfurous acid, sodium sulfite. This was, as in the earlier studies, placed into capsules of varying doses and dished up along with the daily meals.

To the surprise and dismay of the Agriculture Department scientists, only nine of the twelve squad members endured to the end of the sulfite study. At the highest dose (about four grams), two of the volunteers became so ill that the researchers halted the trial before anyone else was badly sickened. They were less sure about a third ailing squad member who was at the time suffering from a bad cold. But every single man had sickened to some degree after being dosed with sulfites, reporting loss of appetite, stomach pains, headaches, dizziness, and a shaky feeling of weakness.

Much more research was needed, but Wiley told the secretary that the government should move toward what he termed a "complete and somewhat speedy suppression" of manufacturing processes that put sulfites into food and drink. "It is evident that the prohibition of its use would necessitate a radical change in methods of manufacture," he wrote. But "assuming that in the manufacturing processes certain added bodies are used which are found on investigation to be injurious to health, the rational conclusions of such an investigation would be, not to excuse or overlook the presence of such bodies, but to institute investigations looking to their suppression." The compounds could never be wholly eliminated. Sulfites formed naturally in wine during the process of fermentation. But why add to those levels?

"The use of sulfurous acid and sulfites never adds anything to the flavor or quality of a food but renders it both less palatable and less healthful," Wiley wrote. "Every fact which has been brought out therefore in the investigation tends to accentuate the justness of the conclusion, namely, that the use of sulfurous acid in foods should be suppressed." A strong stand against these preservatives would, he predicted, encourage research into other, less toxic ways of preserving food and drink.

Wiley must have realized what a regulatory reach this was. To call for a ban of a widely used preservative, to anticipate industries quickly adapting newer, safer methods—these were beyond optimistic. But if he had momentarily forgotten the scale and intensity of the opposition to such ideas, he was soon to be reminded.

In January 1907, before Wiley and his colleagues had managed to put even basic enforcement guidelines into place, James A. Tawney, a congressman from Minnesota, moved to eliminate one of Wiley's favored aspects of the food and drug bill. The fifty-two-year-old Tawney—tall and stylish, sporting an imposing mustache—belonged to a faction of the Republican Party popularly known as the Stand-Patters. In contrast to reformers in general and the Roosevelt-led progressive Republicans, they resisted any move that reeked of change from what they saw as the more noble nineteenth-century approach to government. Tawney's move was to attach an amendment to the agricultural appropriations bill that blocked the use of any federal funds to support food safety work by scientists and officials working at the state level. It was potentially devastating. The Department of Agriculture depended heavily on cooperation with state officials; scientists like Edwin Ladd of North Dakota had shown how much of a difference collaboration could make. Opponents of the food and drug law had already capped its first-year enforcement funding at a mere $700,000, not even enough to cover a national food-inspection program. If the USDA lost its support from state regulators and researchers, there seemed little prospect of making the law work.

Once again Wiley contacted his allies in the pure-food movement; once again he asked them to help him fight back. Alice Lakey of the National Consumers League replied immediately, angrily describing Tawney's amendment as specifically designed to "impair the efficiency of the administration of the food and drugs act. . . . Our committee are doing all we can and please let us know if you have any instructions for us." *Club News*, the newsletter of the General

Federation of Women's Clubs, echoed her outrage. In a nationally circulated editorial, it pointed out that opponents of regulation had first campaigned against the law as a federal violation of states' rights, a claim that had helped array Southern Democrats against the food and drug bill. "The plot failed," the editorial continued. "It would now appear that the same thing is being attempted in a different way—that is, by practically prohibiting all plans for co-operation between the National and State Authorities."

Opposition to Tawney's amendment also came from a new source: the People's Lobby, an organization launched to fight government corruption. Its founders included two well-known muckraking journalists, Henry Beech Needham and Lincoln Steffens, along with crusading Kansas newspaper editor William Allen White; Kentucky food chemist Robert Allen, now secretary of the Interstate Pure Food Committee; James B. Reynolds, who had been part of the investigative team that Roosevelt sent to inspect the Chicago stockyards; and the widely admired and politically liberal novelist Mark Twain. "If anyone is naughty in Congress, he will have to reckon with a new force," Twain wrote in the *New York Times*. The People's Lobby, he said, should be considered an ally to good government, as it would "see, in a methodical manner, that Congress hides no secrets, no secret alliances." Like Steffens, Henry Needham had long been a supporter of Roosevelt's progressive policies, and he was optimistic that the president would favor the new organization. He and Roosevelt had a mostly friendly relationship, based on a shared interest in athletics. Needham was one of the nation's foremost baseball writers and an eloquent critic of excessive violence in football. He often wrote feelingly about his belief in fair play—in sports and in life. He had become so frustrated with American politics that he'd also helped organize the People's Lobby to take on government reform directly. The Tawney amendment became its first target.

Like Hough's presumptuous arrogance, the Tawney amendment

irked Secretary Wilson into abandoning his usual cautious approach
to political issues. He too came out publicly against the measure. The
combined opposition's strength, to the relief of many, caused Tawney's amendment to fail in committee. Wilson's public stance gave
the impression that he was willing to back Wiley as strongly as ever,
but those around them saw signs of strain between the two. Robert
Allen wrote to Needham that the secretary was shutting his chief
chemist out of key decisions regarding food regulation: "Secretary
Wilson absolutely ignores Dr. Wiley."

Wiley and Wilson had, at least, earlier reached an agreement on a
plan to expand their roster of food and drink inspectors; twenty-eight
new men would be on board by year's end. Six new branch laboratories were being opened to handle regional demand for product analysis; the department had plans to add at least another ten facilities the
following year. And Allen himself had successfully recommended a
young lawyer from Kentucky, Walter G. Campbell, to head the Food
Inspection Division: Working with public health officials in Louisville, Campbell had helped shut down numerous swill dairies there.
Allen wrote to Wiley, "I unqualifiedly recommend him as one of the
men that you will make no mistake in appointing and putting close to
you." Campbell proved his worth rapidly, meticulously organizing
the agency's inspection program and working tirelessly to improve
the law and its enforcement. He would eventually direct the regulatory agency that, years later, would inherit the enforcement role of the
Bureau of Chemistry, an agency that in 1930 would become the U.S.
Food and Drug Administration.

Still, Allen's misgivings about Wilson grew. As he also wrote to
Needham, "in thinking over Secretary Wilson's attitude toward the
pure food work, there is nothing to show that he has ever been in
sympathy with it." He recalled that during the embalmed-beef hearings, Wilson had been "unenthusiastic," leaving Wiley to be the public face of the issue. The secretary had even, during the hearings, told

Allen privately that he found Roosevelt's dramatic testimony "a pain in the side." Allen had an uneasy feeling that the People's Lobby would need to come to Wiley's aid "more than once in this fight."

The ever-festering conflict over whiskey was key among matters driving a wedge between Wiley and Wilson. Under the new law, the chief chemist had successfully pushed through one government seizure of rectified whiskey after another. The seizures included two barrels of Choice Old Monongahela Whiskey, which did not "contain enough whiskey to give it character"; fifteen barrels of Clark's Old Blend Rye Whiskey, which contained no rye; four and a half barrels of Old Kimroe Rye Whiskey Blend, which also lacked rye, and a barrel of Old Harmony Whiskey, which was simply a batch of dyed ethanol. In a single week the department had moved to seize more than fifty barrels of so-called whiskey with an eye toward prosecution.

And barely a month after the law went into effect, in February 1907, Wiley had reinforced Hough's fears about his Kentucky bourbon bias when the chief chemist gave some undeniably pro–straight whiskey testimony before the House Committee on Agriculture. House Speaker Joseph Cannon, the fiercely pro-business Republican from Illinois, seeking to protect the numerous bottling businesses in his home district, now wanted blended whiskeys exempted from labeling under the law. When asked before the committee to define "blended whiskey," Wiley gave in to exasperation and replied, "Crooked is the term you mean. If one is straight, the other is crooked. Crooked whisky is not whisky at all but is made of neutral spirits and flavored and colored. It is an imitation."

Politically his outburst did not serve him well. Hough fired off another angry broadside to Wilson. The secretary agreed that such statements could not be described as unbiased scientific commentary. The confrontation added to a sense by Wilson—and, perhaps more important at this point, by the Agriculture Department's powerful solicitor, George P. McCabe—that Wiley's long advocacy for regulation had turned him into more of a crusader than an unbiased researcher.

The argument between Wiley and Cannon had focused on one detail of the new law, a paragraph on misbranding. That section stated that all products that were compounds, imitations, or blends must be accurately labeled. A product could be called a blend only if it was a "mixture of like substances" under the law. This, by Wiley's reading, meant that blended whiskey must be a mixture of genuine whiskeys. If it was one of the rectified versions—whiskey mixed with neutral spirits, water and dye, or just dyed neutral spirits and water—then it should be labeled "imitation whiskey."

The rectifiers had developed a line of additives to mimic the taste of straight whiskey and even its tendency to bead or cling to a glass. These special flavorings and enhancers included bourbon extract, rye oil, rye extract, rye essence, Pittsburg rye essence, Monongahela essence, malt essence, Irish and Scotch essence, essence of gin (made from juniper berries), corn flavoring, aging oil, and bead oil. Hough argued that these coloring and flavoring agents were only trace additives and that all blended whiskeys—his organization was trying to do away with the term "rectified"—could be considered simply a mix of different types of alcohol. In a letter to Wilson he suggested that "everything mixed could be called a blend," rather than using the off-putting word "imitation." The idea—practical and business friendly—appealed to USDA solicitor McCabe. He wrote a recommendation that all alcohols be considered "like substances" in the future.

Wiley pushed back. He didn't buy the idea that synthetic ethanol, dyed with burned sugar and flavored with bourbon extract, was equivalent to aged bourbon. It was cheating the consumer to pretend so. Wilson this time took McCabe's part, rebuffing Wiley. The chief chemist refused to accept their decision and decided that the point was worth appealing over their heads. Requesting and receiving an appointment with President Roosevelt in late March, he took with him to the White House a miniature still and a briefcase loaded with samples of whiskey extracts and additives. For a "very fruitful hour," as Wiley described it, he explained and demonstrated to Roosevelt the differences between types of beverages labeled "whiskey." In a March 30 letter to Robert Allen, he described the president as agreeable to trying the different samples and overall "extremely courteous" and attentive. "At the end, he thanked me most cordially and said I had thrown new light upon the problem. . . . So I think, at least, I did not do any harm."

But in terms of in-house politics, he had also stirred up some trouble. Roosevelt called Wilson in for further discussion. He found the issue "very puzzling," he told the agriculture secretary, and he wasn't satisfied with the department's stand. Wilson, not pleased to find himself in this position, stood by McCabe and did his best to dismiss Wiley's arguments. He urged the president to adopt the single word "blended" for all the mixed whiskeys and alcohols, and Roosevelt agreed to consider it.

The president, though, had been impressed by Wiley's demonstrations and the science behind them. And he was suspicious that, as Henry Needham had recently warned him, the "imitation whisky alliance," having failed to prevent or further weaken the food and drug law, was now focusing its interests on "bulldozing" the Department of Agriculture. Needham pointed out to Roosevelt that if so early in the enforcement process a concession was made to one industry, it would set a precedent that others would easily pursue.

Judging that the department had grown too political within itself—on both sides of the argument—Roosevelt asked his attorney general, Charles J. Bonaparte, to review the evidence from all sides and to issue a formal ruling. Roosevelt considered the fifty-seven-year-old Bonaparte—a grandson of Jérôme Bonaparte, youngest brother of Napoleon I of France—to be thorough, tough, and unafraid of contentious issues.

After reviewing stacks of whiskey-related documents, including a voluminous report from the Bureau of Chemistry, Bonaparte found that he agreed with Wiley that not all whiskeys were created equal. Further, American consumers deserved detailed and accurate labels to help guide their purchases of such products. On April 10, 1907, Roosevelt notified Wilson that Bonaparte had so decided and that he, as president, accepted the ruling. He appended to that notice some instructions: "Straight whiskey will be labeled as such." The definition of a "blended whiskey" would be limited: Only "[a] mixture of two or more straight whiskies will be labeled as blended." If the blend was whiskey mixed with industrially produced ethyl alcohol, then things got more complicated: "Provided that there is a sufficient amount of straight whiskey to make it genuinely a 'mixture,' then the label would call it a 'compound whiskey.'" If there was no straight whiskey in the bottle, if it was simply colored and flavored neutral spirits, then it was a fake version of straight whiskey and needed to be so identified. In other words, "Imitation whisky will be labeled as such. Sincerely yours, Theodore Roosevelt."

Many in the pure-food movement saw the whiskey decision as a test of the government's willingness to address the labeling issue even when powerful business interests opposed it. It was to that end that Wiley had put himself—and his relationship with the secretary—on the line. His friends dared hope that the decision, carrying the clout of Roosevelt's approval, would restore the chief chemist's standing with his boss. "I write to congratulate you on your victory," wrote John Hurty, Indiana's public health officer, to his old friend about the whiskey ruling. "Your ideas in regard to 'blends' are exactly right and thus you see more than the President supporting you." The director of Kentucky's agricultural experiment station wrote, "Let me congratulate you for the victory won. Stick to it."

Wilson, however, saw the decision—especially the way it came about—as proof that his chief chemist could not be trusted. Making his own visit to the White House, he asked Roosevelt for permission to appoint another, more objective scientific expert to provide guidance on the pure-food law. He needed someone "level headed," he said, someone less eager for public attention, a scientist who could be "implicitly trusted in a confidential capacity." Roosevelt had sided with Wiley in the instance, but he valued his agriculture secretary and he was politically astute enough to recognize that the chief chemist had become difficult for Wilson to manage.

As if to underscore this difficulty, another labeling question had arisen. Wiley wanted the government to require the fully detailed listing of all ingredients in food and drink on labels, even those ingredients considered benign. He argued, for example, that sugar should be included on lists of ingredients. Wilson hated the idea. He wrote demanding that his chief chemist back down on the requirement: "It seems to me to be monstrous that we should require mention of salt or sugar or any of these things when we know them to be harmless. If we require mention of one of them we might as well require mention of all." Wiley countered that consumers deserved an all-inclusive listing of what was in their food and drink—he urged the secretary to side with them over industry.

But Wilson instead told the president that the law would place too many unnecessary burdens on manufacturers, and that they would resist it at every turn, stifling progress on the law. Roosevelt decided to give Wilson some additional departmental support and privately agreed to bring another chemist into the Department of Agriculture.

Seeking a scientist with the political savvy that he considered essential for the new job, Roosevelt personally chose Frederick L. Dunlap, a young assistant professor of chemistry from the University of Michigan, recommended by Roosevelt's friend James Burrill Angell, the university's president. Angell said that Dunlap could hold his own in Washington. He put forward a poised and polished presence—well groomed and impeccably dressed, with perfect manners that served his political ambitions. And most important for his new job, Dunlap knew how to keep a secret. Barely two weeks after the whiskey confrontation, on April 24, 1907, Wilson formally appointed Dunlap as "associate chemist," skipping over the normal requirement of a civil service examination. As a demonstration of his own authority, the secretary neither consulted nor warned Wiley in advance.

As Wiley would later tell it, Wilson simply "walked into my office one morning in company with a young man whom I had never before seen, and introduced him as 'Professor F.L. Dunlap, your associate.' I said: 'Mr. Secretary, my what?' He said: 'Your associate. I have appointed an associate in the Bureau of Chemistry who will be entirely independent of the Chief [Wiley] and who will report directly to me. During the absence of the Chief he will be acting chief of the Bureau.' I was astounded and dumbfounded at this action."

After the secretary ordered him to make Dunlap welcome, Wiley gave the newcomer an unsmiling tour of the bureau offices, offering him the smallest and shabbiest quarters available. The bureau staff, intensely loyal to their longtime chief, barely spoke to their new colleague. Even the secretaries were unfriendly. Dunlap, perceiving that he was in hostile territory, decided to rely on McCabe's clerical staff instead. The new associate chemist recognized quickly that McCabe and Wilson would be his friends in the department. They had the real power anyway, so they were more worth cultivating.

Dunlap had no experience as a food chemist. Wiley took the appointment as a "direct insult" to him and to Bigelow, who had always served as acting director in his absence; he fumed that it was poor management to put a man "who knew nothing" of the bureau or its food-law activities in charge of the program. Making matters worse, Wilson at the same time announced the creation of a new entity, the Board of Food and Drug Inspection, within the USDA. There would be three members: Wiley, Dunlap, and George McCabe, the department's solicitor. Wiley would technically be the board's chief, but all decisions were to be made by a simple majority vote. The board would report directly to the secretary and, as Wilson wrote to Wiley, he expected the board to complete its work expeditiously, as "a matter of fairness to the manufacturers of foods and drugs."

To Wiley the new board clearly appeared designed "to take away from the bureau all its power and activities under the food law." Wilson made no effort to disabuse him of that idea.

O n June 19, on Wilson's orders, Wiley embarked on a trip to Bordeaux, France, to join a panel of food judges at the International Maritime Exposition, a world's fair designed to celebrate the range of products carried around the world's oceans by the shipping industry. The U.S. government—which had proudly built a model of the White House to house its exhibits—planned to be well represented. But the State Department also saw in this exposition an opportunity for practical diplomacy. French food and wine exporters were eager to consult with the influential chief chemist on the new U.S. regulations and perhaps even get his help in modifying their own.

Wilson's initial response to France's invitation had reflected his growing dissatisfaction with Wiley. He tabled the request and didn't tell Wiley about it. But several weeks later, Wiley attended a party that also included the French ambassador to the United States, who said to him, "I do not think you are very polite in your country." The ambassador had been waiting three weeks for a response to the consul's invitation. When he heard that Wiley had never received it, the ambassador called the State Department—which insisted Wilson had been sent the invitation immediately—and then called Wilson directly. "In a short time, I received a summons to the Secretary's office and he gave me the invitation and said of course it must be accepted." At this moment, though, Wiley himself hesitated. He wasn't comfortable, he explained, leaving Dunlap as acting head of the Bureau of Chemistry in his absence. In the face of a flat refusal, the

Harvey Washington Wiley, age nineteen, when he was a freshman at Indiana's Hanover College in 1863.

Wiley (*third from right*) with his crew of chemists at the Department of Agriculture in 1883.

Look Before You Eat," from the cover of Britain's satiric *Puck* magazine, mocking the state of the food supply, in 1884.

Notes about poisonous candy from an investigator working for Wiley in 1890.

A state-of-the-art laboratory at the Bureau of Chemistry in the early twentieth century.

Jeremiah Rusk, secretary of agriculture from 1889 to 1893, affectionately nicknamed "Uncle Jerry" by his staff.

Julius Sterling Morton, secretary of agriculture from 1893 to 1897, was a ruthless cost-cutter.

James Wilson, secretary of agriculture from 1897 to 1913, started as a Wiley supporter and ended up as an enemy.

Ira Remsen, codiscoverer of saccharin, was tapped to head an industry-friendly board of scientists for the USDA.

William McKinley, twenty-fifth president of the United States, was assassinated in 1901, near the start of his second term.

Grenville Dodge, a former Union Army general, was named by McKinley to lead an investigation of shoddy meat given to soldiers in the Spanish-American War.

Theodore Roosevelt became the twenty-sixth president of the United States following McKinley's assassination.

President Roosevelt, shown here with his cabinet, signed the country's first food safety legislation in 1906.

Volunteers of the Poison Squad experiments in Wiley's dining room testing the safety of food additives.

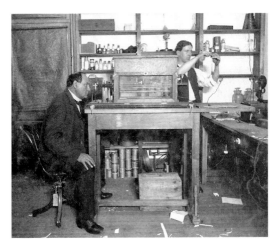

Wiley and one of his chemists in a publicity shot taken during the Poison Squad experiments.

Cover of *The Jungle*, Upton Sinclair's 1906 novel, which exposed the horrors of U.S. meat production.

Novelist Upton Sinclair in 1906.

British postcards satirizing meat produced by the Chicago meatpackers circulated after *The Jungle*'s publication.

The muckraking journalist Ray Stannard Baker, famed for his investigation of the railroad industry, advised Sinclair on his book.

Walter Hines Page, of the publishing firm Doubleday, Page & Company, authorized and supported publication of *The Jungle*.

J. Ogden Armour, president of Armour & Company in Chicago, tried to stop European publication of *The Jungle*.

Journalist David Graham Phillips infuriated President Roosevelt with his searing expose of corruption in the U.S. Senate.

The Heinz Company ran numerous ads promoting the purity of its products in the early twentieth century.

The American meat industry became a favorite target of *Puck* magazine as scandals emerged.

The American magazine *Collier's* took aim at congressional resistance to food safety legislation.

The Beef Trust," which became the nickname for the Chicago meatpackers, satirized in a 1906 *Puck* cover.

The 1906 Food and Drug law made "pure food" labels such as this one extremely popular.

During a lengthy battle to legally define "real" whiskey, distillers made a point of emphasizing the purity of their product.

Cartoon paying homage to Wiley's leadership in the fight for food safety legislation, despite bitter opposition.

One of the U.S. Department of Agriculture's newly authorized food inspection teams, Indiana, 1909.

William Howard Taft (*left*), twenty-seventh president of the United States, meeting with Elihu Root, secretary of state under Theodore Roosevelt.

NEW WINE IN OLD BOTTLES
Cartoon by Darling in the *Des Moines Register and Leader*, reproduced in the *Literary Digest*, December 25, 1909.

A 1909 cartoon in the *Des Moines Register* commenting on President Taft's turn from Roosevelt progressives to congressional leaders who were closely allied with industry.

The *Washington Star's* famed political cartoonist, Clifford Berryman, delighted Wiley with this drawing, mourning his retirement suggesting that his shoes would be impossible to fill.

Photo taken during a U.S. Department of Agriculture inspection of an early twentieth-century candy factory, emphasizing the need for regulation.

Anna Kelton Wiley, in 1920, with sons Harvey (*right*) and John (*left*).

The masthead for Wiley's regular 1920s column about food and nutrition.

A 1956 U.S. postage stamp honoring the fiftieth anniversary of the Pure Food and Drug Act and featuring a portrait of Harvey Washington Wiley.

Portrait of Harvey Washington Wiley in *World's Work* just before he left his government job.

secretary agreed to name Bigelow as acting head for the duration of the trip—at least this time.

In addition to attending the exposition, Wiley did work diligently with the French government on updating its food laws. For his help—and for his dedication to the issue—he was elected a *chevalier* (knight) of the nation's Légion d'honneur. (As an officer of the American government, he was not allowed to take home the medal until after his retirement.)

During the visit, though, Wiley remained uneasy about his status at home. Before leaving Washington, he had given Bigelow very specific instructions to protect the bureau and the law. He asked that Bigelow keep him updated, especially if things started going wrong, which didn't take long. First Dunlap told Bigelow to hand over all correspondence relating to enforcement of the food and drug law. Bigelow replied angrily that the Chemistry Bureau by law had full authority to analyze food and drink and the authority to freely relay those results. Wilson agreed to put the matter on hold until Wiley returned, but Bigelow wrote to the chief chemist that the secretary appeared prepared to support Dunlap's power play. He warned his boss that the two men were meeting in confidence on food-law regulations and he doubted that boded well for the Chemistry Bureau.

It was while Wiley was away that the Agriculture Department issued a major package of rules on food safety. Known as Food Inspection Decision (FID) 76—and announced as a unanimous decision of Wiley, McCabe, and Dunlap—the rules were intended to provide overall guidance on chemical additives in foods. FID 76 reaffirmed that "no drug, chemical or harmful or deleterious dye or preservative" could be used in food. It stated that common salt, sugar, wood smoke, potable distilled liquors, vinegar, and condiments were considered reasonable additives. It barred dyes that were used to conceal damaged, inferior, or faked goods. Wiley had mostly supported those provisions. FID 76 also let it be known that the government would move slowly on additives still under study. Specifically, no prosecutions would be brought against two controversial additives— the greening agent copper sulfate and the preservative sodium benzoate—pending scientific investigation. Wiley had also somewhat reluctantly accepted these delays, but he had recommended a precautionary limit on copper sulfate. This was used mostly cosmetically to deepen the green of canned peas and beans but had a long history of known human health effects. When he'd left for Bordeaux, the ruling had included the precaution: a temporary safe limit for copper sulfate of 11 milligrams per 100 grams of the vegetable contents, an amount equivalent to about 110 parts per million. He considered this a compromise number, suspecting that further research would lead to a lower limit. And Wilson had agreed that it was a reasonable approach.

But in his absence, food manufacturers had put new pressure on the Agriculture Department, arguing the limit was just Wiley's backhanded way of forcing them to take copper out of their products. In response, Dunlap and McCabe had changed the decision's wording without notifying Wiley. The guidelines now merely banned an undefined "excessive" amount. Wiley wired a blistering memo to Dunlap, saying that FID 76 could no longer be considered a unanimous decision from the board. His signature should have been removed from the document if the board was going to make changes that he had not approved. Still steaming when he arrived back in Washington, he discovered his colleagues had quietly made other accommodations to satisfy business complaints.

The original FID 76 had also set a safety limit on sulfites. The department had agreed that Wiley's Poison Squad experiment raised troubling questions about those compounds but also believed that more research was needed. Pending further study, the board had agreed that the government would not act against manufacturers using sulfurous acid or sulfur dioxide in dried fruit, sugar, syrup, molasses, and wine if the produce did not exceed 35 milligrams per gram (about 350 parts per million) and provided the presence of sulfites was cited on the label. But that fairly modest proposal—including the idea of sharing sulfite information with the public—produced an exceptionally bitter outcry from wine and fruit producers in California.

"Telegrams began to come all around me, and it finally reached me that something was seriously the matter," Wilson said. He'd learned that the White House was reporting a similar deluge of complaints. The secretary met with fruit and wine industry representatives, a session that he would later describe as filled with "a very great commotion." The assembled group, as they reminded Wilson, represented a $15 million–a–year (nearly $400 million today) industry that might be damaged by the department's decision. Aside from the labeling requirement, which might scare off consumers, the California coalition said that limiting sulfur use posed potentially devastating problems. East Coast buyers were threatening to cancel contracts for fear that the goods would spoil without the preservative.

"After listening to these good people all day I said, 'I see the condition you are in, gentlemen. I do not think the American Congress in making this law intended to stop your business,'" Wilson related in a speech later that year. He assured them that the Agriculture Department did not want to harm American businessmen in the process of protecting food safety. He went on to reassure the concerned Californians: "I will tell you what to do. Just go on as you used to go on and I will not take any action to seize your goods or let them be seized or take any order into court until we know more about the milligrams to the kilo and all that."

Wiley again protested an action taken while he was away, without his consent, one that yet bore his signature. He reminded Wilson of his own findings and recommendations regarding sulfites. It was better, he insisted, to be overprotective of consumers in the absence of good information. Again he was overruled. The department, Wilson reminded him, had a duty to balance multiple interests, and consumer protection was only one of them. It was "not only that the provisions of the law should be fully executed, but also that there should be no unnecessary burden or annoyance placed on the trade."

Not surprisingly, then, Wilson was unhappy to learn, after the fact, of a speech that Wiley had given to the congregation of the Vermont Avenue Christian Church in Washington, DC, earlier that year. In short order, the chief chemist had managed to offend the flour industry, busy mixing wheat and rye flour and "selling the mixture as rye flour" with no mention of other ingredients. Also the syrup industry: "And when you put sirup on your buckwheat cakes, are you eating maple sirup? There is a nice picture of maple trees on the can and the word 'maple' is very prominent but that is all the maple there is about it." Then the dairy industry, with this appetizing description of ice cream: "I don't want it half gelatin, made of old hides and scrapings of beef, hides that are put down in South America, shipped to Europe and this country and so vile that they have to disinfect them before they will let them into the custom house." The secretary now informed the chief of the Bureau of Chemistry that the Agriculture Department was, in fact, dedicated to the support of agribusiness. From now on, he expected Wiley to do a better job of remembering that.

Ten

OF KETCHUP AND CORN SYRUP

1907–1908

―――――○―――――

And the salad which bears such an innocent look
And whispers of fields that are green

Ketchup (or catsup) was the most everyday of condiments. But its origin story was one of ancient mystery. A sauce made of fermented fish, it derived from China, where it was named *kentia*, according to one version. It was invented in Vietnam, according to another. British sailors first discovered it in Fiji during the 1500s, or possibly in the West Indies. A Chinese recipe, supposedly dating to 544 CE, instructed the sauce maker to "take the intestine, stomach, and bladder of the yellow fish, shark and mullet," wash them well, mix them with salt, seal into a jar, and let "sit in the sun" for up to one hundred days.

The version that made its way to English kitchens was a little tamer than that; the cookbooks of the late seventeenth century suggested methods to produce a golden, anchovy-based "paste of ketchup." During the next hundred years, "ketchup" became shorthand for an array of sauces made with mushrooms or oysters or even walnuts, the latter reportedly a favorite of British novelist Jane Austen. And by the early nineteenth century, James Mease, a Philadelphia physician and amateur horticulturalist, joined those proposing that "love apples"—the popular name for tomatoes at the time—also made "a fine catsup."

"Love apple" ketchup caught on slowly, partly due to an enduring belief that tomatoes could be poisonous. People had noted the painful deaths of tomato-loving aristocrats in Europe. Later investigations would suggest a cause for those fatalities: Acidic juices from tomatoes had caused toxic levels of lead to leach from pewter salad plates. It would take some decades of scientific research—and many healthy years of consumption—before people became fully comfortable with raw tomatoes.

Cooked products like ketchup were believed to be safer, and the earliest commercially bottled version was distributed in the United States in 1837. Such formulations posed challenges to the busy processor. The growing season was summer short, and it was difficult to preserve tomato pulp in containers for any length of time. Too often it provided a rich environment in which bacteria, spores, yeast, and mold thrived. In 1866 the French cookbook author Pierre Blot advised readers to stick to homemade ketchup. The varieties sold in the markets, he wrote, were "filthy, decomposed, and putrid."

Not that bottled ketchups were pure tomato—or pure anything. Food advocates complained that such sauces were too often made from assorted trimmings dumped into barrels after tomatoes were canned, then thickened with ground pumpkin rinds, apple pomace (the skin, pulp, seeds, and stems left after the fruit was pressed for juice), or cornstarch and dyed a deceptively fresh-looking red. Made in less-than-sterile conditions, they required a heavy dose of preservatives to keep microbes at bay. The protective compound of choice was sodium benzoate—in high enough doses to catch Wiley's attention. He added the compound to his list of proposed Poison Squad studies.

Sodium benzoate is a salt of a naturally occurring compound, benzoic acid, found in a wide variety of plants ranging from tobacco to cranberries. Its name refers to the benzoin tree, a plant native to Southeast Asia. Benzoin resin, scraped from tree bark, had been used for centuries in the making of both perfume and incense. And the isolation of benzoic acid was nearly as old; the compound was noted in the records of the French apothecary Nostradamus in 1556. But it had come into wide commercial use in the nineteenth century, following two scientific developments. In 1860 German chemists learned they could make a cheap, synthetic version of benzoic acid from the coal tar–derived solvent toluene. If the acid was neutralized with soda, this caused a salt to precipitate out of the mix. This was sodium benzoate. Some fifteen years later, researchers discovered that sodium benzoate had strong antifungal properties. It was tasteless, easy to make, and inexpensive. Not surprisingly, it became a favorite of the food-processing industry.

Recognizing its natural origins, Wiley's best assumption before he tested the preservative on his Poison Squad diners was that sodium benzoate wasn't especially dangerous. He worried more that the preservative was being used to disguise shoddy food production. Ketchup was a case in point. As noted in the bureau reports, his chemists had found that a sauce made with fresh tomatoes, heat-treated to kill microbes and placed into sterile containers, held up very well without chemical preservatives. It also tasted better.

Most food producers dismissed this recommendation, but there were exceptions. Indiana's Columbia Conserve Company proudly made a tomato ketchup that neither required nor contained any dyes or preservatives. It did so by adapting "housewife methods" to large-scale production, its president said. And Wiley's idea had caught the attention of one of the country's biggest food manufacturers, Henry J. Heinz, founder and president of the H.J. Heinz Company of Pittsburgh.

Heinz was the same age as Wiley—born in the same year and

month—and he had advocated in favor of clean and honest food-stuffs for even longer than the chief chemist had. Heinz had also built a remarkably successful company, one that processed and marketed scores of products. Although he had personally chosen a slogan to advertise "57 Varieties," by the early twentieth century, his canning and bottling plants produced nearly twice that number of foods and condiments. Unlike many of his peers in the food business, Heinz had lobbied in favor of the Pure Food and Drug Act of 1906. Company executive Sebastian Mueller had accompanied such activists as Robert Allen and Alice Lakey when they visited the White House to press the Roosevelt administration, and after its passage, Henry Heinz supported the law's enforcement. Some of his peers called him a traitor. More irked than worried by such remarks, he ordered his company's publicity department to disparage his critics in press releases.

Heinz, like other processors, had frequently used preservatives, following the industry standard. His original recipe for catsup (the spelling on the bottle) was based on his mother's, including a little finely ground willow bark, which added salicylic acid to the mix. The company had later shifted over to sodium benzoate. But Heinz had found himself impressed by the warnings raised in Wiley's Poison Squad studies and had decided to invest in developing an alternative approach. Mueller, in charge of food safety at the company, had at first balked, worrying that the move could prove too expensive. The H.J. Heinz Company had always offered a money-back guarantee, and Mueller feared a preservative-free ketchup would lead to costly returns due to spoilage.

But at his boss's insistence, Mueller ordered the creation of test batches made from recipes like those of homemade versions that were known to have longer shelf lives. His cooks searched for a correct acid balance in the formula, measuring out the right vinegar content to augment the acids that occur naturally in tomatoes. Discovering that he needed both high-quality tomatoes and high pulp content, Mueller developed a sauce that was thicker than the company's previous product, thicker than any on the market.

By 1906 Heinz was selling its new—and, yes, more expensive—ketchup (now spelled that way on the label). The company then launched an aggressive marketing campaign aimed at convincing consumers that it was worth spending a few cents more on a better and healthier condiment. The campaign, like so many run by Heinz, was so successful that in time Americans began to think of all good ketchup as thick and rich—eventually changing production standards industry-wide.

When the food and drug law went into effect, Heinz also proclaimed in newspaper and magazine advertisements that its preservative-free products were "recognized as the standard by Government pure food authorities." Heinz ketchup, as the ads also proclaimed, was not only free of sodium benzoate but was also the preferred choice of the famed Dr. Wiley himself.

Predictably, food processors still using sodium benzoate complained to both Wilson and Roosevelt that the chief chemist had become a shill for H.J. Heinz. Wiley planned to vindicate himself with the publication of his Poison Squad report on sodium benzoate, laying out the evidence that the preservative was clearly suspect in health problems. As 1908 approached, polishing up that report became a top priority, along with other potentially controversial investigations such as a study of the popular artificial sweetener saccharin.

Due to its low cost, saccharin was increasingly used as a sugar substitute in processed foods ranging from canned corn to ketchup itself—although that inclusion rarely appeared on labels. Leaders in the food-processing industry—aside from Heinz and a few others—braced for more bad publicity. The Poison Squad studies had yet to say anything good about food additives. Makers decided to try intervening before the sodium benzoate report was published, hoping to reach an agreement that would prevent its publication.

The National Food Manufacturers Association contacted Roosevelt, Wilson, and every legislator thought to be sympathetic, raising concerns about both the upcoming reports and Harvey Wiley. The chief chemist, the organization complained, was stuck in the old-fashioned past of preindustrial food production and biased against twentieth-century innovation. The association urged the president and the agriculture secretary to create a scientific review board, one that might be more balanced and more favorable toward modern food-production methods.

In January 1908 Roosevelt invited some of the most outspoken among the group's processors and grocers to visit the White House. They included representatives from Curtice Brothers of Rochester, New York, and Williams Brothers of Detroit, both in competition with H.J. Heinz. Also in attendance was Republican congressman James S. Sherman of New York, who was himself president of a New England canning company. Sherman's firm routinely, and surreptitiously, used saccharin instead of more expensive cane sugar to sweeten its canned corn. The Heinz company was not on the invitation list. Intrigued by the conversation, Roosevelt asked his guests to stay over and requested that Wilson, Wiley, McCabe, and Dunlap join them the next morning for a follow-up discussion.

They met in the Cabinet Room of Roosevelt's new office building on the west side of the White House, a precursor to the later West Wing. The meeting required the large chamber because the businessmen had brought along their attorneys. Roosevelt asked the previous day's visitors to repeat their concern that removing sodium benzoate from ketchup would destroy the entire industry. As Wiley would describe it: "There was no way in which this disaster could be diverted except to overrule the conclusions of the Bureau." Wiley was vilified from the outset of the meeting as "a radical, impervious to reason and determined to destroy legitimate business." These businessmen asserted that the Heinz company was an anomaly and its method of ketchup production unlikely to survive.

Roosevelt then turned to Wilson and asked him, "What is your opinion about the propriety and desirability of enforcing your Chief of Bureau?"

Wilson stood by his department's findings. He said to Roosevelt, "Dr. Wiley made extensive investigations in feeding benzoated goods to healthy young men and in every instance he found that their health was undermined." The president then asked McCabe, Dunlap, and Wiley for their individual opinions. Along with Wilson, McCabe and Dunlap had studied the Poison Squad results. In a rare moment of unity, they agreed that the table trial had raised legitimate concerns. The young volunteers in the study had exhibited, as the draft report noted, "unfavorable symptoms and disturbances of metabolism" including irritation, nausea, headache, vomiting, and weight loss. The chemists who had run the experiment were now urging that, "in the interests of health both benzoic acid and benzoate of soda should be excluded from food products."

"On hearing this opinion," Wiley wrote, "the President turned to the protestants, struck the table in front of him a stunning blow with his fist, and showing his teeth in the true Rooseveltian fashion said: 'Gentlemen, if this drug is injurious, you shall not put it into food.'" The battle, Wiley thought, was almost won. But Sherman, the New York congressman and canner, spoke out again. He also wanted to discuss the use of saccharin in canned goods. He strongly objected to Wiley's likely recommendation to restrict its use. "My firm saved $4,000 by sweetening canned corn with saccharin instead of sugar," he said, addressing Roosevelt directly. "We want a decision from you on this question." For decades after the meeting, Wiley would replay this moment and wish he had sat silently and waited for Roosevelt to respond.

By the early twentieth century, saccharin was well known to the public as a diet aid; although most didn't realize that canners like Sherman secretly used it as a cheap alternative to sugar in creating so-called sweet corn. Wiley considered the substitution a deceptive

practice and took a position against such use, at least until the sweetener could be proved benign. It was in his judgment an illegal adulterant under the law. Nor did he care for a move by chemical companies
to avoid the problem by simply rechristening saccharin as a sugar. He
was at that moment pursuing a court case against the Heyden Chemical Company's saccharin product, which was sold under the name
Heyden Sugar. In his cautious approach to the health effects, he differed with Dunlap and McCabe. While the two men agreed that the
sweetener ought to be listed on product labels, and even that it should
be properly described, they thought that until health risks were clearly
shown, the saccharin use should not be restricted.

Now Wiley jumped directly into the conversation: "Everyone who
ate that sweet corn was deceived. He thought he was eating sugar,
when in point of fact he was eating a coal tar product totally devoid
of food value and extremely injurious to health." The interjection was
political bad form. With Roosevelt, it would have been all right in
many cases to venture an opinion without having first been asked for
one. The president was known to tolerate interruptions if he thought
the point that the speaker made was worth being made. In this case,
however, Roosevelt thought the opposite. As he quickly made clear,
the president disagreed strongly with what Wiley had said.

Roosevelt was a regular consumer of saccharin. His personal
physician, Rear Admiral Presley Marion Rixey, had recommended
the sweetener as a healthy alternative to sugar. Roosevelt put a great
deal of faith in what Rixey said as the navy physician was also a
friend. The two of them, both accomplished equestrians, frequently
rode together. Despite regular exercise, the president showed a tendency toward corpulence, and Rixey—having observed the link between weight gain and long-term diseases like diabetes—had advised
Roosevelt to replace sugar with saccharin as a diet aid. "You tell me
that saccharin is injurious to health?" Roosevelt said to Wiley. "Yes,
Mr. President, I do tell you that," Wiley said firmly. No one had

clearly proved injury yet; the research was still going on. But Wiley believed it and he said so.

"Dr. Rixey gives it to me every day," the president said in rising anger. By this time Wiley had recognized his error and attempted to recover the moment: "Mr. President, he probably thinks you may be threatened with diabetes." Roosevelt would have none of it. "Anyone who says saccharin is injurious to health is an idiot," he snapped. Shortly later, he called the meeting to a close.

The following day, Roosevelt announced the appointment of a scientific review board—in fact, the very board that had been requested by the food-processing industry. It would reassess Wiley's research, starting with sodium benzoate and saccharin. Further, Roosevelt had decided on its alternative chief chemist. Ira Remsen of Johns Hopkins, the chemist who had in 1879 co-discovered saccharin along with Constantin Fahlberg, would lead the investigations.

Wiley protested to no avail. Remsen, he thought, had a clear conflict of interest. "According to the ordinary conception of a juror, Dr. Remsen would not have been entitled to sit on the subject of saccharin. Such little matters as those, however, were not dominating with the President of the United States." But although he was angry with Roosevelt, Wiley was angrier with himself for further alienating the president. Ever since the 1902 incident in which he had exasperated Roosevelt over the proposed import of Cuban sugar, he had tried to steer clear of disagreements with the chief executive—until this misstep. He knew that by giving Roosevelt a new reason to be annoyed with him, he had just made things more difficult for himself and his cause. And "I fear that I deserved it."

Not that he'd made an outright enemy. Roosevelt was quick to take offense, but his rational side often overruled his ire. The president would continue to back some of the chief chemist's positions, notably the regulation of whiskey. Wiley's chemists continued to demonstrate fraud in that industry. They had recently revealed that

University Club Whiskey contained no whiskey at all, merely industrial ethanol dyed brown, and that Sherwood Rye Whiskey contained not a trace of a rye product. Despite continued industry pressure to accept such products as simply the modern way, Roosevelt still stood by his attorney general's decision regarding whiskey, and he supported Wiley's determined insistence on accuracy in labeling.

Yet the president also found himself annoyed by other instances of Wiley's staunch unwillingness to compromise. The chief chemist continued to reject the term "corn syrup." Since his earliest food-analysis study, for the state of Indiana in 1881, Wiley had insisted that the word "glucose" was the only accurate way to describe this sugary liquid derived from corn. Within the corn industry, however, that name had long been disliked. It sounded unappetizing, manufacturers feared, and was likely to alienate consumers. A new firm called the Corn Products Refining Company, created by a merger in 1906, had recently petitioned the government to be allowed to call its new corn-derived sweetener a syrup. This appeal carried behind it the clout of company founder Edward Thomas Bedford, a longtime executive and current director of the Standard Oil Company.

E. T. Bedford, as he was known, sought to bottle and market a thick liquid product under the name "Karo Corn Syrup." He knew full well that "Karo Glucose" was never going to succeed in the market. He'd done his best to convince Wiley that the name was aptly descriptive and overall more accurate than the unappetizing word "glucose," which sounded too much like "glue."

Wiley was unmoved. The food and drug law's protective measures should not be "suspended or abandoned because it is hurtful to any interest or is displeasing to any men," he insisted. Bedford responded by appealing to Wilson instead, protesting the Agriculture Department's apparent indifference to what he called the "impossibility of popularizing our product under the name Glucose." He thought Wiley's refusal to reconsider was rooted in hostility toward industry in general and, he wrote to the secretary, such a stubborn refusal to listen "very clearly indicates the personal views of Dr. Wiley in a way that tends to cause us a lot of trouble."

Representatives of the corn industry had also petitioned Roosevelt. In a meeting attended by Wilson and Dunlap but not Wiley, the president had made it clear that he thought "glucose" was a ridiculous name for a syrupy material derived from corn. "You must make the manufacturers call a spade a spade," the president had said. "But don't make them call it a damn shovel." Wilson discussed the issue privately with McCabe and Dunlap. They had earlier sided with Wiley on the term but, at the secretary's request, now agreed to withdraw their support for Wiley's stance on the definition. A majority of the three-man Board of Food Inspection now favored the term that the industry wanted to use, and the department issued a formal endorsement of the term "corn syrup." Karo Corn Syrup was cleared for the grocery store market.

Such moves by Roosevelt and Wilson had established a precedent. Industry advocates now saw a way around Wiley and his insistence on strictly limiting chemical additives to food. This came to bear as French canning companies, which used toxic copper salts to make their peas and other vegetables look especially green, looked to bypass the new standards. Fearing that Americans would reject vegetables without the familiar bright green color, a delegation representing canners and importers took the issue not to the Department of Agriculture but to the Department of State. It proved an effective decision. Secretary of State Root pushed for an exemption to satisfy the French manufacturers. In response, Roosevelt suggested that Wilson refer the copper salts question to the newly created consulting panel—already better known as the "Remsen Board" after chairman Ira Remsen. Until the board reviewed the science—whenever that was—the French were free to continue greening up their canned vegetables as they chose.

Emboldened, makers and importers of other French food products started complaining directly to Roosevelt about Wiley's interference with the labeling of their wares. In May 1908 the issue came to a head regarding a so-called wine vinegar, which was, in truth, a synthetic acetic acid dyed to a golden tone. Manufactured by a company called Cessat of Bordeaux, it bore a cheerful label decorated with bunches of grapes and leaves meant to suggest a product fresh from the vineyard. At Wiley's insistence, Cessat had added the words "Distilled, colored with caramel" to the label. In addition, he wanted the company to remove all the vineyard imagery—grapes, leaves, and vines—which, he thought, erroneously gave the impression of a vineyard product. Cessat executives resisted. They would remove the grape clusters, they said, but leave the decorative vines.

But Wiley refused to compromise, believing that if he gave up on small details for one product he would be forced to give up on all. When the next shipment of Cessat of Bordeaux vinegar reached a U.S. harbor, he ordered that because it was deceptively labeled it could not be brought ashore. The company, encouraged by recent events, appealed directly to Roosevelt. The president promptly fired off an angry letter to Wilson, ordering that the shipment be released and demanding that the responsible officials (meaning Wiley) explain their "useless, illegal and improper interference with shipments of food from a friendly nation." In an impetuous, scrawled postscript to that letter, the president stressed that he did not mean to undercut the food and drug law. It was "one of the best laws on the statute book." He did, however, want it to be administered without "a nagging, vexatious, foolish or corrupt spirit toward honest business."

Meanwhile, Roosevelt worked with Wilson in appointing four other scientists, besides chairman Ira Remsen, to the board that was to review Wiley's work on chemical hazards in food. He wanted scientists with strong reputations. The final list included Russell Chittenden, John H. Young, Christian A. Herter, and Alonzo E. Taylor.

Chittenden, a Yale physiologist who specialized in food and

nutrition, was the best known. Chittenden had early on been cautious about food additives, but more recently his views, especially regarding preservatives, had stood in contrast to Wiley's. The chief chemist attributed that to industry influence; Chittenden, who had publicly endorsed the use of borax, received funding from the borax-mining industry. He also consulted with corn syrup producers. Bedford, the manufacturer of Karo, had cited him to both the president and Wilson as believing that "a strong solution of sugar made from a starch is entitled to be called a syrup."

Wiley was dismayed by the roles of Remsen and Chittenden but had no criticisms of the other board members. Young was a chemist specializing in pharmacology at Northwestern University. Herter, a Columbia University pathologist, was known for his work in diseases of the digestive tract. Taylor, a physiological chemist at the University of Pennsylvania, studied the role of grains in the human diet.

But overall Wiley's relationships with many of his more traditional scientific colleagues were beginning to deteriorate. The Society of Chemical Engineers—an industry-allied group—passed a public resolution criticizing his position on compounds such as sulfur dioxide. The leaders of the New York section of the American Chemical Society suggested that he was now more an advocate than a chemist. He refused to admit discouragement over such actions. "The men who led in such a ridiculous fight can only injure themselves," Wiley told a worried friend in a New York laboratory. "These little fellows do not bother me in the least. You can rest assured of that."

The Remsen Board, though, bothered him, and deeply. It seemed intended specifically to undercut and countermand the findings of the Bureau of Chemistry. He was dismayed that Remsen himself, the "alleged discoverer" of saccharin, as Wiley put it, was given authority to rule on the sweetener's safety. He was dismayed that Chittenden, so obviously pro-industry, was on the board at all. He saw both the creation of the board and its business-friendly composition, he told friends, as a betrayal not just of him but of the American consumer.

Wiley took the uncompromising position that "the creation of the Remsen Board of Consulting Scientific Experts was the cause of nearly all the woes that subsequently befell the Pure Food Law." Other voices agreed. "The Remsen Board," said a *New York Times* editorial, "was created on February 20, 1908 for the specific purpose of overruling the findings of Dr. Harvey Wiley of the Bureau of Chemistry with respect to the purity of food and drugs." The *Times*, along with Wiley's pure-food allies and a considerable swath of those Americans who followed the news from Washington, had come to realize that despite the successful passage of the 1906 law, there were forces within the Roosevelt administration, within the federal government at large, that were more than willing to adjust the law's requirements for the benefit of industry, and not necessarily with the public good in mind.

Eleven

EXCUSES FOR EVERYTHING

1908–1909

————●————

Is covered with germs, each armed with a hook
To grapple with liver and spleen.

I n April 1908, as his Poison Squad study of sodium benzoate and
benzoic acid was being readied for publication, Wiley gave a
somewhat defiant speech to a meeting of the venerable American
Philosophical Society in Philadelphia, an organization that Benjamin
Franklin had founded in 1743. He provided information about his
preliminary results on sodium benzoate, pressed his case for strict
enforcement of the pure-food law, and advocated for tighter limits
on what processors could put into commercial foodstuffs.

"The use of chemical preservatives and artificial colors is of quite
recent date," he told his audience. "I think I may say with safety that
if one could go back thirty, or at most forty, years he would find a
food supply practically free" of such additives. Rapid advances in
chemistry had brought about the change, he continued, making it
possible to "offer manufacturers chemical preservatives of high
potency . . . at prices which make it entirely possible to use them
freely in food products."

He emphasized that it was this ability to make a cheaper product—not safety, not quality—that drove the industry's embrace of industrial food chemistry. And it wasn't that much more expensive to do it right, he argued. A "conscientious manufacturer" of ketchup (clearly Heinz) had shown that it cost only an additional fifteen to twenty cents per case to make a preservative-free version of the product.

Previewing the impending official report, Wiley called sodium benzoate "highly objectionable." It "produced a very serious disturbance of the metabolic functions, attended with injury to digestion and health." This was a study, as he'd earlier told Congress, in which only three of the twelve volunteers had lasted until the end of the experiment. Wiley finished this speech by once again stressing that any compound proven dangerous or that was used only to support the "convenience, carelessness or indifference of the manufacturer" should be removed from the American food supply "entirely."

The sodium benzoate trials had deeply dismayed the chief chemist. He'd predicted minor or no ill effects in his Poison Squad volunteers and seen the opposite. As he'd told legislators, "The most pronounced symptoms were burning sensations in the throat and esophagus, pains in the stomach, some dizziness, bad taste, and when the limit of endurance was reached, the subject suddenly became nauseated and ill." Eleven of the twelve volunteers lost a measurable amount of weight during the trial and—except in two of the men—recovery was proving painfully slow. Following the other findings, this study cemented his conviction that industrially made preservatives posed a more serious health risk than he'd previously realized. "I was converted by my own investigation," he wrote.

But even as Wiley grew more alarmed about processed foods, and more anxious to police them, his boss was moving in the other direction. Secretary Wilson had grown tired of what he considered alarmist investigations. He'd also started blocking publication of what he considered industry-unfriendly findings. Over the course of 1907, he had forbidden the printing of a report on "Corn Sirup as a

Synonym for Glucose" and a Bigelow-authored paper on "Investigations of a Substitute (Weak Brine) for Sulfur Dioxide in Drying Fruits." Already, in 1908, he had prevented the release of a rather damning survey of "Sanitary Conditions of Canneries" at the urging of Congressman Sherman and his peers in that branch of the industry. Wilson had also squelched two other Poison Squad reports, one on the controversial issue of copper sulfate and the other on the old-time preservative potassium nitrate (saltpeter). Wiley had just returned from Philadelphia when Wilson sent for him to tell him that the sodium benzoate report, too, would not be published as scheduled. The secretary wanted it shelved, at least until after the Remsen Board had concluded its own study.

Colleagues around the department noticed and commented upon Wiley's obvious frustration. He didn't deny it. But his exasperation, he would insist, had not pushed him to secretly countermand Wilson's order halting publication of the sodium benzoate report. He swore that he hadn't done anything of the kind. When the Poison Squad report was unexpectedly published on July 20, 1908, Wiley protested that he was as shocked as anyone. He argued that it must have been the result of a misunderstanding at the Government Printing Office. And the people in the printing office backed him in that assertion; its administrators formally apologized for the inadvertent release of information. Wilson wasn't buying it. He knew that Wiley had good friends throughout not only the Agriculture Department but many government agencies, including the printing office. The secretary, already annoyed by the chief chemist's unbending nature, now saw signs of something worse: an instance of possible treachery by a willful and duplicitous subordinate.

In August 1908 the National Association of State Dairy and Food Departments held its annual conference at the elegant Grand Hotel on Michigan's Mackinac Island. The setting might have been beautiful and harmonious, the luxurious 1887 hostelry might serenely overlook a shining stretch of water, but the attendees—as journalists could plainly see—were spoiling for a fight.

"The convention will probably manifest the signs that are now being seen in various parts of the country," warned the *New York Times* on July 30. "Contrary to what was expected, the let down in food legislation has not been popular. . . . Consumer's leagues, clubs of different sorts and others are taking the subject up and making their ideas known to the authorities here." Among the discontents, the newspaper said, were officials of the Bureau of Chemistry and delegates from some of the western states, "where the pure food agitation is strong."

Edwin F. Ladd, the activist food chemist from North Dakota, was both president of the association and lead organizer of the protest movement. He opened the conference on August 4 with a tirade against secretary of agriculture James Wilson, noting the man's suppression of valuable food safety reports, his resistance to tough regulation, and his apparently cozy relationship with the food industry. Roosevelt, Ladd stated, was not much better, and the appointment of the Remsen Board—clearly an end run around the law—was evidence of both men's cold indifference to consumer protection. The actions by the federal government, he continued, were an insult to all who believed in allowing good science to help make good decisions.

The Mackinac conference included carefully selected representatives from the food-manufacturing industry, there to testify in favor of Wiley's views on food safety enforcement. A manager from the Columbia Conserve Company in Indianapolis noted that he'd been at first hostile to the new regulations. Columbia had been profitably selling a cheap "strawberry jelly" made of glucose, apple waste, and red food coloring and had strongly resisted calling it "imitation" for fear of losing customers. But the company had since discovered that it could make even more money by selling well-labeled, high-quality goods. Representatives of the Heinz company also appeared in starring roles. Following its success in removing preservatives from ketchup, the firm had developed a whole line of preservative-free products ranging from mustard to sweet pickles. Heinz's marketing director reported that a year of experience with these products, exposed to "the heat and cold of changing seasons, or wide distribution at home and abroad," had been one of "pronounced and unqualified success. Spoilage is less than one-fourth of one percent." Sebastian Mueller, now a vice president at Heinz, blasted competing manufacturers who insisted on preservative use. He stated firmly that sodium benzoate was being promoted by food manufacturers who found it profitable to use rot-prone waste and scraps in their "bulk" ketchups, sometimes at four times the proposed government standard of 0.10 percent.

Wiley added that food quality and safety represented not only good science but also moral decision-making. The wealthy, he pointed out, could easily afford fresh food and well-made condiments. The trade in cheap, chemically enhanced imitations catered to the poor. If the country could work to standardize good food, then it also would be promoting good health for all. "Whenever a food is debased in order to make it cheap, the laboring man pays more for any given nourishment than the rich man does who buys the pure food," he pointed out.

The attendees voted to adopt a series of resolutions, including a condemnation of the practice of bleaching flour—increasingly criticized for the resulting chemical by-products—and support for a contentious proposal that the weight of the contents should be listed on every food container, allowing consumers to know the actual quantity being purchased. Manufacturers and grocers stood fiercely opposed to such a "weight on the package" law, which suggested to the delegates that they were onto something. By a 42–15 vote, the food and dairy association also put itself clearly in the Wiley camp on the issue of preservatives and other food additives: "Resolved: That this association is convinced that all chemical preservatives are harmful in foods and that all kinds of food products are and may be prepared and distributed without them, and pledges its best efforts to use all moral and legal means at its disposal to exclude chemical preservatives from food products." As another indication of their dissatisfaction with the federal government, the convention attendees agreed to work on a uniform food-purity law that they proposed to pass at the state level across the nation. Ladd appointed a committee to work on drafting such a law, including himself, Robert Allen of Kentucky, and Willard Bigelow of the Bureau of Chemistry.

Of all the actions taken at the conference, the most controversial and potentially dangerous, especially for Harvey Wiley, was an organizational censure of Wilson, sparked by Ladd's opening tirade against the secretary of agriculture. Wiley had warned his friend Ladd in advance that a public attack might not be a good idea, that further alienating Wilson might backfire and hurt their shared cause. But Ladd, who clearly felt a deep sense of betrayal over the change of direction by the federal department, refused to keep his peace. Wiley and other bureau colleagues in attendance prudently abstained from voting on any of the resolutions, let alone the one condemning their department head. And when one particularly irate conventioneer proposed charging Wilson with criminal negligence, they joined other Agriculture Department employees in walking out of the room.

Wiley did not, however, publicly stand up to defend Wilson against the attacks, and some in attendance felt the chief chemist neglected an obvious duty to do so. "Those who watched events at Mackinac were astonished at the course pursued by Dr. Wiley and the rest of the Washington contingent, in absenting themselves from the meeting that 'roasted' Secretary Wilson," said one dismayed attendee, who felt that the chief chemist might have defused the bitterness that accompanied the confrontation. Wilson agreed completely with that assessment. With some heat, he afterward told Wiley that he would never again send anyone to a convention who refused to defend the secretary and the department against unwarranted attacks. Yet as both Ladd and Wiley later noted, there were strong voices speaking up for the secretary, and they came from the food-processing industry. *American Food Journal*, a leading trade magazine, blamed Wiley for embarrassing the secretary and predicted that the chemistry chief would be fired over this "brazen attack." Corporations including Dow Chemical also jumped on the moment, urging that Wiley be replaced.

Shortly after the Mackinac meeting, an Agriculture Department inspector visited Dow's plant in Midland, Michigan, and met with founder Herbert Dow, who complained of a drop in sales of sodium benzoate following both the passage of the food law and Wiley's pernicious attacks on the compound. Dow was "not sparing in his criticism of Dr. Wiley," whom he characterized as playing to the uneducated and temperamentally fearful public. The chemical industry, Dow asserted, was planning its own public education campaign to counter misinformation being spread by Wiley and his friends.

By now the rift between the agriculture secretary and the head of the Chemistry Bureau was public knowledge; their every action was suddenly scrutinized for political nuance. As newspapers including the *New York Times* pointed out with interest, even when Wilson backed Wiley on a point of food safety enforcement, his reasons often differed from those put forward by the chief chemist. A recent and clear example of that could be seen in departmental decisions regarding the controversial practice of bleaching wheat flour.

Snowy-white baked goods had become a measure of household status in the late nineteenth century. The traditional method of whitening flour was simply to expose it to direct sunlight or allow it to age in a well-ventilated room. But these methods took time—hours or even days. By the turn of the twentieth century, millers had turned to far more rapid techniques, mostly involving chemical oxidation of the flour with nitrogen peroxide or ozone. A review of industry practices after passage of the food and drug law found that chemical bleaching of flour had become nearly standard. The exception was usually small companies that could not afford to set up the oxidation process; they typically advertised in magazines with ads promoting the advantages of the old-fashioned ways: "no artificial pallor . . . no fictitious simulation of age."

Edwin Ladd, the North Dakota food commissioner, had the previous year begun investigating bleaching techniques at the request of the state's smaller millers; his friend and ally James Shepard, food commissioner of South Dakota, did the same. Ladd's investigation found that bleached flours, at least those processed with nitrogen oxides, were heavily tainted with nitrates, which are derivative nitrogen-oxygen based salts. These compounds, Ladd felt, should be considered a possible health risk and further studied in that regard. Pending the publication of his report, in 1907 Ladd issued a North Dakota state ruling prohibiting the sale of any bleached flour that contained nitrates.

Wiley's Bureau of Chemistry proceeded more cautiously, advocating at first only that flours be labeled clearly as bleached or not so that consumers could make a choice. But Wiley also authorized an investigation of bleached flour and any chemical fallout, such as nitrates, that might result from the process. The scientists in his laboratory proceeded to show a direct connection between bleaching and nitrates: The more nitrogen peroxide was used, the higher the nitrate residues in flour. Further, they discovered that most of these chemical residues survived even through the baking of bread. They found no evidence that levels of nitrates in either raw flour or baked products diminished over time. Further, according to a report from the department's Food and Drug Inspection Laboratory: "A summary of our results will tend to show that the bleaching of flour by nitrogen peroxide never improves the flour from the consumer's standpoint."

Wilson showed himself willing to at least consider the bleached flour issue. He followed the bureau report by convening a formal hearing on the subject in the fall of 1908. During that session, Ladd, Shepard, and Wiley formed a consensus on three main points: that daily consumption of nitrates could pose a health risk, that this question deserved further study, and that until such consumption was declared safe, the chemical bleaching of flour, which produced those compounds, should be disallowed.

Not surprisingly, the industry disagreed, as did a cadre of scientists whom milling firms hired to respond to the proposed ban. Seventy-five industry members attended the hearing and they had combined resources to employ a phalanx of experts, including well-known Chicago toxicologist Walter S. Haines, who had earlier defended the use of borax in foods. Haines testified that the nitrate amounts in bleached flour clearly were too small to do any real harm. That December, though, Wilson startled the millers by apparently agreeing with Wiley. He announced that the Agriculture Department would indeed declare bleached flour an adulterated product under the new law. That would mean, among other things, that it could no longer be transported across state lines. Ladd and Shepard hoped the decision was a sign of a healed rift between the secretary and his department's chief chemist. "Bleached flour is a dead duck," Wiley wrote happily in response to a query from the Indiana food commissioner, celebrating what appeared to be a rare instance in which he and the secretary of agriculture had worked in harmony.

The details of the decision revealed, however, that Wilson and Wiley had different motives for supporting a ban. Wiley opposed chemical bleaching of flour because of the health risk, but Wilson blocked publication of the Chemistry Bureau's toxicological findings on the subject. Wilson had ruled against bleached flour because he considered the practice a tool for deceptive marketing. With powerful bleaching techniques, millers could disguise cheap grades of flour and sell them for a much higher price. Newspaper coverage of the decision emphasized the political differences involved: "Secretary

Wilson and Dr. Wiley have disagreed again," reported the New York–based *Journal of Commerce*, and the chemist "has once again been turned down by his chief."

Wilson also remained responsive to flour-industry concerns. He allowed for a six-month grace period to review his decision and respond before initiating any prosecutions or product seizures. The secretary appeared so hesitant about enforcement, in fact, that millers decided to test his resolve by continuing to produce bleached flour and ship it as they chose.

Rumors began to circulate that Wiley had finally pushed his boss too hard and was in imminent danger of losing his job. Alarmed members of the National Association of State Food and Dairy Departments wrote directly to Roosevelt to defend their friend. In October, Ladd joined with two other state food commissioners, John G. Emery of Wisconsin and Arthur C. Bird of Michigan, in a letter that noted, "There is a persistent rumor that the Secretary of Agriculture will dismiss Dr. Wiley or ask him to resign," because of Wilson's assumption that the chief chemist was responsible for the confrontation in Mackinac. "His assumption is without foundation," the letter continued. Ladd took full credit, or blame, for organizing the protest. He and his cosigners hoped that Roosevelt would work to prevent any such unfair and harmful actions. But if things got worse, Bird wrote to Wiley, they were prepared to visit the White House in person.

Roosevelt, they acknowledged, would be in office only a few months longer. He had earlier announced that he would not seek another term (a decision he came to regret) and the upcoming November election pitted Roosevelt's chosen successor, William Howard Taft, against returning Democratic candidate William Jennings Bryan. If need be, the food chemists declared, they would take up defense of the food law—and of Wiley—with the next president as well. Even after Taft won the presidential election in November, new rumors flourished, suggesting that Roosevelt would dismiss Wiley before leaving office. Newspaper coverage made it clear that the nation's editors—and by proxy their readers—saw that idea as an industry-backed threat to American food safety.

The *New York World*, December 20, 1908: "Dr. Wiley says 'I have not been asked to resign but I have been fought at every turn of the road by adulterators of food and I am ready to go if the Government wants to take their recommendation. Otherwise, I will remain to defend the food law, no matter how thick the bullets fly.'"

The *Boston Evening Record*, December 29, 1908: "Pure Food Doc Wiley . . . has made hundreds of enemies but he has made them for the sake of the public. If the food tinkerers ever do actually get him removed, the consumer will pay the freight."

The *New York Evening Mail*, December 31, 1908: "It is earnestly hoped that Mr. Wiley will fight his enemies, open and secret, and that he will continue to denounce the modern system of mixing poison with food to increase the profit."

The chorus of public dismay became so loud that Roosevelt's executive secretary, William Loeb Jr., issued a statement declaring that he "knew of no friction" between the president and the popular chief chemist and had heard of no plans to replace Wiley. Roosevelt agreed that he had no plans to remove the chief chemist but he qualified that expression of support shortly later. He told a reporter that he had personally reviewed Wiley's opinions on the issues of corn syrup, accurate labeling of imported French vinegar, and the safety of saccharin, and he had disagreed with him every time. "Those instances gave me a great distrust of Wiley's good judgment." On the other hand, the president continued, "I have such confidence in his integrity and zeal that I am anxious to back him up to the limit of my power wherever I can be sure that doing so won't do damage instead of good."

If regulations became too rigid or petty, Roosevelt emphasized,

then a backlash could lead to "upsetting of the whole pure food law."
He hoped that reasonable men could agree that such a result would
serve no one well.

That same December, the Bureau of Chemistry issued a summary
report on formaldehyde as a food preservative. It was a straightforward condemnation of the practice: Formaldehyde, still heavily
used in milk, especially in summer, was a poisonous additive with an
"insidious effect on the cells." The compound had sickened every single one of the Poison Squad members who had taken it with meals;
they'd suffered sleeplessness, headaches, dizziness, vertigo, nausea,
and vomiting. They'd lost weight. An analysis of their blood and urine
had found that in every case calcium oxalate crystals were forming in
the urine and white blood cell counts were dropping, suggesting im-
mune system harm. The bureau concluded with a flat statement: The
use of formaldehyde in food "is never justified." Despite the forceful
language, this was one of Wiley's least controversial findings.

A review of findings in the *New York State Journal of Medicine*
cited a litany of evidence that formaldehyde was a "violent poison."
Examples ranged from the death of a teenager (who drank a 4 percent solution of formaldehyde and died twenty-nine hours later) to a
study in which five kittens were given milk containing 1/50,000
formaldehyde. Three of the five died within hours. Despite their
many differences, Wilson, McCabe, and Dunlap all concurred with
Wiley that the federal government should bar formaldehyde as a
food additive.

Wiley also could take comfort in the fact that he'd successfully
argued against borax as a food additive and that his position had
been upheld within the department. At Wilson's direction, the agency
began seizing borax-laced products to get them off the market. After
a seizure of a train carload of its cheese, the MacLaren Imperial
Cheese Company (a Canadian manufacturer later purchased by the

J.L. Kraft & Brothers Company) asked Wilson to refer the borax question to the Remsen Board. Wilson refused to do so.

The secretary also had endorsed a November decision to seize fifty-two industrial-sized cans of eggs preserved in a 2 percent solution of boracic acid. The Hipolite Egg Company of St. Louis sold these huge cans—forty-two pounds each—to the baking industry at a price much lower than that of fresh eggs. Hipolite specialized in salvaging dirty, cracked, and even rotting eggs for use in breads and cakes. The company was particularly known for using "spots" (decomposing eggs); mixing their contents into a thick, homogenous mass; using boracic acid, a by-product of borax, to halt further decomposition; and then selling the eggy soup by the can. Wilson not only approved the seizure but also initiated a legal action against the company to halt its use of the preservative. As with the move to ban formaldehyde, this was a politically astute decision. Borax had fallen out of favor precipitously since Wiley's first Poison Squad report—and since the unscrupulous propaganda tactics of the Pacific Coast Borax Company had come to light.

For some years, magazines and newspapers across the country had been printing the anti-Wiley, pro-preservative opinions of H. H. Langdon, who identified himself as a public health advocate with a scientific background. Langdon's ideas usually appeared in letters to the editor but also in the occasional magazine essay. After Wiley had published in 1907 a book compiling the bureau's analyses under the title *Foods and Their Adulteration*, the apparently science-savvy Langdon had written a fiercely critical review of the work. But "Langdon" was a fictional creation of H. L. Harris, the chief publicist for the Pacific Coast Borax Company. Harris planted his Langdon letters in large publications and small. In a missive to a newspaper in eastern Ohio, the *Alliance Review*, he wrote, "A recent case of ptomaine poisoning in Alliance has caused the thought that it is certainly appalling to learn how rapidly ptomaine poisoning cases have increased since the passage of the pure food law."

To the *New York Times* the fictional Langdon described Wiley as an untrustworthy scientist of "radical views." In *Scientific American* he insisted that the health of the Poison Squad volunteers was improved by eating borax-laced food. His work even appeared in Paul Pierce's *What to Eat*, where he wrote that the Poison Squad experiments could not be trusted because the bureau's dining room was so shabby and dirty as to depress anyone's appetite. These entirely fictional statements were reprinted with enough effect that scientists hostile to Wiley—such as the German industrial chemist Oscar Liebreich, who had helped bring borax into favor—sometimes included them in their own testimony.

It was the adoption of the Harris/Langdon statements by high-profile pharmaceutical chemists like Liebreich that led the American Medical Association to investigate. AMA physicians reviewed the cases of ptomaine poisoning reported in the fake letters and discovered that many had never occurred; most of the illnesses ranged from indigestion to a few suicidal "self-administrations of arsenic." In other words, there had been no sudden increase in bacterial food poisoning due to the reduction in use of borax and other preservatives. In an article titled "Press Agents and Preservatives," the editors of the *Journal of the American Medical Association* (*JAMA*) faulted other periodicals for the tendency of the lazy editor to "calmly appropriate Harris's 'dope' as fact and print it as his own." They advised the group's physician members to report any Langdon letters to newspaper editors. In some cases, newspapers had started adding editors' notes to the Langdon opinions, a positive step that the AMA noted, "must cause chagrin and disgust at the headquarters of the Pacific Coast Borax Company."

But despite such evidence of skullduggery by the food industry, and despite his support for prohibiting additives such as borax and formaldehyde, Wilson remained deeply wary of Wiley and his activist tendencies. He again refused to consider restrictions on the use of sulfur compounds in food. He again said that he was waiting for the

Remsen Board's recommendation on sodium benzoate before he would make any decision. It surprised neither Wiley nor his allies when the board's report, issued on January 26, 1909, found no problem worth mentioning with sodium benzoate. "You will find it rich reading," Wiley wrote to a friend after reading the published report and noting that he had not been shown an advance copy. "Excuses for everything."

Three of the board members—Long, Herter, and Chittenden—had independently conducted their studies, loosely following Wiley's design, and failed to replicate the signs of serious illness seen in the Poison Squad study. They had tested the preservative on a group of young men, but they had added several additional months to the testing and they had experimented with a wider range of doses. All three of the Remsen Board researchers saw some signs of ill health in their subjects but dismissed them as "slight modifications in certain physiological processes, the exact significance of which modifications is not known." To a man, they suggested that the causes were anything from lack of sleep to the weather. Chittenden, for instance, blamed the nausea and diarrhea that he observed on a "hot, dry New England summer." The Remsen Board announced that it could reassure the government and the public that sodium benzoate—at an industry-standard dose of 0.01 percent—was perfectly safe.

Preservative makers declared the Remsen report a victory over an "arrogant official scientist." Once again, the food-manufacturing association called for Wiley's removal from office and predicted that the food additives he had criticized—from copper sulfate to saccharin—would be found innocuous. But such public celebration, as the *New York Times* reported, almost immediately backfired. Pure-food advocates immediately charged that the Remsen report was biased, beginning a new round in what the paper called "a first class fight."

The *Journal of the American Medical Association* wrote that the Remsen Board seemed determined to find no health implications.

"[T]his decision of the board leaves the question of the physiologic action of sodium benzoate on the community practically where it was before; that is, that while the substance is known to be a bacterial poison, its deleterious action on the human organs is, in the words of the Scotch verdict, 'not proven.'" A Scottish "not proven" verdict meant, in this context, that although the charge had not been established as true, the defendant had not been absolved of guilt, either. "It is to be hoped that Dr. Wiley will be in no way discouraged and will remain at his post and continue to hew to the line," the piece continued. "He is a government official of a type that happily is becoming more common—one of those men who appreciate that they represent the public and that they are expected to look after the interests of the public and not the interests of any class. . . . No wonder he is so cordially hated by those who heretofore fattened at the expense of public health and well-being."

Women's clubs, consumer leagues, newspaper editorial writers, even the Canners Association and the National Wholesale Grocers Association all came angrily to Wiley's defense. On the day that the Remsen report was published, Paul Pierce announced the formation of a new advocacy group, the American Association for the Promotion of Purity in Food Products, which included representatives from industry including the Shredded Wheat Company, the Franco-American Food Company, the Beechnut Packing Company, and the H.J. Heinz Company. Heinz paid for the association's press agent, who kept journalists supplied with pamphlets detailing both the risks of preservatives and the corporate corruption of the Agriculture Department. "If you could see the letters, telegrams and newspaper clippings pouring in upon me," Wiley wrote to Edwin Ladd, "you would think the Referee [Remsen] Board had not a single supporter in the country."

Wilson was unmoved by such political drama. He accepted the Remsen report without criticism, simply recommending that the preservative be allowed at a low enough level to be considered safe until proven otherwise by objective science. In March 1909, just before leaving office, President Roosevelt approved a regulation permitting the use of sodium benzoate in food at a level set at 0.01 percent. If he'd been less on the defensive, Wiley could have celebrated the fact that he'd at least gotten a limit put in place. But he, his allies, and the press took the decision as a resounding defeat for the chief chemist and his cause. The assessment was that the army of pure-food advocates had flexed their political muscle to an impressive extent, but they had lost.

Wiley thought again about quitting but rejected that idea. He'd come too far and he felt he owed his loyalty and allegiance to his many like-minded comrades in battle. As he wrote to a friend, it would be cowardly for "a general to resign his command because one part of his army was engulfed." He had flaws, he acknowledged, but he could say proudly that cowardice was not one of them.

Twelve

OF WHISKEY AND SODA

1909

———●———

The banquet how fine, don't begin it

William Howard Taft won the presidency largely thanks to the support of Theodore Roosevelt, and he shared his patron's wariness of the Agriculture Department's crusading chief chemist: "I expect to give Dr. Wiley the reasonable and just support he is entitled to have," Taft wrote, shortly after taking office, to one of Wiley's anxious supporters. "But when I feel he has done an injustice I expect to differ with him even at the expense of having my motives questioned."

He expected, on the other hand, that his relationship with Roosevelt would stay cordial. But the sitting president and the former one grew apart over the next four years. A simple and widely cited explanation for the split is that the office brought out Taft's conservative tendencies even while Roosevelt, restless and unhappy at being out of power, grew more progressive. Their differences came to a head when a very public disagreement over wilderness protection prompted Taft in 1910 to fire the popular Gifford Pinchot from his position as U.S. Forest Service chief. The move alienated not just Roosevelt, who had appointed Pinchot to the position, but other progressive Republicans as well, creating a serious rift within the party.

Yet the alienation between the Taft and Roosevelt factions was rooted in more than one big dispute. From his earliest days in office, Taft showed a willingness to reconsider Roosevelt's rulings, including some controversial new positions on enforcement of the food law.

For example, the question of which alcoholic beverages could rightly be called "whiskey" arose yet again. Roosevelt and Attorney General Bonaparte considered that they had settled the matter. But bottling interests represented by that tireless lobbyist Warwick Hough never resigned themselves to the designations "compound whiskey" and "imitation whiskey." Roosevelt had quietly tried to appease the angry liquor wholesalers by appointing an informal "whiskey commission," supposedly to review the situation. It consisted of Wilson, Dunlap, and John G. Capers, head of the Department of Internal Revenue. The commission was so informal, and also apparently so secret, that Wilson and Dunlap at first denied it existed when reporters asked them about its rumored actions. This deceptiveness became a political embarrassment when Roosevelt and Capers acknowledged the panel's formation. Further, Hough acquired a copy of a pro-industry letter from the commission to the president and leaked it to newspapers in order to press his cause. The document, which infuriated Wiley and his purist allies, read in part: "[T]he term 'whiskey' should not be denied to neutral spirits diluted with water to a proper strength and colored with caramel."

Hough welcomed Taft's election—largely because he remembered that at the height of the whiskey deliberations, the then-secretary of war had spoken out in favor of the wholesalers' position. Not long after the 1909 inauguration, Hough brought members of the National Wholesale Liquor Dealers Association and his copy of the whiskey commission letter to a meeting with the new president. Afterward, with Taft's encouragement, the association filed a formal petition to once again revisit the question of how to define whiskey.

In response, Taft asked Solicitor General Lloyd W. Bowers for a formal review of Roosevelt's earlier decision and, at Bowers's recommendation, a new series of whiskey hearings began on April 8, 1909. It continued for almost a month. The resulting 1,200-page volume of testimony retraced the ground that had been covered in earlier hearings before congressional committees. Hough again represented the wholesale liquor dealers. As he had in the past, Edmund Haynes Taylor Jr.—now in his seventies but still an outspoken advocate for aged Kentucky bourbon—represented the straight-whiskey interests. And Wiley, yet again, was called as an expert witness on alcohol analysis and purity. The subject matter may have been somewhat dry, but the hearings were not. Participants repeatedly gathered around a table to taste the samples of whiskey—straight, blended, imitation—submitted in evidence. Henry Parker Willis, an economics professor at Washington & Lee University who served as an adviser on whiskey tax issues, noted a corresponding rise in noise and described the hearings as often "reminiscent of a German drinking club."

Typically impassioned, Wiley once again accused Hough and his association of dishonesty: "The evidence shows convincingly," he said, "that the protestants in this case did not come into court with clean hands; that they have been for half a century guilty of taking neutral spirits and from these neutral spirits making all forms of so-called whiskey." The use of dyes, he reminded the listeners, was purely to give products the false appearance of aged whiskey and to "make the article appear better than it really is, thus contravening the fundamental principles of the Food and Drug Act." After all, the act required many manufacturers to place the term "imitation" on their label—imitation vanilla extract, for instance—when they were made primarily of other ingredients. And he concluded: "There is no hardship, therefore, in imposing the word 'imitation' upon a beverage made in imitation of old genuine whiskey."

In late May, Bowers issued his opinion, agreeing with Wiley that neutral spirits—dyed, flavored, oiled—should not be called whiskey in an unqualified way. He ordered them to be labeled "imitation." But he also agreed with the rectifiers that a blend of alcohols, if it contained primarily straight whiskey, could fairly be called a "blended whiskey," even if it was dyed to a richer color. If this was "coloring matter of a harmless character," such as a vegetable dye, Bowers said he would not call the whiskey adulterated. After all, he noted, "Whisky is not a natural product. It is always a thing manufactured by man."

Wiley wearily accepted the verdict; he was, to the relief of his allies, ready to let the whiskey fight go. The ruling satisfied neither Hough nor Taylor, however, and on behalf of their respective groups both challenged Bowers's decision. Taft then announced he would make a presidential decision to end the argument, possibly later that year. Taylor was optimistic; he and his straight-whiskey colleagues had filed a detailed brief establishing the solid legal precedent for precise labeling of whiskey and its ingredients. In this they had the support of Senator McCumber, one of the powers behind the passage of the food law, who had written to the president that he considered it consumer fraud to allow cheap alcohol enhanced with "drugs and oils and colors . . . to be sold for a good brand of whiskey."

Less openly, Taft also reviewed another Roosevelt decision, the creation of the Remsen Board. Shortly after taking office, the new president had asked deputy attorney general James Fowler to affirm that the board had legal standing. Fowler responded with a memo, copied to Wilson, that dismayed both the secretary and the president. It warned that the board represented an illegal use of department funds: "I do not think the Secretary of Agriculture was authorized by law to employ scientific experts to be paid out of the fund named." Startled, Taft privately asked Attorney General George Wickersham to review Fowler's finding. Wickersham concurred. Indeed, the attorney general's office expressed concern over how much money Wilson was lavishing on these industry-friendly scientists—annual salaries of up to $60,000 and, from 1908 to 1909, an additional $40,000 for expenses. At Wilson's urging, however, Taft decided to keep the board in place. Both men agreed that the department needed a counterweight to Wiley's purist extremes. And both men agreed to keep the Justice Department ruling secret—another decision that would later prove a very public embarrassment.

At the Agriculture Department, Dunlap and McCabe now routinely joined hands against Wiley on every decision. McCabe had announced a "three-month rule," stating that if cases were reported to the board more than three months after samples were collected, they would not be prosecuted. Wiley protested, pointing out that the Chemistry Bureau was understaffed and not always able to turn analyses around so quickly. "I consider there is neither justice nor reason in the three months rule," he wrote. "I have never consented to it nor was I consulted in its adoption." McCabe responded by requiring him to attach justification to every delayed analysis. The attorney continued to think Wiley far too quick to prosecute violations and too resistant to work with companies on solving problems. There was some merit in slowing things down, he thought, even though some wrongdoers might slip by along the way.

In June 1909 Wiley recommended that eight barrels from Ohio labeled "Sweet Catawba Wine" be seized and the company reprimanded. Departmental inspectors had discovered that the barrels contained not wine but an alcoholic liquid made from fermented corn sugars sweetened with saccharin. McCabe and Dunlap took the position that rather than fraudulent, the wine was merely poorly labeled. They blocked the seizure and scheduled a hearing with the manufacturer to work out a compromise. At least, Wiley suggested, the department might keep the mislabeled—and again, he would argue, fake—product out of the market until the situation was resolved. McCabe wrote back with undisguised hostility that he considered that a "ludicrous recommendation."

Many of their disagreements centered on defining the risk of a poorly studied compound. In a typical argument with Dunlap that July, Wiley recommended barring the compound sodium acetate—a salt of acetic acid used widely by the textile industry—from also being used as an additive in candy. He worried, he said, that sweets were largely eaten by children, one of the groups that most needed extra protection. A clause in the law forbade the addition of mineral substances to confectionary. Admitting it was a stretch, he argued that, as sodium was a mineral, the department could apply the law in a protective sense until more was known. Dunlap countered that the action would pose a troubling scientific precedent: "If sodium acetate is a mineral substance, so is cane sugar, for cane sugar is composed of over 40 percent carbon and no one could possibly deny the fact that carbon is mineral." True, Wiley admitted, but wasn't it worth risking interpretive overreach in the interest of protecting the most vulnerable consumers? "I have not time to go into all the reasons that would lead me to exclude sodium acetate from confectionary. The fact that confections are eaten especially by children and others whose digestive systems are not the strongest is a good and sufficient reason to me," wrote Wiley in a memo arguing his case. Dunlap again replied that he found that unconvincing and would not support enforcing the law in such an arbitrary way.

They also quarreled over whether the label "Norway Boneless Cod Strips" could be applied to cod from New England that still contained some of the smaller bones. "I do not know of but one meaning of the word 'Norway' and that is probably the signification of the word on this package," Wiley wrote. The three-man panel eventually decided to order that "Norway" be removed from the package but, in a two-to-one decision, allowed small bones to be considered acceptable in a "boneless" product.

In another dispute they differed over whether a cookie could be called an "arrowroot biscuit" when it contained only 15 percent arrowroot starch. Predictably, Wiley took the stance that a higher percentage was needed to justify the name; McCabe countered that if they were so literal in applying the law, it would become a joke. This kind of stance on arrowroot biscuits, he declared, "would lead to the proposition that one product of the baker's art, now styled 'Lady Finger,' is misbranded unless actually the result of mayhem.'"

The battle over sodium benzoate, meanwhile, had not abated. Frustrated with federal government inaction, the state of Indiana had independently banned the product's use in foods. In 1908, fearing that Indiana's action would trigger similar moves by health officials in other states, two large food processors, Curtice Brothers of Rochester, New York, and Williams Brothers of Detroit, filed suit, petitioning the U.S. District Court in Indianapolis to block the state law, describing it as economically crippling. The court issued a temporary injunction and scheduled a full hearing on the issue for the spring of 1909.

In anticipation of the hearing, the manufacturers quietly asked James Wilson for two favors. They wanted representatives from the Remsen Board to testify in their favor and they wanted Wiley and his loyal chemistry staff kept out of the courtroom. Wilson agreed to both requests, arranging to fund members of the Remsen Board to testify in Indiana, preparing to block any opposite viewpoints. When James Bingham, attorney general of Indiana, asked to have Wiley and some of his bureau staff testify in support of the state's case, Wilson refused permission. When Bingham protested, Wilson sought Taft's approval for the refusal, emphasizing that representatives of the Department of Agriculture should not so publicly take opposite sides in a lawsuit over preservatives. The president readily agreed and the secretary prepared to block all access to the recalcitrant chemists in his bureau.

Bingham, however, cabled the department that he now would get on a train and come to them for the depositions. Harvey Wiley agreed to give his statement, despite knowing that it was against department policy and that he would once again anger his boss by doing so. But others in the Agriculture Department declined, telling the Indiana attorney general they feared Wilson's retribution. Now genuinely angry, Bingham filed suit in the Supreme Court of the District of Columbia (what is now called the U.S. District Court for the District of Columbia). Naming Wilson and the department, the suit sought to compel the department's full testimony in the Indiana case. The federal court agreed with Indiana's attorney general that the Agriculture Department could not suppress expert testimony. Bingham gathered all his requested depositions and put Wilson into a legal bind, forcing the secretary, against his will, to send Wiley to testify in the state case.

But the standoff between the federal government's quarreling experts doomed the state law. The court ruled that without a consensus it could not find the preservative to be a health problem: "Ingredients and processes may be prohibited as unwholesome or causing deception but not merely because they preserve." Further, the justices had been impressed by the manufacturers' arguments that they were wholly dependent on chemical additives to stay in business: "While it may regulate," they said, "the legislature may not destroy an industry."

Paul Pierce's magazine—its name now changed from *What to Eat* to the more serious-sounding *National Food Magazine*—responded with renewed attacks on sodium benzoate. The issue featured a strong warning from William Williams Keen—a Philadelphia physician acclaimed as the country's first brain surgeon—on the risks of repeated low doses of chemical agents in food: "It must be evident that any drug used as a food preservative, eaten constantly, must affect the general health deleteriously and hence is most undesirable. . . . I have warned my grocer that I shall not accept such food for use and, if furnished me, I shall simply change my grocer."

The issue also featured a full-page ad from H.J. Heinz. Titled "A Health Problem That Confronts the Nation," it read in part: "Are you sure that your own state of health justifies you taking, for an indefinite period, drugged foods into your system? Are you willing to drug your family according to the prescription of any food manufacturer?

"Benzoate of soda is not necessary in any food. Every food product sold in a preserved state can be and is put up without it. Reputable manufacturers (and there are many) who do not use waste products of canneries, evaporating plants and other refuse raw materials and who do not permit untidiness and unsanitary practices about their factories find it unnecessary and do not use it. . . .

"Heinz 57 varieties are prepared from fresh, sound, wholesome fruits and vegetables; by neat uniformed work people; in model kitchens that are open to the public every day and visited annually by thousands from all parts of the world.

"Our products do not—and regardless of any legislative action or Government ruling—they will never contain Benzoate of Soda or any drug or chemical." The ad concluded by suggesting that despite the new law, consumers still needed to protect themselves by reading food labels carefully.

Wilson knew that Ladd, Shepard, and many of the other critics who had so savaged his reputation the previous summer in Michigan would have another opportunity that August as the Association of State and National Food Dairy Departments was scheduled to convene in Denver. Just weeks earlier, the secretary had authorized Agriculture Department agents to start seizing bleached flour shipments and publicly proclaimed his vigilance against dishonest manufacturing practices. "I am utterly hostile to having the people's foods tampered with," he told the *American Food Journal*. "We want to know that what we eat is the pure product."

More privately, Wilson acknowledged that his decision had been urged as a test case by department solicitor George McCabe, who believed the bleaching issue offered a chance to sharpen up some vague wording in the law. The law, as McCabe correctly pointed out, did not provide clear definitions for what constituted an injurious additive or adulteration. On that point he agreed with Wiley, who had long complained about the vague standards. The solicitor thought judicial clarification was needed to improve the situation. "This can come only from the courts," he wrote, "and there is not a single serious administrator connected with the law who does not join in the opinion that further progress must depend very largely on judicial rulings. If the bleached flour people bring their case to trial, they will do a valuable public service whether they win or lose."

Despite agreeing to seizures for legal purposes, Wilson appeared increasingly hostile to his department's role in tackling public health issues. He moved to block a bureau report on the chemical risks inherent in bleaching flour. He had also, not surprisingly, refused a provocative request from Wiley in June to reprint the report on benzoic acid and benzoates. He'd also shut down a series of other planned publications: on the use of the sugar alcohol glycerin in processing meat, on preventing spoilage of tomato ketchup, on pathogenic bacteria growing in frozen and dried eggs, and even an assessment of the arsenic content of confectioner's shellac, the glaze used on chocolate candies. He'd further blocked the release of a troubling report from Lyman Kebler, chief of the bureau's Drug Division, on the growing problem of medicated soft drinks.

Wilson also tried to prevent Wiley from taking his case to popular publications. "I regret that I shall have to withdraw my offer to write you an article which would be truthful, readable and useful on the subject of 'The Campaign for Pure Food, up to Date,'" wrote Wiley to an editor at *Century* magazine. "As I told you, I submitted your request to the Secretary of Agriculture and he informed me that if I would write an article which he would approve I could publish it. The Secretary and I are so diametrically opposed in our view in regard to this matter that I am convinced it would be useless for me to try to secure his approval to any article which in my opinion would do anything like justice to the subject. . . . I reluctantly ask you to cancel the engagement."

When the Association of State and National Food Dairy Departments convened in Denver that summer, little of the previous year's bitterness from the Mackinac Island convention had faded. "James Wilson, secretary of agriculture, and Dr. H.W. Wiley, chief chemist of the department, have come to the parting of the ways on the subject of food," reported the *Chicago Tribune* in a story predicting a "battle royal" over preservatives, especially sodium benzoate. Wilson brought the entire Remsen Board with him to Denver, paying for their rooms at the city's Brown Palace Hotel, convention headquarters. Despite the luxurious setting, Ira Remsen would later describe the conference as "a bear pit." He found himself repeatedly defending the board against charges that it favored industry at the cost of public health and safety. The secretary had prepared an aggressive strategy. He demanded that a scheduled vote on the sodium benzoate question be decided on an open ballot. Then he privately assured attendees that the Department of Agriculture would withdraw funding to all those who voted against him.

Food commissioners from Pennsylvania and Michigan, both sodium benzoate critics, protested Wilson's heavy-handed approach by angrily walking out of the meeting. The walkout backfired, as the final tally—absent those votes and the influence of the two protesting officials—went narrowly in support of both the Remsen Board and its finding that sodium benzoate was a fully safe additive. An editorial in the *Los Angeles Herald* decried Wilson's tactic and its result: "As the inside facts concerning the Denver convention become more generally known it is revealed as one where the artifices of the politicians were considerably more in evidence than the sober thought of the expert charged with protecting the public health."

But Wilson was wholly satisfied. He wrote to President Taft that "we fully smashed the program, turned things end for end, fully endorsed the Referee Board and its findings." Wiley, Wilson added, was a troublesome "low class fellow" but he believed that the Denver vote had sent the chief chemist a warning to Wiley that his policy of defiance would not be tolerated much longer.

B etween his fight to maintain some level of toxicity research and his battles for enforcement and public awareness, Wiley's staff worried that their chief was beginning to sound exhausted. They were also angry over Wilson's dismissal of their own work and increasingly willing to push back. One of the most determined to do so was Lyman Kebler, still steaming over the suppression of his investigation of medicated soft drinks.

Kebler had left a lucrative job at Smith, Kline, French & Co. in Philadelphia for the Department of Agriculture, because he believed that it was critical to establish honest practices for pharmaceutical products. Now forty-three, he led the Chemistry Bureau's oversight of the drug industry and had earned a reputation as meticulous and, on occasion, ruthless. The *Bulletin of Pharmacy*, while not entirely an enthusiast, had described Kebler, with some respect, as the country's most eminent "foe to fakers."

Kebler, with Wiley's backing, decided to counter Wilson's suppression of his report with an even more in-depth investigation. To do so, he reviewed more than one hundred brands of medicated soft drinks and bottled waters on the market. The manufacturers ranged from small companies such as New Hampshire's Londonderry Lithia, which made a drink rich in the element lithium, to large ones, such as the Atlanta-based Coca-Cola Company, which had famously made its fortune through a nineteenth-century formula that had included the potent stimulant cocaine. By withholding his report, Kebler told Wiley, the department was hiding both knowledge and risk from American consumers. He knew Wiley was under constant attack; he knew that Wilson had very little patience with the bureau. He also knew that his planned publication had a very provocative title: "Habit-Forming Agents: Their Indiscriminate Sale and Use a Menace to Public Welfare." But, he added, that title realistically summed up a national problem.

The indiscriminate use of narcotics remained an enormous risk to public health, Kebler pointed out. Many "soothing syrups" for children were laced with morphine, heroin, and chloral hydrate, among other sedatives; cough syrups and asthma medications for adults could contain a mixture of several of these narcotics. Further,

Kebler considered the problem of medicated soft drinks particularly troubling because consumers often had no idea that the sodas contained stimulants and/or intoxicating agents. Doctors reported cases of soft-drink addiction, and insurance companies, he said, were trying to develop a plan to deal with "soft drink habituees [sic]." Wiley agreed to make the case to Wilson yet again. But, he told Kebler ruefully, he could make no promises that his argument would work.

The yet-to-be published "Habit-Forming Agents" offered a damning review of the unrestricted use of narcotics in over-the-counter remedies. It was equally unsparing on the subject of counter drinks: "During the last 20 years, a large number of soft drinks containing caffeine and smaller or greater amounts of coca leaf and kola nut products have been placed on the market. Preparations of this class, on account of insufficient information, were formerly looked upon as harmless, but they are now known to be an impending evil." Kebler had drawn up a list of the worst offenders, many of which were named to hint at their stimulant content: Mello-Nip, Dobe, Kola-Kok, Pillsbury's Koke, Kola-Ade, Kos Kola, Café-Coca, and Koke. As a further example, the department had ordered the seizure of two products from the American Beverage Corporation: Great American Coca Cream and Great American Pepsette. An analysis found that Coca Cream contained saccharin, benzoic acid, cocaine, and caffeine; and Pepsette, which advertised itself as a pepsin-based, fruit-flavored soft drink, contained no pepsin at all but plenty of cocaine.

It was one thing for the department to find fault with any of those companies—most of them serving limited regional markets—and even to take enforcement action against one or a few. It was quite another to take on Atlanta-based Coca-Cola. The *National Druggist* estimated that the company sold more than ten million gallons of Coca-Cola to American soda fountains alone, "representing 300,000,000 glasses" consumed annually. This combination of money and influence played a role in the careful approach of James

Wilson toward the company; he was especially wary of provoking the company's influential and combative president, Asa Candler.

The Georgia tycoon had publicly supported the 1906 food and drug law, emphasizing the "pure and wholesome" nature of Coca-Cola. And after the law passed, Candler's company also stopped secretly sweetening the beverage with cheap saccharin and returned to the old sugar formula. To Candler's unhappy surprise—expressed loudly to Wilson and others—those measures had not led to a perfectly harmonious relationship with government regulators.

The U.S. Army in 1907 dropped Coca-Cola from its list of approved beverages, responding to rumors that the drink contained a possibly intoxicating level of alcohol. Arguing its innocence, the company requested an analysis by the Bureau of Chemistry to prove such suspicions wrong. The results convinced the army to take Coca-Cola back: Wiley's chemists found only a trace amount of alcohol residue from the oils and extracts used in the soda, nothing even close to a level that could cause intoxication. The bureau analysis also confirmed that the soft drink was cocaine free. The only notable stimulant in Coca-Cola was caffeine. A glass of the soft drink, served at a soda fountain, contained slightly more than half the amount of caffeine in a cup of coffee and close to twice that in an average cup of tea. Candler assumed these findings were as reassuring to the Agriculture Department as to the Department of War. But as would gradually become clear, the tests raised other issues to trouble Wiley and Kebler.

Wiley, who, as his colleagues often complained, was given to literal-mindedness about labels, thought the word "coca" implied to consumers the existence of that ingredient; some of the labels even depicted the fruit of a coca plant. Kebler was more bothered by the caffeine levels. This was a drink marketed directly to children, without any disclosure of the stimulant involved, and he took that worry to the chief chemist and again asked his aid in raising the issue with the secretary of agriculture. "I am not a believer in the promiscuous

use of caffeine," wrote Wiley to Wilson in a memo detailing his concerns about "so-called soft drinks." As always, the chief chemist had
a list of other concerns, such as the artificial flavoring (industrial
citric acid instead of real lemon juice, pepper dust instead of ginger),
coal-tar dyes, and cheap saccharin as an unlabeled sugar substitute.
These methods were "highly objectionable both on ethical grounds
and because of their possible injury to health." But he'd come to
agree with Kebler that the unlabeled caffeine issue should be addressed first.

They got support from an unexpected quarter. George McCabe
thought Coca-Cola might offer a test case on the unlimited use of
stimulants in products sold to children and urged Wilson to at least
consider the idea. Meanwhile, Wiley continued to urge the secretary
to act: "Coca-Cola is one of the most widely sold beverages in the
country. Its use is to a certain extent habit-forming and great injury
may come to health by the continued and excessive use of an alkaloid
of this kind." In his memo to Wilson, Wiley emphasized that he
wasn't deliberately singling out the soft-drink industry; it was a
healthy alternative to alcohol for adult drinkers, and "there is much
to be said good about it and little bad," he wrote. But publicly, the
chief chemist was starting to take a harder stance.

In a spring 1909 speech at the Holy Cross Academy in Washington, DC, Wiley warned the students: "If you only knew what I know
about these soft drinks you would abstain from them," he said. "It
would surprise you that most of them have more caffeine in them
than coffee—and a drug even more deadly." After newspaper accounts of the talk provoked angry complaints from the American
Bottlers Association, he clarified that, emphasizing that caffeine was
his major concern. "What I did say to the young girls at that academy is that parents often forbid their children to drink coffee or tea
and yet they could get caffeine, the most injurious part of those
drinks, at the soda fountain."

What he didn't mention was that, following the Coca-Cola

analysis, he'd sent Lyman Kebler down south to take a closer look at both the company and the culture surrounding soft-drink consumption. Kebler had combined a visit to the company headquarters and production facilities with some time spent lurking at Atlanta soda fountains. He was dismayed to observe children as young as four years old drinking glasses of stimulant-rich Coca-Cola. It was this report, in part, that had led Wiley to urge a legal test case, arguing that caffeine was an unlabeled additive that posed a genuine health risk to children.

Wilson, still annoyed, sent Wiley a memo ordering him to drop the subject—and again refused to publish Kebler's report. Wiley had no evidence that the Coca-Cola Company had helped influence the decision, but he thought it highly likely. "I was, of course, surprised and grieved at this action on the part of Mr. Wilson, but as usual I could see behind it the manipulation of powerful hands." He suspected that an action against Coca-Cola was never going to happen. And then a visit from a muckraking Atlanta journalist changed that prediction.

In October 1909 Wiley sat down for an unexpectedly hostile interview with Fred L. Seely, editor of the reform-minded newspaper the *Atlanta Georgian*. Seely was a longtime critic of the Coca-Cola Company's indifference to others and he saw the federal government as complicit in the company's bad behavior. He demanded to know why the Agriculture Department had never gone after Coca-Cola for the health issues linked to consumption of its product. Wiley responded defensively that he had in fact recommended that the company be prosecuted. His chemists had even done research suggesting that the soft drink might be both "habit-forming and nerve-racking." He then showed the journalist a handful of the memos he'd written to Wilson on the subject—all of which had been rebuffed.

There was, for instance, the memo telling the secretary that "this product contains an added ingredient [caffeine] which may render the product injurious to health." There was also one regarding false labeling, noting that "the name Coca-Cola would indicate that it contained the substances and active principals of the coca leaf and the kola nut, when as a matter of fact it contains only an extract derived from exhausted coca leaves, which is a refuse product obtained in the manufacture of cocaine." There was another memo urging that "an effort should be made to stop the traffic in a dangerous beverage."

In that last note, Wiley had written to his boss that Coca-Cola "contains an alkaloidal, habit-forming drug of a character which is forbidden to be used by hundreds of thousands of parents in this country who refuse to allow their children to drink either tea or coffee, which contain caffeine in its natural state and in a much less injurious form than this misbranded and adulterated beverage. Our duty is clearly in this case to protect the people of our country in every possible way."

Seely studied the memos that Wiley brandished at him. Then, newly outraged, he marched over to Wilson's office and demanded a meeting on the spot. When it was granted, he told Wilson that he planned to write a story about the department's refusal to protect consumers from a dangerous product. He would feature the secretary's order telling Wiley to leave Coca-Cola alone. He planned to make an example of Wilson as government corruption at its worst. The following day, Wilson called Wiley into his office and told him that it was time to make a formal seizure of Coca-Cola products. "It is remarkable," Wiley noted sarcastically, "what the fear of publicity will do!" The secretary also told Wiley that he would schedule Kebler's medicated-soft-drink report for the following spring.

On October 21, 1909, two weeks after Seely's visit, the U.S. government moved to seize a shipment of Coca-Cola syrup bound for the company's bottling plant in Chattanooga, Tennessee. The action meant that the government would need to schedule a formal court hearing into the company's famous and lucrative product. A date had not yet been set for the hearing, but the legal action was already gaining attention based on its title alone: *United States v. Forty Barrels and Twenty Kegs of Coca-Cola.*

Toward the end of 1909, rumors began circulating that Taft was preparing to announce his whiskey decision. The rumors also predicted which side the president would take. Newspapers began writing mockingly about the new "Taft Whisky," which would be "neutral spirits made from molasses and beet refuse."

On December 26 the president announced his decision, officially changing the Roosevelt rules and establishing final definitions. The president ruled that the term "whiskey" could and should be used for any and all liquors made from grain alcohol. The government would require some "subordinate" description—whether the product was blended and a list of ingredients, such as coloring agents or neutral spirits. But there would be no requirement to label a quick-stilled and well-dyed product as imitation and there would be no describing barrel-aged whiskeys as the only real thing. Taft said that he agreed with the wholesale group that all alcohols were basically "like" substances. Or as economics professor Henry Parker Willis put it, "Whiskey appears to be virtually anything that will serve to intoxicate."

Lloyd Bowers, the solicitor general who had issued the more nuanced decision earlier in the year, called Wiley the next morning. As Wiley described the conversation, Bowers, who was an old friend of the president, said that he was about to depart on a much-needed vacation. But before he left he wondered, "What do you think of Mr. Taft's decision?" Wiley replied ruefully that he felt as if he'd been spanked. "He laughed and said so do I."

Not everyone took Taft's decision with such grace. In January 1910 Arthur Stanley, head of the Louisville-based Glenmore Distillery, wrote to Wiley that he thought the president was mostly a very good friend to Joe Cannon and his Peoria rectifiers: "What I fear is that wine distillers of Illinois will be allowed to brand their output as whisky, it will then be shipped to the rectifiers and mixed with real whisky and then called a 'Whisky Blend.'" It was a terrible precedent for those who cared about honest labeling, Stanley said bitterly, and had the potential of "virtually nullifying the Pure Food Law."

Alice Lakey felt the same. Her organization, the National Consumers League, issued a formal resolution to that effect: President Taft's statement "that neutral spirits, which the most eminent food chemists have declared an unlike substance to whisky, may be added to whisky and the whole product colored with burnt sugar or caramel without stating the latter fact on the label, etc. is destined to open the door for the return of all the evils of adulterated foods, drugs, liquors and medicines that have for a time been held in check by the operation of the pure food law. . . . We the executive board protest against this action and urge state officials to stand up."

Lakey also wrote to magazines and newspapers: "We believe that Mr. Taft's decision is the most serious blow to the pure food legislation this country has had. We believe that it is class legislation. We believe it permits special rulings for one product coming under the pure food law which was designed to make uniform regulations specific. . . . If this decision holds, it opens the door for every other product to demand the same 'immunity bath.' . . . If we follow this reasoning when, then, should blackberry brandy contain any blackberry juice? . . . This decision robs the consumer and the honest manufacturer of the protection designed by the pure food law."

To Wiley she wrote privately that she doubted the decision could be changed: "It is a very strong illustration of how clever the rectifiers are." But Wiley, increasingly besieged at the Department of Agriculture, put most of the blame on Wilson, who he suspected had quietly moved to undermine the law. In a letter to Lakey, he wrote, "There is but little we can do as long as the present Secretary of Agriculture is in the saddle."

Thirteen

THE LOVE MICROBE

1910–1911

———————◦———————

Till you think of the past and the future and sigh

Wiley wasn't prepared to give up. As Wilson knew all too well, his chief chemist never was. With the idea of pressing his beleaguered cause outside the department, by the start of 1910, Wiley had lined up months' worth of public talks.

In January he had promised to talk to the Men's Club of Newark, New Jersey, on the "morality of business"; to testify about aluminum levels in baking powder at a state trial in Harrisburg, Pennsylvania; to talk about food additives to the Montgomery County Medical Society and the Medical Society of New York. In February, the Harvard Club in Philadelphia; in March, the New York State Department of Health; in May, the Historical and Art Society; in July, the United States Pharmaceutical Convention in Washington, DC, and the National Dental Association in Denver. He'd also tentatively accepted engagements in Oklahoma City; Des Moines; Lawrence, Massachusetts; and Brooklyn, Newburgh, and Buffalo, New York.

In March, at Lakey's urging, Wiley agreed to add a trip to Cincinnati for a presentation at the national convention of the General

Federation of Women's Clubs. More than ever he recognized how important politically motivated women were to the pure-food cause. The same month, he accepted an invitation to speak to a women's suffrage club in Washington, DC. Although that decision was perhaps less political. The invitation came from Anna Kelton.

Kelton, now thirty-two years old, was still single and living at home, still working as a clerk at the Library of Congress. Still elegant, intelligent, well read, still a deep supporter of progressive change, she was also, these days, a passionate advocate for equality. She'd joined the National American Woman Suffrage Association (NAWSA) to help in the drawn-out, frustrating fight for women's right to vote. The association worked closely with other women's organizations, from the WCTU, which now had a ratification committee, to the General Federated Women's Clubs. And like them, the suffragettes had begun to take on consumer issues such as the struggling food and drug law. That interest encouraged Anna Kelton—Nan to her friends—to draw on an old relationship and invite Wiley to speak to her group about the importance of the national food law. He was happy to say yes—and just as happy that she still embodied the kind of crusading zeal that had always appealed to him.

I n May 1910 Wilson issued a formal directive (General Order 140) giving George McCabe full authority over the regulation of food and drugs, including the ability to revoke earlier decisions by the Bureau of Chemistry.

Wiley, now perpetually on edge, told his friends that he feared that with this new power McCabe would enact further rollbacks on the regulation of preservatives. But the attorney surprised him by tackling a different contentious issue. Responding to industry complaints, McCabe moved to loosen restrictions on food dyes, one of the more successful enforcement actions taken after the passage of the 1906 law.

Before the law, even food manufacturers had become alarmed about the toxic nature of industrial coloring agents. Some still used the old-time vegetable-based dyes, such as saffron or annatto for yellow. But those dyes were both comparatively expensive and muted in tone. They did not offer the eye-popping yellows, reds, and greens that could be achieved by using metallic elements such as arsenic, mercury, lead, and copper. Yet thanks to a combination of toxicology studies and occasional poisoning episodes, such metallic additives were increasingly regarded as more trouble than they were worth. The National Confectioners Association had recommended back in 1899 that to avoid injuring customers, members voluntarily avoid almost two dozen coloring agents in their candy and other sweets.

New options arose with synthetic dyes made from coal tars—dense, chemically complex residues left over from the processing of coal. These compounds dated back to work by the English chemist Sir William Henry Perkin, a student of August Wilhelm von Hofmann, who pioneered analysis of coal tars and whose lectures Wiley had attended on his 1878 sabbatical in Germany.

Some decades earlier, in 1856, Perkin had used the coal-tar derivative benzene to create a purple dye that he called "mauvine" (a name later shortened to "mauve"). Benzene, a neatly linked ring of carbon and hydrogen atoms, also proved a handy base for other synthetic dyes, offering up a vivid chemical rainbow. The new dyes were durable, cheap, and potent—and rapidly adopted by industrial processors of everything from fabric to food. Chemists called them "aniline" dyes but they were widely known by a more direct description as coal-tar dyes. By the time the food and drug law passed, more than eighty such coloring agents were being used in American food and drink, without any safety review or restriction.

After passage of the 1906 law, the USDA had quickly banned food dyes based on lead, mercury, arsenic, and other toxic metals. And Wiley had hired an outside expert, a respected German food dye chemist named Bernhard Hesse, to evaluate the safety of the coal-tar dyes. Hesse's research led him to conclude that only seven of eighty such dyes on the market could fully be considered safe. A resulting 1907 Food Inspection Decision approved only those seven—three red, one orange, one yellow, one green, and one blue—as "certified colors." Predictably, makers of colorful foodstuffs sought to lengthen that list. But Hesse had stockpiled an arsenal of evidence showing that many of these other dyes could be directly linked to health problems. Wiley had firmly kept the list short, moving to block any coloring agents that weren't clearly identified as safe.

Newly employed by James Wilson in 1910 to guide the law's enforcement, McCabe decided to review Wiley's consumer-friendly decision. Deliberately splitting legal hairs, he wrote that "certification" was not a strictly approved process under the food and drug law. The legislation provided a framework for banning food products and additives considered injurious, but not for official sanction of others as safe.

Wiley pointed out in return that prior certification was less punitive to manufacturers than after-the-fact seizure and prosecution—something that he thought McCabe should find appealing. Further, the process had removed some very risky products from the food supply. He warned that weakening the certification provisions would allow unsafe dyes back onto the market. McCabe, unmoved, joined with Dunlap on the three-member Food Inspection Board to remove the certification requirement from the rules governing dyes. Wiley refused to sign the paperwork. The department issued the decision without his signature but the chief chemist decided to fight that move. He asked Hesse to prepare for Secretary Wilson a full report on the safety of coal-tar dyes. Perhaps the actual evidence would prove persuasive.

W hile Hesse worked on the new report, McCabe moved ahead with his legal test of bleached flour. He had a major enforcement question that needed clarifying. The nitrates that occurred as a result of bleaching were but by-products of processing. Did the government have the authority to regulate by-products as well as additives? It was an issue that needed a quick resolution. The Agriculture Department had that spring seized 625 sacks of bleached flour en route from the Lexington Mills and Elevator Company of Lexington, Nebraska, to a large grocery company in Missouri. The National Millers Association—also seeking a test case—decided to fight the seizure in the U.S. District Court in Missouri.

In court, the millers' group argued that bleaching did not degrade flour; rather it enhanced it. Thus the practice rose above the standard of adulteration under the law. The manufacturers further asserted that residual nitrates and nitrogen peroxide were not unsafe or injurious industrial additives but products of nature, created by a whitening process that used such harmless methods as electricity and naturally occurring gases, "a blast of God's own pure fresh air." Bruce Elliott, the attorney representing the millers, pointed out in court that nitrates occurred in nature, including in the human body. Even if they carried some hazard, he continued, the average American undoubtedly had a natural tolerance for them.

The Agriculture Department's experts countered with evidence that bleached baked goods contained an unnaturally high nitrate level. In a courtroom demonstration, a bureau chemist brought in two batches of biscuits, one made with unbleached flour and the other with some of the seized bleached flour. Both had been treated with a compound that turned red when exposed to nitrates. He offered to the jury a choice between a plate of golden brown biscuits and a plate of bright pink ones.

The defense did not deny that the bleached-flour biscuits

contained nitrates, enough to produce a rosy color in the chemical test. But, changing tactics, the millers' attorneys argued that even if nitrates were indeed injurious to health no safe level had been established scientifically. Therefore, it was impossible to argue how much was too much. The government's insistence on a low and "harmless" level of the compounds could then not be based on solid evidence and ought not to be admitted. The Missouri judge found that final assertion completely reasonable.

As he told the jury, "The fact that poisonous substances are to be found in the bodies of human beings, in the air, in potable water . . . does not justify the addition of the same or other poisonous substances to articles of food, such as flour, because the statute condemns the adding of poisonous substances." But it was the character of the additive, not the amount, that should guide the rules, the judge said, and if nitrates had no clearly defined toxicity levels, then they did not meet the law's definition of a poisonous substance. The jury, composed of bread-eating citizens clearly unhappy about the addition of nitrates to their daily meals, did not embrace such over-legal reasoning. As their verdict made clear, they wanted their food to be safe before all. The jurors found for the government, rejecting the judge's advice, firmly declaring that the bleached flour was both adulterated and misbranded and had been seized legally.

On behalf of his shocked clients, Elliott responded— embarrassingly for the White House—by complaining to newspaper reporters that he'd been promised better results. In fact, he had personally met with President Taft and been assured of a fair trial, which he took to mean a decision in his favor. He added that he had also met with Wilson and been assured that the flour studies would be taken away from Wiley and turned over to the far more sympathetic Remsen Board. In his opinion, the case was evidence of the unreliable nature of administration officials, not to mention government failure to support good American businessmen. He made it clear that he and his clients would appeal the decision and were prepared to fight for years if necessary. This government overreach would never stand, Elliott declared, and he predicted that the U.S. Supreme Court would agree.

Bernhard Hesse's eighty-page report, *Coal-Tar Colors Used in Food*, described experiments in which he had supplied colored food and water to test subjects—dogs and rabbits—over periods of not less than thirty days. The dosage of the dyes was calculated to be comparable to a possible high end of human exposure in a daily diet. The resulting health effects on the animals included weakness, nausea, vomiting, irritation of the intestinal tract, damage to the mucous membranes, fatty degeneration of the liver, swelling and discoloration of the kidneys, and, on occasion, evidence of dyes in the brain or the lining of the lungs.

The most common effect seemed to be a lingering stupor, sometimes followed by a gradual slide into a coma and on rare occasions the death of the test animal. He also noted minor side effects such as mild diarrhea and low levels of albuminuria, or protein in the urine, a symptom of kidney disease.

"It must be remembered," Hesse noted, "that smaller amounts of drugs, and therefore coal-tar colors, affect children as a rule than are effective upon adults." He suggested that a three-year-old child's dose should be about one-fifth that of an adult's—a twelve-year-old should receive no more than half. "All of this should be taken into account in drawing conclusions as to the harmfulness of coal-tar dyes on humans." As a large variety of dyed foods—candies, decorated cakes and pastries, soft drinks—were marketed largely to children, he worried that animal research–based "deductions" about the risks to adults might well underestimate the problem. To the surprise of some in the department, Hesse's thorough job, impassive and scientific, won over Secretary Wilson. The certification program, he announced, would remain in place—a decision that allowed Wiley a moment to savor an increasingly rare victory.

B y 1910 Wiley had been at the USDA for twenty-seven years. There'd been tumult and struggle at the department, but he had prospered personally. He had good friends in Washington and across the country. After twenty years rooming with a Washington family, he had acquired his own house, a three-story brownstone, just a short walk from Dupont Circle in northwest Washington. He turned sixty-six that year and had confided in letters and in his daily journal that he had considered retiring—especially after recent professional setbacks—and he'd bought himself a modest country place in anticipation, a farm in Loudoun County, Virginia, in the eastern lee of the Blue Ridge Mountains. Admiring its rolling meadows, he'd named it Grasslands. He'd even purchased a newfangled steam-powered automobile, among the first in Washington, with the idea of driving himself out to his country property. The car, however, had been almost immediately damaged in a collision with a horse-drawn wagon, an incident that Wiley would describe, with some amusement, as a collision between past and future.

The accident would also return him, while repairs were under way, to traveling by public transportation. In late October 1910, Wiley was waiting for a streetcar when he found himself standing near Nan Kelton. She appeared genuinely glad to see him again. Before they parted, he impulsively asked her if he could come call, perhaps take her to a show or out to dinner. To his surprise and happiness— confided to his journal—she said yes. Over the next month, he embarked on a renewed courtship. They quickly rekindled their relationship, and in the first week of December Wiley again proposed. This time she accepted without reservation. The engagement announcement was received with pleasure—and amusement—by the nation's newspapers.

DR. WILEY WILL TAKE A BRIDE, began a headline in the *Chicago Tribune*. PURE FOOD EXPERT TO DESERT CAFES FOR HOME COOKED MEALS. The paper added a cheerful subhead: "Fiancée Not Terrified." As the story that followed put it: "Dr. Harvey Washington Wiley, pure food expert and rampant foe of the near-lamb chop and almost-chocolate drop, conserver of the national digestion and chief exponent of the we-must-have-pure-food-to-be-happy cult, is getting married."

The *Los Angeles Examiner* headlined its story GREATEST ENEMY OF FOOD GERMS FALLS VICTIM OF LOVE MICROBE. The writer speculated that the wedding cake "will have no old eggs, no alum, no clay-clad eggs or near-butter. Nothing but the purest of flour and baking powder and dairy out put [sic] will be used." The *Denver Post* printed a cartoon showing a fainting Kelton being carried away as her relentless husband searched the kitchen for chicory in coffee and preservatives in jam.

Kelton, swamped by interview requests, took the attention in stride. She used the opportunity to advocate for women's right to vote. A newspaper in Bangor, Maine, headlined its resulting story WILEY TO WED SUFFRAGETTE. She cheerfully told the *Boston Journal* that she didn't know how to cook. "I have been in the Congressional Library almost since I left college so I have had little time for domestic science." Fortunately, she added, her husband-to-be happened to be an excellent chef. That made Wiley laugh. He appreciated the story, which described her as a woman who "admires and takes pride in her fiancé and doesn't hesitate to say so."

At work he was so visibly happy that Wilson permitted himself to hope that his obsessive chief chemist would finally have another interest besides pure food. "There is a shade of hope for Wiley's future," the secretary wrote to Ira Remsen. "He is going to marry a suffragette, I believe, which may result in a change for the better; at least in these Christmas holidays, let us hope so."

After the passage of the 1906 law and his savage evaluation of its shortcomings, David Graham Phillips, the journalist whose work had so enraged President Roosevelt, had been undaunted by presidential insults. He saw nothing wrong with being described as a "muckraker." Phillips had continued to expose backroom deals between federal lawmakers, state legislatures, and the corporate interests—including food processors and their ilk—to whom so many officeholders were in deep financial debt. His articles detailing those well-financed connections would eventually help spur passage of the Seventeenth Amendment to the U.S. Constitution. That amendment threw out the old and increasingly corrupt system in which state legislators chose the U.S. senators to represent their respective states, and put in place public elections. The reform would not happen, though, until 1913, and Phillips would not live to see it.

After completing the last of his exposés of senatorial corruption, Phillips decided to take a break from muckraking and return to the relative tranquility of writing fiction. The choice, ironically, proved more dangerous than investigative journalism. Fitzhugh Coyle Goldsborough, a well-born member of a Baltimore family, who apparently suffered from mental illness, arrived at the deluded notion that a character in Phillips's novel *The Fashionable Adventures of Joshua Craig* was based on Goldsborough's sister. He confronted the author in front of the Princeton Club in New York, shot him multiple times, and then fatally shot himself. Taken to Bellevue Hospital, Phillips, just forty-four years old, died the next day, January 24, 1911. It marked an unhappy start to a year that would become one of the most stressful in Wiley's career.

Barely two months later, in Tennessee, the matter of *United States v. Forty Barrels and Twenty Kegs of Coca-Cola* at last went to trial. Wiley, McCabe, Wilson, and the whole Bureau of Chemistry had been conferring for months on how to approach the lawsuit. The government's case rested on three main points. First, it objected to what it described as the company's shoddy manufacturing processes. Second, on Wiley's recommendation, it challenged the very name "Coca-Cola" as false advertising because it implied that the drink contained both cocaine and kola (or bissy) nut extracts in its formula. This had been true in the nineteenth century but was no longer so; the Chemistry Bureau's latest analysis of the drink showed that its primary ingredients were water, sugar, phosphoric acid, caffeine, caramel, glycerin, and lime juice.

The government's third point—and this would become the primary focus of the trial—was that the drink did, however, contain another potent stimulant, namely caffeine. This charge immediately caught the attention of a dedicated nation of coffee drinkers as well as soft-drink imbibers. The Coca-Cola trial was going to put caffeine—and early-twentieth-century scientific understanding of its effects—at center stage. Not surprisingly, reporters flocked to Chattanooga for the show.

Newspaper coverage was constant and varied widely according to the editors' perspectives. EIGHT COCA-COLAS CONTAIN ENOUGH CAFFEINE TO KILL, the *Atlanta Georgian* announced based on testimony in the trial's first week, continuing its ongoing crusade against Asa Candler and his company. COCA-COLA DRINKERS SAY IT IS NOT BAD, the *Chattanooga News* countered. Wiley hadn't wanted the trial to be held in that southern city, where a large Coca-Cola bottling plant was one of the city's main employers. He had urged McCabe to get a change of venue to Washington, DC. But McCabe refused, fueling conspiracy theories among Wiley's allies that the solicitor—and the agriculture secretary—wanted the case to fail as a means of further crippling the influence of the chief chemist.

McCabe began the prosecution by calling J. L. Lynch, an Agriculture Department food and drug inspector. Lynch promptly provided a detailed and alarming portrait of Coca-Cola production methods. Describing the way the syrup soft-drink base was made, he said: "The Negro cook engaged in dumping the ingredients in the kettle was scantily attired in a dirty undershirt, old dirty trousers and broken shoes. His bare feet were protruding from his shoes in places and he was perspiring freely. He was chewing tobacco and spitting from time to time, the expectorate falling on the floor and on the platform from which he was dumping the sugar." Excess sugar also fell onto the platform, and the cook would shove it into the kettle with either a board or his feet, Lynch said. The caramel coloring was added on another floor of the building, he continued, and that level was so slimy with tobacco spit and other substances—"it had apparently never been scrubbed"—that the inspector declared that he'd been afraid of slipping and falling.

After Lynch came two scientists—H. C. Fuller, a pharmaceutical industry chemist, and W. O. Emory of the Bureau of Chemistry—who had independently analyzed the syrup. Both verified it no longer contained either coca leaf or kola nut extracts—although pictures of the plant leaves still decorated Coca-Cola barrels. Both verified that the primary stimulant now found in the drink was caffeine. They also noted some other unexpected ingredients—such as dirt, straw, and insect parts.

The government's main expert on caffeine was Henry Hurd Rusby, professor of botany and *materia medica* at Columbia University's College of Pharmacy and a longtime editor for *U.S. Pharmacopeia*, the publication that set uniform standards for pharmaceutical compounds. Rusby—fifty-six, slight, fair haired, brisk of manner—was a former physician who had developed a passionate interest in medicinal botany. Among other research projects, he'd spent more than a year in South America researching the plant sources of cocaine and caffeine. He was relieved to find the former missing from Coca-Cola but testified that caffeine was "apt to be deleterious to human health."

Given the quantity of caffeine in the soft drink, as described by Fuller and Emory, Rusby testified, if the "product known as Coca-Cola were taken into the system in repeated doses it would be injurious." Some twenty other government witnesses supporting Rusby's claim were also part of McCabe's expert list, a roster that showed he intended to win, despite rumors to the contrary. Expert after expert spoke of the risks involved in continually consuming the alkaloid, some telling the jurors about animal studies with alarming outcomes.

USDA chemist F. P. Morgan had found that a regular dose of Coca-Cola appeared to cause inflammation and lesions in the stomachs of rabbits. Boston-based toxicologist William Boos of Massachusetts General Hospital had looked at caffeine's effect on frogs, finding that it interfered with heart rate and affected the nervous system and caused "reflex irritability." The jurors also heard about unsettling effects on humans. "I consider caffeine a habit-forming drug," said Dr. John Musser of the University of Pennsylvania. His patients who drank caffeinated beverages rarely consumed a single glass or cup: "Once taken, there is a desire or craving of the system to repeat the dose." Dr. Oliver Osborne of Yale Medical School testified that several glasses of Coca-Cola a day registered above the recommended dose for caffeine set by *U.S. Pharmacopeia*. Dr. Maurice Tyrode of Harvard University testified that eight glasses of Coca-Cola contained so much caffeine that their rapid consumption was potentially fatal.

The court also heard from "Coca-Cola addicts." A patient from Philadelphia reported that he had found the soft drink a helpful stimulant—at first. "When I felt tired or fagged a glass or two of Coca-Cola would revive me. As the habit increased, I consumed about a dozen drinks a day." He sought treatment after developing insomnia and a state of constant jitters: "After I quit using Coca-Cola my general health improved and has continued to improve."

Lyman Kebler represented the Bureau of Chemistry position. "I have traveled extensively in the United States and have observed that Coca-Cola is sold indiscriminately to all comers at soda fountains, without distinction as to youth or old age, nervous or robust persons. I have seen children as young as four years old drinking Coca-Cola at fountains," Kebler said. Both as a scientist and a family man, he found this irresponsible and dangerous. He'd accompanied Fuller on the tour of the Coca-Cola plant, where he'd also been appalled by the filthy conditions; he'd been particularly struck by the spiderwebs' dangling over the vats and the workers dripping sweat all over the floors and spitting tobacco juice everywhere: "I saw no cuspidors." But Kebler had also noticed the two-hundred-pound containers of caffeine, in crystalline form, sitting alongside the cooking vats.

Like everything else in the plant, Kebler testified, the caffeine had appeared somewhat grimy. It was "not as white as the ordinary article." There was a reason, Kebler continued, that Coca-Cola had two popular nicknames. One was "dope" and the other was "Coke," and both referred, he said, to its well-known stimulant effects. That had been true when it contained cocaine and it was true now. "Caffeine is a drug having poisonous tendency," Kebler said.

Coca-Cola was angrily prepared to counter these accusations. Its defense began with testimony from two members of the company's founding family. First, John S. Candler, who had partnered with his brother, Asa, and other investors in forming the soft-drink company in 1892, declared that he consumed at least one glass of Coca-Cola a day—and sometimes six or more—but did not consider that evidence of addiction. He just liked it. "I have never experienced any inordinate craving for it or observed any tendency to form a habit." In other words, he stated, "My health is good."

Asa Candler's oldest son, Charles Howard Candler, who was vice president and general manager of the company, directly contradicted the government's accusations of cheapjack production standards. "About eight men, three white and five colored, are employed in making the Coca-Cola syrup," he said. "The sugar is dumped into the kettle by a Negro who has been employed since 1906. He does not chew tobacco." And that cook wore good protective gear while working on a well-cleaned factory platform, Candler added. The company called the cook, James Gaston. He said that he wore coveralls and heavy shoes while working in the factory—and for good reason. It would be dangerous to wear shoes with holes in them, he said, because "the stuff splashes out of the kettle and would scald my feet."

Candler suggested that the government was untrustworthy. Certainly he doubted the veracity of its finding of dirt and insect parts in the soft-drink syrup. And he dismissed Kebler's reference to the beverage's drug-linked nicknames as unfair. The street terms were unauthorized and unwanted by the makers of Coca-Cola. "The company has never advertised or sold Coca-Cola under the names 'Dope' or 'Coke.'" (This was true at the time; the company wouldn't trademark the name "Coke" until 1945.) Further, the company disputed the idea that it was selling just another version of a stimulant—or a toxic substance—because its formula happened to include caffeine.

It also offered a lineup of expert witnesses. Rudolph Witthaus, a New York toxicologist known for his testimony in high-profile murder trials, promised, "I know of no case of caffeine in any quantity causing death." John Marshall, of the University of Pennsylvania, one of the founders of American toxicological analysis, said that he'd tested caffeine's effect on protein metabolism and found no measurable impact. Charles F. Chandler of Columbia University, an industry-allied sixty-five-year-old chemist who had testified for the meatpackers in the oleomargarine hearings before the U.S. Senate in the 1880s, declared, "I am familiar with caffeine. It is not a toxic or poisonous substance."

Victor Vaughan, a chemist from the University of Michigan, who had earlier disputed Wiley's contention that sodium benzoate might pose a health risk, also came forward as a soft-drink company witness. In his testimony Vaughan said he'd based his analysis on the possibility of imbibing an ounce of Coca-Cola syrup, mixed with a cup of carbonated water, six or seven times a day. "I have no doubt it would be stimulating to the brain and muscles, and to some extent, possibly the kidneys, slightly, but such stimulation would be normal." Vaughan had fed guinea pigs Coca-Cola for almost four months and, he said, seen no ill effects worth mentioning.

Coca-Cola had also hired Columbia University psychologist Harry L. Hollingworth to run tests on caffeine's effect on human mental processes and physical reactions. Later hailed as doing the most impressive research presented during the trial, Hollingworth's study involved sixteen subjects, ten men and six women, between the ages of nineteen and thirty-nine. All had swallowed capsules daily during a four-week period. The capsules contained either no caffeine or caffeine in a range of different doses.

It was a classic double-blind study; neither the participants nor Hollingworth knew who received what capsule. At regular intervals, every subject was tested to evaluate motor skills and cognitive function. Each was also required to keep a journal recording sleep patterns and noting periods of either alertness or fatigue. By the end of the study, Hollingworth had accumulated 64,000 data points that he presented to the slightly stunned jury through a series of complex charts.

The psychologist found that caffeine did speed up motor reactions briefly. Its influence on cognitive processes was more gradual and more persistent. He described caffeine as a mild stimulant that, overall, seemed to enhance general performance across the spectrum of given tasks, without measurable harm that he could identify. The journalists covering the trial, many of them regular coffee drinkers, reported these results in great detail.

John F. Queeny, founder of the Monsanto Chemical Company in St. Louis, followed Hollingworth. The company was, as it was proud to say, the maker of both saccharin and the crystalline caffeine used by the soft-drink company. Queeny testified that Coca-Cola's caffeine contents remained modest compared with other beverages such as coffee and tea. His company's chemical analyses suggested that a strong cup of tea, for instance, could contain almost three times the caffeine in a glass of Coca-Cola.

The company then focused on consumers. A group of Atlanta doctors testified that none of the children they treated ever drank Coca-Cola—a counter to Kebler's assertions. Witnesses also included ten carefully selected adult Atlanta residents—ranging in age from twenty-four to fifty-seven. These upright citizens, Coca-Cola's attorneys said, had been consuming their product for an average of seven years, some drinking fifteen or more glasses a day. None of them had reported ill effects. The physicians hired by Coca-Cola were also confident that the adults who did imbibe Coca-Cola handled it without side effects. One doctor told of a traveling salesman who regularly knocked back nearly two dozen drinks a day. Or as the *Chattanooga Daily Times* put it—to the undoubted annoyance of the Candler family—the salesman had consumed "20 dopes daily" but remained in "perfect health."

Before McCabe could assemble his rebuttal witnesses, Coca-Cola's lawyers made a surprise appeal to Judge Edward T. Sanford to dismiss the case. They did not argue that Coca-Cola had proved that caffeine was harmless or that heavy soft-drink consumption was without risk; clearly that remained a matter of scientific debate. Rather the company now made an entirely new argument: The scientific debate was irrelevant because the company had made a new reading of the law. Coca-Cola now argued that caffeine was not an "added ingredient" but a basic part of the soft-drink formula. The law addressed additives and adulterants. If caffeine was not an additive, as Coca-Cola now argued, then the Agriculture Department had no standing to prosecute.

It was something of a legal gamble at this stage of a three-week trial. But to the surprise—not to say shock—of those on both sides, Judge Sanford readily accepted the company's position. He agreed that the inclusion of caffeine in a soft-drink formula—regardless of whether the compound posed a health risk—was legally different from, say, adding formaldehyde to milk or copper sulfate to canned peas. On Friday, April 7, the day after Coca-Cola presented the new argument, Sanford dismissed the jury and closed the case: "I am constrained to conclude that the use of the word 'added,' when applied to poisonous and deleterious ingredients . . . cannot be considered meaningless."

COCA COLA IS THE WINNER, announced the *Chattanooga Daily Times* headline, adding with some partisan pleasure, "Case is practically thrown out of court." The paper speculated that the judge had taken sides, to protect not only the soft-drink company but also American business in general. The *Daily Times* claimed to have discovered that "if the government proved successful in the Coca-Cola case, it was the first of 2,500 prosecutions planned." That number was a journalistic exaggeration, but it was true that the Agriculture Department had hoped for a clear legal precedent that would support better enforcement of the law and smooth the way for other cases.

For once, George McCabe and Harvey Wiley were united in dismay; on the same day that Sanford announced his decision, McCabe announced the government's decision to appeal the Coca-Cola verdict.

The defeated delegation from the Agriculture Department had barely returned from Chattanooga to their jobs in Washington when the increasingly contentious saccharin question reemerged—and this time in ways that did not please Monsanto and its allies. A just-completed report by the Remsen Board, based on a review initiated at industry request, had found that the sweetener did indeed present a potential health risk if consumed in large enough doses.

And those large doses were made the more likely because of the common practice among food processors of substituting cheaper saccharin for more expensive sugar without informing the consumer, leading to a cumulative exposure. This was what Wiley had been warning about since before his unfortunate confrontation with the previous president. It underscored not just the chief chemist's belief that saccharin could damage health but also his near obsession with truth in labeling. The finding, from the supposedly industry-friendly Remsen Board, headed by saccharin codiscoverer Ira Remsen himself, was a shocker to McCabe and Wilson—and one that infuriated Monsanto's head, John Queeny.

It had come about in part because Remsen had prudently recused himself from the investigation. The lead investigator had been board member Christian Herter, a physician on the faculty of Columbia University and cofounder of the *Journal of Biological Chemistry*. In December 1910 Herter had unexpectedly died, at age forty-five, of what his doctors called a neurological wasting disease. His friend and colleague Otto Folin, a professor of biological chemistry and molecular pharmacology at Harvard University, had then completed the research.

Swedish-born Folin had used a Poison Squad–style method of adding capsules containing saccharin to the meals of healthy male volunteers. A tally of the results after four weeks found that tiny amounts of saccharin (less than 0.3 grams) taken daily did not produce any signs of obvious injury. In trace amounts, Folin reported, it appeared to be safe.

But in subjects given higher doses, both Herter in the early stages of the study and Folin in his follow-up work had recorded signs of digestive upset, ranging from nausea to stomach pain. Further, such higher doses were a real possibility for average American consumers, the report reminded the authorities, given that unlabeled saccharin was now found in products including canned fruits and vegetables, jams, jellies, wines, and other spirits. The Remsen Board also, again to industry dismay, concurred with Wiley that saccharin lacked any of the nutritive (caloric) value of natural sugar and therefore lessened the quality of food.

McCabe had long believed, along with Theodore Roosevelt and

Secretary Wilson, that saccharin was relatively harmless, too benign to merit Agriculture Department regulation. That belief had become a de facto federal policy, reflected in the way that the U.S. War Department now included saccharin tablets in its military rations. But department policy was also to consider the Remsen Board findings the final word. In late April, just three weeks after the Coca-Cola trial ended, the Agriculture Department announced that starting in July 1911, all foods containing saccharin would be considered adulterated and therefore subject to prosecution.

Queeny, energized by the Coca-Cola trial, hurried to Washington to mount an immediate counterattack. He summoned Monsanto's new attorney, Warwick Hough, the same Hough who had so ably represented the liquor wholesalers on the whiskey question. Together they gathered a cadre of chemical and food industry representatives, secured a meeting with Wilson, and asked the secretary to rethink the decision. First they contended that the government had moved too fast. They recognized that Wilson was a supporter of the Remsen Board. But the manufacturers, Hough now said, had a right to read and respond to the Remsen report before a rule was issued. Second he asserted that if the rule was to be issued, it should be amended to allow industry time to adapt, particularly time to gradually sell and reduce existing saccharin inventories.

Following the Coca-Cola debacle, Wilson was reluctant to rush into another industry showdown. He accepted both points. Following the meeting, and without consulting either Wiley or Ira Remsen, the secretary announced that the saccharin ban would be delayed until January 1912. He also reassured the business leaders that the Remsen Board had not been co-opted by the overly purist Wiley faction. "I want to say frankly to you gentlemen," Wilson told the assembled group of saccharin industry representatives "that the referee board was organized and put into action for the very purpose of conserving the interests of manufacturers." He then took a sly swipe at Wiley. The board, he added, was there to give industry a "sane hearing."

The conversation was meant to be private, and Wilson would deeply regret both that it didn't stay that way and, even more so, the reason it became national news. The exchange would soon be reported during a Senate investigation of a scandal at the Agriculture Department, one that would eventually involve not only the secretary and his underlings but also the president, drawing unwanted comparisons to the political storm over Taft's 1910 firing of forestry chief Gifford Pinchot.

This new mess—and it would be publicly revealed to be one of many in the Agriculture Department—grew out of a plot hatched by Dunlap, backed by McCabe and Wilson, with the goal of removing Wiley and his allies from the department. The ill-managed conspiracy was rooted in the Coca-Cola trial and particularly focused on the government's prominent expert witness, Henry Rusby, the prosecution's prized critic of caffeine.

At first Rusby had refused to testify because of a reduction in federal pay for scientific consultants. The rate for such work had been $20 a day under Roosevelt. Taft's thrift-minded attorney general, George W. Wickersham, however, had cut it to a mere $9 a day. With reluctance, Rusby had accepted the lower pay for his drug-analysis work for the government. He thought it too important to give up, he explained. But he said he couldn't afford to accept so little for testifying in the Coca-Cola case. At that rate, by the time he had paid for unreimbursed travel from New York to Tennessee, not to mention hiring a substitute to teach his classes, it would be a money-losing endeavor.

Wiley pointed out to McCabe that Wickersham's ruling allowed for some independence; several federal departments, also confronting witness reluctance, were still paying $20 a day for trial testimony. But McCabe refused to consider any additional money for chemistry experts. So, quietly, Wiley's lieutenant Willard Bigelow devised a work-around arrangement. The bureau would hire Rusby for an annual fee of $1,600 a year. This would cover any expert testimony and all analytic work that might be required over the next year.

The Agriculture Department's respected pharmaceutical expert, Lyman Kebler, wrote to Rusby, urging him to take the offer and pointing out that the flat fee would guarantee a regular monthly stipend no matter what the workload. "Personally, I am of the opinion that your new option is much better than the old." Rusby accepted the deal and Wiley approved it, making a point of sending it to the department secretary. Wilson signed off as well, although, once the scandal blew up, he would hastily deny responsibility, saying that he had not been fully informed about the details.

The correspondence and records regarding the Rusby arrangement were filed in Wiley's office before he left for Tennessee. There, Frederick Dunlap "discovered" them while searching through the chief chemist's documents when he was gone. Dunlap was serving as acting bureau chief while Wiley attended the Coca-Cola trial, and he had requested and received access to Wiley's office. After pulling the Rusby file and studying the arrangement, Dunlap—knowing of Wilson's discontent with the chief chemist—realized that he could use Rusby's hiring arrangement as the basis for charges that the chief chemist and his allies had defrauded the government.

In May 1911, he prepared a memo accusing Wiley, Kebler, and Bigelow of illegal misuse of government money, carefully keeping his action secret. Dunlap had his memo typed outside the department so that none of the secretaries or clerks—whom he had found to be distressingly loyal to Wiley—knew anything about it. He then took the memo to Wilson. The agriculture secretary did indeed see Dunlap's memo as a political gift, an opportunity to remove a perpetual thorn in his side.

Not surprisingly, Wilson also decided to keep the memo secret from Wiley and his staff, referring it directly to the department personnel committee chaired by McCabe. The solicitor, also weary of Wiley's endless arguments, instructed the committee to find that

Wiley, Kebler, and Bigelow had acted "in defiance" of Wickersham's ruling on pay. McCabe recommended that Rusby's contract be declared invalid, that Kebler be demoted, and that Wiley and Bigelow be offered the opportunity to resign. Wilson then reported the affair to Wickersham and asked him, as the country's attorney general, to move the recommendations forward.

It was a politically fraught recommendation, as all would recognize belatedly. Wickersham carried the scars of the embarrassing Pinchot affair, in which he had favored the controversial firing, but his critics would complain that he appeared not to have learned from the experience. Major Archie Butt, an aide to Taft, described the attorney general as having the "political judgment of an ox." Despite that earlier fiasco, in mid-May Wickersham wrote to Taft supporting McCabe's decision.

It was the president himself who hesitated. He had warned Wilson earlier about having "too great of a disposition to charge people with bad faith and too great encouragement to newspaper controversy." Taft remembered well the catastrophic fallout of the Pinchot decision and, recognizing that Wiley too was immensely popular in the country, saw a real risk of repeating it. He didn't need another political struggle, especially within his own party, with an election year approaching. Also, Taft was himself a legal scholar. The president worried that Wilson's procedure in this case had violated due process. None of the accused employees had been shown any of the charges against them or allowed to respond to them. Further, some of Taft's most trusted confidants, such as U.S. senator W. Murray Crane of Massachusetts, had recently warned him that legislators were beginning to consider the Agriculture Department something of a snake pit.

Taft took some weeks to consider the recommendation. Finally he decided to proceed—but with caution, and with an eye to due process. On Monday, July 11, 1911, the president ordered Wilson to inform his subordinates of the accusations and proposed actions. No decisions would be made until the accused scientists had a chance to respond. Even so, Taft expected some blowback, maybe some bad press. But, as with the earlier Pinchot decision, he underestimated the popularity of the civil servant involved and the extent of public anger that would greet the news. Although not, perhaps, as much as James Wilson had done.

Fourteen

THE ADULTERATION SNAKE

1911–1912

———— ○ ————

How I wonder . . .

After he received the president's instructions, Wilson had no choice but to inform the bureau chemists of the impending charges. He decided to have McCabe handle the problem. The attorney waited until week's end, hoping to deliver the news and then escape for the weekend. Wiley was not at the department on the afternoon of Friday, July 15. He had left with Anna for a few days at Grasslands, their Virginia farm. As a shocked Kebler and Bigelow absorbed McCabe's news, the solicitor indicated that he had no wish to confront Wiley in any case. Perhaps one of his subordinates might want to relay the details to their boss.

The next day Bigelow drove unhappily to Grasslands. As he would recall it, he was shocked once again by Wiley's reaction. The chief chemist sat silently, carefully reading through the written charges. Then, to Bigelow's surprise, he leaped up, waving the papers above his head, shouting, "Victory, victory!"

Walking the farm's sunny fields with Bigelow, Wiley explained: For years there'd been rumors of political plots against Wiley and his work. Now he had clear documentation of an actual plot, one that included Dunlap rummaging through his desk, secret meetings, and trumped-up charges. If he handled it right—and he'd been in federal service long enough to think he could—his enemies had just put a weapon in his hands. Back at his desk on Monday, he was even more confident. He was also touched to find himself surrounded by secretaries, clerks, other bureau scientists, and officials from other sections within the department, all of them offering to help prepare a defense. To the bureau's chief clerk, Fred Linton, who offered his services, Wiley simply smiled his thanks. "We need no defense," he said. "I am planning an attack."

That Wednesday, July 20, the *New York Times* broke the carefully leaked story. "After having failed in many vigorous attempts to separate Dr. Harvey W. Wiley, the pure food expert, from his place at the head of the Bureau of Chemistry, his opponents seem in a fair place to at last achieve their desire," it said, describing the plot in detail. If his opponents succeeded, Wiley's resignation "will be hailed with delight by the food and drug adulterers and misbranders from all over the country." The story quoted Rusby, who defended the pay arrangement, and Wiley, who emphasized that Wilson had approved the compensation. The secretary, the paper reported, refused to answer any questions at all.

Newspapers nationwide picked up the story and expanded on it, painting a portrait of corruption not by the dedicated food chemists but by Wilson, McCabe, and Dunlap. The *Evening Star* of Washington, DC, reported that other cabinet secretaries in the Taft administration had begun ducking for cover. "They . . . showed a tendency to sharply criticize Secretary Wilson for not having settled the whole thing without letting it get outside of his department." The *Evening Star* article also trumpeted the fact that the federal Agriculture Department had spent more than $175,000 (more than $4 million in today's dollars) on the Wilson-backed Remsen Board. Ira Remsen alone had received an $11,631 annual salary (more than twice

Wiley's) and been given $4,000 in expenses. Board members Russell Chittenden and John Long had both received more than $13,000 in salary and a combined $15,000 in expenses. The remaining board members had received almost $10,000 each in salary and an average $4,000 each in expenses. The *Evening Star* also revealed, with some glee, that the members' expense accounts covered—in addition to monkeys, dogs, ice cream, Belgium peas, and electric griddles—chiffoniers (mirrored chests of drawers) and horoscopes.

Embarrassed and angry, Ira Remsen called reporters into his office at Johns Hopkins to decry what he saw as an unwarranted, gratuitous attack. He received a chilly hearing from the DC newspapers. In fact, the *Evening Star* wasn't finished digging up dirt. It next reported on the existence of the attorney general's memo that Wilson and Taft had tried to keep secret, the one warning that the Remsen Board payment system was illegal. An *Evening Star* correspondent who had attended Wilson's early meeting with the saccharin makers now revealed just how industry-friendly the arrangement was, quoting the Secretary telling the businessmen that "the Remsen referee board was organized for the purpose of conserving the interests of manufacturers." When some Wilson supporters expressed doubt about the accuracy of the statement, the Agriculture Department stenographer who had been in the meeting confirmed that the secretary had said exactly that.

Such revelations further stoked public outrage. Wiley received encouragement and offers of support from fellow chemists, from state food commissioners, from the director of publicity at the Shredded Wheat Company—"You have had a hard struggle against the manufacturers of impure foods and drugs and we don't propose to desert you at this critical moment"—from women's groups, from the head of Old Dutch Mill Coffee Roasters—"I shall do all I possibly can to aid the work"—from medical societies and insurance executives—"I am prompted to write you personally about the disgraceful and detrimental exposition now being conducted at the nation's capital."

President Taft was also inundated with messages of support for

Wiley. The telegrams received at the White House that week didn't deviate from that point. From the board of trustees of the American Medical Association: "to express the hope that Dr. Wiley, Chief of the Bureau of Chemistry, will be continued in office as the chief exponent in the execution of the pure food law. The manufacturers of impure foods and drugs would rejoice in his dismissal." From the American Association for the Advancement of Science's committee on national health: "The services of Dr. Wiley and Dr. Rusby are of such value we earnestly hope that no action be taken against them. We respectfully urge that a technicality ought not to be employed to afford a reason for dismissing two such honorable and loyal servants." From the president of the Florida Board of Pharmacy: "I wish to assure you of my full confidence in Dr. Wiley. I feel that after due personal investigation by yourself you will find the charges groundless." From the pastor of the Methodist Episcopal Church in south Baltimore: "Dr. Wiley is worth more to the people of this country than the whole aggregation of his traducers combined." From a chemical engineer in New York City: "I most respectfully and earnestly request that your Excellency see that Dr. Wiley not be hampered in the prosecution of the splendid work he has been doing for more than a quarter century to protect the food and drug supply of this country." From Ballard and Ballard Company, a flour mill in Louisville, Kentucky: "We think it would be a public calamity for Dr. Wiley to be allowed to leave the service." Not unexpectedly, Alice Lakey also telegraphed the president that Wiley's removal would cause "manufacturers who wish to deprive the law of its efficiency" to rejoice.

The same scenario played out in Congress. A consulting engineer in Pottsville, Pennsylvania, wrote to his congressman, Robert Difenderfer, that the charges against Wiley were so childish and overwrought that he thought the accusers should instead be dismissed. Difenderfer replied, "The case against Dr. Wiley, to which you refer, is only another evidence of the infamies that are so evident and have grown to such mammoth proportions in the last few years that it seems appalling that such a system could be propagated in a country such as ours. . . . It seems to me the minute a man has the courage to attack dishonesty, he becomes a mark."

Congressman William Hughes of New Jersey wrote to Wiley: "Just a line to let you know that I am in hearty sympathy with you and the work you have been doing. If there is anything I can do to help you defeat the 'Poison Brigade' let me know." Congressman Burton Harrison of New York wrote, "I observe your enemies are trying to put a crimp in you. You have a lot of friends in the House and perhaps we can turn the crimping process on the other fellows." And Congressman Ralph W. Moss of Indiana, chairman of the House Committee on Expenditures in the Department of Agriculture, scheduled a hearing in which he promised a thorough investigation of internal politics at what appeared to be a very troubled agency. The *Wall Street Journal* suggested that for the good of the service, James Wilson should resign. And "if Mr. McCabe is a sample of the growths fostered by the Department of Agriculture, some weeding out might be in order."

Appalled, George Wickersham wrote to President Taft, apologizing for pitching the administration into "all the worriment of another Pinchot affair." But although Taft was annoyed with his attorney general, he was angrier with Wilson. Taft wrote bitterly to his wife, Nellie, who was at their "summer White House" in Massachusetts, that Wilson was "as weak as water and shows how poor a secretary he is. He has very little grasp of his department. I ought to get rid of him but I don't know how I can do so now."

The Moss committee hearings on "expenditures in the Department of Agriculture" now became front-page news, filled with daily dramatic detail. In a story rather unfortunately headlined HAD GIRL ON GRILL, the *Evening Star* reported testimony by USDA stenographers who said McCabe had taken them into his office, locked the door, and grilled them about any possible secret doings of Wiley,

Kebler, and Bigelow. Other employees testified about McCabe's "third degree methods," including bringing in a fake Secret Service agent to threaten them and hiring private detectives to spy on them. Kebler testified that McCabe had told him that sharing information with any member of Congress or any U.S. attorney was a fireable offense. He was "arrogant and domineering," Kebler said, and deliberately intimidating.

The *Washington Star* wrote, "Lawyer McCabe has been bossing the whole department," and the *New York Times* said, "By the clever framing and manipulation of departmental rules, he [McCabe] became the sole judge of whether cases against manufacturers of food and drugs should be prosecuted."

McCabe admitted that he had refused to prosecute more than five hundred cases recommended by the chief chemist, but he pointed out that hundreds of other recommendations had been either prosecuted or worked out in arbitration or more informal discussions. He also admitted that he had blocked Wiley from appearing in court hearings regarding preservatives, notably sodium benzoate, because he didn't want him contradicting Remsen Board findings. But he absolutely denied that he had "the real power" in the department. That belonged to Wilson. Secretary Wilson, who was called next, admitted to the committee that he'd suppressed the publication of almost twenty reports from the Bureau of Chemistry. He'd also suppressed information internally, blocking Wiley and his men from knowing much about the Remsen Board or its findings. But like McCabe, he blamed those decisions on Wiley. The chief chemist had become too stringent, too rigid, and too prone to become angry over such matters, he said. Wilson explained that he was a man who preferred to operate in a more peaceful atmosphere than Wiley allowed.

The committee also called Frederick Dunlap, who admitted that he'd drafted the accusatory memo, the main subject of the hearings, in secret and delivered it to Wilson on a day when he knew that Wiley would be out of town. He also acknowledged that when he and

Wiley disagreed on a matter of food safety, he routinely deferred to McCabe in making the final decision on any regulatory issue. "And Mr. McCabe is not a chemist, is he?" asked one committee member pointedly. "Not that I ever heard of," Dunlap replied. Legislators from both sides of the aisle, the newspapers reported, were unanimous in finding that the Agriculture Department was a personal and political mess.

Taft, who had joined his wife for the summer in Massachusetts, followed the daily newspaper reports as well as consulted with his staff as he tried to decide how best to handle the situation. In mid-September 1911, just before returning to Washington, he announced his decision on the charges related to the Rusby affair. Considering the tenor of the Moss hearings, his findings surprised no one. WILEY UPHELD BY PRESIDENT IN RUSBY CASE read the *New York Times* headline.

In a letter to Wilson that he made available to the public, the president declared that he'd found no evidence of conspiracy to defraud the government in the payment arrangements to Henry Rusby. In fact, Taft wrote, the payment of the Remsen Board was among many precedents that showed that Rusby's contract was justified by ordinary government procedure.

By presidential order, Rusby and Wiley both were cleared of all charges. In a diplomatic concession to Wilson, Taft recommended that Kebler and Bigelow be reprimanded for overzealousness in recruiting the New York expert, although he also praised their effort to pay an expert witness fairly. The president stopped short of ordering a reorganization of the department or punishing McCabe or Dunlap. But he signaled his dissatisfaction. "The broader issues raised by the investigation, which have a much weightier relation than this one on the efficiency of the department, may require much more radical action than the question I have considered and decided," Taft wrote.

In response, Wiley issued a statement to the Associated Press, thanking the president for his sense of justice, the American press for "the practically unanimous support which it has given me during this ordeal," and especially the many people who had written to encourage him. Neither James Wilson nor George McCabe responded to requests for comment, which the newspapers made a point of emphasizing in their coverage of Taft's decision.

"My heartiest congratulations," wrote the muckraking journalist Samuel Hopkins Adams, whose exposé of patent medicine, "The Great American Fraud," had been central to some of the regulations written into the food and drug law. "I didn't think Taft had the nerve to come out flat-footed. The slap against Kebler (and the same for Bigelow) was unfair, I thought, and rather cowardly. But everyone who knows Taft will read between the lines and know it for what it is worth. A slight sop to the forces of the enemy."

In the public view, Wiley had triumphed against his oppressors. Certainly he'd kept his job. But privately he was keenly aware that he hadn't really shifted the balance of power regarding food regulation. The "adulteration snake," he told one reporter, still coiled through the department. Again he wondered how long he could persevere. Along with the letters of encouragement and congratulation, he began receiving job offers—most of them from businesses in the food and drink industry. The R.B. Davis Company (makers of phosphate food products, baking powder, and starch) of Hoboken, New Jersey, for example, proposed to create a position for him and match his $5,000-a-year government salary, if he wanted to "leave the pressures of federal service." He firmly declined them all, replying to R.B. Davis that "I am still in my present job and I intend to hold onto it until I am forcibly ejected." But at home, talking to Anna, he was thinking very seriously about whether he had outlasted his usefulness.

In January 1912 the Moss committee issued its report, reinforcing the president's decision and approving Taft's dismissal of the Rusby charges. The committee dismissed any suggestion that the bureau chemists had conspired to defraud the government. It emphasized the importance of Rusby's testimony in the Coca-Cola case, praising the bureau's strategy to accommodate him as part of an essential effort to build a strong regulatory system for food and drink: "One cannot withhold one's sympathy with an earnest effort on the part of Dr. Wiley to pay proper compensation and secure expert assistance in the enforcement of so important a statute, certainly in the beginning, when questions arising under it are of capital importance to the public."

The committee reprimanded McCabe and Dunlap for their heavy-handed tactics. It joined the president in criticizing Wilson for the secretive support lent to industry by the Remsen Board and for his direction of that body, which, said the report, often paralyzed reasonable enforcement of the law. It characterized the department as poorly managed, which was yet another embarrassing blow to Wilson, but it did not find that the USDA was, as Wiley suggested, entirely in thrall to industry. Wilson, McCabe, and Dunlap might not believe in Wiley's consumer-before-all approach, but they had prosecuted businesses, worked to build a regulatory structure, proved willing to fight questionable practices such as the bleaching of flour all the way to the Supreme Court. A willingness to work with manufacturers, the committee noted, was not always the evidence of corruption that Wiley and his allies believed. Sometimes it was merely evidence of practicality.

Publicly Wiley declared the double whammy of Taft's decision and the committee report a "sweeping victory" for his side. To his friends he was a little more cautious, writing to one of them that "while the verdict was not as sweeping as I had hoped it is nevertheless a good one."

Following the Moss report, Wilson made visible efforts to repair the damage. He removed McCabe from the Food and Drug Inspection Board and appointed an ally of Wiley's, Roscoe Doolittle, director of the department's New York–based food laboratory, as its chairman. But he kept Dunlap on the board in order to maintain some of that practicality. And Wilson, who had served under three presidents, remained as agriculture secretary. (He'd privately asked to finish out the current term, his fourth, and Taft had consented.) He calmly assured the president and Congress that the situation in the department was much improved. But the calm was deceptive; he was furious about having his reputation so tarnished. Within a few weeks following Taft's decision, Wiley was increasingly aware of that, noting that Wilson had become "alertly antagonistic."

"I found that my recommendations to the secretary were being returned unapproved," he said. It was obvious that "I would have continually to fight my own associates on the Board of Food and Drug Inspection in carrying out my orders and policies." The scandal, the Moss hearings, the fact that little had changed at the Agriculture Department—all had made it clear to both Wiley's allies and his enemies that though he had survived the attack, though he had undaunted public support, he lacked vital internal support for his strict approach to food regulation.

"Be sure of your ground for the conspirators will not cease to lay pitfalls for you," warned J. G. Emery, Wisconsin food and dairy commissioner. The food industry was now neatly sidestepping Wiley on a regular basis, taking complaints directly to Wilson. The chief chemist had just recently tried to regulate mold and dirt in grain shipped across state lines, and Wilson, responding to pressure from the industry, had directly overruled him again.

Wiley had declared that he would stay as long as the department would have him, but he had begun to see the futility of remaining in such a hostile environment. He wasn't interested in going to work for a baking soda company, but he thought there might be somewhere else that he could make a difference. If he could find a place that would allow him to fight as he chose, he wondered if he should now explore such opportunities. And there were also welcome family reasons for considering a job that might pay better. To their surprise and delight, he and Nan were expecting their first child in the spring.

The women's magazine *Good Housekeeping*, known for its crusading tendencies, had offered him $10,000 a year—double his current salary—to become director of a new department of "food, health and sanitation." It would include his own state-of-the-art laboratory, based in Washington, DC, that would test products on the market, offer advice to readers on their safety and merits, and perhaps even award them a *Good Housekeeping* "seal of approval" where deserved. He could also write a column in the magazine on both food safety and nutrition.

The Redpath Lyceum Bureau, an agency that booked lecturers and performers into halls across the country, also contacted Wiley to offer him a lucrative speaking contract. The agency, founded as the Boston Lyceum Bureau in 1868, had represented such luminaries as Mark Twain, Julia Ward Howe, Susan B. Anthony, and Frederick Douglass. Wiley was honored by the opportunity to join that list. It was a pleasant reminder that, due to both his public successes and his public failures, he had become an influential celebrity.

Anna Wiley was also becoming a well-known reform advocate. She was president of the Elizabeth Cady Stanton Suffrage Club in Washington, DC, lobbying not just for women's right to vote but also for bank reform. In December 1911 she'd also been elected to the Congressional Committee of the American Women's Suffrage Association. "As I read the papers and I diagnose the signs, I find you are slowly but surely becoming known as the husband of Anna Wiley," wrote Nathaniel Fowler to his friend Wiley. Fowler, a Boston-based journalist and author, joked that Wiley would soon find himself featured in a new *Ladies' Home Journal* series titled "Unknown Husbands of Great Women."

By March 1912, rumors had begun circulating again that Wiley might finally leave the department. Wilson, who might have welcomed such news, was slow to believe it. He told his friends that Wiley himself had planted such rumors, probably to angle for further concessions. When a reporter for the *New York Times* asked the secretary about the possibility of the chief chemist resigning, Wilson snapped, "That story isn't ripe yet." But on the morning of March 15, Wiley sent a notice to his favorite newspaper reporters, telling them that he had an important message to share. He also prepared a simple resignation letter for Wilson, extending not even a day's notice to his employer: "I hereby tender my resignation as chief of the bureau of chemistry at a salary of $5,000 per annum in the Department of Agriculture, to take effect at the termination of the 15th day of March 1912."

He asked for a meeting with Wilson to deliver the letter. The two men talked for almost an hour. Wiley said, as he had before, that he would gladly stay if Wilson would clear the department of opponents of honest regulation, particularly Dunlap—whom he described as a sneak and a liar—and the equally devious George McCabe. Wilson replied, as he had before, that he would not consider it, that he did "not see his way clear" to dismissing the people in question. At the end of the discussion, the secretary scrawled, "Your resignation is accepted," on Wiley's note and handed it back to him.

Later that day—mostly for the benefit of the press—Wiley released a "supplementary statement" of resignation, emphasizing his long dedication to the civil service and adding, "It is also a matter of extreme gratification to me that in the twenty-nine years which I have been chief of this bureau, there has not been a cent, to my knowledge, wrongfully expended." He reminded reporters that he was quitting the government, but not the cause. "I propose to devote the remainder of my life with such ability as I may have at my command and with such opportunities as may arise, to the promotion of the principles of civic righteousness and industrial integrity, which underlie the Food and Drugs Act."

Wiley also made a point of thanking Wilson for "the personal kindness and regard which he has shown me during his long connection with the department." He was grateful that one of his most trusted lieutenants, Willard Bigelow, had been appointed acting chief of the Bureau of Chemistry in his absence. But, he added, the situation in the department had become intolerable for him, and he saw no other "self-respecting" course but to leave.

To members of the press who gathered for an afternoon news conference at the department, Wilson praised Wiley's long and valuable service but said that he had chosen to respect his chief chemist's decision. He had told Wiley, he said, "that I should not for a moment stand in his way" if he felt that he could better himself by resigning. "I could only acquiesce and wish him Godspeed." The listening reporters maintained their skepticism; a number of the resulting stories described the secretary as looking relieved. The *Druggist Circular* described Wilson's response to the resignation with that ironic American saying "Here's your hat, what's your hurry?"

Like Wilson, President Taft was moderate in his public statement. He praised the outgoing chief chemist, commenting, "I would be very glad if he could continue in the service of the government. I feel that I shall have difficulty finding a man to fill his place." But he then added that he was already moving to consult with university presidents in search of an appropriate replacement.

But elsewhere in the Department of Agriculture, the news brought an almost universal outpouring of grief. As McCabe and Dunlap had often noticed with irritation, Wiley had many more loyal friends on staff than they, or Secretary Wilson, could ever hope for, especially among the many women who served in clerical positions, the clerks whom he'd always made a point of treating with kindness and respect. Employees from throughout the building rushed to Wiley's office to wish him well.

WOMEN WEEP AS WATCH DOG OF THE KITCHEN QUITS AFTER

TWENTY-NINE YEARS, read the headline in the *Buffalo Courier*: "With tears streaming down their cheeks, hundreds of women clerks, many of them employed in other sections of the Department of Agriculture, filed in to say goodbye. So crowded were the elevators leading to Dr. Wiley's office that numerous women walked up four long flights of stairs." It was, the *New York Times* wrote, a remarkably affecting scene: "Some of the employees had worked with him for more than a quarter-century and they left crying like children."

Wiley's allies and supporters were both surprised and deeply disappointed by his decision. Paul Pierce wrote in *National Food Magazine* that he feared his friend had been secretly threatened or pressured out of the job. "Dr. Wiley is known to be a man of indefatigable will and courage; it is not reasonable to believe that he would thus quit under fire. . . . It is hard, therefore, to account for his strange action unless there be a cause back of it all which has not yet come to light." Alice Lakey interpreted the resignation as a triumph for Wiley's enemies, blaming the agriculture department for putting Wiley in an impossible situation: "his hands have been tied so far as possible to hinder the strict enforcement of the pure food law." Secretary Wilson and his alliance of corporate friends had worked toward this end, she said, so that the Agriculture Department, instead of enforcing the law, could "make everything easy for the food adulterer."

The *Journal of Commerce* pointedly headlined its story THE SACRIFICE OF DR. WILEY. The editor of a consumer-advocacy publication called the *Oil, Paint and Drug Reporter* began his lament by quoting from *Macbeth*: "So clear in his great office that his virtue will plead like angels, trumpet tongued, against the deep damnation of his taking off." Ralph Moss, the congressman who had chaired the investigative hearings into the Rusby case, sounded a similar note. "I regard the passing of Dr. Wiley from public service as the greatest loss that the American people have sustained in a generation," wrote Moss, who was also from Indiana. Like Lakey, though, he acknowledged that it might have been an unavoidable choice. "I have known that the conditions of administration in the Department were such that he could not remain in his place. . . . He has done more, in my judgment, than any other man in the country for mankind in general."

Wiley saved the testimonials and newspaper clippings for years, but his favorite of all the tributes was a cartoon in the *Washington Star*. It pictured his office, containing tables cluttered with test tubes and beakers. A pair of battered shoes was sitting on the floor. Next to the desk stood Uncle Sam, looking sadly down at those shoes. They were labeled as belonging to Harvey Wiley. The shoes were unmistakably oversized, unmistakably far too large for anyone else to fill.

Fifteen

THE HISTORY OF A CRIME

1912–1938

———◦———

. . . I wonder, what's in it.

Theodore Roosevelt's unhappiness with Taft as president, combined with his absolute belief that he himself would do a far better job, had drawn him back into national politics. During the same spring, of 1912, he campaigned to be the Republican nominee for the fall election. His odds looked promising; he'd started sweeping presidential primaries, including in Taft's home state of Ohio.

The embattled Taft realized that just one more controversy would end his chance of staying in office. With outrage over Wiley's resignation still simmering, he put off naming a replacement to the position of chief chemist. Quietly he and Wilson replaced Bigelow as temporary acting chief, but with another ally of Wiley's—Roscoe Doolittle, who had recently taken McCabe's place on the Food Inspection Board.

In a report to Wilson that May, Doolittle reported that fakery and adulteration continued apace. Products most frequently at fault, he wrote, included "cordials containing artificial color without declaration . . . figs unfit for consumption because of worms and excreta . . . flour bleached to conceal inferiority, eggs decomposed and unfit for food, arsenic in baking powders [also in gelatin and the shellac used to give chocolate a shine], so-called egg noodles containing artificial color but little or no eggs . . . black pepper containing added pepper shells, maple products adulterated with cane products, confectionary products containing talc and unpermitted colors, misbranded mixtures of olive oil and cotton seed oil," and more.

Doolittle wasn't the only one noticing that manufacturers seemed newly emboldened. A *New York Globe* series that spring bore the headline SODA WATER SOLD TO CITY CHILDREN IS FULL OF POISONS. For the *Globe*, writer Alfred W. McCann hired chemical analysts who found that many of the "fruit syrups" used to mix fizzy drinks contained anything but fruit. Both "raspberry" and "wild cherry" extracts were mostly alcohol, glycerin, acetic acid, succinic acid, benzoic acid, alcohol, and coal-tar dyes. The drinks were heavily sweetened with unlabeled saccharin; of the more expensive sugar there was barely a trace. As McCann made a point of concluding: "There wasn't a single sign hanging at any soda fountain in New York City advertising the artificial and chemical character of the drinks."

At the Republican National Convention that June in Chicago, Roosevelt failed to unseat Taft as the nominee. Despite the fact that he'd won the popular vote in the primaries, the GOP's conservative leaders blocked Roosevelt's return to the ballot. Believing that party bosses had stolen the nomination from him, he marched out of the convention. And shortly later, declaring himself "fit as a bull moose" going into the contest, he mounted a third-party bid for president under the Progressive banner. Predictably, the GOP vote in November split between Taft and Roosevelt, allowing Democrat Woodrow Wilson to win the presidency with only 41.8 percent of the popular vote.

With James Wilson surely on his way out at Agriculture, Wiley partisans pushed for the former chief chemist to become the next secretary. Wiley's longtime foes—such as the National Association of Food Manufacturers—united instantly in opposition. The *Chemical Trade Journal* editorialized in near panic, "We cannot conceive of Mr. [Woodrow] Wilson inviting to his cabinet a secretary to create turmoil, commotion, confusion, tumult, disturbance, disquiet, annoyance, vexation, uneasiness, agitation, affliction, calamity, misfortune, anxiety, sorrow and misery. If Mr. Wilson wants that, Dr. Wiley is well-equipped."

"I have no cabinet aspirations," Wiley wrote in December of 1912, to a physician in Oregon who urged him to apply for the position. ". . . I shall hope to continue on the lecture platform and with my pen to speak a forceful word for pure food and the public health along many lines." Since taking the magazine job, he had been offered several much more lucrative industry positions—one from his longtime fan the Kentucky distiller Edmund Haynes Taylor Jr.—now past eighty but still a force in politics. But Wiley turned them all down; for the first time in many years, he said, he was enjoying his work again.

On December 11 Wiley's secretary at *Good Housekeeping* wrote to J. G. Emery, the food commissioner of Wisconsin, that Wiley was traveling but had left instructions for how to respond to any call for his return to government service. "The doctor doesn't expect that the secretaryship will be offered to him and is not a candidate in any way; in fact, he is discouraging his friends from making any efforts in that direction and his enemies are very busy in the opposition direction. The National Retail Druggists Association has passed resolutions to the effect that the doctor's appointment to the cabinet would be a national disaster."

The retail druggists' group was especially opposed to Wiley because of his longtime advocacy of honest and detailed labeling of food and drug products. Cure-all manufacturers had been fighting that requirement ever since the passage of the Food and Drug Act. In

1911 lawyers for the over-the-counter industry had convinced the U.S. Supreme Court that the 1906 law did not explicitly forbid "false therapeutic claims" but only misleading statements about individual ingredients. The decision sparked such public outrage that in 1912 Congress amended the act (a change known as the Sherley Amendment) to specify that "false therapeutic claims intended to defraud the consumer" were in violation of the law. Yet the industry successfully pushed back on that law too, repeatedly tying up enforcement attempts in the courts. Many Wiley advocates had urged him to return to the Agriculture Department, if not as secretary then to his old job, specifically to deal with the drug-labeling problems that continued to put so many at risk. He considered it but worried that such a move would involve a deep pay cut. As his secretary also wrote, in a message passed along from Wiley, "I do not think he would consider at all going back to the Bureau of Chemistry as it would be a great sacrifice financially."

In late December 1912, James Wilson picked Dr. Carl L. Alsberg as the new chief of the Bureau of Chemistry. Taft, in the last month of his presidency, promptly approved the appointment. Alsberg, a biochemist, had been working in the USDA's Bureau of Plant Industry and was known as a careful scientist and a far-less-flamboyant personality than his predecessor. But Alsberg surprised those expecting him to quickly drop the agenda set by the former chief chemist. He began determinedly pursuing some of the key cases that had arisen during Wiley's tenure—returning to the issues of caffeine content in Coca-Cola and the regulation of saccharin as a food additive. More than Wiley had, he would put an emphasis on the investigation and regulation of pharmaceutical products—and even Wiley's long-time supporters would come to admire the way he could do so without being hampered by political baggage. Or, as it turned out, by Wiley's long-standing opponents. Secretary Wilson, as expected, stepped down just a few days into Woodrow Wilson's term (now having served under four presidents). Frederick Dunlap also left the department later that year. George McCabe left government service in January 1913 for a position with an Oregon law firm.

President Wilson chose David Houston, chancellor of Washington University in St. Louis, to be the next secretary of agriculture. Houston kept Alsberg on as chief of the Bureau of Chemistry and—to the surprise and dismay of the food industry—the new secretary proved far less willing than Wilson to change the rules at corporate demand. This change was highlighted after a new federal policy on saccharin—banning it from foods as a nonnutritive additive with pharmaceutical properties—was formally instituted in April 1912.

Once again Warwick Hough, representing Monsanto, prepared for battle. He contacted Houston directly, pushing him to reverse that policy, which, he complained, was rooted in outdated research done during the Wiley days. Hough again cited the company position: The artificial sweetener was harmless, possibly helped preserve food, and had "value from an economic standpoint." Houston merely referred him to the new chief chemist, who dismissed such points as lacking any real merit. Alsberg countered by pointing out that the soft-drink industry was now generally using such high levels of saccharin that a consumer's daily intake, when other artificially sweetened foods were considered, could easily exceed the safe levels identified by even the Remsen Board. Following yet another hearing on the subject in June 1913, Houston further backed his chief chemist. He refused to lift the ban on saccharin and—in the face of warnings from Hough that Monsanto would fight this in court—merely encouraged Alsberg to continue building his case against it.

Meanwhile, as promised, the organization of millers that had lost the bleached-flour trial in Missouri had appealed their case all the way to the U.S. Supreme Court. In February 1914 the court issued a business friendly decision. The justices agreed that—as Wiley had always argued—vulnerable populations should be considered in drafting regulations. Flour offered a perfect example of why the most vulnerable must be considered, because the product "may be used in many ways, in bread, cake, gravy, broth, etc. . . . It is intended that if any flour, because of any added poisonous or other deleterious ingredient, may possibly injure the health of any of these, it shall come within the ban of the statute." But the court also said that just because a product contained a compound considered toxic didn't mean that said compound was harming the bread and gravy consumers. Toxic effects had to be demonstrated for the law to apply, and the burden of proof was on the government. Thus nitrates, though poisonous in large quantities, could not be considered poisonous as residues in bleached flour unless the government could prove that they were directly harming consumers. The high court concluded that in the Lexington Mill case, the government had failed to prove such harm. The ruling, though, ignored the fact that the government did not have the resources to safety-test all products and that the law did not require businesses to do so at all. It thus threatened to cripple the existing regulatory process. The justices had not only found in favor of the millers—they had set a formidably high standard, especially given the state of toxicology in the early twentieth century, for the banning of any additive as "injurious."

Appalled, Wiley sent a furious statement to the wire services, complaining that the Supreme Court seemed set on delivering "knockout blows" to the food and drug law. "To permit the unrestricted addition of poisons into foods unless such can be proved specifically injurious paralyzes that section of the law relating to harmful adulterations," he warned. "Under the present decision, a man may add traces of arsenic or strychnine to a food with impunity." Further, the court decision left the responsibility for product safety entirely in the hands of regulatory agencies. Without a legal requirement—explicit or implied—for companies to safety-test their products in advance of selling them to the public, the consumer safety net would only continue to fray.

Over the following several years, the millers and the Agriculture

Department would wrestle with how the court decision should be applied specifically to flour. They would finally agree on three main points: (1) bleached flour had to be labeled as such; (2) the government would withdraw the charge that such flour contained "deleterious" compounds; and (3) the millers would accept the original charge of misbranding their flours. Recognizing that the federal government had basically lifted all restrictions on bleaching flour, some states tried tackling the issue on their own, but to little effect. Only a few unbleached-flour cranks—Harvey Wiley being the most notable—continued to argue in favor of "natural flour." In *The Pure Food Cookbook*, published in 1914 by *Good Housekeeping*, he explained with uncharacteristic diplomacy, "I am not an enemy of white flour but I am a friend of whole wheat flour."

Good Housekeeping was now his public platform—and it was an effective one. At the magazine, a Hearst publication with some 400,000 subscribers, he had the title of director of the bureau of foods, sanitation and health, and he was free to write what he chose in a monthly column. Not surprisingly, he wrote in support of state food safety regulations and better federal protections. He also reported on scientific developments in food and nutrition. An essay on everything wrong with poultry was typical, beginning, "There is perhaps a greater quantity of unfit poultry offered on the American markets than any other kind of food," before exploring the causes of food poisoning and the need for sanitary practices at both farms and processing plants.

He produced a detailed series on the significance of vitamins, a new and exciting area of nutritional science. When his editors complained that housewives were unlikely to appreciate so much technical chemistry, he brushed off the criticism. Women should be treated as intelligent human beings, not as children, he stated. His contract with the magazine specified that no advertisements of food, drugs, or cosmetics would be run without his approval. He sent samples of all advertised products to a commercial laboratory for analysis. Based on the results, advertisements received a star (approved by Wiley) or not (a noncommittal rating). If he found the products deceptive or risky, he had the power to censor the ad—and he did so. He enjoyed the ability to say what he thought so freely. "I had no longer to restrict myself on account of official propriety. What I thought would be good for the people at large and for the readers of *Good House-keeping*, in particular, I was at liberty to express in my own way."

In 1915 the members of the Remsen Board, ruthlessly ignored by the new secretary of agriculture, resigned from federal service. Carl Alsberg had ignored them too. He was less publicly combative than Wiley but he shared his predecessor's zeal for investigating business practices, which made him almost as disliked by the food-processing industry. In 1916 Alsberg authorized an undercover sting operation aimed at McCormick & Company's pepper production. The bureau's inspectors had discovered that McCormick was importing large amounts of pepper shells in addition to the pepper itself. The company refused to explain why; tests of McCormick's "Pure Black Ground Pepper" suggested impurities but at levels too low to identify. The chief chemist of the New York station, which had been tracking the imports, suggested that the Agriculture Department intercept the shells as they came into port and secretly spray them with an identifying agent. The department sprayed almost two hundred bags of pepper shells with the drug quinine and then followed their delivery to the McCormick plant in Baltimore. In May 1916 the government seized six barrels of black pepper, heavily contaminated with quinine, and charged the company with misbranding.

Embarrassed and angry, the company fought the accusation in court. And lost. The judge in the case ordered McCormick to label its adulterated product accurately as "ground black pepper containing from 10 percent to 28 percent added pepper shells." The company also was required to offer that product at a public sale to be conducted by U.S. Marshals, to pay all legal costs, and to pay a fine of $750.

The same year, Alsberg again took on the issue of deceptive use of saccharin. That spring the chief chemist ordered the seizure of a one-pound can of saccharin sent from the St. Louis Monsanto plant to a Chicago soft-drink supply house. He formally charged Monsanto with misbranding, citing the company's dishonest statements on the label, ones that described the artificial sweetener as "positively harmless" and "healthful." Alsberg's action set the stage for a legal fight over the sweetener, and there, he would later admit, he was perhaps too optimistic.

But he, Wiley, and just about everyone involved in consumer protection had been buoyed by a U.S. Supreme Court decision, also in 1916, regarding the Coca-Cola case. In a decision written by Chief Justice Charles Evans Hughes, the court overturned the lower court's finding that the soft-drink company's use of caffeine was merely part of a brand-name formula and therefore could not be classed as an adulterant.

The ruling had created a dangerous loophole, Evans wrote, in which any compounded product could be deemed out of reach of federal regulation. Coca-Cola, "like any formulaic product," was subject to the law's primary intent, "which was to protect the public from poisonous and deleterious substances which might pose a danger to public health." Further, Evans declared, "Coca-Cola" was not the distinctive generic name of a substance, like coffee, but the brand-name hyphenation of two common words. Caffeine, therefore, should be considered not integral to the product but an added ingredient; the Supreme Court ordered the case back for retrial.

Hoping to avoid another deluge of bad press coverage and uncertain that this time it would prevail, the soft-drink company moved to settle the case. Alsberg rebuffed the offer and instead authorized new research into the risks of caffeine. The company's lawyers, noting that the new chief chemist was known primarily as a thorough and careful researcher, again warned the Candler family that they might well lose this round. Secretly the company began experimenting with reducing caffeine levels in the soft drink. In late 1917, surprising the Agriculture Department, the company entered a no-contest plea to the original charges of adulteration. And by providing proof that it had now reduced the amount of caffeine in the drink by half, it negotiated a final settlement to the court case.

This time the Coca-Cola machinations received little public notice. World affairs had by that time taken over the nation's newspaper headlines. In April 1917 the United States had made a belated entry into the Great War (later known as World War I). As Alsberg wrote to Secretary Houston, "the urgent demands of the various war agencies" meant that most of his scientists had been reassigned to military duty, the regulatory teams were for the most part disbanded, and projects that had "no immediate bearing on the prosecution of war" had been closed down. He assured his boss that enforcement of the food law continued, however. The bureau had managed that year to prosecute an impressive eight hundred cases of adulterated or misbranded products.

Even in the shadow of war, the Wiley family managed to annoy a U.S. president. Anna Kelton Wiley, now the mother of two young sons—Harvey Washington Jr. and John Preston—went to jail for picketing the White House on behalf of women's right to vote. After a 1917 demonstration in which she and fellow activists in the suffrage movement demanded that President Wilson stop stalling and put his support behind equal voting rights for all, the president impatiently requested an end to "women howlers" and recommended a more dignified approach from equal-rights supporters. Wilson, who had been reelected in 1916, had deeply disappointed voting rights activists. He'd flatly rebuffed calls for federal action on suffrage, insisting that voting rights should be decided on a state-by-state basis.

In protest of such an unrealistic position, the militant National Women's Political Union mounted another demonstration, one that Anna Kelton Wiley proudly joined. Dressed in a gray carriage dress and her best hat, she marched carrying a sign reading: MR.

PRESIDENT: HOW LONG MUST WOMEN WAIT FOR LIBERTY? On November 10 she and other protest leaders were arrested and she was sentenced to fifteen days in the city jail. On appeal, she accepted a five-day sentence. Harvey Wiley at first encouraged her to ask for a pardon and stay out of jail. But when she refused, he supported the decision. He was proud of her suffragette activities; shortly after starting at *Good Housekeeping* he'd prompted the magazine to do a feature story on her right-to-vote work: "She believes the ballot to be a necessary tool for the advancement of women." To his friends who wondered how he could let his wife and the mother of his children serve jail time, Wiley answered that "he had fought all his life for a principle and hardly could deny her the same privilege."

The U.S. entry into the Great War had helped speed its end, although not before more than fifty thousand U.S. troops had died in combat. American losses were a mere fraction of the total, however; military deaths from the more than two dozen countries involved in the war topped eleven million, and civilian deaths exceeded those. The war concluded, on notes of both relief and grief, with the Treaty of Versailles in November 1918. The following January, Theodore Roosevelt died in his sleep during a stay in his Oyster Bay, New York, home at the age of sixty. Many attributed his decline into illness to the death of a favored son during the war. NATION SHOCKED, PAYS TRIBUTE TO FORMER PRESIDENT read the *New York Times* headline. "Our flag on all seas and in all lands at half-mast."

But Harvey Wiley spared no mourning for Roosevelt, who remained central to his grievances over the fate of the food and drug law. "Even if . . . the President favored the food bill, it is perfectly clear that he took the most active part in preventing the Bureau of Chemistry from enforcing it," he would write bitterly some years after Roosevelt's death. He had been further disillusioned by Woodrow Wilson's complete indifference to issues of food safety—although being ignored by the president had tended to reduce interference and work in the Chemistry Bureau's favor. Still, when Wilson had run for reelection in 1916, Wiley had campaigned for Republican challenger Charles Evans Hughes.

Wiley, by contrast, came to appreciate Wilson's presidency, at least regarding her leading cause. In 1918, after a series of meetings with suffrage leaders, the president changed course and backed a constitutional amendment favoring women's right to vote, publicly urging Congress to draft language that would enable that action. On June 4, 1919, after much argument and presidential pressure, both houses passed an amendment granting women's right to vote, and it was sent out for ratification as the Nineteenth Amendment to the U.S. Constitution. In just over a year, the required thirty-six states ratified it—the last being Tennessee, by a single vote from a young legislator whose mother ordered him to cast it or be forever barred from the house—and it became national law on August 18, 1920.

The case against saccharin had been halted during the war, due in part to its use as a substitute sugar in military supplies, a use that Alsberg publicly criticized. He remained committed to regulating the controversial sweetener. In December 1919, his case against saccharin as a food additive at last went to court in St. Louis, home of Monsanto. Government attorneys began the trial by demonstrating how widespread the unlabeled use of saccharin was in the food supply: in sodas and ice cream, candies, cakes, pies, breads, canned fruits and vegetables, sweet wines. American consumers, often without their knowledge, now consumed the artificial sweetener with almost every meal. "Unrestricted consumption" of saccharin had been shown to be dangerous, the Agriculture Department insisted, and it had plenty of evidence in that regard.

The government's leading expert during this round was Anton Carlson, professor of physiology at the University of Chicago. Born in Sweden and with a PhD from Stanford University, Carlson was known for his evidence-based approach to toxicology. He liked to

sarcastically describe scientists who theorized without studies to support their ideas as "chicks who chirp but don't scratch."

Carlson pointed out that the saccharin (an easily identifiable
compound that meshed the well-known elements sodium, carbon,
nitrogen, hydrogen, and oxygen) "gets into every place in the body
and appears in every secretion in the body; it appears in the saliva; it
may appear in the tears; it appears in the bile; just the same as it appears in the urine." If fed to goats, it appeared in their milk. In every
place, in every cell, he said, it had a physiological effect. His own
studies on the digestive tract found saccharin caused an increase in
stomach acids and a decrease in protein absorption. He absolutely
would not describe it as "positively harmless," the phrase used by the
chemical industry. Monsanto's lawyers didn't attempt to rebut his
studies but instead used a defense strategy inspired by the Supreme
Court's bleached-flour decision. Yes, saccharin might pose some
risks, they argued, but the government had failed to positively show
that putting it in the U.S. food supply caused active harm. Therefore,
the Agriculture Department could not restrict it.

The jury failed to reach a verdict, splitting with seven in favor of
the government's case to five against. Against Monsanto's urging,
the judge agreed to a new trial, and Alsberg again directed his staff
to begin building a case.

For many involved in the pure-food cause, these battles had become seemingly unending, largely because of the inadequacy of the
1906 food law itself. For example, the "Wiley law," as everyone still
called it, required ingredient labels but did nothing to address the
problems of deceptive containers, designed to mislead consumers as
to the amount of product they contained. Nor did it require manufacturers to reveal the number of ounces within those containers.
Echoing the battles over the 1906 law, a "slack-fill" bill, introduced
in 1919 and meant to improve regulation of such chicanery, was
firmly opposed by the food industry and had failed in both houses of

Congress that year. It then failed again the following year for the same reason.

In 1921, just before Republican Warren G. Harding took office as president, Carl Alsberg, himself battle weary, resigned as chief chemist. He took a position at Stanford as founding director of its new Food Research Institute. His replacement as chief of the Bureau of Chemistry was Walter G. Campbell, the Kentucky attorney whom Wiley had selected to direct the food-inspection programs created by the 1906 law. Wiley was pleased, although the two would not always agree on how to address the limitations of the old food and drug law. Campbell, for instance, would come to believe that an updated law was needed to address the deficiencies. Wiley fiercely defended his signature legislation, insisting that it simply needed better enforcement.

In the summer of 1923, President Harding suddenly died—doctors thought probably from a cerebral hemorrhage—during a visit to San Francisco. His vice president, Calvin Coolidge, succeeded him and won 1924's election to continue in the office. Coolidge, a small-government conservative and former Massachusetts governor, had earned a well-deserved reputation as a friend to business and staunch opponent of regulation.

That same year the government's prosecution of Monsanto and saccharin again ended in a mistrial, again on a 7–5 split in the government's favor. Despite the president's reputation for siding with industry, Coolidge's secretary of agriculture, Henry Wallace, wrote to Monsanto's Queeny, saying that the department was not giving up. This was echoed by a statement from the Bureau of Chemistry that "it would be a serious mistake to accept any form of compromise which would in any way, even partially, sanction the use of saccharin in food." But the judge in St. Louis told the government attorneys that he was done with the case. He was prepared to strike it from the docket rather than revisit the issue. Further, if the government pursued it, he warned, then he was prepared to simply declare for the defendant. Angry Agriculture Department officials suspected that Monsanto, a major employer in the judge's hometown, had finally applied enough pressure to end the case in the company's favor. But they were stymied as to how to go forward.

The following year the government dropped its effort to regulate the artificial sweetener but issued a formal statement reiterating its lack of enthusiasm for the product: "The Government has much scientific evidence to show that saccharin is harmful to health and believes that it should not be used except as a drug under direction of a physician. It is sometimes prescribed for patients suffering with diabetes who demand some sweetening agent but who are prohibited the use of sugar. As a drug, saccharin has its uses. In our opinion, it has no legitimate use as food and is harmful to health." The department used its authority to formally require that saccharin be listed as an ingredient on product labels, a measure that proved surprisingly effective in limiting its use. Many food companies, rather than reveal that they were surreptitiously using saccharin, removed it from their products. Others, inspired by the government's preference for its health-related uses, began marketing saccharin and saccharin-sweetened products to diabetics and others who either needed or wanted to limit their sugar intake.

Wiley fumed over the decision to drop the case. He was increasingly disenchanted with everything about the federal approach to consumer protection. Upon Coolidge's election, he'd written him an open letter, published in *Good Housekeeping*, urging newly aggressive enforcement and a reversal of decisions that allowed nitrates, sulfites, preservatives like sodium benzoate, and additives like saccharin and caffeine in the food supply. The letter closed: "It is the crowning ambition of my career before I die to see these illegal restrictions, which now make a prisoner of the Food Law, removed and the Law restored to the functional activity which Congress prescribed for its enforcement at the time of its enactment."

Coolidge did not reply. Instead Wiley received a letter from assistant secretary of agriculture Renick W. Dunlap (no relation to Frederick Dunlap). In diplomatic language, it emphasized the department's essential support on protection issues and agreed that the compounds listed by Wiley were "for the most part undesirable from the broad general standpoint of human health and nutrition" and that to eliminate them was "an object greatly to be desired." But Dunlap also emphasized a growing consensus that the 1906 law was inadequate. Its primary enforcement mechanism—seizure of goods followed by prosecution—had turned out to be a cumbersome tool. More important was its failure to define key terms, such as "injurious," or to provide a mechanism for doing so. Due to that failure, the court decisions, notably the bleached-flour ruling, had ended up hobbling enforcement. "To bring cases and fail," Dunlap pointed out, "invited an increased employment of these [harmful] substances."

Wiley had known since before the food and drug law passed that it was flawed. He'd argued in 1906 that it should include exactly the kinds of specifics that Renick Dunlap now cited as lacking, but away from the bureau, he had grown increasingly protective of "his" law. It was a position that would alienate him from some of his longtime friends at the agency, but not one that he could bring himself to change.

Still, in 1926, at age eighty-one, he joined former colleagues in a campaign to protect the law against a new push from an old enemy. The Corn Products Company, the corporation that had persuaded Roosevelt to allow the term "corn syrup" instead of "glucose," had now persuaded a friendly Iowa senator to introduce an amendment to the food law that would have stripped away any power to regulate corn sweeteners in the food supply. The new language had been slipped in as part of an agricultural relief bill, and it specifically exempted dextrose—another name for sugar made from cornstarch, especially in its dry form—from being indicated on any label. Under the proposed amendment, dextrose would just be called sugar.

The proposal had gone through the Senate's committee process without a single dissenting vote when Wiley, Campbell, and the alarmed regulators at the Agriculture Department learned of it. They also learned that Monsanto was providing lobbying money in support of the amendment; the company hoped that this exemption would pave the way for others to follow. Walter Campbell immediately organized an Agriculture Department pushback against the amendment, warning publicly that this move was designed to mislead consumers into believing they were purchasing a cane sugar– or beet sugar–sweetened product.

Wiley, back in warrior mode, canceled plans for a Florida vacation with his family. He sounded the alarm in newspapers, giving a widely printed interview to United Press in which he said: "I had hoped to do my small share in protecting the country from the wicked actions of food adulterers but I am afraid the battle is going against us." Congress, he warned, was moving to allow food manufacturers to deliberately cheat American consumers, "mak[ing] legal the grossest kind of food adulteration in this case," opening the door for countless other cheats and basically nullifying the good done by the 1906 law.

He said the same in his *Good Housekeeping* column, he personally wrote to all senators and congressmen, and he requested a private meeting with Coolidge to urge a veto if the law did pass. He did not gain the president's help but he attracted the attention and support of Senator Matthew M. Neely of West Virginia, who took up the cause and, when the bill reached the floor of the Senate, conducted a filibuster. Throughout it Neely held a copy of *Good Housekeeping* in one hand, and he interspersed his speech with paragraphs read aloud from Wiley's column, including the plea "Why should legislation be used to deceive the public?" The proposed amendment failed shortly later. The following day, Wiley wrote a glowing note to Neely: "The country owes you a vote of thanks for your heroic and successful endeavor yesterday to block the approval of the so-called 'Corn-Sugar Bill.'"

In a 1927 efficiency move, the Agriculture Department split the old Bureau of Chemistry in two. It created a Food, Drug and Insecticide Administration to handle consumer protection duties, with Campbell as its head. The other division was the Bureau of Chemistry and Soils, with a focus on more basic agricultural research. The former chief hated the change, which he felt dismantled the agency that he had nurtured and shaped. He feared, as he wrote in his column, that the government had split and weakened the unit and would next simply set pure-food issues aside. Despite the positive signs—three years later Campbell's agency was renamed the Food and Drug Administration, a clear sign of sharpened focus—he saw nothing but his own work being undermined and dismissed. He was now eighty-two years old and he was weary of the war. He stepped down from his full-time job at *Good Housekeeping* and decided to channel his remaining energy into detailing his grievances.

Wiley poured his anger and disappointment into a self-published book, *The History of a Crime Against the Food Law*. It appeared in 1929, bearing the unwieldy subtitle *The Amazing Story of the National Food and Drugs Law Intended to Protect the Health of the People, Perverted to Protect Adulteration of Food and Drugs*. A four-hundred-plus-page tirade, it detailed the many often-vicious attacks on Wiley and derided his attackers. It revisited in detail the early corruption of the law's enforcement and leapfrogged into the enforcement failures of the 1920s.

The government had gotten it wrong, he wrote, on everything from toxic food dyes to imitation whiskeys, preservatives, labeling, corn syrup and soft drinks, and, most recently, saccharin. He decried "the ignominy and disgrace of great scientific men bending their efforts to defeat the purpose of one of the greatest laws ever enacted for protection of the public welfare." If successive administrations had not bent to industry pressure, he asserted, the government would have avoided "outraged public opinion," the American people would have become stronger and healthier, and "this History of a Crime would never have been written."

The book's bitter tone dismayed Wiley's old colleagues, but they could recognize that his weariness and anger came partly from his declining health. Suffering from heart disease, he kept mostly to his home. But he too felt that his angry screed should not be his last word. Wiley began working with freelance writer Orland "O.K." Armstrong on another book, an autobiography to be published by the Bobbs-Merrill Company of Indianapolis.

It may have been the influence of Armstrong, a social activist and reform-minded journalist (and later a member of Congress from Missouri), but the resulting work reflected a personality much closer to that of the younger Wiley—the Indiana-born chemist and occasional versifier with a lively sense of humor. It reflected his old passion to do good and his abiding belief in the power of science to benefit society. "The freedom of science should be kept inviolate," he urged in its conclusion, and he returned to his old call for moral standards in research—that science should live up to its ultimate calling, which was "to search for truth and thereby to elevate and improve mankind."

Harvey Washington Wiley: An Autobiography was published in late 1930, but Wiley never had a chance to hold that last book or learn how it was received. He died on June 30 of that year exactly twenty-four years to the day after Theodore Roosevelt had signed into law the Pure Food and Drug Act. He was buried in Arlington National Cemetery with a full military service, and his tombstone, on Anna Wiley's orders, bore the legend FATHER OF THE PURE FOOD LAW. She'd also asked the minister to base his final tribute in a sermon on St. Paul's words in the second Gospel of Timothy: "I have fought a good fight, I have finished my course, I have kept the faith."

Walter Campbell was at the graveside to pay his respects. Despite Wiley's late-life doubts about him, Campbell would continue to lead the fight for stronger food and drug regulation. In this he would be joined by activist groups formed in the 1930s, such as the Consumers' Union, as well as longtime Wiley allies such as the American Medical Association and the still-powerful women's organizations. New adulteration abuses would also come to light, ones that again highlighted the weaknesses of the old law. In a scathing book on the country's health policies, *100,000,000 Guinea Pigs*, the founders of the Consumers' Union stated flatly, "Pure food laws do not protect you" and provided instances of everything from fake antiseptics to mascaras thick with lead to apples tainted by arsenic-rich pesticides. The consumer group directly blamed the pro-business U.S. government for the "squeezing out of Dr. Wiley and his policies," a program that daily put American citizens at risk.

Consumer advocates renewed those charges to real effect when, horrifically, more than one hundred people—many of them children—died in late 1937, poisoned by cough syrup sweetened with the solvent diethylene glycol (often found in antifreeze). The Tennessee company that made the lethal concoction had, of course, not been required to safety-test it under the 1906 regulation. In fact, the only charge possible under the law was mislabeling; the syrup had been labeled an "elixir" despite the fact that it did not contain alcohol.

Campbell's FDA had mounted an investigation of the event and now put it to political use. He'd been pushing the administration of Franklin D. Roosevelt on this issue for years, with limited success. Now, with everyone from pediatricians to parents expressing deep anger at government inaction, the cough syrup tragedy spiraled into a national scandal, one that soon sparked passage of that better law, the Food, Drug, and Cosmetic Act of 1938. The legislation replaced and greatly expanded on the 1906 legislation, correcting many of its deficiencies and enlarging the authority of the U.S. Food and Drug

Administration. And although he did not live to see it, the new law, signed by President Roosevelt on June 25, 1938, marked the moment that Harvey Wiley's once-tiny, six-man Division of Chemistry achieved one of his long-held dreams. The newly empowered FDA would become an independent agency with the real authority to protect American citizens against risky drugs and tainted food.

Wiley might have seen, at last, in the new agency that "more perfect" regulatory structure he'd hoped would arise from the 1906 law. He would have also undoubtedly continued to harangue the FDA to pursue even more perfect protection of his fellow citizens. "I believe," he said while lobbying year after year for the first food and drug law, "in the chemistry of inward and spiritual grace. And I believe in its application to the welfare of humanity," and nothing less would do.

EPILOGUE

The story of consumer protection in the United States is often the story of a country playing defense, an account of government regulators waking up, time and time again, to yet another public health crisis.

The 1906 food and drug law, which established federal food regulation, was propelled into being largely by a series of scandals over food processing, including the gruesomely spectacular case of the Chicago meatpackers. The 1938 law, which created the modern U.S. Food and Drug Administration, was passed following the deaths of dozens of children who were poisoned by a cough syrup legally sweetened with the antifreeze ingredient diethylene glycol. A 1956 decision by the FDA to ban some of the old coal-tar dyes arose from the sickening of children by Halloween candy that contained unsafe levels of orange and red coloring agents. A 1976 law authorizing the agency to regulate medical devices was passed after some 200,000 women reported injuries from an intrauterine birth control device called the Dalkon Shield.

More recently, the Food Safety Modernization Act (FSMA), a sweeping update to the FDA's protective authority, was signed into law after one of the most severe food-poisoning outbreaks in American history, one that continued for months—from late 2008 to early 2009—and derived from one of the country's most trusted and ordinary food staples.

The cause was a line of peanut butters made by the Virginia-based Peanut Corporation of America. The company used factories that were deliberately unregistered to avoid government attention. Many of the jars and containers of peanut butter, produced in notably unsanitary conditions, contained the pathogenic bacteria salmonella. People in forty-six states were sickened; the U.S. Centers for Disease Control and Prevention linked the products to an estimated nine deaths and up to 22,000 illnesses. To the dismay of consumers and legislators alike, the source of the contamination was identified not by the federal government but by state laboratories in Minnesota, Georgia, and Connecticut, harking back to nineteenth-century failures in enforcing nationwide consumer protection.

Two years later, in 2011, President Barack Obama signed the FSMA into law. The act once again enhanced the FDA's ability to prevent food safety problems. It included new requirements that food growers, food importers, and food processors adhere to specific, agency-determined safety practices and keep records of compliance. The first stricter rules for crop management began to go into effect in the summer of 2017, prompting some farmers—in language eerily reminiscent of early-twentieth-century complaints—to protest that the government now expected their fields to be as sterile as hospitals. Agricultural business groups have asked that the federal government tone down the regulations and expressed optimism that the current administration, under President Donald J. Trump, will do so.

During his successful 2016 campaign for the White House, Trump promised to have his cabinet "submit a list of every wasteful and unnecessary regulation which kills jobs, and which does not improve public safety, and eliminate them." His FDA commissioner, Scott Gottlieb, followed that promise by saying that while he recognizes the importance of food safety legislation he wants to "strike the right balance" in its implementation. Consumer groups now anticipate delayed and reduced protections from agencies facing deep budget cuts. The Earthjustice Institute has warned of the "Trump administration's willingness to accommodate even unfounded and partial industry opposition to the detriment of the health and welfare of people and families across the country."

Such a warning, with its mix of theatrical anger and genuine dismay, could have been written, almost word for word, by Harvey Washington Wiley more than a century ago. This sense of déjà vu, echoing down the years, should remind us of the ways that food safety practices have dramatically changed in this country—and of the ways they have changed hardly at all.

Thanks to the work of people like Wiley and his colleagues at the turn of the twentieth century, thanks to generations of consumer advocates, scientists, attorneys, journalists, and, yes, dedicated public servants, we've come a long way from the unregulated and unsafe food and drink that imperiled American citizens in the past. Today we are buffered by rules and institutions created over the past century to protect American citizens from deceit and danger in the food supply.

If we pay attention, we see signs of those protections every day, in large ways and small. Food labels, for instance, contain a wealth of information about ingredients and nutrition—not as much as some of us might want, but more than many of us will ever take the time to read. New products are safety-tested. Food-poisoning outbreaks are monitored and traced; tainted products are subject to recall; food and drug manufacturers who cause harm can be criminally prosecuted. In 2015 the chief executive of the Peanut Corporation of America was sentenced to twenty-eight years in prison for fraud, conspiracy, and the introduction of adulterated food into interstate commerce.

And these same principles, also built on lessons learned from crises, have been applied to other protective measures— environmental regulations being an outstanding example of that. About a half century after Wiley's crusade for food and drug protections, Americans became increasingly alarmed over evidence of industrial and agricultural pollution. In her influential 1962 book *Silent Spring*, Rachel Carson drew a vivid portrait of the destructive nature of untested pesticides. In 1969 Congress passed the National Environmental Policy Act, and the following year President Richard Nixon established the U.S. Environmental Protection Agency. The EPA has, over the years, been a central force in cleaning up our land, air, and water, but again new fears have risen about the agency's increasingly corporate-friendly policies. Agency administrators, appointed by President Trump, have shifted the EPA's direction toward protection of the oil and gas industry, including removing all reference to scientifically proven links between fossil fuels and climate change from the agency websites. In addition, the EPA has shut down a program that helped document that connection by collecting information on gas emissions from industrial sites. "The number of environmental rollbacks in this time frame is staggering," said Harvard University environmental law professor Richard Lazarus after agency administrator Scott Pruitt had been in office for just six months.

We have succeeded in creating a protective system that at its best protects all of us impartially. But it's our responsibility to value and maintain that system. We still need those who will fight on the public's behalf; we still need our own twenty-first-century version of Harvey Washington Wiley—or rather a cadre of them—to fight for those protections if we are to remain safe.

And that, in part, is why stories like his remain so important today. If we are to continue moving in a direction that preserves what's best in this country, we need not romanticize the past but we must learn from what it tells us about our earlier mistakes. The people who fought to correct those long-ago errors still have lessons to share. The story of Harvey Washington Wiley, at his fierce and fearless best, should remind us that such crusaders are necessary in the fight. That the fight for consumer protection may never end. But if it does, if that long-awaited final victory is achieved, it will be because we, like Wiley, refused to give up.

Gratitudes

When I finish a book, one of my first thoughts—after those of cartwheeling around the room—is to thank everyone I know for putting up with me. A book of this nature is an obsessive and often antisocial project. So as I return from this sojourn into the nineteenth and early twentieth centuries, I'd like to thank all for their patience with the time traveler.

At the top of that long list is my editor, Ann Godoff, not only for her patience but also for her deep interest and often brilliant counsel during the book-writing process; my terrific agent, Suzanne Gluck, who is ever both encouraging and wise; my husband, Peter Haugen, for his generosity and invaluable help in pulling a very messy story into a coherent one; my sons, Marcus and Lucas Haugen, for their savvy twenty-something perspective on fake food and for their help in prioritizing my enormous stack of early-twentieth-century publi-cations with a special thanks to Lucas for his smart analysis of *What to Eat*; my former graduate student Kate Prengaman for her tireless investigations of the history of food safety, including a visit to the Library of Congress that involved days of sorting through a daunting stack of boxes from the Wiley papers; and the truly wonderful librarians in the Science Reading Room and the Manuscript Division of the Library of Congress, who collect and watch over some of our country's most important history. As always, thanks to my friends Kim Fowler, Denise Allen, and Pam Ruegg for their interest and encouragement throughout this book and others.

And a special thanks to my mother, Ann Blum, who never failed to listen to my food horror stories with grace and humor and who frequently kept me on track with the question about the book's progress, beginning, "My friends are wondering when . . ."

Finally, that there is a "when" at all owes more than I can say to the many dedicated professionals at Penguin Press. Special thanks to Casey Denis, Will Heyward, Hilary Roberts, Eric Wechter, Sarah Hutson, and Matt Boyd. They are the often unsung heroes of every book you pick up and it is a pleasure to thank them here.

Notes

Harvey Washington Wiley was married to an outspoken and widely admired Washington, DC, suffragette—Anna Kelton Wiley—who had also worked for years at the Library of Congress. Not surprisingly, she donated his carefully kept and voluminous (70,000 items spanning almost 250 file containers) papers to the library. They are kept in the manuscript division there, and the online finder's guide can be found at http://findingaids.loc.gov.

In the course of researching this book, I made several visits to study these papers; many of the details in this book are drawn from letters, memos, telegrams, invitations, programs, diaries, newspaper and magazine articles, and other resources in the archive. For those interested in food, history, and public health, I also spent time at the remarkable Cookery, Nutrition and Food Technology collection at the Library of Congress, where I found everything from magazines like *What to Eat* to a collection of cookbooks that are in themselves a history of the United States: www.loc.gov/acq/devpol/cookery.pdf.

All other resources—books, papers, documents, and other publications—are described below with, on occasion, some additional context and explanation.

Introduction

1 **Milk offers a stunning:** Many of these outrages are cited in *The Milk Trade in New York and Vicinity*, by John Mullaly (New York: Fowler and Wells, 1853). The *New York Times* also published a series of exposés on the subject in the 1850s that reflected Mullaly's outrage in stories such as "How We Poison Our Children" (May 13, 1858). The many problems with nineteenth- and early-twentieth-century milk are noted in numerous other publications, both contemporary, such as Thurman B. Rice, "The Milk Problem," in *The Hoosier Health Officer: The History of the Indiana State Board of Health to 1925* (Indianapolis: Indiana State Board of Health, 1946), pp. 161–68, and more recently, in food safety histories such as James Harvey Young, "Mercury, Meat and Milk," in *Pure Food* (Princeton, NJ: Princeton University Press, 1989), pp. 18–39.

2 **Fakery and adulteration:** These fakeries were studied by Harvey Wiley and his chemistry group for years. He summarized many of the findings in Harvey Washington Wiley, *Foods and Their Adulteration* (Philadelphia: P. Blackiston's Sons, 1907), and in Harvey W. Wiley and Anne Lewis Pierce, *1001 Tests of Foods, Beverages and Toilet Accessories, Good and Otherwise* (New York: Hearst's International Library Company, 1914).

3 **"Ingenuity, striking hands":** La Follette's speech can be found in *Congressional Record*, 49th Cong., 1st sess., vol. 17, appendix, pp. 223–26, and is noted in Young's book *Pure Food*, which also focuses on the pure-food crusade that gained power in the late nineteenth century, notably in chapter 6, titled "Initiative for a Law Resumed," pp. 125–46.

4 **This especially galled:** The comparison of unregulated U.S. alcoholic beverages with those in Europe can be found in Charles Albert Crampton, U.S. Department of Agriculture, "Fermented Alcohol Beverages, Malt Liquors, Wine and Cider," part 3 of U.S. Department of Agriculture, bulletin 13, *Foods and Food Adulterants* (Washington, DC: Government Printing Office, 1887). Between 1887 and 1893, the Bulletin 13 series, established by Wiley, investigated dairy products, spices and condiments, alcoholic beverages, lard, baking powders, sweetening agents, tea, coffee and cocoa, and canned vegetables. These are summarized in Oscar E. Anderson Jr., *The Health of a Nation: Harvey W. Wiley and the Fight for Pure Food* (Chicago: University of Chicago Press, 1958), pp. 73–74.

4 **"this great country":** This is a quote from Frank Hume, chair of the Local Call Committee of the National Pure Food and Drug Congress of 1898. The quote is highlighted in *Pure Food*, p. 125, and the full presentation can be found in the *Journal of Proceedings of the National Pure Food and Drug Congress Held in Columbia University Hall* (Washington, DC, March 2, 3, 4–5, 1898). Further description can be found in Suzanne Rebecca White, "Chemistry and Controversy: Regulating the Use of Chemicals in Foods, 1883–1959" (PhD diss., Emory University, 1994).

6 **great food safety chemist:** Anderson, *Health of a Nation*, p. 148.

Chapter One: A Chemical Wilderness

11 **"I am not possessed":** This quote can be found on page 20 of Harvey Washington Wiley, *An Autobiography* (Indianapolis: Bobbs-Merrill, 1930), which served as one of the primary sources for this section. For the biographical material in this chapter, I also drew upon the letters and diaries archived at the Library of Congress and voluminous biographical material, including that found in Oscar E. Anderson Jr., *The Health of a Nation: Harvey W. Wiley and the Fight for Pure Food* (Chicago: University of Chicago Press, 1958); James Harvey Young, *Pure Food* (Princeton, NJ: Princeton University Press, 1989); and Laurine Swainston Goodwin, *The Pure Food, Drink and Drug Crusaders, 1879–1914* (Jefferson, NC: McFarland, 1999), among many other sources.

12 **"can not climb to Heaven":** Anderson, *Health of a Nation*, pp. 10–11.

14 **In 1820 a pioneering book:** Accum's *A Treatise on Adulterations of Food, and Culinary Poisons* is cited by many food safety historians as one of the most influential nineteenth-century publications. It can be found (along with its wonderful cover featuring a skull peering out of a cooking pot) as a public-domain publication on the Internet Archive: https://archive.org/stream/treatiseonadulte00a ccurich#page/n5/mode/2up. The British physician Arthur Hill Hassall built on Accum's work, publishing many accounts of toxic foods, such as candies, in the *Lancet* and summarizing those reports in *Food and Its Adulterations* (London: Longman, Brown, Green and Longmans, 1855).

14 **"millions of children are thus":** This quote is from another book on arsenic: John Parascandola, *King of Poisons: A History of Arsenic* (Lincoln, NE: Potomac Books, 2012), p. 128. A remarkable overview can also be found in environmental historian James C. Whorton's book *The Arsenic Century: How Victorian Britain Was Poisoned at Home, Work and Play* (New York: Oxford University Press, 2010), in a chapter titled "Sugared Death," pp. 139–68.

15 **"They poison and cheat"**: Angell's push to protect the food supply is described in Young, *Pure Food*, pp. 45–48.

16 **"Not only are substances"**: Young, *Pure Food*, p. 51.

16 **In 1881 the Indiana**: Wiley's investigation of fraud in sweetening agents was titled "Glucose and Grape Sugar" and was published in *Popular Science Monthly* 19 (June 1881). The article can be found online at https://en.wikisource.org/wiki/Popular_Science_Monthly/Volume_19/June_1881 /Glucose_and_Grape-Sugar. His comment about entering the fray over "Wiley's Lie" can be found on p. 151 of Wiley, *An Autobiography*.

19 **"The dangers of adulteration"**: Anderson, *Health of a Nation*, p. 22.

21 **"These were the first"**: Wiley, *An Autobiography*, p. 165.

21 **In 1883, the Agriculture**: Wiley's decision to leave Purdue, his battle with Peter Collier, including the quotes about "public attacks," his impressions of the Division of Chemistry, the political background of his start in federal service, and his decision to ban smoking can be found in Wiley, *An Autobiography*, pp. 159–75. Wiley was early in his belief that tobacco smoking was harmful to health; in 1927 he even warned that it might contribute to cancer, a fact noted in his official FDA biography: www.fda.gov/aboutfda/whatwedo/history/centennialoffda/harveyw.wiley/default.htm.

23 **"I have every year"**: John Mullaly, *The Milk Trade in New York and Vicinity* (New York: Fowler and Wells, 1853). Further investigation of "swill dairies," which used cheap waste products from breweries as the food source for milk cattle, can be found in "Swill Milk: History of the Agitation of the Subject: The Recent Report of the Committee of the New York Academy of Medicine," *New York Times*, January 27, 1860, p. 1. The issue is also explored in Bee Wilson, *Swindled: The Dark History of Food Fraud, from Poisoned Candy to Counterfeit Coffee* (Princeton, NJ: Princeton University Press, 2008). Wilson offers in particular a vivid description of swill dairies (pp. 159–62).

23 **"so numerous a proportion"**: Albert Leeds, "The Composition of Swill Milk," *Journal of the American Chemical Society* 42 (1890): pp. 451–52.

23 **"sticks, hairs, insects"**: Thurman B. Rice, *The Hoosier Health Officer* (Indianapolis: Indiana Department of Health, 1946), pp. 162–63.

23 **It revealed, as expected**: "Dairy Products," part 1 of U.S. Department of Agriculture, *Foods and Food Adulterants*, bulletin no. 13 (Washington, DC: Government Printing Office, 1887).

24 **The ability of producers**: The history of oleomargarine is detailed in Ethan Trex, "The Surprisingly Interesting History of Margarine," *Mental Floss*, August 1, 2010; and Rebecca Rupp, "Butter Wars: The Margarine Was Pink," *The Plate*, August 13, 2014, http://theplate.nationalgeographic.com/2014/08/13/the-butter-wars-when-margarine-was-pink/; among others. The battle over the first margarine law is described in those articles, in Young, *Pure Food*, pp. 71–94, and in detail in Geoffrey P. Miller, "Public Choice at the Dawn of the Special Interest State: The Story of Butter and Margarine," *California Law Review* 77, no. 1 (January 1989): 81–131.

25 **"We face a new situation"**: Young, *Pure Food*, p. 66. The other comments from legislators—such as Grout on "bastard butter," are from the same source at pp. 71–80. The congressional debate over oleomargarine, including many of the same quotes, can also be found in chapter 10 of Douglass Campbell M.D., *The Raw Truth About Milk* (Rogers, AR: Douglass Family Publishing, 2007).

27 **"It is undoubtedly true"**: "Dairy Products," p. 10.

27 **"nearly the same chemical"**: "Dairy Products," p. 73.

27 **"the use of mineral coloring"**: "Dairy Products," p. 107.

27 **That same year**: Jesse P. Battershall, *Food Adulteration and Its Detection* (New York and London: E. & F. N. Spon, 1887) can be found online at https://books.google.com/books?id=i-AMAAAY AAJ&pg=PP11&lpg=PP11&dq=battershall,+food+and+detection&source=bl&ots= EB3hZWz-BN&sig=9qeRqV_92ipt89D1dY27qthifHM&hl=en&sa=X&ved=0ahUKEwjm27um 3q7WAhUHySYKHeFxAtEQ6AEINDAC#v=onepage&q=battershall%2C%20food%20and% 20detection&f=false.

28 **"Could only a portion"**: Clifford Richardson, "Spices and Condiments," part 2 of U.S. Department of Agriculture, *Foods and Food Adulterants*, Bulletin 13 (Washington, DC: Government Printing Office, 1887).

Chapter Two: Cheated, Fooled, and Bamboozled

29 **Yet Battershall's 1887 book**: Jesse P. Battershall, *Food Adulteration and Its Detection* (New York and London: E. & F. N. Spon, 1887).

30 **Richardson, writing in the bulletin:** Clifford Richardson, "Spices and Condiments," part 2 of U.S. Department of Agriculture, Bulletin 13, *Foods and Food Adulterants* (Washington, DC: Government Printing Office, 1887).

32 **The third and final:** C. A. Crampton, "Fermented Alcoholic Beverages, Malt Liquors, Wine, and Cider," part 3 of U. S. Department of Agriculture, Bulletin 13, *Foods and Food Adulterants* (Washington, DC: Government Printing Office, 1887).

32 **Found in plants:** The backstory of salicylic acid is widely published, in places ranging from Daniel R. Goldberg, "Aspirin: Turn-of-the-Century Miracle Drug," *Distillations*, summer 2009, www .chemheritage.org/distillations/magazine/aspirin-turn-of-the-century-miracle-drug, to T. Hebner and B. Everts, "The Early History of Salicylates in Rheumatology and Pain," *Clinical Rheumatology* 17, no. 1 (1998): 17–25.

33 **"In this country but little":** Crampton, "Fermented Alcoholic Beverages," p. 35.

34 **"This report closes":** Crampton, "Fermented Alcoholic Beverages," pp. 142–44.

34 **"a healthy stomach can":** Harvey Wiley, "Introduction," in Crampton, "Fermented Alcoholic Beverages," p. 4.

35 **Like Wiley, Rusk had:** Wiley describes Rusk's tenure in Harvey Washington Wiley, *An Autobiography* (Indianapolis: Bobbs-Merrill, 1930), pp. 181–83, as "the golden epoch in my service in the Department of Agriculture."

35 **The lard study again:** H. W. Wiley, "Lard and Lard Adulterations," part 4 of U.S. Department of Agriculture, Bulletin 13, *Food and Food Adulterants* (Washington, DC: Government Printing Office, 1891).

36 **Increasingly frustrated that:** Harvey Young, *Pure Food* (Princeton, NJ: Princeton University Press, 1989), p. 106.

36 **"utter recklessness and hard-heartedness":** Alexander Wedderburn, U.S. Department of Agriculture, "A Popular Treatise on the Extent and Character of Food and Drug Adulteration" (Washington, DC: Government Printing Office, 1890).

36 **The division's 1892 investigation:** Guilford L. Spencer and Ervin Edgar Ewell, "Tea, Coffee and Cocoa Preparations," part 7 of U.S. Department of Agriculture, Bulletin 13, *Food and Food Adulterants* (Washington, DC: Government Printing Office, 1892).

36 **"This substance, as its name":** Spencer and Ewell, "Tea, Coffee and Cocoa Preparations," p. 886.

36 **"there is probably":** Spencer and Ewell, "Tea, Coffee and Cocoa Preparations," pp. 933–45.

37 **"Dear Sir," began one:** Spencer and Ewell, "Tea, Coffee and Cocoa Preparations," p. 915.

38 **Lawmakers had taken:** Oscar E. Anderson Jr., *The Health of a Nation: Harvey W. Wiley and the Fight for Pure Food* (Chicago: University of Chicago Press, 1958), pp. 77–79; Young, *Pure Food*, pp. 95–100; Suzanne Rebecca White, "Chemistry and Controversy: Regulating the Use of Chemicals in Foods, 1883–1959" (PhD diss., Emory University, 1994), pp. 1–15.

38 **"The devil has got hold":** Young, *Pure Food*, p. 95.

38 **"as nearly nonpartisan":** Young, *Pure Food*, p. 99.

39 **"To be cheated, fooled":** Harvey W. Wiley, "The Adulteration of Food," *Journal of the Franklin Institute* 137 (1894): p. 266.

39 **"Angry waves of popular":** Young, *Pure Food*, p. 99.

39 **The new secretary was:** Background on Morton can be found at https://en.wikipedia.org/wiki /Julius_Sterling_Morton, which includes links to his biography and his stature as a founder of Arbor Day. His contentious time at the Agriculture Department is detailed in Wiley's autobiography, in *Health of a Nation* at pp. 86–94, and in the internal correspondence of the Agriculture Department archived at the Library of Congress.

40 **"well on the way":** Anderson, *Health of a Nation*, p. 87.

40 **"Is there any necessity":** Morton's increasingly exasperated exchanges with Wiley, regarding both Wedderburn and the budget of the Chemistry Division, can be found in the Harvey Washington Wiley Papers, Library of Congress, Manuscript Division, box 29, folders 1892–93. The work of Wedderburn is further described in Steven L. Piott, *American Reformers 1870–1920: Progressives in Word and Deed* (Lanham, MD: Rowman and Littlefield, 2006), pp. 168–70, and in Courtney I. P. Thomas, *In Food We Trust: The Politics of Purity in American Food Regulation* (Lincoln: University of Nebraska Press, 2014).

41 **The secretary also ordered:** Anderson, *Health of a Nation*, pp. 86–94; Wiley, *An Autobiography*, pp. 183–84. Further budget-cutting measures and exchanges over test tubes, typewriter ribbons, and other reductions, as well as notes from members of Congress regarding the Agriculture budget, can be found in the Wiley Papers, box 29, folder 1894.

42 "The sentiment and truths": Alexander Wedderburn, U.S. Department of Agriculture, *Report on the Extent and Character of Food and Drug Adulteration* (Washington, DC: Government Printing Office, 1894).

42 "President of all": Wiley, *An Autobiography*, p. 186.

43 Wiley wasn't happy: Wiley Papers, box 29. The chemistry exhibits at the 1893 World's Columbian Exposition, including Wiley's speech, are described in "The American Chemical Society at the World's Fair 1893 and 1933," *Chemical & Engineering News* 11, no. 12 (June 20, 1933): pp. 185–86.

44 In the last week: Helen Louise Johnson to Harvey Wiley, October 31, 1893, Wiley Papers, box 29.

45 "I was the manager of": W. L. Parkinson to C. F. Drake, July 28, 1895, Wiley Papers, box 33.

Chapter Three: The Beef Court

47 "I was plunged at once": Harvey Washington Wiley, *An Autobiography* (Indianapolis: Bobbs-Merrill, 1930), p. 180.

48 the nickname "Tama Jim": Wiley described his early days with James Wilson in less than glowing terms. "He had the greatest capacity of any person I ever knew to take the wrong side of public questions, especially those relating to health through diet." Wiley, *An Autobiography*, pp. 190–91. But there are a host of more objective Wilson biographies online, including this one from Iowa State University: www.public.iastate.edu/~isu150/history/wilson.html.

48 Perhaps it was under: Wiley, *An Autobiography*, pp. 194–97.

49 The term dated to: The battles over how to define "real" whiskey and how to define "good" whiskey began in the late 1890s and continued throughout the rest of Wiley's time in office. For an outstanding overview of magazine length, I recommend H. Parker Willis, "What Whiskey Is," *McClure's*, April 1910, pp. 687–99. At book length, the issues are covered in depth in Gerald Carson, *The Social History of Bourbon* (Lexington: University Press of Kentucky, repr. ed. 2010), including the political maneuverings of Kentucky's Edmund Taylor. Regarding the Bottled-in-Bond Act, the Web site Bourbon & Banter offers "A Brief History": www.bourbonbanter.com/banter/bottled-in-bond-a-brief-history/#.WcEGbJOGM0Q.

49 "carelessly made whiskeys": Reid Mitenbuler, *Bourbon Empire: The Past and Future of America's Whiskey* (New York: Penguin Books, 2016), p. 163.

50 Although they could not: The blended whiskey makers, including the Hiram Walker Company, saw Wiley as hostile to their interests. Walker's efforts to protect its brand, as well as its political stance and actions over defining whiskey, are outlined in Clayton Coppin and Jack High, *The Politics of Purity: Harvey Washington Wiley and the Origins of Federal Food Policy* (Ann Arbor: University of Michigan Press, 1999). They get an even more detailed focus in Clayton Coppin and Jack High, "Wiley and the Whiskey Industry: Strategic Behavior in the Passage of the Pure Food and Drug Act," *Business History Review* 62, no. 2 (Summer 1988): 286–309, and in James Files, "Hiram Walker and Sons and the Pure Food and Drug Act" (master's thesis, University of Windsor, 1986). The subtitle of Files's thesis, "A Regulatory Decision Gone Awry," will tell you that he is not a fan of Wiley's position, and Coppin and High are similarly hostile to Wiley's regulatory approach.

51 To the president's dismay: Many of the issues regarding army mismanagement are summarized in Burtin W. Folsom, "Russell Alger and the Spanish American War," Mackinac Center for Public Policy, December 7, 1998, www.mackinac.org/V1998-39. Russell A. Alger was secretary of war during the conflict.

52 The "embalmed beef" scandal: This was news in newspapers across the country, starting in 1898, when the first stories began to appear, and continuing into 1899. As Chicago was home to the meatpacking industry, the *Chicago Tribune* was one of the first to report on the charges by General Miles and to repeat the term "embalmed beef." A December 22, 1898, story, at the top of page 7, was headlined simply "Miles Tells of Embalmed Beef." The scandal was covered by many other newspapers. Coverage in the *New York Times*, for instance, included "The Army Meat Scandal," February 21, 1899, p. 1; "Chemists to Inspect Beef," March 10, 1899, p. 1; "Roosevelt on Army Beef," March 26, 1899, p. 2; "The Army Beef Inquiry," April 14, 1899, p. 8; and "Army Beef Report Is Made Public," May 8, 1899, p. 1.

The scandal is neatly summarized in Andrew Amelinckx, "Old Time Farm Crime: The Embalmed Beef Scandal of 1898," *Modern Farmer*, November 8, 2013, https://modernfarmer.com/2013/11/old-time-farm-crime-embalmed-beef-scandal-1898/, and gets a more academic treatment in Edward F. Keuchel, "Chemicals and Meat: The Embalmed Beef Scandal of the Span-ish American War," *Bulletin of Medical History* 48, no. 2 (Summer 1974): pp. 249–64.

52 **"had to retire to a distance":** "Inspector Fears Embalmed Beef Men," *Chicago Tribune*, October 29, 1899, p. 3. This story also detailed the threats made by the meatpackers against investigators.

52 **"apparently preserved by injected":** Miles's remarks are cited in "Eagan and Embalmed Beef," *New York Times*, February 2, 1899, p. 6.

53 **"He lies in his throat":** "Charles P. Eagan," Wikipedia, https://en.wikipedia.org/wiki/Charles _P._Eagan.

53 **The Dodge hearings satisfied:** "Army Beef Report Is Made Public," *New York Times*, May 8, 1899, p. 1; Harvey Young, "Trichinous Pork and Embalmed Beef," *Pure Food* (Princeton, NJ: Princeton University Press, 1989), pp. 135–40.

54 **In anticipation, the president:** Correspondence concerning the hearings and details of the specific findings can be found in the Harvey Washington Wiley Papers, Library of Congress, Manuscript Division, box 41, folder 1899.

54 **"fill all the interstices":** Memo, Harvey Wiley to James Wilson, January 18, 1899, Wiley Papers, box 41. In addition, Wiley's testimony and his results are in the *Report of the Commission Ap-pointed by the President to Investigate the Conduct of the War Department During the War with Spain* (Washington, DC: Government Printing Office, 1899), pp. 854–62.

54 **"Packingtown," as the locals:** A portrait of the old Chicago stockyards can be found in Ron Gross-man, "'Hog Butcher to the World,'" *Chicago Tribune*, February 19, 2012: http://articles.chicago tribune.com/2012-02-19/site/ct-per-flash-stockyards-0219-2-20120219_1 _union-stock-yard-butcher-shop-packingtown. Another retrospective look is Anne Bramley, "How Chicago's Slaughterhouse Spectacles Paved the Way for Big Meat," NPR, *The Salt*, Decem-ber 3, 2015, www.npr.org/sections/thesalt/2015/12/03/458314767/how-chicago-s-slaughterhouse -spectacles-paved-the-way-for-big-meat. And there's a fine overview also at Wikipedia: https: //en.wikipedia.org/wiki/Union_Stock_Yards.

55 **The average housewife:** Food prices are taken from "Prices from the 1899 Sears, Roebuck Gro-cery Lists," Choosing Voluntary Simplicity, no date, www.choosingvoluntarysimplicity.com /prices-from-the-1899-sears-roebuck-grocery-lists/.

55 **The Beef Court convened:** Testimony and later comments, such as from Carl Sandburg, are cov-ered in Young, *Pure Food*, pp. 135–39, and in Edward F. Keuchel, "Chemicals and Meat: The Embalmed Beef Scandal of the Spanish American War," *Bulletin of Medical History* 48, no. 2 (Summer 1974): 253–56. Miles's testimony and grievances are reviewed in Louise Carroll Wade, "Hell Hath No Fury Like a General Scorned: Nelson A. Miles, the Pullman Strike, and the Beef Scandal of 1898," *Illinois Historical Journal* 79 (1986): 162–84.

56 **"It was a disgrace":** "The Army Meat Scandal," *New York Times*, February 21, 1899, p. 1.

59 **The army also sought:** Coverage of the soldier's death can be found in "Poisoned by Army Ra-tion," David B. McGowan, *New York Times*, May 27, 1898, p. 2.

59 **Metal poisoning from canned:** K. P. McElroy and Willard D. Bigelow, "Canned Vegetables," part 8 of U.S. Department of Agriculture, Bulletin 13, *Foods and Food Adulterants* (Washington, DC: Government Printing Office, 1893).

60 **In a *Munsey's* article:** Frank Munsey to Harvey Wiley, July 14, 1899, with a copy of Wiley's article attached, Wiley Papers, box 41.

61 **"embalmed milk" causing:** "Embalmed Milk in Omaha: Many Infant Deaths Believed to Be Due to a Preservative Fluid," *New York Times*, May 30, 1899, p. 1; *Sanitarian* (publication of the Medico-Legal Society of New York) 42 (1899): p. 372; "Sale of Embalmed Milk Less Frequent," Preliminary Report of the Dairy and Food Commissioner for the Year 1907, bulletin 168, Com-monwealth of Pennsylvania, p. 25; A. G. Young, "Formaldehyde as a Milk Preservative," Report to the Maine Board of Public Health, 1899, www.ncbi.nlm.nih.gov/pmc/articles/PMC2329554 /pdf/pubhealthpap00032-0152.pdf; "The Use of Borax and Formaldehyde as Preservatives of Food," *British Medical Journal*, July 7, 1900, pp. 2062–63.

61 **"an epidemic of stomach trouble":** "Embalmed Beef Troubles in Cincinnati," *New York Times*, June 16, 1899, p. 4.

62 **"It is noticeable":** "Embalmed Milk in Omaha: Many Infant Deaths Believed to Be Due to a Pre-servative Fluid," *New York Times*, May 30, 1899, p. 1.

62 **"Two drops of a":** Thurman B. Rice, *The Hoosier Health Officer: The History of the Indiana State Board of Health to 1925* (Indianapolis, Indiana State Board of Health, 1946), p. 162.

63 **"Well, it's embalming":** Rice, *Hoosier Health Officer*, p. 165.

63 **"state confidently that":** Rice, *Hoosier Health Officer*, p. 163.

Chapter Four: What's in It?

65 **In 1899 U.S. senator:** Mason and his role in the hearings are profiled in "Senator Mason, the Champion of Liberty," *San Francisco Call*, January 10, 1899, p. 1. Hearing overviews can be found in Harvey Young, "The Mason Hearings," in *Pure Food* (Princeton, NJ: Princeton University Press, 1989), pp. 140–45; Oscar E. Anderson Jr., *The Health of a Nation: Harvey W. Wiley and the Fight for Pure Food* (Chicago: University of Chicago Press, 1958), pp. 127–32; and Michael Lesy and Lisa Stoffer, *Repast: Dining Out at the Dawn of the New American Century 1900–1904* (New York: W.W. Norton, 2013), which on pages 29–31 includes some of Wiley's most pointed testimony to the committee. A complete summary of the hearings can be found in *Hearings Before the Committee of Interstate and Commerce of the U.S. House of Representatives, on Food Bills Prohibiting the Adulteration, Misbranding and Imitation of Foods, Candies, Drugs and Condiments in the District of Columbia and the Territories, and for Regulating Interstate Traffic Therein and for Other Purposes* (Washington, DC: Government Printing Office, 1902).

69 **sodium borate, or borax:** A basic chemical profile of borax can be found on the Azo Materials Web site, www.azom.com/article.aspx?ArticleID=2588. The history of Pacific Coast Borax Company can be found at the Santa Clarita Valley history Web site, https://scvhistory.com/scvhistory/borax -20muleteam.htm; and at Wikipedia, https://en.wikipedia.org/wiki/Pacific_Coast_Borax_Com pany; and an interactive time line of its most positive moments can be found on the company's own Web site, https://www.20muleteamlaundry.com/about.

69 **During the Mason hearings:** *Hearings Before the Committee.*

70 **In the early spring:** William E. Mason, *Adulteration of Food Products: Report to Accompany S. Res. 447, Fifty-fifth Congress* (Washington, DC: U.S. Government Printing Office, 1900), https:// catalog.hathitrust.org/Record/011713494.

70 **"This is the only civilized":** https://books.google.com/books?id=XelP2FtgWxkC&pg=PA17 &lpg=PA17&dq=Senator+Mason,+1900,+adulteration,+speech,+Senate&source=bl&ots=j51z dLIgP8&sig=NU1WBa_7ePzHO6g7spTpiRpgNv8&hl=en&sa=X&ved=0ahUKEwiDvfmrwqzX AhXB7yYKHaygAfsQ6AEINDAC#v=onepage&q=Senator%20Mason%2C%201900%2C %20adulteration%2C%20speech%2C%20Senate&f=false.

71 **"before the public eye":** Marriott Brosius to Harvey Wiley, November 23, 1899, Harvey Washington Wiley Papers, Library of Congress, Manuscript Division, box 41.

71 **applauded the action:** Anderson, *Health of a Nation*, p. 127.

72 **That same spring:** Anna Kelton to Harvey Wiley, May 22 and 25, 1900, Harvey Washington Wiley Papers, Library of Congress, box 43; Harvey Wiley to Anna Kelton, May 19, 1900, Wiley Papers, box 43.

72 **"When I left for Paris":** Harvey Wiley to William Frear, July 29, 1900, Wiley Papers, box 43.

73 **"You say, 'Why don't'":** Harvey Wiley to Anna Kelton, May 24, 1900, Wiley Papers, box 43.

73 **Secretary Wilson wrote:** James Wilson to Harvey Wiley, August 7, 1900, Wiley Papers, box 43.

74 **In 1901, shortly after:** Anheuser-Busch to Harvey Wiley, June 4, 1900, Wiley Papers, box 45.

74 **The Woman's Christian Temperance:** The Woman's Christian Temperance Union provides a history on its Web site at www.wctu.org/history.html, and there's another from the Frances Willard House museum: https://franceswillardhouse.org/frances-willard/history-of-wctu/. The organization's role in the pure-food fight is covered in detail in Laurine Swainston Goodwin, *The Pure Food, Drink and Drug Crusaders, 1879–1914* (Jefferson, NC: McFarland, 1999). Frances Willard's vision for the organization is outlined on pp. 31–35 and the WCTU's work on a state-by-state basis is noted throughout.

75 **Wisconsin-based Pabst:** Pabst to Harvey Wiley, July 13, 1901, Wiley Papers, box 45.

75 **"This is our secret":** Anheuser-Busch to Harvey Wiley, June 4, 1900, Wiley Papers, box 45.

75 **In May 1901 the Pan-American:** The adulterated food exhibit is described in E. E. Ewell, W. D. Bigelow, and Logan Waller Page, *Exhibit of the Bureau of Chemistry at the Pan-American Exhibition, Buffalo, New York, 1901*, Bulletin 63, U.S. Department of Agriculture, Bureau of Chemistry. It can be found in full at https://archive.org/stream/exhibitofbureauo63ewel/exhibi tofbureauo63ewel_djvu.txt.

77 **Reporter John D. Wells:** John D. Wells, "The Story of an Eye-Witness to the Shooting of the President," *Collier's Weekly*, September 21, 1901; Lewis L. Gould, *The Presidency of William McKinley* (Lawrence: University Press of Kansas, 1981); William Seale, *The President's House: A History* (Washington, DC: White House Historical Association, 1986); "The Assassination of President William McKinley, 1901," EyeWitness to History, 2010, www.eyewitnesstohistory.com/mckinley.htm.

77 **"I told William McKinley":** "1904: Alton Parker vs. Theodore Roosevelt," The Times Looks Back: Presidential Elections 1896–1996, *New York Times*, 2000, http://events.nytimes.com/learning/general/specials/elections/1904/index.html.

78 **"In this hour of":** James Ford Rhodes, *The McKinley and Roosevelt Administrations 1897–1909* (New York: Macmillan, 1922), p. 218.

78 **Wiley feared that if:** Anderson, *Health of a Nation*, pp. 100–102.

79 **"'If I go up there'":** This quote, as well as the excerpt of Wiley's testimony and exchange in Congress on the sugar policy, Roosevelt's response, and Wiley's rueful acknowledgment of the long-lasting effect of this episode, can be found in Harvey Washington Wiley, *An Autobiography* (Indianapolis: Bobbs-Merrill, 1930), pp. 221–23. Wiley also recounts this episode in a self-published and angry book reviewing the fate of food safety legislation: Harvey W. Wiley, *The History of a Crime Against the Food Law* (Washington, DC, 1929), pp. 270–74.

79 **"I consider it a very unwise":** Wiley, *An Autobiography*, pp. 220–21.

79 **"I will let you off":** Wiley, *An Autobiography*, pp. 220–21.

Chapter Five: Only the Brave

80 **By 1901 the Bureau:** Suzanne Rebecca White, "Chemistry and Controversy: Regulating the Use of Chemicals in Foods, 1883–1959" (PhD diss., Emory University, 1994), pp. 8–10.

80 **The American chemical industry:** White, "Chemistry and Controversy," pp. 20–27. Additional information on the well-known Herbert Dow can be found at www.encyclopedia.com/history /encyclopedias-almanacs-transcripts-and-maps/dow-herbert-h and on the less well-known Jacob Baur, of the Liquid Carbonic Company, at http://forgottenchicago.com/articles/the-last-days -of-washburne/.

82 **combative Edwin Ladd:** State Historical Society of North Dakota, "Edwin F. Ladd and the Pure Food Movement," no date, http://ndstudies.gov/gr8/content/unit-iii-waves-development-1861 -1920/lesson-4-alliances-and-conflicts/topic-6-progressive-movements /section-4-edwin-f-ladd-and-pure-food-movement.

83 **"By God, no Eastern":** Culver S. Ladd, *Pure Food Crusader: Edwin Fremont Ladd* (Pittsburgh: Dorrance Publishing, 2009).

83 **To showcase the problem:** Shepard's menu appears in Mark Sullivan, *Our Times*, vol. 2 (1927; repr. New York: Charles Scribner and Sons, 1971), pp. 506–7.

84 **"According to this menu":** Sullivan, *Our Times*, p. 507. See also James Shepard, "Like Substances," Association of National Food and Dairy Departments, Eleventh Annual Convention (1907), pp. 165–74.

85 **Wiley had long worried:** Wiley's hygienic table trials, renamed the "Poison Squad" by newspaper reporters, grew out of his concerns about the lack of good—or often any—science behind chemical additives in the food supplies. He summarizes some of this backstory in Harvey W. Wiley, "The Influence of Preservatives and Other Substances Added to Foods upon Health and Metabolism," *Proceedings of the American Philosophical Society* 47, no. 189 (May–August 1908): pp. 302–28. His subsequent investigations on compounds ranging from borax to formaldehyde to salicylic acid cite in the introductory sections the previous research or lack of it. The Poison Squad studies themselves have been widely covered, both by newspapers and magazines of the time and by more recent food safety historians. For simplicity's sake, I'll provide here some of the most comprehensive summaries: White, "Chemistry and Controversy," pp. 46–91; Laurine Swainston Goodwin, *The Pure Food, Drink and Drug Crusaders, 1879–1914* (Jefferson, NC: McFarland, 1999), pp. 219–24; Harvey Young, *Pure Food* (Princeton, NJ: Princeton University Press, 1989), pp. 151–57; Oscar E. Anderson Jr., *The Health of a Nation: Harvey W. Wiley and the Fight for Pure Food* (Chicago: University of Chicago Press, 1958), pp. 149–52; Michael Lesy and Lisa Stoffer, *Repast: Dining Out at the Dawn of the New American Century 1900–1904* (New York: W.W. Norton, 2013), pp. 31–34; Bruce Watson, "The Poison Squad: An Incredible History," *Esquire*, June 27, 2013; Natalie Zarelli, "Food Testing in 1902 Featured a Bow Tie–Clad 'Poison Squad' Eating Plates of Acid," *Atlas Obscura*, August, 30, 2016, www.atlasobscura.com/articles/food -testing-in-1902-featured-a-tuxedoclad-poison-squad-eating-plates-of-acid.

85 **"young, robust fellows":** Harvey Washington Wiley, U.S. Department of Agriculture, *Influence of Food Preservatives and Artificial Colors on Digestion and Health: Boric Acid and Borax* (Washington, DC: Government Printing Office, 1904), p. 10.

85 **"whether such preservatives":** Wiley, *Influence of Food Preservatives*, p. 23.

86 **"enable the Secretary":** Wiley, *Influence of Food Preservatives*, p. 8.

86 **"Cheerful surroundings, good company"**: Wiley, *Influence of Food Preservatives*, pp. 13–14.

87 **"open, for the first time"**: Carol Lewis, "The 'Poison Squad' and the Advent of Food and Drug Regulation," *U.S. Food and Drug Administration Consumer Magazine*, November–December 2002, http://esq.h-cdn.co/assets/cm/15/06/54d3fdf754244_-_21_PoisonSquadFDA.pdf.

87 **"They are clerks"**: Lewis, "The 'Poison Squad.'"

87 **"Dear Sir," wrote one**: Bruce Watson, "The Poison Squad: An Incredible History," *Esquire*, June 26, 2013, http://www.esquire.com/food-drink/food/a23169/poison-squad/.

87 **"You will begin"**: Harvey Wiley to H. E. Blackburn, August 15, 1901, Wiley Papers, box 45.

88 **"so they came to us"**: Wiley, *Influence of Food Preservatives*, p. 10.

88 **"Did you explain"**: *The Borax Investigation: Hearings Before the Committee of Interstate and Foreign Commerce*, U.S. House of Representatives (Washington, DC: Government Printing Office, February 1906).

88 **As the details of the project**: Newspaper coverage of Wiley's toxicity studies is discussed in wonderful detail in Kevin C. Murphy, "Pure Food, the Press, and the Poison Squad: Evaluating Coverage of Harvey W. Wiley's Hygienic Table," 2001, www.kevincmurphy.com/harveywiley2.html.

89 **"Should they become hungry"**: Murphy, "Pure Food, the Press, and the Poison Squad."

89 **"pursue their ordinary"**: Wiley, *Influence of Food Preservatives*.

90 **One of them involved**: John C. Thresh and Arthur Porter, *Preservatives in Food and Food Examination* (London: J & A Churchill, 1906), pp. 16–52.

90 **Unlike Wiley, who**: F. W. Tunnicliffe and Otto Rosenheim, "On the Influence of Boric Acid and Borax upon the General Metabolism of Children," *Journal of Hygiene* 1, no. 2 (April 1901): 168–201.

91 **Wiley knew his study**: H. W. Wiley, "Results of Experiments on the Effect of Borax Administered with Food," *Analyst*, January 1, 1904, pp. 357–70.

91 **"It is pointed out"**: Wiley, "Results of Experiments on the Effect of Borax."

92 **"Those who thought"**: Wiley, "Results of Experiments on the Effect of Borax."

92 **his experiment had attracted**: Brown's approach to covering the Poison Squad is described in Murphy, "Pure Food, the Press, and the Poison Squad." Among his stories published in the *Washington Post*: "Dr. Wiley and His Boarders," November 21, 1902, p. 2; "Borax Ration Scant: Official Chef Falls in Disfavor with Guests," December 23, 1902, p. 2; "Dr. Wiley in Despair: One Boarder Becomes Too Fat and Another Too Lean," December 16, p. 2; and "Borax Begins to Tell—at Least the Six Eaters Are All Losing Flesh," December 26, 1902, p. 2.

92 **"I can't say anything"**: "Borax Begins to Tell."

93 **"The authorities are apprehensive"**: Murphy, "Pure Food, the Press, and the Poison Squad."

93 **"braving the perils"**: "Dr. Wiley and His Boarders."

94 **Christmas dinner menu**: Murphy, "Pure Food, the Press, and the Poison Squad," p. 3.

94 **That December he'd been**: American Association for the Advancement of Science to Harvey Wiley, November 22, 1902, Harvey Washington Wiley Papers, Library of Congress, Manuscript Division, box 48. Harvey Wiley, "Poison Dinner Invitation," 1902, Wiley Papers, box 48.

95 **Molineux was one of**: Deborah Blum, *The Poisoner's Handbook: Murder and the Birth of Forensic Medicine in Jazz Age New York* (New York: Penguin Books, 2010), pp. 61–63.

95 **"F.B. Linton, who weighs"**: "Borax Begins to Tell."

96 **"Dr. Wiley is in despair"**: This and the other comedic lines from Brown's reporting are in Murphy, "Pure Food, the Press, and the Poison Squad."

96 **"The change in the complexion"**: "The Chemical Food Eaters," *Summary* (Elmira, NY), April 18, 1903, available at https://books.google.com/books?id=OgFLAAAAYAAJ&pg=PR116&lpg=PR116&dq=borax+turns+boarders+pink,+wiley&source=bl&ots=wCg8DwtqXr&sig=U1hq-ozDBsBsC2rQaX5IcnkNgew&hl=en&sa=X&ved=0ahUKEwiy97LB2azXAhWE7iYKHeD2B00Q6AEISDAI#v=onepage&q=borax%20turns%20boarders%20pink%2C%20wiley&f=false.

96 **By that time, the once sedate**: Dockstader's song is reprinted in Murphy, "Pure Food, the Press, and the Poison Squad," p. 4, and in most accounts of the studies.

97 **the paper's editors had to**: Scott C. Bone (editor of the *Washington Post*) to Harvey Wiley, December 24, 1902, Wiley Papers, box 48.

Chapter Six: Lessons in Food Poisoning

98 **In 1903 Fannie Farmer**: A basic biography can be found here: www.notablebiographies.com/Du-Fi/Farmer-Fannie.html.

98 "Food," the book began: Fannie Merritt Farmer, "Food," in *The Boston Cooking-School Cook-book* (1896; repr. Boston: Little, Brown, 1911), full text available at https://archive.org/stream/bostoncookingsch00farmrich#page/n21/mode/2up.

100 Farmer may have been: Fanny Farmer, *Food and Cookery for the Sick and Convalescent* (Boston: Little, Brown, 1904), full text available through the Historic American Cookbook Project: http://digital.lib.msu.edu/projects/cookbooks/html/books/book_56.cfm.

100 "unappetizing and unhealthful": Farmer, *Food and Cookery for the Sick and Convalescent*, pp. 50–58.

100 "The pathogenic germs": Farmer, *Food and Cookery for the Sick and Convalescent*, pp. 50–58.

100 "borax, boracic acid, salicylic acid": Farmer, *Food and Cookery for the Sick and Convalescent*, pp. 50–58.

100 Earlier cookbook authors: To give a couple of examples: Mary Johnson Bailey Lincoln, *Mrs. Lincoln's Boston Cookbook* (Boston: Roberts Brothers, 1884), discusses adulteration of cream of tartar and baking powder (pp. 49–55) and chemicals used to disguise bad chicken (p. 251); and Sarah Tyson Rorer, *Mrs. Rorer's New Cookbook* (Philadelphia: Arnold, 1902), http://digital.lib.msu.edu/projects/cookbooks/html/books/book_54.cfm, cites adulterated arrowroot powder, flour, coffee, mustard powder, and vanilla.

100 "eating poisons under": "Borax Preservatives Found Injurious," *New York Times*, June 23, 1904, p. 9.

101 But the *Times* anticipated: "Borax Preservatives Found Injurious," *New York Times*, June 23, 1904, p. 9; Wiley, *Influence of Food Preservatives and Artificial Colors on Digestion and Health*, vol. 1, *Boric Acid and Borax* (Washington, DC: Government Printing Office, 1904).

101 In June the Department: Wiley, *Influence of Food Preservatives*.

103 Congress once again weighed: Hepburn, McCumber, and their push for food and drug legislation are reviewed in Harvey Young, *Pure Food* (Princeton, NJ: Princeton University Press, 1989), pp. 164–82; Oscar E. Anderson Jr., *The Health of a Nation: Harvey W. Wiley and the Fight for Pure Food* (Chicago: University of Chicago Press, 1958), pp. 158–82; and Mark Sullivan, *Our Times*, vol. 2 (1927; repr. New York: Charles Scribner's Sons, 1971), pp. 268–70.

104 As Warwick Hough, the chief: Young, *Pure Food*, pp. 165–68; James Files, "Hiram Walker and Sons and the Pure Food and Drug Act" (master's thesis, University of Windsor, 1986).

105 "will seriously impair": Warwick Hough to Harvey Wiley, quoted in Files, "Hiram Walker and Sons," p. 120.

105 The issue of drug fakery: In Harvey Washington Wiley, *An Autobiography* (Indianapolis: Bobbs-Merrill, 1930), pp. 203–9, Wiley discusses his concerns about the issue. The hiring of Lyman Kebler, signifying that he was prepared to put more emphasis on the issue, is discussed in Anderson, *Health of a Nation*, p. 103; and Young, *Pure Food*, pp. 118–19. Kebler's meticulous research and reputation for undaunted investigation are profiled in D. B. Worthen, "Lyman B. Kebler: Foe to Fakers," *Journal of the American Pharmaceutical Association* 50, no. 10 (May–June 2010): pp. 429–32.

106 The Proprietary Association: James Harvey Young, *The Toadstool Millionaires: A Social History of Patent Medicines Before Federal Regulation* (Princeton, NJ: Princeton University Press, 2015), pp. 227–35.

106 "If the Federal Government": Young, *Toadstool Millionaires*, p. 229.

106 "It will take more": Sullivan, *Our Times*, p. 270.

107 He also began courting: The importance of women and women's organizations in the battle for regulation is a main focus of Laurine Swainston Goodwin, *The Pure Food, Drink and Drug Crusaders, 1879–1914* (Jefferson, NC: McFarland, 1999); "Women Join the Pure Food War," *What to Eat* 18, no. 10 (October 1905): pp. 158–59; and "Women's Clubs Name Special Food Committee," *What to Eat* 18, no. 12 (December 1905): pp. 191–92.

107 In his Hanover College days: Wiley, *An Autobiography*, pp. 55–65. See also speech to USDA researchers, 1904, Harvey Washington Wiley Papers, Library of Congress, box 189 ("we regard women as human beings").

108 "Man's highest ambition": Harvey Wiley, speech to USDA researchers, 1904, transcript in Harvey Washington Wiley Papers, Library of Congress, box 189.

108 "I know she is not intended": H. M. Wiley in "Men's Views of Women's Clubs: A Symposium by Men Who Are Recognized Leaders in the Philanthropic and Reform Movements in America," *Annals of the American Academy of Political and Social Science* 28 (July–December 1906): p. 291.

108 Born in 1856, Lakey: Nina Redman and Michele Morrone, *Food Safety: A Reference Handbook*, 3rd ed. (Santa Barbara, CA: ABC-Clio, 2017), pp. 130–65; Sullivan, *Our Times*, pp. 521–22.

109 **Addams to begin to speak:** Goodwin, *Pure Food, Drink and Drug Crusaders*, pp. 258–75.

109 **"I think women's":** Wiley in "Men's Views of Women's Clubs."

110 **Lakey urged Wiley:** Alice Lakey, "Adulterations We Have to Eat," *What to Eat* 18, no. 6 (June 1905): pp. 9–10.

110 **"For the purpose of":** Thomas H. Hoskins, M.D., *What We Eat: An Account of the Most Common Adulterations of Food and Drink* (Boston: T.O.H.P. Burnham, 1861), p. iv, text available at https://archive.org/details/whatweeatanacco00hoskgoog.

111 **"flour is present":** John Peterson, "How to Detect Food Adulterations," *What to Eat* 16, no. 2 (February 1903): pp. 11–12.

111 *Some Forms of Food Adulteration:* Willard D. Bigelow and Burton James Howard, U.S. Department of Agriculture, *Some Forms of Food Adulteration and Simple Methods for Their Detection* (Washington, DC: Government Printing Office, 1906), text available at https://archive.org/details/someformsoffooda10bige.

111 **"Sir," wrote Wiley:** Bigelow and Howard, *Some Forms of Food Adulteration*, p. 1.

111 **"It is not in their":** Bigelow and Howard, *Some Forms of Food Adulteration*, p. 34.

113 **On April 30, 1904:** The pure food exhibit at the St. Louis World's Fair is described in "Novel Exhibit of Food Adulteration," *What to Eat* 17, no. 4 (April 1904): pp. 131–32; and Mark Bennett, "Lessons in Food Poisoning," *What to Eat* 17, no. 7 (July 1904): pp. 161–62; Sullivan, *Our Times*, pp. 522–25; Goodwin, *Pure Food, Drink and Drug Crusaders*, pp. 229–32; and Marsha E. Ackermann, "Promoting Pure Food at the 1904 St. Louis World's Fair," *Repast, Quarterly Newsletter of the Culinary Historians of Ann Arbor* 20, no. 3 (Summer 2004): pp. 1–3. The food served at the fair is described in Kate Godfrey-Demay, "The Fair's Fare," *Sauce*, April 9, 2004, pp. 1–4.

114 **"Now let the food adulterer":** Paul Pierce, "Our Allies in the Pure Food," *What to Eat* 16, no. 5 (May 1903): p. 1.

115 **"increase public interest":** Robert Allen to Harvey Wiley, January 24, 1902, Wiley Papers, box 48.

115 **"While potted chicken":** E. F. Ladd, "Some Food Products and Food Adulteration," bulletin 57, North Dakota Agricultural College, Fargo, ND, 1903.

115 **"If you want to":** Bennett, "Lessons in Food Poisoning."

116 **"one of the most":** Sullivan, *Our Times*, p. 522.

117 **"It is true that":** Harvey Wiley, speech given at City College of New York, November 7, 1904, Wiley Papers, box 197.

117 **"There are times in life":** *Journal of Proceedings of the Eighth Annual Convention of the National Association of State Dairy and Food Departments*, September 26–October 1, 1904, St. Louis, Missouri, p. 64.

118 **Hough was also in attendance:** Warwick M. Hough, "The Pure Food Bill and Bottled in Bond Whiskey," *What to Eat* 18, no. 2 (February 1905): pp. 74–75; Anderson, *Health of a Nation*, pp. 159–62.

118 **"I agree with you":** Warwick Hough to Harvey Wiley, quoted in Anderson, *Health of a Nation*, pp. 159–62.

Chapter Seven: The Yellow Chemist

119 **In early November 1904:** The background here for Upton Sinclair's research on the Chicago stockyards and the creation of *The Jungle*, first as a series for *Appeal to Research* and then for book publication, is based on numerous sources. The story is woven through this chapter, and sources for those sections include Anthony Arthur, *Radical Innocent: Upton Sinclair* (New York: Random House, 2006), pp. 43–85; Doris Kearns Goodwin, *The Bully Pulpit: Theodore Roosevelt, William Howard Taft and the Golden Age of Journalism* (New York: Simon & Schuster, 2013), pp. 459–55; Michael Lesy and Lisa Stoffer, *Repast: Dining Out at the Dawn of the New American Century 1900–1904* (New York: W.W. Norton, 2013), pp. 37–61; Mark Sullivan, *Our Times*, vol. 2 (1927; repr. New York: Charles Scribner and Sons, 1971), pp. 471–80; Harvey Young, *Pure Food* (Princeton, NJ: Princeton University Press, 1989), pp. 221–40; and "Upton Sinclair, Whose Muckraking Changed the Meat Industry," *New York Times*, June 30, 2016, www.nytimes.com/interactive/projects/cp/obituaries/archives.

120 **The novel's main character:** Upton Sinclair, *The Jungle* (1906), full text available at www.online-literature.com/upton_sinclair/jungle/.

121 **And a new senator:** Sullivan, *Our Times*, pp. 525–27. A biographical sketch of Heyburn plus a guide to his papers at the University of Idaho can be found at www.lib.uidaho.edu/special-collections/Manuscripts/mg006.htm.

121 **"I am in favor":** Lorine Swainston Goodwin, *The Pure Food, Drink and Drug Crusaders 1879–1914* (Jefferson, NC: McFarland, 1999), p. 227.

121 **The confrontational Heyburn:** Oscar E. Anderson Jr., *The Health of a Nation: Harvey W. Wiley and the Fight for Pure Food* (Chicago: University of Chicago Press, 1958), pp. 173–78.

122 **Meanwhile, the blended-whiskey:** Clayton Coppin and Jack High, "Wiley and the Whiskey Industry: Strategic Behavior in the Passage of the Pure Food and Drug Act," *Business History Review* 62, no. 2 (Summer 1988): pp. 297–300.

122 **"suffer to an extent":** "Labeling Ruinous to Liquor Trade," *New York Journal of Commerce* 131, no. 30 (December 1, 1904): p. 3.

123 **"There is a bill":** Goodwin, *Pure Food, Drink and Drug Crusaders*, p. 242.

123 **"Who is that":** Gerald Carson, *The Social History of Bourbon* (Lexington: University Press of Kentucky, repr. ed. 2010), p. 164.

123 **"What now?" wrote:** Goodwin, *Pure Food, Drink and Drug Crusaders*, p. 243.

123 **"Let somebody muzzle":** "Chemistry on the Rampage," *California Fruit Grower* 15, no. 2 (February 1905): p. 3.

123 **"The greater part of":** "Grocers Stand Against Food Bill Excesses," *Grocery World* 39, no. 12 (March 5, 1905): p. 41.

124 **"I believe in chemistry":** Harvey Wiley, "Food Adulteration and Its Effects" (lecture, Sanitary Science class, Cornell University, 1905).

124 **"On the platform":** Sullivan, *Our Times*, p. 520.

124 **It was a "great battle":** Harvey Washington Wiley, *An Autobiography* (Indianapolis: Bobbs-Merrill, 1930), p. 231.

126 **"it is useless to tell":** Carl Jensen, *Stories That Changed America: Muckrackers of the Early Twentieth Century* (New York: Seven Stories Press, 2002), p. 55.

126 **"I had to tell":** Jensen, *Stories That Changed America*, p. 57.

127 **Meanwhile, other writers:** Charles Edward Russell, *The Greatest Trust in the World* (New York: Ridgeway-Thayer, 1905), full text available at https://archive.org/details/greatesttrustin01russ goog; Henry Irving Dodge, "The Truth About Food Adulterations," *Woman's Home Companion* 48 (March 1905): pp. 6–7; Henry Irving Dodge, "How the Baby Pays the Tax," *Woman's Home Companion* 49 (April 1905): pp. 5–8.

128 **"The Senate does not indulge":** Henry Irving Dodge, "How the Baby Pays the Tax," *Woman's Home Companion* 49 (April 1905): p. 8.

129 **Also in 1905, Pierce's magazine:** The series, "The Slaughter of Americans," appeared in five issues of *What to Eat: What to Eat* 18, no. 2 (February 1905): pp. 1–4; *What to Eat* 18, no. 3 (March 1905): pp. 1–3; *What to Eat* 18, no. 4 (April 1905): pp. 1–5; *What to Eat* 18, no. 5 (May 1905): pp. 1–3; and *What to Eat* 18, no. 6 (June 1905): pp. 1–5.

132 **"I recommend that a law":** Theodore Roosevelt, "Fifth Annual Message," December 5, 1905, transcript available at www.presidency.ucsb.edu/ws/index.php?pid=29546.

132 **"Are we to take up":** Horace Samuel Merrill and Marion Galbraith Merrill, *The Republican Command 1897–1913* (Lexington: University Press of Kentucky, 2015), p. 27.

132 **"On the contrary":** Young, *Pure Food*, pp. 182–83.

133 **"Heyburn said he could":** Sullivan, *Our Times*, pp. 533–34.

134 **Back at the Bureau:** Carol Lewis, "The 'Poison Squad' and the Advent of Food Regulation," *U.S. Food and Drug Administration Consumer Magazine*, November–December 2002, pp. 1–15, http://esq.h-cdn.co/assets/cm/15/06/54d3fdf754244_-_21_PoisonSquadFDA.pdf.

134 **"It is hardly necessary":** Harvey W. Wiley, *Influence of Food Preservatives and Artificial Colors on Digestion and Health*, vol. 2, *Salicylic Acid and Salicylates* (Washington, DC: Government Printing Office, 1906), p. 5, text available at https://archive.org/details/influenceoffoodp84wile_0.

135 **"exerts a depressing":** Wiley, *Influence of Food Preservatives*, p. 8. A critical rebuttal of Wiley's conclusions was published in the industry magazine *American Food Journal* under the title "Salicylic Acid and Health," November 1906, pp. 6–15.

Chapter Eight: The Jungle

137 **To the *Washington* (DC) *Star*:** Harvey Wiley to the *Washington Star*, January 30, 1906, Harvey Washington Wiley Papers, Library of Congress, box 60.

138 **To *Everybody's Magazine*:** Harvey Wiley to *Everybody's Magazine*, February 12, 1906, Wiley Papers, box 60.

138 **"My attention is called":** Arthur H. Bailey to Harvey Wiley, February 26, 1906, Wiley Papers, box 60.

139 **"The attacks which are":** H. C. Adams (27th district, Wisconsin) to Harvey Wiley, February 5, 1906, Wiley Papers, box 60; Harvey Wiley to H. C. Adams, February 12, 1906, Wiley Papers, box 60.

139 **In late February Wiley gave:** Harvey Washington Wiley, *An Autobiography* (Indianapolis: Bobbs-Merrill, 1930), pp. 212–15.

141 **"From the newspapers we notice":** F. H. Madden (director, Reid, Murdoch & Co., Chicago) to Harvey Wiley, February 12, 1906, Wiley Papers, box 60.

141 **"Your wonderful tenacity":** J. E. Blackburn (National Bond and Securities Company) to Harvey Wiley, March 5, 1906, Wiley Papers, box 60.

141 **Charles Reed of the AMA:** Charles Reed to Harvey Wiley, March 6, 1906, Wiley Papers, box 60.

141 **In early March:** Anthony Arthur, *Radical Innocent: Upton Sinclair* (New York: Random House, 2006), pp. 43–85.

142 **"did not care to":** Arthur, *Radical Innocent*, p. 71.

143 **"what is going on":** George Bernard Shaw, *John Bull's Other Island* (New York: Brentano's, 1910), p. 179.

143 **The hostile *Chicago Tribune*:** Arthur, *Radical Innocent*, p. 57.

143 **"I aimed for the public's":** Eric Schlosser, *Chicago Tribune*, "'I Aimed for the Public's Heart, and . . . Hit It in the Stomach,'" May 21, 2006, http://articles.chicagotribune.com/2006-05-21/features/0605210414_1_upton-sinclair-trust-free.

143 **"Tiddy was toying":** Mark Sullivan, *Our Times*, vol. 2 (1927; repr. New York: Charles Scribner and Sons, 1971), p. 535.

144 **The question threw Wilson:** Sullivan, *Our Times*, p. 547. The conflict is covered in his book on pages 536–51. Accounts can also be found in Doris Kearns Goodwin, *The Bully Pulpit: Theodore Roosevelt, William Howard Taft and the Golden Age of Journalism* (New York: Simon & Schuster, 2013), pp. 459–65; and Michael Lesy and Lisa Stoffer, *Repast: Dining Out at the Dawn of the New American Century 1900–1904* (New York: W.W. Norton, 2013), pp. 37–61.

145 **"ignoring at the same":** Theodore Roosevelt, "The Man with the Muck-rake," speech delivered April 14, 1906, transcript available at www.americanrhetoric.com/speeches/teddyrooseveltmuckrake.htm.

145 **The president's attack:** David Graham Phillips, *The Treason of the Senate*, ed. George E. Mowry and Judson A. Grenier (Chicago: Quadrangle Books, 1964), pp. 9–46.

146 **"The men with the muck rakes":** Roosevelt, "Man with the Muck-rake."

146 **"Really, Mr. Sinclair":** Maureen Ogle, *In Meat We Trust: An Unexpected History of Carnivore America* (Boston: Houghton Mifflin, 2013), p. 78.

146 **"Tell Sinclair to go":** Gary Younge, "Blood, Sweat and Fears," *Guardian*, August 4, 2006, www.theguardian.com/books/2006/aug/05/featuresreviews.guardianreview24.

146 **"Many inside rooms":** "Conditions in Stockyard Described in the Neill-Reynolds Report," *Chicago Tribune*, June 5, 1906, p. 1.

148 **"clean and wholesome":** "Conditions in Stockyard Described."

148 **"If a commission of men":** "Discuss New Meat Bill," *Chicago Tribune*, June 4, 1906, p. 4.

148 **"I am sorry to have":** Sullivan, *Our Times*, p. 548.

149 **"In Armour's own establishment":** Lesy and Stoffer, *Repast*, p. 54.

149 **In early June, exasperated:** David Moss and Marc Campasano, "*The Jungle* and the Debate over Federal Meat Inspection in 1906," Harvard Business School case no. N9-716-045, February 10, 2016, https://advancedleadership.harvard.edu/files/ali/files/the_jungle_and_the_debate_over_federal_meat_inspection_in_1906_716045.pdf.

149 **"Roosevelt has a strong":** Lesy and Stoffer, *Repast*, p. 57.

150 **"The momentum of the":** Sullivan, *Our Times*, p. 552.

150 **There were still those:** Phillips, *Treason of the Senate*, pp. 204–7.

151 **Roosevelt's secretary replied:** William Loeb Jr. to Thomas Ship (clerk, Committee on Territories, U.S. Senate), July 12, 1906, Wiley Papers, box 60.

151 **Roosevelt had a different:** Daniel Ruddy, ed., *Theodore Roosevelt's History of the United States (in His Own Words)* (New York: Smithsonian Books, 2010), pp. 211–12; Oscar E. Anderson Jr., *The Health of a Nation: Harvey W. Wiley and the Fight for Pure Food* (Chicago: University of Chicago Press, 1958), p. 190.

Chapter Nine: The Poison Trust

155 **"How does a general feel":** Harvey Washington Wiley, *An Autobiography* (Indianapolis: Bobbs-Merrill, 1930), p. 231.

155 **"I have long contemplated":** L. D. Waterman, MD, to Harvey Wiley, March 15, 1906, Harvey Washington Wiley Papers, Library of Congress, Manuscript Division, box 60.

155 **"I suppose you are pleased":** James Shepard to Harvey Wiley, April 27, 1906, Wiley Papers, box 60.

156 **On July 24 Wilson:** Memo, James Wilson to Harvey Wiley, July 24, 1906, Wiley Papers, box 60.

156 **"is not as good":** Oscar E. Anderson Jr., *The Health of a Nation: Harvey W. Wiley and the Fight for Pure Food* (Chicago: University of Chicago Press, 1958), p. 228.

156 **It did at least contain:** Federal Food and Drugs Act of 1906 (noted on the U.S. Food and Drug Administration Web site as the "Wiley Act"), Pub. L. No. 59-384, 34 Stat. 786 (1906), www.fda.gov/regulatoryinformation/lawsenforcedbyfda/ucm148690.htm; and Robert McD. Allen, "Pure Food Legislation," *Popular Science Monthly* 29 (July 1906): pp. 1–14.

157 **"establish standards of purity":** Robert McD. Allen, "Pure Food Legislation," *Popular Science Monthly* 29 (July 1906): pp. 1–14.

157 **"No set of authorities":** Anderson, *Health of a Nation*, p. 198.

158 **"For seventeen years":** David Graham Phillips, *The Treason of the Senate*, eds. George E. Mowry and Judson A. Grenier (Chicago: Quadrangle Books, 1964), pp. 204–6.

159 **"Naturally when the battle":** Wiley, *An Autobiography*, p. 223.

159 **"The word FOOD does not":** Warwick Hough to James Wilson, November 26, 1906, Wiley Papers, box 60.

160 **"discriminate against one class":** Warwick Hough to James Wilson, December 3, 1906, Wiley Papers, box 60.

160 **He told the lobbyist:** James Wilson to Warwick Hough, December 22, 1906, Wiley Papers, box 60.

160 **"Since you have objected":** Warwick Hough to James Wilson, December 23, 1906, Wiley Papers, box 60.

160 **In a mid-December speech:** Harvey Wiley, lecture at the Atlas Club, Chicago, December 14, 1906, Wiley Papers, box 60.

160 **In 1907 the Bureau:** Harvey W. Wiley, *Influence of Food Preservatives and Artificial Colors on Digestion and Health*, vol. 3, *Sulphurous Acid and Sulphites* (Washington, DC: Government Printing Office, 1907), https://archive.org/details/preservafood00wilerich.

161 **"microscopical examination of":** Wiley, *Influence of Food Preservatives*, p. iii.

161 **"The relations of sulfurous":** Wiley, *Influence of Food Preservatives*, pp. 761–66.

162 **"complete and somewhat":** Wiley, *Influence of Food Preservatives*, pp. 761–66.

162 **"The use of sulfurous":** Wiley, *Influence of Food Preservatives*, pp. 761–66.

163 **In January 1907:** James Tawney's maneuvers to limit food regulations and pure food advocate responses are described in Anderson, *Health of a Nation*, pp. 200–218; and Laurine Swainston Goodwin, *The Pure Food, Drink and Drug Crusaders, 1879–1914* (Jefferson, NC: McFarland, 1999), pp. 275–77.

163 **"impair the efficiency of":** Alice Lakey to Harvey Wiley, February 14, 1907, Wiley Papers, box 63.

164 **"The plot failed":** Goodwin, *Pure Food, Drink and Drug Crusaders*, p. 276.

164 **Opposition to Tawney's amendment:** Samuel Merwin, "The People's Lobby," *Success Magazine* 10 (January 1907): pp. 17–18; People's Lobby to Harvey Wiley, December 13, 1906, Wiley Papers, box 60.

164 **"If anyone is naughty":** "A People's Lobby to Watch," *New York Times*, September 18, 1906, p. 6.

165 **"Secretary Wilson absolutely":** Robert Allen to Henry Needham, March 3, 1907, Wiley Papers box 63.

165 **And Allen himself had:** Anderson, *Health of a Nation*, pp. 211–12.

165 **"I unqualifiedly recommend him":** Robert Allen to Harvey Wiley, May 14, 1907, Wiley Papers, box 63.

165 **Still, Allen's misgivings:** Robert Allen to Henry Needham, April 20, 1907, Wiley Papers, box 63.

166 **The ever-festering conflict:** Harvey Washington Wiley, "1908 Report of the Bureau of Chemistry (from June 1907 to June 1908)," Bureau of Chemistry, U.S. Department of Agriculture, September 14, 1908, Washington, DC.

166 **And barely a month after:** Harvey Young, *Pure Food* (Princeton, NJ: Princeton University Press, 1989), pp. 206–18.

166 **"Crooked is the term":** Anderson, *Health of a Nation*, p. 202.

167 **In a letter to Wilson:** Warwick Hough to James Wilson, October 4, 1906, Wiley Papers, box 60.

168 **In a March 30 letter:** Harvey Wiley to Robert Allen, March 30, 1907, Wiley Papers, box 63; Wiley, *An Autobiography*, pp. 257–59.

168 **But in terms of in-house:** Young, *Pure Food*, pp. 206–18; H. Parker Willis, "What Whiskey Is," *McClure's*, April 1910, pp. 687–99; Mark Sullivan, *Our Times*, vol. 2 (1927; repr. New York: Charles Scribner and Sons, 1971), pp. 509–10.

168 **After reviewing stacks of:** William Wheeler Thomas, *The Law of Pure Food and Drugs* (Cincinnati: W. H. Anderson, 1912), pp. 450–455; Clayton Coppin and Jack High, *The Politics of Purity: Harvey Washington Wiley and the Origins of Federal Food Policy* (Ann Arbor: University of Michigan Press, 1999), pp. 100–110.

169 **On April 10, 1907:** Theodore Roosevelt to James Wilson, April 10, 1907, Wiley Papers, box 63.

169 **"I write to congratulate you":** James Hurty to Harvey Wiley, April 18, 1907, Wiley Papers, box 63.

169 **"Let me congratulate you":** M. A. Scovell to Harvey Wiley, April 20, 1907, Wiley Papers, box 63.

170 **"level headed," he said:** Anderson, *Health of a Nation*, p. 204.

170 **As if to underscore:** James Wilson to George McCabe, March 23, 1907, Wiley Papers, box 63.

170 **"It seems to me":** Wilson to McCabe, March 23, 1907.

170 **But Wilson instead told:** Wiley, *An Autobiography*, pp. 237–39; memo, James Wilson to Harvey Wiley, April 24, 1907, Wiley Papers, box 63.

171 **"walked into my office":** Wiley, *An Autobiography*, p. 238.

172 **"a matter of fairness":** James Wilson to Harvey Wiley, memo, April 24, 1907, Wiley Papers, box 63.

172 **"to take away from the":** Wiley, *An Autobiography*, p. 239.

172 **On June 19, on Wilson's:** Department of State to James Wilson, June 8, 1907, Wiley Papers, box 63.

172 **"In a short time":** Wiley, *An Autobiography*, p. 319.

173 **During the visit, though:** A week after Wiley left, Dunlap moved to take over his duties. Willard Bigelow, who was acting chief of the Bureau of Chemistry, tried strenuously to prevent this, eventually insisting on meeting with Secretary Wilson. Bigelow also found himself battling George McCabe on the solicitor's efforts to undermine food safety enforcement. "I am sorry to trouble you," he wrote to Wiley on July 26, 1907, while the chief chemist was still in France, and warned him that the department was moving to a probusiness stance. These actions are contained in a memo from Dunlap to Bigelow on June 27, 1907, demanding that he be given authority over all bureau correspondence; a reply from Bigelow, on the same day, flatly refusing to do so; a letter of warning from Bigelow to Wiley on June 29, 1907; a memo of reassurance from Wilson to Bigelow on July 1, 1907; and the letter of dismay from Bigelow to Wiley, cited above, on July 26, 1907, all contained in the Wiley Papers, box 63.

173 **Known as Food Inspection Decision (FID) 76:** Anderson, *Health of a Nation*, pp. 206–7.

175 **"Telegrams began to come":** "Question of Sulfur in Dried Fruit at Rest for the Present," letter from James Wilson, *California Fruit Grower*, March 21, 1908, p. 1.

175 **"After listening to these":** *Pacific Rural Press,* August 17, 1907, p. 1; Suzanne Rebecca White, "Chemistry and Controversy: Regulating the Use of Chemicals in Foods" (PhD diss., Emory University, 1994), p. 57.

175 **The department, Wilson reminded:** Memo, James Wilson to Harvey Wiley, August 24, 1907, Wiley Papers, box 63.

176 **Not surprisingly, then:** Harvey Wiley, "What Pure Food Laws Are Doing for Our People," speech at Vernon Avenue Christian Church, Washington, DC, September 5, 1907, transcript in Wiley Papers, box 63.

Chapter Ten: Of Ketchup and Corn Syrup

177 **Ketchup (or catsup) was:** Jasmine Wiggins, "How Was Ketchup Invented?" *The Plate* (blog), *National Geographic*, April 21, 2014, http://theplate.nationalgeographic.com/2014/04/21/how-was-ketchup-invented/; Dan Jurafsky, "The Cosmopolitan Condiment," *Slate*, May 30, 2012, www.slate.com/articles/life/food/2012/05/ketchup_s_chinese_origins_how_it_evolved_from_fish_sauce_to_today_s_tomato_condiment.html.

177 **"take the intestine":** John Brownlee, "How 500 Years of Weird Condiment History Designed the Heinz Ketchup Bottle," *Co.Design*, December 21, 2013, www.fastcodesign.com/1673352/how-500-years-of-weird-condiment-history-designed-the-heinz-ketchup-bottle.

179 **Sodium benzoate is:** James Harvey Young, "The Science and Morals of Metabolism: Catsup and Benzoate of Soda," *Journal of the History of Medicine and Allied Sciences* 23, no. 1 (January

1968): pp. 86–104; Floyd Robinson, "Antiseptics in Tomato Catsup," *American Food Journal*, August 1907, pp. 39–41.

179 **Indiana's Columbia Conserve:** Harvey Washington Wiley, *An Autobiography* (Indianapolis: Bobbs-Merrill, 1930), pp. 234–36.

179 **Heinz was the same age:** Anna Slivka, "H.J. Heinz: Concerned Citizen or Clever Capitalist?" no date, The Ellis School, www.theellisschool.org/page/default?pk=29093.

181 **When the food and drug law:** Heinz Co. Food Products to Harvey Wiley, May 7, 1907, Harvey Washington Wiley Papers, Library of Congress, Manuscript Division, box 63.

181 **Due to its low cost:** "Saccharin from Coal Tar," *New York Times*, February 16, 1897, p. 3; Jesse Hicks, "The Pursuit of Sweet," *Distillations*, Spring 2010, www.chemheritage.org/distillations/magazine/the-pursuit-of-sweet.

182 **The National Food Manufacturers:** The anger of industry is outlined in the food manufacturers' publication, "Benzoate of Soda in Food Products," *American Food Journal*, January 15, 1908, pp. 7–9, in which Wiley is described as a man with "total lack of consideration for the financial interests involved." The meeting with Roosevelt has been widely covered, including in Young, "Science and Morals of Metabolism," pp. 89–92, and in Harvey Washington Wiley, *The History of a Crime Against the Food Law* (Washington, DC: self-published, 1929), pp. 160–68.

182 **"There was no way":** Wiley describes his meeting with the president in rueful detail in *An Autobiography*, pp. 239–41.

183 **"in the interests of":** Harvey W. Wiley, *Influence of Food Preservatives and Artificial Colors on Digestion and Health: Benzoic Acids and Benzoates* (Washington, DC: Government Printing Office, 1908).

183 **"On hearing this opinion":** Wiley, *An Autobiography*, pp. 239–41.

183 **"My firm saved $4,000":** Wiley, *An Autobiography*, pp. 239–41.

184 **"Everyone who ate":** This quote and the discussion that followed are found in Wiley, *An Autobiography*, pp. 240–43.

185 **The following day, Roosevelt:** Wiley, *An Autobiography*, pp. 242–43; James C. Whorton, *Before Silent Spring: Pesticides and Public Health in Pre-DDT America* (Princeton, NJ: Princeton University Press, 1974), pp. 105–10.

185 **"According to the ordinary":** Wiley, *History of a Crime Against the Food Law*, pp. 160–65.

185 **Wiley's chemists continued:** Harvey Wiley to Charles Bonaparte, October 3, 1907, Wiley Papers, box 63; Harvey Wiley to James Wilson, October 7, 1907, Wiley Papers, box 63; Charles Bonaparte to Warwick Hough, October 21, 1907, Wiley Papers, box 63; summary of Wilson's memo to Bonaparte, October 25, 1907, Wiley Papers, box 63.

186 **Yet the president:** "Effect of the Food Law on the Glucose Interests," *American Food Journal*, December 1906, p. 10; Anthony Gaughan and Peter Barton Hutt, "Harvey Wiley, Theodore Roosevelt, and the Federal Regulation of Food and Drugs" (third-year paper, Harvard Law School, Winter 2004), https://dash.harvard.edu/bitstream/handle/1/8852144/Gaughan.html?sequence=2.

186 **E. T. Bedford, as he was:** E. T. Bedford to James Wilson, December 16, 1907, Wiley Papers, box 63; memo, James Wilson to Harvey Wiley, December 20, 1907, Wiley Papers, box 63; Harvey Wiley to William Frear, December 27, 1907, Wiley Papers, box 63.

186 **the unappetizing word:** E. T. Bedford to Frederick Dunlap, January 9, 1908, Wiley Papers, box 65.

187 **"You must make the manufacturers":** Oscar E. Anderson Jr., *The Health of a Nation: Harvey W. Wiley and the Fight for Pure Food* (Chicago: University of Chicago Press, 1958), pp. 205–6.

187 **This came to bear as:** Anderson, *Health of a Nation*, pp. 207–8.

187 **In response, Roosevelt suggested:** Whorton, *Before Silent Spring*, pp. 107–9.

188 **"The president promptly fired":** Theodore Roosevelt to Harvey Wilson, July 30, 1908, Wiley Papers, box 64.

188 **Meanwhile, Roosevelt worked:** Charity Dye, *Some Torch Bearers in Indiana* (Indianapolis: Hellenbeck Press, 1917), pp. 210–15, quotes Wiley as saying, "This board was created by President Roosevelt in direct violation of the food and drug act"; Samuel F. Hopkins, "What Has Become of Our Pure Food Law?" *Hampton's Magazine* 24, no. 1 (January 1910): pp. 232–42; "The Referee Board," Expenditures in the U.S. Department of Agriculture, Report No. 249 (Moss Hearings), 62nd Cong., Government Printing Office, Washington, DC, January 22, 1912, pp. 2–17; "The United States Referee Board: How It Came to Be Appointed," *American Food Journal* 6, no. 9 (September 15, 1911): pp. 48–50.

189 **"a strong solution of":** E. T. Bedford to James Wilson, December 19, 1907, Wiley Papers, box 63.

189 But overall Wiley's relationships: *Proceedings of the American Chemical Society*, Easton, Pennsylvania, 1907, p. 83.

189 "The men who led": Harvey Wiley to C. A. Brown, New York Sugar Trade Laboratory, November 20, 1907, Wiley Papers, box 63.

190 "the creation of the": Wiley, *History of a Crime Against the Food Law*, p. 160.

190 "The Remsen Board": "Getting Results in the Fight for Pure Food," *New York Times*, May 10, 1908, p. 33.

190 The *Times*, along with Wiley's: An example is this letter to Roosevelt from Thomas McElhenie, a pharmacist in Brooklyn, on January 25, 1908: "The makers of food products are besieging you to appoint for their benefit a commission of chemists to be the superiors in Dr. Wiley's office. . . . I hope they will not prevail. In shotgun practice other birds are bound to be hit. Let them flutter. . . . The Food Law is a right law and should therefore stand."

Chapter Eleven: Excuses for Everything

191 "The use of chemical": Harvey Wiley, "Influence of Preservatives and Other Substances Added to Foods upon Health and Metabolism" (lecture, Annual Meeting of the American Philosophical Society, Philadelphia, April 25, 1908), Harvey Washington Wiley Papers, Library of Congress, Manuscript Division, box 190.

192 The sodium benzoate trials: Harvey W. Wiley, *Influence of Food Preservatives and Artificial Colors on Digestion and Health; Benzoic Acids and Benzoates* (Washington, DC: Government Printing Office, 1908). The Remsen Board's report, "The Influence of Sodium Benzoate on the Nutrition and Health of Man," was released in preliminary form in the summer of 1908 and formally published in January 1909 by the U.S. Department of Agriculture through the Government Printing Office in Washington, DC. To no one's surprise, where Wiley found health problems, the Referee Board found none.

192 Over the course of 1907: The publications suppressed by Wilson are listed by Wiley in a section titled "Data Refused Publication" in his self-published book *The History of a Crime Against the Food Law* (Washington, DC, 1929), pp. 62–64.

193 In August 1908 the: "Report of the Proceedings of the Twelfth Annual Convention of the Association of State and National Food and Dairy Departments," *American Food Journal* 3, no. 8 (August 15, 1908): pp. 1–12; Ronak Desai, "James Wilson, Harvey Wiley, and the Bureau of Chemistry: Examining the 'Political' Dimensions of the Administration and Enforcement of the Pure Food and Drugs Act 1906–1912" (student paper, Harvard Law School, May 2011), https://dash.harvard.edu/handle/1/8592146.

194 "The convention will probably": "Food and Drug Disagreements Become Public," *New York Times*, August 5, 1908, p. 7.

195 "the heat and cold": "Report of the Proceedings of the Twelfth Annual Convention," p. 8.

195 "Whenever a food": "Report of the Proceedings of the Twelfth Annual Convention," p. 10.

195 "Resolved: That this association": "Report of the Proceedings of the Twelfth Annual Convention," pp. 11–12.

196 "Those who watched events": Desai, "James Wilson, Harvey Wiley, and the Bureau of Chemistry."

197 this "brazen attack": Clayton Coppin and Jack High, *The Politics of Purity: Harvey Washington Wiley and the Origins of Federal Food Policy* (Ann Arbor: University of Michigan Press, 1999), pp. 123–26.

197 "not sparing in his": Suzanne Rebecca White, "Chemistry and Controversy: Regulating the Use of Chemicals in Foods, 1883–1959" (PhD diss., Emory University, 1994), pp. 108–10.

197 Snowy-white baked goods: White, "Chemistry and Controversy," pp. 112–34.

198 Edwin Ladd, the North Dakota: E. F. Ladd and R. E. Stallings, *Bleaching of Flour*, bulletin 72 (Fargo, ND: Government Agricultural Experiment Station of North Dakota, November 1906), pp. 219–35; James Shepard, "Nitrous Acid as an Antiseptic," *Monthly Bulletin of the Pennsylvania Department of Agriculture* 10 (November 1919): pp. 4–12. Shepard describes nitrous acid as a "vicious" additive in this article.

198 Wiley's Bureau of Chemistry: Aaron Bobrow-Strain, *White Bread: A Social History of the Store-Bought Loaf* (Boston: Beacon Press, 2012), pp. 51–72.

198 "A summary of our": *Annual Reports of the Department of Agriculture, Bureau of Chemistry* (Washington, DC: Government Printing Office, 1908), pp. 402–408.

198 **Wilson showed himself willing:** "Hearings of the Food and Drug Inspection Board," Preliminary Hearing #155, September 1908, National Archives, U.S. Food and Drug Administration, boxes 3 and 4.

199 **"Bleached flour is a":** Harvey Wiley to H. E. Barnard (Indiana food and drug commissioner), May 5, 1909, Wiley Papers, box 71.

199 **The details of the decision:** White, "Chemistry and Controversy," pp. 125–27.

199–200 **"Secretary Wilson and Dr. Wiley":** "Food Inspection Decision 100: Bleached Flour," *American Food Journal* 4, no. 1 (January 15, 1909): p. 26.

200 **Rumors began to circulate:** Michigan Dairy and Food Department to Theodore Roosevelt, October 22, 1908, Wiley Papers, box 65. The convention lived up to the promised drama, and both the events and their fallout appear in Clayton Coppin and Jack High, *The Politics of Purity: Harvey Washington Wiley and the Origins of Federal Food Policy* (University of Michigan Press, 1999), pp. 125–27; Andrew E. Smith, *Pure Ketchup: A History of America's National Condiment* (University of South Carolina Press, 2011), pp. 77–118, in a stunningly good chapter titled "The Benzoate Wars," which covers not only the convention but also Wiley, the Remsen Board, and the battles between Heinz and other manufacturers in the most fascinating way; Ronak Desai, "James Wilson, Harvey Wiley, and the Bureau of Chemistry: Examining the 'Political' Dimensions of the Administration and Enforcement of the Pure Food and Drugs Act, 1906–1912" (student paper, Harvard Law School, May 2011), https://dash.harvard.edu/bitstream/handle/1/8592146/Desai%2C%20Ronak.pdf?sequence=1; and Oscar E. Anderson Jr., *The Health of a Nation: Harvey W. Wiley and the Fight for Pure Food* (Chicago: University of Chicago Press, 1958), pp. 230–31.

201 **Newspaper coverage made it clear:** All newspapers quoted are from a clippings file, Wiley Papers, box 229, folder 1908.

201 **The chorus of public dismay:** James Harvey Young, "Two Hoosiers and the Food Laws of 1906," *Indiana Magazine of History* 88, no. 4 (1992): 303–19.

202 **That same December:** Harvey W. Wiley, *The Influence of Preservatives and Artificial Colors on Digestion and Health*, vol. 5, *Formaldehyde* (Washington, DC: Government Printing Office, 1908), https://archive.org/details/influenceoffoodp84wile_3.

202 **a "violent poison":** Wiley, *Influence of Preservatives and Artificial Colors*, p. 30.

202 **Wiley also could take:** Anderson, *Health of a Nation*, pp. 234–35.

203 **For some years, magazines:** "Booming the Borax Business," *Journal of the American Medical Association* 49, no. 14 (October 5, 1907): 1191–92; "Preservatives and Press Agents," *Journal of the American Medical Association* 303, no. 1 (January 6, 2010): p. 81 (reprint of January 1, 1910, article).

205 **It surprised neither:** James C. Whorton, *Before Silent Spring: Pesticides and Public Health in Pre-DDT America* (Princeton, NJ: Princeton University Press, 1974), pp. 106–8.

205 **"You will find it":** James Harvey Young, "The Science and Morals of Metabolism," *Journal of the History of Medicine and Allied Sciences* 23, no. 1 (January 1968): p. 97.

205 **"slight modifications in":** U.S. Department of Agriculture, Referee Board of Consulting Experts, *The Influence of Sodium Benzoate on the Nutrition and Health of Man* (Washington, DC: Government Printing Office, 1909), pp. 9–13.

205 **"hot, dry New England":** U.S. Department of Agriculture, *Influence of Sodium Benzoate*, pp. 88–90.

205 **Preservative makers declared:** Smith, *Pure Ketchup*, pp. 97–103.

205 **"a first class fight":** Young, "Science and Morals of Metabolism," p. 100.

206 **"[T]his decision of":** E. E. Smith, MD, "Benzoate of Soda in Foods," *Journal of the American Medical Association* 52 , no. 11 (March 13, 1909): p. 905.

206 **"If you could see":** Anderson, *Health of a Nation*, p. 218.

206 **Wilson was unmoved:** *Literary Digest* 38 (March 20, 1909): pp. 463–64; J. F. Snell, "Chemistry in Its Relation to Food," *Journal of the Chemical Industry* 28 (January 30, 1909): pp. 52–53.

207 **Wiley thought again:** Harvey Washington Wiley, *An Autobiography* (Indianapolis: Bobbs-Merrill, 1930), pp. 241–43.

Chapter Twelve: Of Whiskey and Soda

208 **"I expect to give Dr. Wiley":** Oscar E. Anderson Jr., *The Health of a Nation: Harvey W. Wiley and the Fight for Pure Food* (Chicago: University of Chicago Press, 1958), p. 224.

208 **But the sitting president:** Nicholas Lemann, "Progress's Pilgrims: Doris Kearns Goodwin on T.R. and Taft," *New Yorker*, November 18, 2013, www.newyorker.com/magazine/2013/11/18 /progresss-pilgrims; Doris Kearns Goodwin, *The Bully Pulpit: Theodore Roosevelt, William Howard Taft and the Golden Age of Journalism* (New York: Simon & Schuster, 2013), pp. 605–21.

209 **Roosevelt had quietly tried:** H. Parker Willis, "What Whiskey Is," *McClure's*, April 1910, pp. 687–99.

209 **"[T]he term 'whiskey'":** Willis, "What Whiskey Is," p. 696.

210 **In response, Taft asked:** James Files, "Hiram Walker and Sons and the Pure Food and Drug Act" (master's thesis, University of Windsor, 1986), pp. 84–89.

210 **"reminiscent of a German":** Willis, "What Whiskey Is," p. 697.

210 **"The evidence shows":** Willis, "What Whiskey Is," pp. 693–95.

210 **In late May, Bowers:** Harvey Washington Wiley, *An Autobiography* (Indianapolis: Bobbs-Merrill, 1930), pp. 257–59; memo, Harvey Wiley to Frederick Dunlap, October 2, 1909, Harvey Washington Wiley Papers, Library of Congress, Manuscript Division, box 71 ("My opinion of the letter of Mr. Hough, addressed to the commissioner of the IRS, is that Mr. Hough will use every effort in his power to protect the adulterers and debasers of distilled spirits from receiving the penalty they should under the law.").

211 **"drugs and oils and colors":** Willis, "What Whiskey Is," p. 698.

211 **Less openly, Taft also:** The background on Taft's inquiry about the legality of the Remsen Board and the suppression of the findings comes from congressional testimony during hearings held by U.S. senator Ralph Moss of Indiana in August 1911. Full coverage of the hearing can be found in a report from the U.S. Senate, "The Referee Board," Expenditures in the U.S. Department of Agriculture, Report No. 249 (Moss Hearings), 62nd Cong., Government Printing Office, Washington, DC, January 22, 1912.

211 **"I do not think":** "The Remsen Board's Opinion," *New York Times*, August 6, 1911, p. 8.

212 **"I consider there is":** Harvey Wiley to George McCabe and Frederick Dunlap, memo, July 2, 1909, Wiley Papers, box 71.

212 **a "ludicrous recommendation":** George McCabe to Harvey Wiley and Frederick Dunlap, memo, July 6, 1909, Wiley Papers, box 71.

212 **Many of their disagreements:** By the fall of 1909, the departmental warfare among Wiley, Dunlap, and McCabe was ceaseless, at least judging by the memos archived at the Library of Congress. And Wiley's tone was shifting from outrage to resignation. Two examples: On October 30, 1909, Dunlap rejects Wiley's concern about phosphoric acid as a health issue and demands evidence. On November 9, 1909, Wiley's response begins, "I have no time to hunt up information to convince you that articles are injurious to health. It is too much of a task." On December 21, 1909, Wiley writes to Dunlap, "I regret that I have no time to expound all the reasons which lead me to believe that the addition of a substance to foods which is not a food and which takes no part in nutrition need not be proved absolutely harmful before it can be excluded under the law." Wiley Papers, box 71.

213 **"If sodium acetate is":** Frederick Dunlap to Harvey Wiley, memo, July 15, 1909, Wiley Papers, box 71.

213 **"I have not time":** Harvey Wiley to Frederick Dunlap, memo, August 2, 1909, Wiley Papers, box 71.

213 **In another dispute:** C. D. Regier, "The Struggle for Federal Food and Drug Regulation," *Law and Contemporary Problems* 1 (1933): pp. 11–12.

214 **The battle over sodium:** Andrew E. Smith, *Pure Ketchup: A History of America's National Condiment* (Columbia: University of South Carolina Press, 2011), pp. 105–13; Samuel F. Hopkins, "What Has Become of Our Pure Food Law?" *Hampton's Magazine* 24, no. 1 (January 1910): 232–42.

214 **In anticipation of:** Anderson, *Health of a Nation*, pp. 228–32.

215 **But the standoff between:** "Injunction Granted in Favor of Benzoate of Soda," *American Food Journal* 4, no. 4 (April 15, 1909): pp. 15–16; the decision is outlined in the legal record of the ruling, *Curtice Brothers v. Harry E. Barnard et al.*, United States Circuit Court of Appeals, 4:2987–3043, National Archives Great Lakes Region, Chicago.

215 **"It must be evident":** William Williams Keen, "The New Pure Food Catsup," *National Food Magazine* 28, no. 1 (July 1910): pp. 108–9.

216 **Wilson knew that Ladd:** Smith, *Pure Ketchup*, pp. 105–13; Clayton Coppin and Jack High, *The Politics of Purity: Harvey Washington Wiley and the Origins of Federal Food Policy* (Ann Arbor: University of Michigan Press, 1999), pp. 128–32.

218 **Just weeks earlier:** Suzanne Rebecca White, "Chemistry and Controversy: Regulating the Use of Chemicals in Foods, 1883–1959" (PhD diss., Emory University, 1994), pp. 127–34.

216 **"I am utterly hostile":** "Bleached Flour Men Try to Get Wilson Reversed," *American Food Journal* 4, no. 3 (March 15, 1909): p. 25.

216 **"This can come only":** Anderson, *Health of a Nation*, pp. 220–22.

217 **Despite agreeing to seizures:** Anderson, *Health of a Nation*, pp. 220–22.

217 **He moved to block:** Suppressed documents are listed in Harvey W. Wiley, *The History of a Crime Against the Food Law* (Washington, DC: self-published, 1929), pp. 62–64.

217 **"I regret that I shall":** Harvey Wiley to R. U. Johnson, September 13, 1909, Wiley Papers, box 71.

217 **"James Wilson, secretary":** "Pure Food Feud Nearing a Climax," *Chicago Tribune*, August 26, 1909, p. 4.

218 **"a bear pit":** Anderson, *Health of a Nation*, p. 230.

218 **"As the inside facts":** "Politics Reign at the Agriculture Department," *Los Angeles Herald*, September 3, 1909, p. 3.

218 **"We fully smashed the":** Ronak Desai, "James Wilson, Harvey Wiley and the Bureau of Chemistry: Examining the 'Political' Dimensions of the Administration and Enforcement of the Pure Food and Drugs Act 1906–1912" (student paper, Harvard Law School, May 2011), p. 29, https:// dash.harvard.edu/handle/1/8592146.

218 **"low class fellow":** Desai, "James Wilson, Harvey Wiley and the Bureau of Chemistry."

219 **"foe to fakers":** Dennis B. Worthen, "Lyman Frederick Kebler (1863–1955): Foe to Fakers," *Journal of the American Pharmacists Association* 50, no. 3 (May–June 2010): pp. 429–32, www.japha .org/article/S1544-3191(15)30834-7/abstract.

219 **The indiscriminate use of:** Lyman F. Kebler, U.S. Department of Agriculture, *Habit-Forming Agents: Their Indiscriminate Sale and Use a Menace to Public Welfare* (Washington, DC: Government Printing Office, 1910), https://archive.org/details/CAT87202997; "Medicated Soft Drinks," 1910 Report of the Bureau of Chemistry, U.S. Department of Agriculture, p. 156; and backgrounder on "so-called soft drinks" by Harvey W. Wiley for James Wilson, Wiley Papers, box 208. The issue had also been gaining some public health attention, as seen in "Drugged 'Soft' Drinks: The Food Law Has Partly Revealed Their Character," *New York Times*, July 7, 1909, p. 8.

220 **"representing 300,000,000 glasses":** "All Doubts About Coca-Cola Settled," *National Druggist*, August 1908, p. 274.

221 **he was especially wary:** Coca-Cola Company, "The Chronicle of Coca-Cola: The Candler Era," January 1, 2012, www.coca-colacompany.com/stories/the-chronicle-of-coca-cola-the-candler-era; Mark Pendergrast, *For God, Country & Coca-Cola* (New York: Basic Books, 2013), pp. 45–66.

221 **The U.S. Army in 1907:** Stephen B. Karch, *A Brief History of Cocaine* (Boca Raton, FL: CRC Press, 2005), p. 126.

221 **Wiley, who, as his colleagues:** White, "Chemistry and Controversy," pp. 134–39.

221 **"I am not a believer":** Harvey Wiley to James Wilson, October 28, 1909, Wiley Papers, box 71.

222 **"highly objectionable both":** Harvey Wiley to George McCabe, November 2, 1909, Wiley Papers, box 71. (The memo also argues that "an effort should be made to stop traffic in this dangerous beverage.")

222 **They got support from:** White, "Chemistry and Controversy," p. 139.

222 **"Coca-Cola is one of":** Harvey Wiley to James Wilson, November 13, 1909, Wiley Papers, box 71.

222 **"there is much":** Wiley to Wilson, November 13, 1909.

222 **"What I did say":** "Dr. Wiley Throws a Stone at Our Industry and Then Runs," *American Bottler*, December 1909, p. 182.

222 **What he didn't mention:** Pendergrast, *For God, Country & Coca-Cola*, pp. 107–9.

223 **"I was, of course":** Wiley, *An Autobiography*, pp. 261–63.

224 **"contains an alkaloidal":** Pendergrast, *For God, Country & Coca-Cola*, pp. 109–10.

224 **"It is remarkable":** Wiley, *An Autobiography*, pp. 261–63.

224 **On October 21, 1909:** *United States v. Forty Barrels and Twenty Kegs of Coca-Cola*, 241 U.S. 265 (1916), http://caselaw.findlaw.com/us-supreme-court/241/265.html.

225 **"Taft Whisky," which would:** Bob Eidson, "The Taft Decision," *Bourbon Review*, February 17, 2014, www.gobourbon.com/the-taft-decision/.

225 **On December 26 the president:** Wiley, *An Autobiography*, pp. 257–59; Michael Veach, "20th Century Distilling Papers at the Filson," *Filson Newsmagazine* 7, no. 4 (no date), www.filsonhis torical.org/archive/news_v7n4_distilling.html.

225 **"Whiskey appears to be"**: H. Parker Willis, "What Whiskey Is," *McClure's*, April 1910, pp. 698–99.
225 **"What do you think"**: Wiley, *An Autobiography*, p. 258.
225 **"What I fear is"**: A. O. Stanley (Glenmore Distilleries) to Harvey Wiley, January 14, 1910, Wiley Papers, box 81.
226 **"that neutral spirits, which"**: Alice Lakey to Harvey Wiley, January 12, 1910, Wiley Papers, box 81. Wiley too was deeply unhappy. He prepared a rebuttal, should the occasion occur again, arguing strongly for the old classifications of whiskey: whiskey folder, 1908–1910, Wiley Papers, box 209.
226 **"We believe that"**: from Alice Lakey to *Detroit News*, January 12, 1910, Wiley Papers, box 81. This letter is also cited in "Pure Food Progress," *Collier's*, March 12, 1912, p. 3.
226 **"It is a very"**: Alice Lakey to Harvey Wiley, January 12, 1910, Wiley Papers, box 81.
226 **"There is but little"**: Harvey Wiley to Alice Lakey, January 22, 1910, Wiley Papers, box 81.

Chapter Thirteen: The Love Microbe

227 **In January he had promised**: Wiley's schedule, Harvey Washington Wiley Papers, Library of Congress, Manuscript Division, box 81.
228 **That interest encouraged**: Oscar E. Anderson Jr., *The Health of a Nation: Harvey W. Wiley and the Fight for Pure Food* (Chicago: University of Chicago Press, 1958), p. 242.
229 **Before the law, even**: Adam Burrows, "A Palette of Our Palates: A Brief History of Food Coloring and Its Regulation" (paper submitted as a Food and Drug Law course requirement, Harvard Law School, May 2006); H. T. McKone, "The Unadulterated History of Food Dyes," *ChemMatters*, December 1999, pp. 6–7.
230 **A resulting 1907 Food**: Dale Blumenthal, "Red Dye No. 3 and Other Colorful Controversies," *FDA Consumer* 24 (May 1990): pp. 18–21.
230 **McCabe decided to review**: Daniel Marmion, *Handbook of U.S. Colorants* (New York: John Wiley and Sons, 1991), pp. 11–12.
231 **While Hesse worked**: The Lexington Mill case and the first stages of litigation are described in Suzanne Rebecca White, "Chemistry and Controversy: Regulating the Use of Chemicals in Foods, 1883–1959" (PhD diss., Emory University, 1994), pp. 127–33; and William G. Panschar, *Baking in America: Economic Development*, vol. 1 (Evanston, IL: Northwestern University Press, 1956), pp. 235–39. The first public victory was celebrated in newspaper stories such as "Bleached Flour Is Adulterated: Government Wins Important Test Case," *Sacramento Union*, July 7, 1910, p. 2; and deplored in great detail in "Government Wins Bleached Flour Case," *American Food Journal* 5, no. 7 (July 15, 1910): pp. 1–11.
231 **"a blast of God's"**: and "Flour Bleachers to Be Prosecuted Pending Appeal," *American Food Journal* 5, no. 8 (August 15, 1910): pp. 8–12.
233 **Bernhard Hesse's eighty-page**: Bernhard C. Hesse, U.S. Department of Agriculture, Bureau of Chemistry, *Coal-Tar Colors Used in Food Products*, (Washington, DC: Government Printing Office, 1912), https://archive.org/details/coaltarcolorsuse14hess. (The report was first circulated in 1910.)
234 **he'd named it Grasslands**: Eldsley Mour, "Dr. Wiley and His Farm," *Country Life in America* 28, no. 4 (August 1915): pp. 19–21.
234 **he'd even purchased a**: Harvey Washington Wiley, *An Autobiography* (Indianapolis: Bobbs-Merrill, 1930), pp. 279–80.
234 **In late October of 1910**: Anderson, *Health of a Nation*, p. 242.
235 **DR. WILEY WILL TAKE A BRIDE**: The *Tribune* story and other newspaper clippings regarding the engagement can be found in Anna Wiley's scrapbook, Wiley Papers, box 227; Wiley, *An Autobiography*, pp. 281–83.
235 **"There is a shade"**: James Wilson to Ira Remsen, December 11, 1910, Wiley Papers, box 189.
236 **After the passage of the**: Peter Duffy, "The Deadliest Book Review," *New York Times*, January 14, 2011, www.nytimes.com/2011/01/16/books/review/Duffy-t.html.
236 **Barely two months later**: The Coca-Cola trial appears in Mark Pendergrast, *For God, Country & Coca-Cola* (New York: Basic Books, 2013), pp. 110–15; White, "Chemistry and Controversy," pp. 139–47; and countless newspaper stories, including the one cited in the next note and others which can be found in the Coca-Cola clippings file, Wiley Papers, box 200. The *American Food Journal*'s coverage of the trial, "Coca-Cola Litigation Ends with Defeat for the Government," April 15, 1911, pp. 10–17, provides an invaluable witness-by-witness review of the case.

237 **McCabe began the prosecution:** "Candler Cursed Me, Says the Inspector," *Atlanta Georgian*, March 4, 1911, p. 1.

242 **Coca-Cola had also hired:** Ludy T. Benjamin, "Pop Psychology: The Man Who Saved Coca-Cola," *Monitor on Psychology* 40, no. 2 (2009): p. 18, www.apa.org/monitor/2009/02/coca-cola.aspx. For more about Hollingworth and the trial, it's worth checking out Anne M. Rogers and Angela Rosenbaum, "Coca-Cola, Caffeine, and Mental Deficiency: Harry Hollingworth and the Chattanooga Trial of 1911," *Journal of the History of the Behavioral Sciences* 27 (1991): pp. 42–55, www.researchgate.net/publication/229960591_Coca-Cola_caffeine_and_mental_deficiency_Harry_Hollingworth_and_the_Chattanooga_Trial_of_1911.

243 **"20 dopes daily":** "Coca-Cola Drinkers Suffer No Harm," *Chattanooga Daily Times*, March 16, 1911, archived in Wiley Papers, Coca-Cola files, box 200.

244 **"if the government proved":** "Coca-Cola Trial Was Only the Start," *Chattanooga Daily Times*, April 30, 1911, archived in Wiley Papers, Coca-Cola files, box 200.

244 **The defeated delegation:** Referee Board of Consulting Scientific Experts, U.S. Department of Agriculture, *Influence of Saccharine on the Nutrition and Health of Man*, report 94 (Washington, DC: Government Printing Office, 1911).

245 **It had come about:** James Harvey Young, "Saccharin: A Bitter Regulatory Decision," in *Research in the Administration of Public Policy*, ed. Frank B. Evans and Harold T. Pinkett (Washington, DC: Howard University Press, 1974), pp. 40–50.

245 **McCabe had long believed:** Board of Food and Drug Inspection, U.S. Department of Agriculture, Food Inspection Decision (FID) 35, April 29, 1911.

246 **Queeny, energized by:** "Saccharin Makers at Washington," *Oil, Paint, and Drug Reporter* 79, no. 22 (May 1911): p. 28.

246 **"I want to say frankly":** Testimony before the U.S. Senate, hearings held in August 1911 by Senator Ralph Moss of Indiana, recorded in "The Referee Board," Expenditures in the U.S. Department of Agriculture, Report No. 249 (Moss Hearings), 62nd Cong., Government Printing Office, Washington, DC, January 22, 1912. The statement is also cited in "The Remsen Board's Opinion," *New York Times*, August 6, 1911, p. 8.

247 **This new mess:** Anderson, *Health of a Nation*, pp. 244–45; Harvey W. Wiley, *The History of a Crime Against the Food Law* (Washington, DC, self-published, 1929), pp. 174–82.

248 **"Personally, I am of":** Anderson, *Health of a Nation*, p. 244.

249 **"political judgment of an ox":** L. F. Abbott, ed., *Taft and Roosevelt: The Intimate Letters of Archie Butt*, vol. 2 (New York: Doubleday, Doran, 1930), p. 696.

249 **"too great of a disposition":** Ronak Desai, "James Wilson, Harvey Wiley, and the Bureau of Chemistry: Examining the 'Political' Dimensions of the Administration and Enforcement of the Pure Food and Drugs Act 1906–1912" (student paper, Harvard Law School, May 2011), https://dash.harvard.edu/handle/1/8592146, p. 29.

Chapter Fourteen: The Adulteration Snake

251 **Then, to Bigelow's surprise:** Oscar E. Anderson Jr., The *Health of a Nation: Harvey W. Wiley and the Fight for Pure Food* (Chicago: University of Chicago Press, 1958), p. 246.

252 **"We need no defense":** Anderson, *Health of a Nation*.

252 **"After having failed":** Harvey W. Wiley, *The History of a Crime Against the Food Law* (Washington, DC: self-published, 1929), p. 258.

252 **"They . . . showed a tendency":** "Row over Wilson," *Evening Star* (Washington, DC), August 1, 1911, p. 1.

253 **"The Remsen referee board":** "Row over Wilson."

253 **Such revelations further stoked:** Telegrams and letters regarding the Rusby affair, July 13–August 18, 1911, Harvey Washington Wiley Papers, Library of Congress, Manuscript Division, box 88. I do not cite them all here, but the file contains dozens. One of my favorite uncited ones was dated August 18, 1911, to Wiley from J. H. Hunt of the canning company Hunt Brothers. It concludes, "Give 'em H—l Doctor!"

255 **Appalled, George Wickersham wrote:** Anderson, *Health of a Nation*, p. 247.

255 **"as weak as water":** Anderson, *Health of a Nation*, p. 247.

255 **The Moss committee hearings:** My description is based on numerous sources, including "The Referee Board," Expenditures in the U.S. Department of Agriculture, Report No. 249 (Moss Hearings), 62nd Cong., Government Printing Office, Washington, DC, January 22, 1912; and Wiley, *History of a Crime Against the Food Law*, pp. 88–210 (citing directly from the report). See

also the *Herald*'s highly critical coverage, Wiley Papers, box 221, 1911 clippings folder. The *Evening Star* clippings can also be found in this folder.

256 **"Lawyer McCabe has been":** "McCabe Ruled Hard, Scientists Assert," *Evening Star* (Washington, DC), August 11, 1911, p. 3.

256 **"By the clever framing":** "Big Fees Were Paid by Remsen Board, Dispersing Officer Admits," *New York Times*, August 2, 1911, p. 2.

257 **"The broader issues raised":** Anderson, *Health of a Nation*, pp. 247–48.

258 **"My heartiest congratulations":** Samuel Hopkins Adams to Harvey Wiley, September 17, 1911, Wiley Papers, box 88. Among dozens of notes of congratulations, "I believe there is rejoicing all over the country," wrote Arthur Bailey of Bailey's Extract of Clams, Boston, on September 16.

258 **The R.B. Davis Company:** R.B. Davis Company to Harvey Wiley, July 14, 1911, Wiley Papers, box 88; Harvey Wiley to R.B. Davis Company, July 21, 1911, Wiley Papers, box 88.

258 **In January 1912 the Moss:** "The Referee Board"; Wiley, *History of a Crime Against the Food Law*, pp. 88–210 (citing directly from the report).

259 **"while the verdict was":** Harvey Wiley to Frank McCullough (Green River Distillery, Kentucky), January 29, 1912, Wiley Papers, box 88.

260 **Within a few weeks following:** Harvey Washington Wiley, *An Autobiography* (Indianapolis: Bobbs-Merrill, 1930), pp. 288–89.

261 **"As I read the papers":** Nathaniel Fowler to Harvey Wiley, January 15, 1912, Wiley Papers, box 88.

261 **By March 1912:** Wiley, *An Autobiography*, pp. 288–89; Wiley, *History of a Crime Against the Food Law* (coverage of the conversation with Wilson at pp. 55–56; copy of the resignation letter at p. 92).

262 **"That story isn't":** "Dr. Wiley Resigns," *Druggists Circular*, April 1912, p. 211.

262 **"I hereby tender my":** Harvey Wiley to James Wilson, March 15, 1912, Wiley Papers, box 88.

262 **"It is also a matter":** Wiley, *History of a Crime Against the Food Law*, pp. 92–94.

263 **"that I should not":** Wiley, *History of a Crime Against the Food Law*, pp. 92–94.

263 **"Here's your hat":** "Dr. Wiley Resigns," *Druggists Circular*, April 1812, p. 211.

263 **Like Wilson, President Taft was:** Anderson, *Health of a Nation*, pp. 252–53.

263 **But elsewhere in the Department:** Wiley, *An Autobiography*, pp. 290–91.

264 **"With tears streaming down":** Wiley, *An Autobiography*, p. 292.

264 **"Some of the employees":** "Dr. Wiley Is Out, Attacking Enemies," *New York Times*, March 16, 1912, p. 1.

264 **"Dr. Wiley is known":** "Dr. Wiley Resigns," *National Food Magazine* 30, no. 4 (April 1912): p. 2.

264 **"his hands have been":** "Dr. Wiley Resigns," *Druggists Circular*.

264 **"So clear in his great":** "Dr. Wiley Resigns," *Druggists Circular*.

264 **"I regard the passing":** Wiley, *An Autobiography*, p. 292.

Chapter Fifteen: The History of a Crime

266 **In a report to Wilson:** Roscoe Doolittle, Acting Chief, U.S. Department of Agriculture, *1911 Report of the Bureau of Chemistry* (Washington, DC: Government Printing Office, July 30, 1912).

267 **"There wasn't a single":** Alfred W. McCann, "Food Frauds as Revealed at the National Magazines Exposition," *National Food Magazine* 31, no. 9 (September 1912): pp. 505–6.

268 **"We cannot conceive":** "A New Head for the U.S. Department of Agriculture," *Chemical Trade Journal*, November 17, 1912, archived in Harvey Washington Wiley Papers, Library of Congress, Manuscript Division, clippings file, box 199.

268 **"I have no cabinet aspirations":** Harvey Wiley to R. W. Ward (Oregon physician), December 4, 1912, Wiley Papers, box 88.

268 **"The doctor doesn't expect":** Harvey Wiley to J. G. Emery, December 11, 1912, Wiley Papers, box 88.

268 **The retail druggists' group:** "United States Supreme Court; The Sherley Amendment to the Pure Food and Drugs Act Is Constitutional; A Misbranded 'Patent Medicine' Condemned; *Seven Cases Eckman's Alterative v. United States, U.S.* (Jan. 10, 1916)," *Public Health Reports (1896–1970)* 31, no. 3 (January 21, 1916): pp. 137–40; Nicola Davis, "FDA Focus: The Sherley Amendment," *Pharmaletter*, October 11, 2014, www.thepharmaletter.com/article/fda-focus-the-sherley-amendment.

269 **"I do not think":** Wiley to Emery, December 11, 1912.

269 **Alsberg, a biochemist:** U.S. Food and Drug Administration, "Carl L. Alsberg, M.D.," March 15, 2017, www.fda.gov/AboutFDA/WhatWeDo/History/Leaders/Commissioners/ucm093764.htm.

270 **This change was highlighted:** "Clearing the Atmosphere in the Saccharin Controversy," *American Food Journal* 7, no. 1 (January 15, 1912): 16–17; "An Opinion on the Saccharin Decisions," *American Food Journal* 7, no. 9 (September 15, 1912): p. 7.

270 **Following yet another:** Suzanne Rebecca White, "Chemistry and Controversy: Regulating the Use of Chemicals in Foods, 1883–1959" (PhD diss., Emory University, 1994), pp. 154–60; James Harvey Young, "Saccharin: A Bitter Regulatory Decision," in *Research in the Administration of Public Policy*, ed. Frank B. Evans and Harold T. Pinkett (Washington, DC: Howard University Press, 1974), pp. 40–50; Deborah Jean Warner, *Sweet Stuff: An American History of Sweeteners from Sugar to Sucralose* (Lanham, MD: Rowman and Littlefield, 2011), pp. 185–94.

270 **Meanwhile, as promised:** White, "Chemistry and Controversy," pp. 131–33; *United States v. Lexington Mill & Elevator Co.*, 232 U.S. 399 (1914), www.law.cornell.edu/supremecourt/text/232/399.

270 **Appalled, Wiley sent:** Harvey W. Wiley, *The History of a Crime Against the Food Law* (Washington, DC: self-published, 1929), pp. 381–82.

272 **"I am not an enemy":** Harvey Washington Wiley and Mildred Maddocks, *The Pure Food Cookbook* (New York: Hearst's International Library, 1914), p. 71.

270 *Good Housekeeping* **was now:** Harvey Washington Wiley, *An Autobiography* (Indianapolis: Bobbs-Merrill, 1930), pp. 302–6; "The Original Man of the House," *Good Housekeeping*, April 10, 2010: www.goodhousekeeping.com/institute/about-the-institute/a18828/about-harvey-wiley/.

272 **"There is perhaps":** Wiley and Maddocks, *Pure Food Cookbook*, p. 171.

273 **"I had no longer":** Wiley, *An Autobiography*, p. 304.

273 **In 1916 Alsberg authorized:** Carl Alsberg, U.S. Department of Agriculture, *1916 Report of the Bureau of Chemistry* (Washington, DC: Government Printing Office, July 30, 1917).

274 **But he, Wiley, and just about:** Mark Pendergrast, *For God, Country and Coca-Cola* (New York: Basic Books, 2013), pp. 114–15; White, "Chemistry and Controversy," pp. 149–50; *United States v. Forty Barrels and Twenty Kegs of Coca-Cola*, 241 U.S. 265 (1916), http://caselaw.findlaw.com/us-supreme-court/241/265.html.

275 **As Alsberg wrote:** Carl Alsberg, U.S. Department of Agriculture, *1917 Report of the Bureau of Chemistry* (Washington, DC: Government Printing Office, July 30, 1918).

275 **Even in the shadow:** Roxie Olmstead, "Anna Kelton Wiley: Suffragist," History's Women, no date, www.historyswomen.com/socialreformer/annkeltonwiley.html.

276 **"She believes the ballot":** Katherine Graves Busbey, "Mrs. Harvey W. Wiley," *Good Housekeeping*, January 1912, pp. 544–46.

276 **To his friends who wondered:** Oscar E. Anderson Jr., *The Health of a Nation: Harvey W. Wiley and the Fight for Pure Food* (Chicago: University of Chicago Press, 1958), p. 264.

276 **"Our flag on all seas":** "Theodore Roosevelt Dies Suddenly at Oyster Bay Home; Nation Shocked, Pays Tribute to Former President, Our Flag on All Seas and in All Lands at Half Mast," *New York Times*, January 6, 1919, p. 1.

276 **But Harvey Wiley spared no:** Wiley wrote an entire bitter chapter about Roosevelt's hostility toward him and his perceived undermining of food regulations: "Attitude of Roosevelt," in *The History of a Crime Against the Food Law*, pp. 263–75.

277 **The case against saccharin:** White, "Chemistry and Controversy," pp. 155–66.

277 **The government's leading expert:** R.M. Cunningham and Williams Greer, "The Man Who Understands Your Stomach," *Saturday Evening Post* (September 13, 1947): pp. 173–75; A. J. Carlson, "Some Physiological Actions of Saccharin and Their Bearing on the Use of Saccharin in Foods," in *Report of the National Academy of Sciences for the Year 1917* (Washington, DC: Government Printing Office, 1918).

278 **"slack-fill" bill:** *Food and Drug Law* (Washington, DC: Food and Drug Institute, 1991), p. 46.

279 **"it would be a serious":** Suzanne Rebecca White, "Chemistry and Controversy: Regulating the Use of Chemicals in Foods, 1883–1959" (PhD diss., Emory University, 1994), pp. 160–62.

280 **"The Government has much":** "Chronology of Food Additive Regulations in the United States," Environment, Health and Safety Online, no date, www.ehso.com/ehshome/FoodAdd/foodaddi tivecron.htm.

280 **Upon Coolidge's election:** Harvey W. Wiley, "Enforcement of the Food Law," *Good Housekeeping*, September 1925, www.seleneriverpress.com/historical/enforcement-of-the-food-law/?.

281 **"for the most part undesirable":** Wiley's letter to Coolidge and Dunlap's reply to Wiley can be found in this digital text version maintained by the Library of Congress: https://memory.loc.gov /mss/amrlm/lmk/mk01/mk01.sgm.

282 **"I had hoped to do":** UPC News Services, "'Food Poisoning General,' Says Wiley; Expert Charges Pure Food Law Is Being Ignored, Attacks Proposed Starch Sugar Law as Fraud," July 26, 1926.

282 **"Why should legislation be":** Anderson, *Health of a Nation*, p. 275.

282 **"The country owes you":** Anderson, *Health of a Nation*, p. 275.

284 **"The freedom of science":** Wiley, *An Autobiography*, p. 325.

285 **In a scathing book:** Arthur Kallet and F. J. Schlink, *100,000,000 Guinea Pigs* (New York: Grosset and Dunlap, 1933), p. 196.

285 **Consumer advocates renewed:** Barbara J. Martin MD, *Elixir: The American Tragedy of a Deadly Drug* (Lancaster, PA: Barkberry Press, 2014).

285 **Food, Drug, and Cosmetic Act of 1938:** The full text of the act can be found at www.fda.gov/regu latoryinformation/lawsenforcedbyfda/federalfooddrugandcosmeticactfdcact/default.htm.

286 **"I believe," he said:** Harvey Wiley, "Food Adulteration and Its Effects" (lecture before the sanitary science class at Cornell University, 1905), Wiley Papers, box 198.

Epilogue

287 **A 1956 decision by:** Deborah Blum, "A Colorful Little Tale of Halloween Poison," *Speakeasy Science* (blog), PLoS, October 31, 2011, http://blogs.plos.org/speakeasyscience/2011/10/31/ a-colorful-little-tale-of-halloween-poison/.

287 **A 1976 law authorizing:** Gina Kolata, "The Sad Legacy of the Dalkon Shield," *New York Times Sunday Magazine*, December 6, 1987, www.nytimes.com/1987/12/06/magazine/the-sad-legacy-of-the-dalkon-shield.html.

288 **More recently, the Food Safety:** The full text of the act and additional information on it can be found at www.fda.gov/food/guidanceregulation/fsma/.

288 **The cause was a line of peanut butters:** A history of the issue can be traced through multiple articles at *Food Safety News*: www.foodsafetynews.com/tag/peanut-corporation-of-america/# .WcfMUZOGM0Q.

288 **as sterile as hospitals:** Donita Taylor, "R.I. Farmers Push Back on New Federal Food Safety Rules," *Providence Journal*, July 25, 2017, www.providencejournal.com/news/20170625/ri-farmers-push-back-on-new-federal-food-safety-rules.

289 **During his successful:** Scott Cohn, "Food Safety Measures Face Cuts in Trump Budget," CNBC .com, July 1, 2017, www.cnbc.com/2017/06/30/american-greed-report-food-safety-measures-face-cuts-in-trump-budget.html.

289 **The Earthjustice Institute:** "Food Watchdog Groups Sue FDA over Menu Labeling Day," *Quality Assurance and Safety*, June 8, 2017, www.qualityassurancemag.com/article/food-watchdog-groups-sue-fda-over-menu-labeling-delay/.

290 **In her influential 1962 book:** Rachel Carson, *Silent Spring* (Boston: Houghton Mifflin, 1962).

290 **"The number of environmental":** Coral Davenport, "Counseled by Industry, Not Staff, EPA Administrator Is Off to a Blazing Start," *New York Times*, July 1, 2017, p. 1, www.nytimes.com/ 2017/07/01/us/politics/trump-epa-chief-pruitt-regulations-climate-change.html.

Photo credits

Page 1: (Top) Dr. Harvey W. Wiley, 1863, by Gorgas & Mulvey, Madison, Ind. Library of Congress, Prints and Photographs Division, LC-USZ61-732; (bottom) U.S. Food and Drug Administration, via Wikimedia Commons.

2: (Top left) *Look Before You Eat*, by Frederick Burr Opper. Illustration in Puck, v. 15, no. 366, (1884 March 12), cover. Library of Congress, Prints and Photographs Division, LC-DIG-ppmsca-28300; (top right) National Archives, Records of the Bureau of Chemistry, 1890; (bottom) Agrl. Dept., Bureau of Chemistry, 1920. Library of Congress, Prints and Photographs Division, LC-DIG-npcc-29499.

3: (Top) Rusk, Hon. Jeremiah, governor of Wisconsin. secretary of agriculture. Library of Congress, Prints and Photographs Division, Brady-Handy Collection, LC-DIG-cwpbh-04525; (bottom) J. Sterling Morton, 1895. Library of Congress, Prints and Photographs Division, LC-USZ62-14802.

4: (Top) U. S. Department of Agriculture via Wikimedia Commons; (bottom) Portrait of Ira Remsen from The World's Work, 1902, via Wikimedia Commons.

5: (Top) William McKinley, 1896, by Courtney Art Studio. Via Wikimedia Commons; (bottom) Illustration from *History of Iowa From the Earliest Times to the Beginning of the Twentieth Century*, by Benjamin F. Gue, 1903, via Wikimedia Commons.

6: (Top) Theodore Roosevelt by Pach Brothers, 1915. Library of Congress, Prints and Photographs Division, LC-USZC2-6209; (bottom) Roosevelt Cabinet group, 1903. Library of Congress, Prints and Photographs Division, LC-USZ62-96155.

7: (Top) U.S. Food and Drug Administration, via Wikimedia Commons; (bottom) DCPL Commons, via Wikimedia Commons.

8: (Top left) Cover of the 1st edition of *The Jungle* by Upton Sinclair, via Wikimedia Commons; (top right) Upton Sinclair, 1906 May 29. Library of Congress, Prints and Photographs Division, New York World-Telegram and the Sun Newspaper Photograph Collection, LC-USZ62-132336; (bottom) National Archives, General Records of Department of State.

9: (Top left) Ray Stannard Baker, half-length portrait. Library of Congress, Prints and Photographs Division, LC-USZ62-36754; (middle) Walter Hines. 1915. *Current History of the War*, vii, via Wikimedia Commons; (bottom left) J. Ogden Armour. November 16, 1922. Library of Congress, Prints and Photographs Division, LC-DIG-npcc-07376.

10: (Top left) Photograph of David Graham Phillips, appearing in the *Bookman* (March 1911), p. 8 (Volume 33, Issue No. 1), via Wikimedia Commons; (bottom right) 1906 Heinz advertisement, via https://www.magazine-advertisements.com/heinz-company.html

11: (Top left) "Watch the Professor," illustration in *Puck*, v. 59, no. 1525 (1906 May 23), centerfold. Library of Congress, Prints and Photographs Division, LC-DIG-ppmsca-26062; (middle) *As to the Pure Food Bill*, by Kemble. Illustration in *Colliers*, 1906 March 31. Library of Congress, Prints and Photographs Division, LC-USZ62-55408; (Bottom left) *The Meat Market*, by Carl Hassmann. Illustration in *Puck*, v. 59, no. 1528 (1906 June 13), cover. Library of Congress, Prints and Photographs Division, LC-DIG-ppmsca-26067.

12: (Top left) Ad for Cascade Pure Whiskey, 1909, *Hopkinsville Kentuckian*, 23 December 1909. Library of Congress, Chronicling America: Historic American Newspapers; (top right) National Archives, Records of the Patent and Trademark Office; (middle right) By U.S. FDA, via Wikimedia Commons; (bottom) U.S. Food and Drug Administration, via Wikimedia Commons.

13: (Top) William Howard Taft and Elihu Root seated at desk, Library of Congress, Prints and Photographs Division, LC-USZ62-66346; (bottom) *New Wine In Old Bottles*, by Darling in the *Des Moines Register and Leader*, reproduced in the *Literary Digest*, December 25, 1909. Via Wikimedia Commons.

14: (Top) Cartoon by Clifford Berryman, from the *Washington Star*, March 1912; (bottom) National Archives, Records of the Food and Drug Administration, 1908.

15: (Top) Mrs. H. W. Wiley and John and Harvey, by Underwood & Underwood, Washington, D.C. 1920. Library of Congress, National Woman's Party Records, Manuscript Division; (bottom) the *Tacoma Times*, March 23, 1912, p. 5, image 5. Library of Congress, Chronicling America: Historic American Newspapers.

16: (left) U.S. postage stamp of Harvey W. Wiley, June 27, 1956. Designed by Robert Miller, engraved by C.A. Brooks. Via Wikimedia Commons; (right) Portrait of Harvey Washington Wiley from The World's Work, via Wikimedia Commons.

Index

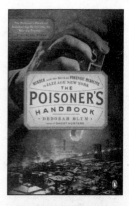